AN YVES R. SIMON READER

CATHOLIC IDEAS FOR A SECULAR WORLD

O. Carter Snead, *series editor*

Under the sponsorship of the de Nicola Center for Ethics and Culture at the University of Notre Dame, the purpose of this interdisciplinary series is to feature authors from around the world who will expand the influence of Catholic thought on the most important conversations in academia and the public square. The series is "Catholic" in the sense that the books will emphasize and engage the enduring themes of human dignity and flourishing, the common good, truth, beauty, justice, and freedom in ways that reflect and deepen principles affirmed by the Catholic Church for millennia. It is not limited to Catholic authors or even works that explicitly take Catholic principles as a point of departure. Its books are intended to demonstrate the diversity and enhance the relevance of these enduring themes and principles in numerous subjects, ranging from the arts and humanities to the sciences.

AN YVES R. SIMON READER

The Philosopher's Calling

YVES R. SIMON

edited by MICHAEL D. TORRE

with John W. Carlson and Anthony O. Simon

University of Notre Dame Press
Notre Dame, Indiana

University of Notre Dame Press
Notre Dame, Indiana 46556
undpress.nd.edu

Copyright © 2021 by the University of Notre Dame

All Rights Reserved

Published in the United States of America

Library of Congress Control Number: 2020950363

ISBN: 978-0-268-10829-8 (Hardback)
ISBN: 978-0-268-10830-4 (Paperback)
ISBN: 978-0-268-10832-8 (WebPDF)
ISBN: 978-0-268-10831-1 (Epub)

For Tony

CONTENTS

An Account of the *Reader*, by Way of Acknowledgment   xi

Simon's Works in the *Reader*   xv

Part I. Introduction

1. The Philosophy of Yves R. Simon   3
   Introduction by Michael D. Torre

2. Method in Philosophy   23
   Introduction by Jude P. Dougherty

Part II. Knowledge

3. Knowledge as Immanent Action   55
   Introduction by Raymond Dennehy

4. The Distinction of Thing and Object   79
   Introduction by John C. Cahalan

5. Analogy and Metaphysical Knowledge   95
   Introduction by Steven A. Long

6. Sensation and Physical Knowledge   115
   Introduction by Ralph Nelson

7. Knowledge of Persons and Society 131
   Introduction by John P. Hittinger

8. Moral Knowledge 149
   Introduction by Ralph McInerny

Part III. Freedom

9. Human Freedom 173
   Introduction by David B. Burrell, CSC

10. Human Reason and Will 201
    Introduction by Laurence Berns

11. Good Use and *Habitus* 221
    Introduction by Catherine Green

12. The Definition of Moral Virtue 240
    Introduction by W. David Solomon

13. Freedom of Intellect 263
    Introduction by V. Bradley Lewis

14. Society and the Formation of Free Persons 285
    Introduction by Joseph W. Koterski, SJ

Part IV. Community

15. Political Society 307
    Introduction by James V. Schall, SJ

16. The Definition of Law 325
    Introduction by George Anastaplo

17. The Common Good and Authority   337
   Introduction by Walter J. Nicgorski

18. Work and Society   352
   Introduction by John A. Gueguen, Jr.

19. Economic Justice   376
   Introduction by Thomas R. Rourke

20. Community, Truth, and Culture   396
   Introduction by Jeanne Heffernan Schindler

Epilogue: Problems in International Order   415
Introduction by Robert Royal

Select Bibliography   447

Contributors   462

Index   471

AN ACCOUNT OF THE *READER*, BY WAY OF ACKNOWLEDGMENT

Aristotle rightly tells us a thing's nature is best seen in its perfect specimen. To know the nature of filial piety, one need look no further than to the lifework of Yves R. Simon's son, Anthony O. Simon (1936–2012). Tirelessly and lovingly, he made the work of his father available to the world. Unquestionably, he was the world's expert on it.[1] All philosophers, and especially those working in the tradition of Aristotle and Thomas, are deeply in his debt, for, through his lifework of filial devotion, he made available to them the riches of his father's thought. And, as this *Reader* makes clear, Yves René Marie Simon (1903–61) was unquestionably a brilliant member of his tradition, one of the truly great philosophical minds of the twentieth century.

Indeed, in large part because of Tony, his father's reputation has only increased with time. This can be seen from the Select Bibliography. As his receiving the Aquinas Medal indicates, Yves was already deeply respected during his lifetime. The decade following his death saw four master's and two PhD theses on his work, yet the 1990s (thirty years later) saw an equal number of master's theses and eight PhD theses. Again, the 1960s bibliography includes four articles on him, but the 1990s saw twenty-three articles along with four books. The twenty-first century has witnessed an issue of the *Cahiers Jacques Maritain* dedicated to him, the publication of his two-volume correspondence with Jacques Maritain, and a book, ten articles, and a PhD thesis on him: he continues to be a significant philosopher in and for our day. As one of our contributors rightly insists, Yves R. Simon touched nothing that he did not adorn.[2]

This *Reader* was Tony's last work, his swan song. Indeed, in it he finishes his work from the other side of the grave. He had intended John W. Carlson (1943–2012) to help him complete his final task, but John's last projects[3] delayed its completion. As the project stalled, and as he sensed that time was also running out on him, Tony asked me to complete what he and John had begun, and John seconded his request. They asked me to write the book's introduction and to work with them to "put the text in order."

With their deaths shortly after their request, it was left to me to do so on my own.[4] I inherited what they had done, but could not work with them to complete their task. Although I have made some slight alterations to it, the book's shape is substantially Tony's. Thus, even though my own preference as editor was for longer and continuous texts, I tended to observe the range and selection of texts if previously given, even when these were shorter and discontinuous

Tony, working with John, had assembled a remarkable collection of contributors, many of them former students of his father, who were tasked with giving brief introductions to the various subjects most central to Yves's work. He had also given each of them a preliminary set of texts he judged most pertinent to their subject. Save where otherwise noted, the contributors then made a selection from those texts. This book thus represents a remarkable collaborative effort of many diverse and well-respected Thomists, working together to honor the achievement of one of the greatest among them, to whom they owe a real debt. The contributors span two generations: from former pupils of Simon (a number of whom died before this could see the light of day) to others young enough to have been their students. I reviewed all their selections, and, again save where noted, the contributors were able to approve of the texts I finally chose. Some overlap in Simon's themes is unavoidable, but this also is instructive, helping to show the links between them. Nevertheless, overlap has been kept to a minimum. It was Tony's hope that the *Reader* thus created would serve as an introduction to the best of his father's thought, both for a university-level philosophy course and for any educated person interested in contemporary philosophy, especially in the tradition of Aristotle and Thomas.

An Account of the Reader, *by Way of Acknowledgment* xiii

Generally, Simon's notes have not been included in the *Reader*. Occasionally, where a note was short or added an important point, it has been kept. The editorial notes found in his posthumous works have also occasionally been kept. All footnotes in this work are formatted the same way, regardless of any other his editors may have used.

I am grateful to the Jacques Maritain Center at the University of Notre Dame for permission to use many of Simon's works (*The Community of the Free*; *A Critique of Moral Knowledge*; *The Definition of Moral Virtue*; *Foresight and Knowledge*; *Freedom and Community*; *Freedom of Choice*; *An Introduction to Metaphysics of Knowledge*; *Practical Knowledge*; *The Road to Vichy*; *The Tradition of Natural Law*; and *Work, Society, and Culture*); Marquette University Press for permission to use Simon's *The Nature and Functions of Authority* (ISBN 9780874621044; Marquette University Press; www.marquette.edu/mupress); the University of Chicago Press for permission to use Simon's foreword to *The Material Logic of John of St. Thomas*; the Philosophy Documentation Center for permission to use Simon's essays "The Philosopher's Calling" (in *Proceedings of the American Catholic Philosophical Association* 32 [1958]: 29–34) and "Order in Analogical Sets" (in *The New Scholasticism* 34, no. 1 [1960]: 1–42); and the *Chicago Review* for permission to use Simon's essay "To Be and To Know" (*Chicago Review* 14, no. 4 [1961]: 83–100).

I am gratified that the University of Notre Dame Press has believed in the value of Tony's final project. Certainly, John and especially Tony must be properly acknowledged, for the shape of the work, its chosen contributors, and a substantial number of the texts to be found in the *Reader* are their doing. Nevertheless, much remained to be completed and a variety of choices needed to be made in regard to the texts used in order to integrate what they had well begun into a final whole. Since I alone am responsible for this whole, any failings in it that have gone uncorrected are to be laid solely at my door.

I want to thank Stephen Little and especially Jane Bonfiglio of UNDP for diligently working with me to bring this collaborative work of philosophers finally into the light of day. I also wish to thank the work's copyeditor, Scott Barker, whose fine eye for detail has improved the text. Throughout, it has been a pleasure for me to have worked with the volume's other contributors to honor our great and common teacher. This work is rightly dedicated to his son, Anthony O. Simon—as discerning and loyal a friend as he was an intelligent and indefatigable champion of his father's oeuvre.

Notes

1. To see the remarkable extent of what he accomplished, consult our Select Bibliography. He was not only the world's expert on *what* his father had written—as is evident from the many bibliographies of his work that he had published (culminating in the one he published in *Acquaintance with the Absolute*)—but also on what was *most valuable* in it, through his intimate knowledge of that work. This can be seen in the selection of texts he made for this *Reader*, with the cooperation of John W. Carlson. Part of his life's work also consisted in furthering writings *on* his father. See the eleven essays featuring his father published in *Freedom in the Modern World* (1989), the five published in *Freedom, Virtue, and the Common Good*, which he edited with Curtis L. Hancock (Washington, DC: American Maritain Association, 1995), and the six he edited in *Acquaintance with the Absolute* (1998). Also, see the four articles in "Yves-René Simon, 1903–1961," special issue, *Cahiers Jacques Maritain* 47 (2003).

2. See Jeanne Heffernan Schindler's concluding sentence (chapter 20 in this volume); the remark can be found in Willis D. Nutting's review of *Work, Society, and Culture*, in *The Review of Politics* 34, no. 1 (1972): 239. Nutting, in turn, was paraphrasing Samuel Johnson's epitaph for Oliver Goldsmith.

3. See John W. Carlson, *Understanding Our Being: Introduction to Speculative Philosophy in the Perennial Tradition* (Washington, DC: Catholic University of America Press, 2008), and Carlson, *Words of Wisdom: A Philosophical Dictionary for the Perennial Tradition* (Notre Dame, IN: University of Notre Dame Press, 2012).

4. Tony, with John quickly concurring, asked that I assume editorial responsibility for this work in the spring of 2012. Tony soon became quite ill, dying shortly thereafter, on August 2, and John then abruptly followed, on December 12.

SIMON'S WORKS IN THE *READER*

The date next to each work refers to its first publication, whether in French or English, even if the work was later revised. A complete entry for each work will be found in the Select Bibliography. Save for one exception (see the editorial note on the first of John C. Cahalan's selected texts, chapter 4), the latest English edition of the work is always used in the *Reader*. The first number given is that of the pages from Simon's text. (A given range of texts may skip one or two pages, but no more. Thus, material found on pages 1, 2, 4, 5, 6, 9, and 12 would simply read "1–12"; but material found on pages 1, 2, 6, 7, 11, and 12 would read "1–2, 6–7, 11–12.") The second number (in parenthesis) is where those pages are found in the *Reader*.

An Introduction to Metaphysics of Knowledge (1934): 39–84 (59–74); 137–54 (83–87)
A Critique of Moral Knowledge (1934): 9–13, 17–21, 41, 48–49, 53 (152–55)
The Ethiopian Campaign and French Political Thought (1936): 74–78 (427–28)
Nature and Functions of Authority (1940): 1–7, 12–18, 28–30 (424–26)
The Road to Vichy (1941): 13–15, 42–43, 50–51, 102–3, 111, 115, 136–37, 163–65, 196–97, 201–4 (429–32)
The March to Liberation (1942): 8–10, 15–18, 23, 33–34, 84–96 (433–37)
Foresight and Knowledge (1944): 1–5 (30–32); 117–25 (134–39)
The Community of the Free (1945): 13–21 (267–72); 88, 104–13, 118–21, 128–30, 134–36 (438–42)
Philosophy of Democratic Government (1951): 1–6 (420–23); 7–9, 19–21, 26–42, 47–48, 70–71, 139–41 (341–47); 62–67 (321–24); 232–53 (379–95); 296–307 (299–303)
Freedom of Choice (1951): 3–15, 18–24, 44–65, 144–58 (176–200); 25–26, 31–34 (310–11); 83–87, 91–97 (44–47); 97–127 (204–20)
The Material Logic of John of St. Thomas (Foreword) (1955): xxii–xxiii (28–29)

A General Theory of Authority (1962): 29–30, 36–39, 122–26 (317–20); 40, 48–49, 55–57, 79, 84, 93, 134, 143–45, 161 (348–51); 100–115 (273–84); 126–31, 148–56 (294–98)

The Tradition of Natural Law (1965): 69–87, 97–98, 107–9 (328–36); 89–96 (312–15); 125–36 (165–68); 138–39, 143–45 (112–14)

Freedom and Community (1968): 33–34 (108–9); 93–101, 109–13 (289–93)

The Great Dialogue of Nature and Space (1970): 94–106 (88–94); 144–49, 153–60 (33–43)

Work, Society, and Culture (1971): 33–59 (356–75); 154–67, 182–88 (399–414)

Jacques Maritain: Homage in Words and Pictures (coauthored with J. W. Griffin) (1974): 3–14 (9–12)

The Definition of Moral Virtue (1986): 19–29, 55–61 (225–39); 109–11 (169–70); 1, 15–16, 69–87, 91–92, 106–8, 116–19, 127–30 (244–62)

Practical Knowledge (1991): 1–5, 15–16, 21–23, 53–61, 65–66, 71–74 (156–64); 88–98 (48–52); 115–20, 123–32 (140–48); 123 (316); 139–44, 149–55 (443–46)

Philosopher at Work (2000)* (the following four essays therein):

"The Philosopher's Calling" (1958): 1–6 (13–22)
"An Essay on Sensation" (1960): 57–111 (118–30)
"On Order in Analogical Sets" (1960): 140–64 (99–107)
"To Be and To Know" (1961): 173–92 (75–78); 183–86, 191–92 (110–11)

* One will find the full bibliographical listing to these essays, where originally published, directly following the bibliographical reference to *Philosopher at Work* in the Select Bibliography. In the *Reader*, these essays when used are again referenced to where they were republished in *Philosopher at Work*.

PART I

Introduction

CHAPTER 1

The Philosophy of Yves R. Simon

The biography of Yves René Marie Simon,[1] intellectual or otherwise, has yet to be written.[2] Facts can be swiftly stated. He was born at Cherbourg in 1903, to August Simon (an industrialist) and Berthe Porquet. He had two older brothers, both of whom died in his youth (the younger in World War I), and one older sister. In 1920, he enrolled at the Lycée Louis-le-Grand in Paris; in 1923, he received a Diplôme d'Études Supérieur de Philosophie from the Sorbonne; and, in 1929, he received a licentiate in philosophy from the Institut Catholique de Paris. In 1930, he married Paule Dromard; they had six children, four born in France, two in the United States. In 1930, he also began teaching at the Catholic University of Lille, and he became a professor there in 1932. He obtained his doctorate in philosophy ("Cum Singulari Prorsus Laude") from the Institut Catholique in 1934.[3] It was there, in 1922, that he had first encountered Jacques Maritain, who became his philosophical mentor and great, lifelong, friend.[4] In 1938, he accepted a position in the Philosophy Department at the University of Notre Dame as visiting professor[5] (until the collapse of France in 1940, at which time he became a member of its regular faculty). He stayed there until 1948, when he went to the University of Chicago, where he taught as a member of its Committee on Social Thought, until cancer forced his retirement in 1959.[6] He died in May 1961. Even more than Maritain, Simon found in the United States a politics and a society dear to his heart. He became a U.S. citizen and never once returned to France after the war. Dying young, he left many projects unfinished. His son Anthony O. Simon, often working with his father's former pupils,[7] saw to the posthumous publication of many of his philosophical works throughout the latter half of the twentieth century.

Socrates is usually seen, and rightly, as the father of Western philosophy as it came to be.[8] He was intensely focused on a two-part problem: what it was to be a good person, and how to become one. Plato argued (e.g., in the *Symposium* and in *Republic*, bk. 7) that his teacher's task could only be accomplished by knowing the standard that measured all goods, and thus by an intuition of the Absolute Good. Simon's philosophical focus was the same as Socrates's, but he had taken Aristotle's point: Plato's "vision of the Good" did not "get the job done" (and it is notable how spare Simon's reflections on God are in his published writings).[9] What was needed, instead, was a sure grasp of the proximate standard and guide to action, namely, human nature, and especially an understanding of the difference between theoretical wisdom and the practical wisdom needed to guide our decisions, so that they might, indeed, accord with the true and the good. This became Simon's central philosophical undertaking: to understand and to articulate the nature of the practical wisdom essential to becoming and remaining a good human being.[10]

This focus extended in two directions. First, backward to a just account of human nature and human knowing (theoretical and practical).[11] Second, forward to the way practical wisdom operated politically and socially,[12] not just in general, but also in relation to contingencies of our own time, especially to the events that led up to World War II and that it then occasioned.[13]

Part I offers, by way of introduction, first this brief account of his life and work and of the *Reader*. This is then followed by what is, in effect, a "prologue" to the rest of the book. As was Bernard J. F. Lonergan (twenty-one months his junior), Simon was very concerned with philosophical method, and so it is fitting that the *Reader* begin by speaking to this abiding concern. Its chosen texts bear witness to his interest both in logic and in the philosophy of science. Simon's attraction to Jacques Maritain owed much to the way the latter explained the relation between empirical science and philosophy, and Simon here follows and deepens that position.

Part II is rightly devoted to human knowing. Better than most in the tradition of Aristotle and Thomas, Simon well articulates the essential immateriality, and the objectivity, of knowledge. His analyses of action and of its analogical character are as trenchant and as profound as anything one will encounter in his tradition. Perhaps even more arresting is his remarkable "An Essay on Sensation," which not only highlights his Aristotelian credentials but underlines the qualified immateriality (and thus the mysterious "inner life") proper to sensitive knowledge and animal life. Although occasional overlaps in the introductions were almost inevitable, these are superficial: each chapter in part II focuses on a different, sparkling, facet of his philosophical analysis. Part II concludes by turning from an analysis of theoretical to practical knowledge.

Part III of the *Reader* is rightly devoted to practical philosophy. It begins with his no less brilliant analyses of human freedom (chapter 9), in his gem of a book devoted to it, *Freedom of Choice*.[14] We begin with his account of freedom fully achieved, one that emphasizes the self-determination and self-mastery proper to it. We then take a closer look at the relation between reason and will at the heart of free choice (chapter 10). The "overlap" here is only apparent: what Adler called the "natural freedom of self-determination" (i.e., "freedom of choice"), when rightly used, then leads to what Adler termed the "freedom of self-perfection" (i.e., "terminal freedom" of self-mastery).[15] (To instance this distinction, we can freely choose to enslave ourselves, to a physical addiction or a life of crime, for example, or we can freely choose to live a life based on the truth, a life that will, in the words of the Apostle John written over the portal of many a university, then set us truly free.) We go on to highlight Simon's careful analyses of "use" and "*habitus*" essential to an account of virtue (chapter 11), and then move on to its careful definition and its contrast with inadequate simulacra often found in contemporary philosophers, ending with the necessary interdependence of the virtues. Part III concludes with analyses of the freedom that is proper to the social and political order.

Part IV details Simon's political philosophy. With Plato and Aristotle he recognized the inseparability of ethics and politics. Perhaps it is fair to say that no other great contemporary Thomist evinced as deep an interest in politics as Simon. And, from some of his earliest work, for example, on Proudhon,[16] Simon indicated that he was a son of the French Revolution and its commitments to liberty, equality, and fraternity. He once remarked to Jacques Maritain that he was the only "sans-culotte" among his many disciples.[17] There is surely no greater Thomistic account and defense of democracy than his *Philosophy of Democratic Government*, now justly translated into a number of languages. Indeed, his may be the finest account of democracy to be found in any contemporary philosopher. His analyses—especially his original and deeply thoughtful development of Thomas Aquinas's account of authority—remain strikingly pertinent to problems that continue to vex contemporary politics. And his insistence both on the virtue of work and on the requirements for economic justice in our present social order are prescient in relation to abiding concerns of recent pontiffs: of St. John Paul the Great and of Pope Francis. Indeed, as the readings in our epilogue clearly attest, Simon was that rare philosopher who combined theoretical brilliance with practical acuity and insight.

Simon, then, attempted nothing less than to show that there could be a living and vital Aristotelianism in his and our own day. He labored to show that the careful analyses of Aristotle's philosophy remained a live option for a contemporary philosopher. He sought to defend his thought (philosophically) in the secular circumstances of his current society and day, thus showing himself to be a true follower of Thomas, who sought to baptize his thought (theologically) in the world of faith of his day. Any Aristotelian (beginning with Aristotle himself) recognizes the need to think within a tradition and the futility of trying to start *ab novo*, and Simon is no exception. Throughout his work, one will find his debt to Maritain, in particular. To site but a few examples: his use of the distinction between "empiriological" and philosophical analyses of nature or of the idea of "superdetermination" in his account of freedom of choice; or, again, his defense of the existence of practically practical knowledge and also of the inadequacy of practical philosophy absent a knowledge of our present fallen condition and of the final happiness offered us in union with God. Through Maritain, Simon also inherited a healthy respect for the commentators of Thomas, be it Cajetan or John of St. Thomas.[18] Simon thinks out of this philosophical tradition.

In recognition of his debt to Maritain, we start in this introduction with an excerpt from his book *Jacques Maritain: Homage in Words and Pictures* (1974).[19] This is then followed by his 1958 acceptance (given in its entirety) of the American Catholic Philosophical Association's Aquinas Medal, a speech from which the title of our *Reader* is taken.

I have detailed the matter of his philosophical thought, but what is most striking and most important is the form of that thought, the way Simon approached his philosophical vocation. For not only is he here most original, but he also provides a philosophical model for present Thomists. Donald Gallagher—the first president of the American Maritain Association and the well-known author of the first bibliography of Maritain's works[20]—once characterized Simon in these terms: "*Simon is preeminently the philosopher adhering closely to philosophical argument.* . . . [he] *is the thinker, the teacher-argumentator, whose discourse in rigorous and careful procedure leads minds to definitive conclusions about reality.*"[21] This is surely right. He could also have added that he was an exceptional teacher, beloved by his students. (Something of "Simon the man" also comes through in his work; it is easy to see why his students loved him.) He was expert at finding concrete examples to illumine an idea. Who can ever forget the contrast he draws between the indifference of a poor man, who is open to any good just because he has nothing, and the indifference of a rich man, whose wealth frees him to buy whatever good he wants to make his own? This perfectly illustrates the difference between the passive indifference that consists in the ability "to receive a multiplicity of influences" and the active indifference (proper to true freedom) that enables us "to produce a multiplicity of effects." Or, again, once encountered, who will fail to recall the difference between the virtually unconscious swerve of a man almost asleep at the wheel, before the blur of an animal in the road ahead, and the conscious decision of a man wide awake, who chooses to swerve, thereby risking his own life to avoid a child in the road? A comparison that again perfectly captures the difference between an Epicurean "indetermination" and the "self-determination" that is properly at the heart of our freedom to choose. Simon also sought to find the right contemporary words to present ancient definitions, in defense of their insightfulness. A perfect example of this is his expression of an "existential readiness to act well" to describe the order to our good proper to moral virtue.

Finally, Simon engaged in the hard task of conceptual analysis, always striving for the rigor that is proper to philosophy. This is above all true in his analyses of being and knowledge that he rightly recognized were what crucially separated his Aristotelian thinking from the heirs of Descartes. All of his work is animated by an intense love of the truth and a desire to state the truth accurately. Simon was a "philosopher's philosopher,"[22] someone it is hard for anyone bitten by the desire for conceptual clarity distinctive to all philosophers not to appreciate, even if he or she may choose to demur on this or that point or honestly acknowledge a different standpoint. In the manner of their philosophizing, Thomists could do worse than to take their cue from Simon.

This intellectual feast, of Simon's finest work, is what our book sets before its readers.

Michael D. Torre

Jacques Maritain:
Homage in Words and Pictures
("Homage in Words," 3–14)

I would like to start with a paradox and say that Maritain was the first non-scholastic among the disciples of St. Thomas. . . .[23] A scholastic philosophy is a philosophy of professors, and Maritain holds that the professor is precisely the worst enemy of St. Thomas's philosophy. A scholastic culture is centered on what takes place between teachers and students, with little or no concern with what goes on in public affairs, in art and literature, and in spiritual life. It is this meaning of Scholasticism that we bear in mind when we set in contrast the Scholastics and the Humanists of the sixteenth century. These scholastics were not always bad at expounding the rational, scientific and philosophic psychology of animals and man. But when there was a question of understanding man in the contingencies of history, in the indefinitely many accidents of his concrete existence, when there was a question of understanding what we would now call the existential man, they were rather poor and the Humanists were much better. Interest in Scholastic philosophies was revived toward the end of the nineteenth century and the old conflict could be observed again. In fact, it had never died out. I know of liberal arts colleges where there is a tendency to center training about philosophy. Because of my professional interest, I might be expected to be enthusiastic about such programs. I am not. I rather think that on the college level it is man considered in the contingencies of his concrete existence who should be the main subject of liberal studies. Although there have been considerable changes in the attitudes and ideas of Maritain, one feature is present in all periods of his life: he has always been in warm contact with the existential man, and his excellence in the rational analysis of the soul has never interfered with his intuitive relation to men such as they are here and now, such as they have been shaped by history, by grace and by suffering, and such as they behave with regard to their eternal destiny. . . .

From the beginning Maritain had the soul of a contemplative and that of an artist. I have some notion of the people whose company he liked, for, over a long period, it was my privilege to visit his home on Sunday afternoons. The living room was generally crowded, less by teachers or students than by writers, poets, painters, musicians, persons interested in mysticism, missionaries and friends of missions. Most of the artists were of the vanguard description....

What "scholasticism" meant when Maritain was a young man has become hard to realize, precisely because of the work he has been doing, for half a century, especially in the domain of the philosophy of art. "Scholasticism" was never in vital communication with the living energies of temporal communities. Even at its best it was an academic and ecclesiastical affair.... The genius of Western nations was producing masterworks in history, the sciences, technology and the fine arts, but there was no communication between these domains of intellectual activity and the sound work that a few seminary teachers offered to the world in a very particular language. It has been said that a word is "a little poem born of people's spontaneity." Such poems are absent from the best as well as the worst products of "scholastic" philosophy in the nineteenth century. After having read the first essays of Maritain on Bergson, Léon Bloy wrote in his diary that philosophy had quite a new appearance when it was treated by his godson. "I [have] read in the *Revue Thomiste* a paper of my godson Jacques Maritain, 'The Two Bergsonisms.' That I have little use for philosophy is well known: In my opinion it is the most boring way of wasting the precious time of our lives and its Hyrcanian dialect discourages me. But with Jacques Maritain things are strikingly different.... It never occurred to me that the shabby jacket of a philosopher could clothe such a strong arm. The arm is that of an athlete and the voice expresses a powerful lamentation. I felt at the time something like a wave of sorrowful poetry, a mighty wave coming from very far"....

I feel that I am no longer young when I see around me boys and girls to whom the Spanish Civil War does not mean so much. It is already an old story. How many Spaniards died in this war? One million is a reasonable estimate, and a rather conservative one. The thing that I cannot say is what fraction of that million died on the battlefield. Beyond doubt, the ratio of those killed outside all military action was very high. Whenever someone says that a huge amount of crime was committed only on the other side, he either lies or does not know all the facts. Besides the slaughter, the Spanish Civil War brought about, and not in Spain alone, an extraordinary indulgence in hatred and in the most debased feelings the human soul ever conceived. The French were close to the Spanish war in more than one respect. Lies about every subject that pertained to the ordeal of Spain were really atrocious. Spanish refugees who were pouring into France comprised all sorts of characters, from the most noble to the most undependable. We all felt that we had an urgent duty to do something about the misfortune of our neighbors and its international consequences. Maritain stood for mediation between the parties at war. So did I. We met in committees with a faint hope that the crushing victory of one side and the slaughter of the other might be avoided. . . .

My first political writing, if I omit a few articles in my student years, was a short study on the Ethiopian war, or more exactly on the attitudes of French political thinkers towards Mussolini's war in Ethiopia. As this pamphlet was about to be published, I happened to describe it to an old friend whom I had known in groups formed for the study of international organizations. He was a man of sharp intelligence and fine education, a jurist by training, and a civil servant of high rank. Some prominent and noisy intellectuals had just given Mussolini the support of an enthusiastic manifesto. My friend listened attentively to my exposition. He interrupted me with this remark: "*You* are trained in the handling of abstract ideas."[24] In another context this remark would have meant that a philosopher is restricted to abstractions and has no sense of political contingencies. But this is not what he had in mind. He plainly meant that to fulfill such a task as the defense of public conscience against corruption by politicians and intellectuals a few so-called abstract ideas, e.g., those of right, law, contract, community, authority, force, legal coercion, violence, autonomy, and civilization have got to be handled, and that in order that they be handled properly, philosophical training is necessary, or very helpful. . . .

In the discussions which have been going on for over thirty years on the notion of "Christian philosophy," Maritain has never failed to recall, against any possible misunderstanding, that this expression designates a *state* of philosophy, not an essence. If it designated an essence, it would be granted that philosophy receives premises from revelation, and of the great statements of St. Thomas concerning philosophy, theology, and their relationship nothing would be left. When these positions are clearly formulated, the question remains as to whether it is desirable that philosophical issues be treated in a state of abstraction or in a concrete condition of association with the problems of our supernatural destiny. I would not hesitate to say that it is, to a large extent, a question of calling. I am strongly attracted to the method of isolation because it furnishes special guarantees of epistemological purity and logical rigor. To be sure, Maritain will never be tempted to use a revealed premise in a philosophical treatment. But there can be no doubt that his calling is that of the Christian philosopher who generally treats philosophical issues in the particular *state* that they assume by reason of their relation to Christian faith and theology.

Likewise, when we come to practical issues, it may be asked whether it is desirable that what is essential and scientific in them should be treated in the state of scientific isolation, or in association with problems of a prudential order. Again, the answer is, to a large extent, determined by one's particular calling. In order that we should, at all times, be aware of what we are doing, in order that epistemological purity be preserved, it is certainly desirable that some men should write treatises of political philosophy or theology where the considerations of contingency and the decisions of prudence play as small a part as possible. But what the calling of Maritain was is not dubious. We have seen that all his writings on political and social subjects were composed under circumstances which, purely and simply, demanded an extensive exercise of historical intelligence and prudential judgment.

In this long exposition, little has been said about the moral personality of Maritain. What would have been the use of expressing admiration for a man to whom I am well known to owe so much? By way of conclusion, I wish, however, to remark that there may well be a difference between the calling of a man and his choice. I mean what he would have chosen if he had had his own way. I suspect that there have been many conflicts throughout Maritain's career between his choice and his calling. And I cannot think of a single case in which his calling was not preferred to his choice. Remote ages may feel it relevant to remark that Maritain is the philosopher who, in case of conflict, never hesitated to fulfill his calling rather than to follow his choice.

Philosopher at Work
("The Philosopher's Calling," 1–6)

Just a year ago, Father George Klubertanz took me by surprise when he telephoned to ask if I would accept the American Catholic Philosophical Association's Aquinas medal for 1958. I said I would, of course. It never occurred to me that anyone would refuse the Aquinas medal. Also I could not miss my only chance to give all of you my thanks for having nominated me. In the difficulties of the work that I hope to do, your friendliness will never cease to be a source of courage: let this be considered an expression of my gratitude.

To be sure, courage is a thing of which a philosopher needs an excess for many reasons, the first of which is the weight of past failure. At the beginning of the *Metaphysics*, Aristotle gives to understand that first philosophy is the limit of the human mind's possibilities. What holds for first philosophy holds also, in varying degree, for the other domains of philosophical inquiry. Generally speaking, the human mind is not at its best in philosophy. The fine arts often fill us with a sentiment of perfection which helps us to understand the meaning of the image of God in man. This was well said by a poet. In a piece entitled *The Beacons*, Baudelaire speaks of Rubens, Leonardo da Vinci, Rembrandt, Michelangelo, Watteau, Goya, Delacroix, and concludes:

> For there is not, O Lord, a better testimony
> That we ever can give our dignity
> Than the ardent sobbing which moves from age to age
> And dies at the fringe of Thy eternity.

Replace these artists by great philosophers: no doubt, some of them were ardently dedicated to the search for truth, and sobbing, at times, accompanied their labors. Their performances bear testimony to our dignity, but they speak more loudly of our wretchedness. Strikingly, philosophers often are most arbitrary and weak in the immediate vicinity of their best accomplishments. As an artist, Plato is at least as great as any of the painters in the list of Baudelaire, and we are short of words when we want to express his philosophical greatness. The dialectician who keeps probing all the time and pledges himself never to deliver a system has established a number of truths definitively. He has refuted empiricism forever. He has manifested, with the most complete success, the infinity of the qualitative distance between intelligible objects and the data of sense experience, no matter how refined. But when this founder of the theory of intelligibility elaborates on the truth that he has so convincingly established, he can hardly do better than leave the way open, for centuries, to suspicious traditions and highly improbable hypotheses about a previous life of the human spirit and its native familiarity with a world of things intelligible. As for the very few philosophers of whom it can be said that they were spared really grave errors, one thing remarkable is how little they have to say about the truths that they consider most fundamental. A decisive advance was made when Aristotelian abstraction displaced Platonic innatism and reminiscence. On the subject of abstraction, a few geniuses have done good work. We have no doubt that the direction of Aristotle is sound and never will be refuted. And yet when we are challenged to explain what it means to say that intelligible representations are abstracted from the data of sense experience, our laborious answers are mostly characterized by large areas of silence. There is no reason to believe that these areas cannot be filled. They should have been filled long ago. Let us go to work, there is no time to waste. But, to be sure, hoping to accomplish some part of the work which should have been done so long ago is an appalling ambition. If this ambition is protected by illusions, it will not do any good. Let it be inspired and made invulnerable by fortitude, I mean by the kind of fortitude that is derived from the sense of a great destiny, of an everlastingly fruitful task, and also from willingness to be unprofitable servants.

This urge to perform the unprecedented is not peculiar to the philosopher. The progressivity of our nature and of our community challenges us, in all domains, to do things that men, as yet, never succeeded in doing. In this respect a great example is set by scientists and technicians. How is it that philosophers seem unable to follow an example which is consistently made glorious by unquestioned success? We are here touching upon a significant cause of our bewilderments: in philosophy, success is never unquestioned. With regard to communication, the destinies of science and philosophy are strikingly different. Ever since the notion of demonstrative thinking became familiar to men, it has been taken for granted that a genuinely demonstrated proposition should win common assent. Indeed, it should, and ability to cause consensus certainly follows upon demonstrativeness. The expectation of consensus, wherever there is claim to certain proof, is stronger than ever in the technological society, where the quest for certainty, as the pragmatists tried to show, obtains new satisfaction from the operation of two vitally related factors, the consensus of the experts and actual success in the control of physical nature. The minds of our contemporaries are filled with patterns of consensus confirmed by technical feats. Under these circumstances the disagreements of the philosophers are, more than ever, considered intolerable. (When the Cartesian reformation took place, it was still possible to tell people that the reason for the philosophers' failure to agree was the lack of the right method, and that the promulgation of four simple rules would bring about, apparently within a short time, the desired consensus.) In the more common opinion, it is an accepted fact that the never-ending disagreements of the philosophers show that there is no obvious objective necessity in philosophy. Some conclude that time spent in philosophical research is time wasted, but many hold that philosophy, without achieving demonstrative certainty, can still serve mankind by keeping alive an interest in issues that remain worth investigating, even though they do not admit of rational determination. At least, philosophical systems should serve to express the sentiments of the human soul in relation to the mysteries of our destiny.

No doubt, any proposition which expresses a rational necessity is, in terms of logical nature, capable of winning universal assent. There is no essential reason why it should not determine consensus. But there are many accidental reasons why certain propositions, though expressive of rational necessity, do not have the slightest chance of being commonly assented to. It would not be sufficient to say that philosophy is uniquely difficult. In the sciences also there are many issues of extreme difficulty: yet, concerning these issues, experts often achieve a remarkable amount of consensus.

It seems that the reasons why philosophers disagree have never been analyzed and set forth adequately. Many of the reasons are but confusedly suspected. To mention only one example, not enough attention has been given to the consequences of philosophy's ability to exist in a multiplicity of states. Physics exists only in the state of a technically developed discipline. Philosophy exists in the state of a technically developed discipline, but it also exists in the state of common intelligence apart from any special education, and it also exists within the thought of the physicist, and within the thought of the mathematician, and within the thought of the biologist, and within the thought of the humanist, and within the ways of thought of many other learned people. The ability to exist in a multiplicity of states is a glorious privilege of philosophic intelligence and the ground of its significance to culture at large. But when philosophical intuitions born of scientific thought, or of a moral or aesthetic experience, or of a sense for the history of ideas, are built into philosophical systems, all sorts of accidents are likely to take place. The examination of these and similar contingencies would make it clear that the disagreements of the philosophers are abundantly accounted for, without there being any need to question the possibility of establishing philosophic truth demonstratively.

If it is true that philosophic propositions may express objective necessity, and that accidental, but overwhelming reasons will always prevent them from winning factual consensus, the position of the philosopher in society raises embarrassing problems. Some philosophers have access to demonstratively established truths. What are these poor fellows going to do? They certainly have nothing to brag about, for access to rare truth is the most undeserved of all privileges. And yet they have to express their well-founded convictions with firmness and zeal, they have to fight for these precious convictions, they would be unfaithful to truth if they consented to have them described as more or less personal opinions. This is really what is strangest in the philosopher's calling: this duty of fighting an often solitary fight against learned and dignified persons, against Descartes and Spinoza and Berkeley and a few others, with the inescapable implication that he, the solitary fighter, knows better about the really important issues than most of the greatest among the philosophical geniuses. It looks as if a painter of fair talent went to war with

Leonardo da Vinci, Michelangelo, and Rubens. How can the philosopher convince people that he is not just yielding to insane pride? The audacity with which he discusses, criticizes, and refutes genius bears all the appearances of the worst kind of conceit. Can anything be done to remove these damaging appearances? Much can be done indeed, but to conceal certainty by proposing truth under the externals of socially acceptable opinion is not always the right method. The job has to be done through things that are much more difficult to acquire than good social manners. These things are virtues, and accordingly they are hard to get. In the fulfillment of the philosopher's duty there is no substitute for the fearless love of truth, for selflessness, fortitude, and humility.

Addressing especially the younger members of this audience, I wish also to remark that, all well considered, the life of the philosopher is worth the troubles of which we have spoken, and many more troubles that we shall not speak of. The team work that brings so much comfort to the scientist is rarely possible in philosophy, and the huge amount of research, analysis, trials and errors, and endeavors of every description that a philosophic life demands has to be done, for the most part, in solitude. This is not an effect of essential necessity: it is just a situation generally inevitable. But in such a meeting as this it would be particularly unfair to indulge in a gloomy view of the case. This is the very proper time and place to speak of what happens when the philosopher breaks out of his solitude and succeeds in communicating, together with a particle of truth, something of the aspiration, something of the dedication, something of the hope and the love that keep him going through never-ending difficulties. A philosopher who has ever succeeded in communicating his inspiration together with his demonstration, and who has experienced the joy of a friendship born of such communication, will always feel that if he had to choose again, philosophy would again be his calling.

Notes

All notes below are those of the editor.

1. His son Anthony rightly insisted that he be referred to as "Yves R. Simon," in order to distinguish him from another "Yves Simon," a French

singer, often referenced on the internet. During his lifetime, however, he was often referred to simply as "Yves Simon," as will sometimes be seen in various publications referred to herein; however, the *Reader* is faithful to his son's judgment and includes the "R." throughout.

2. Simon was born on March 3, 1903, and died on May 11, 1961. For brief summaries of his work, see Marie-Vincent Leroy, OP, "Yves R. Simon (1903–1961): A Bio-Bibliography," in Yves R. Simon, *The Definition of Moral Virtue*, edited by Vukan Kuic (New York: Fordham University Press, 1986), ix–xiv, and Anthony O. Simon, "Editor's Note" and "A Brief Chronology," in *Acquaintance with the Absolute: The Philosophy of Yves R. Simon, Essays and Bibliography*, ed. Anthony O. Simon (New York: Fordham University Press, 1998), ix–xiii and xviii–xix. For a complete bibliography of his works through 1996, see Anthony O. Simon, "Yves R. Simon: A Definitive Bibliography, 1923–1996," in *Acquaintance with the Absolute*, 185–293. We have very little on Simon's person and life. He left a few memories of the latter: see Yves R. Simon, "Philosophy and Faith: Extracts from the Memoirs of a French Philosopher," Part 1, in *Notes et Documents*, n.s., 23 (1988): 76–82, and Part 2, in *Notes et Documents* 14 (1979): 5–8 (both originally published in French in *La Nouvelle Relève* [Montreal], 1942); Simon, "My First Memories of Jacques Maritain," in *Notes et Documents*, n.s., 2–3 (1983): 106–10 (first published in French in *The New Scholasticism*, 1982); and especially Simon, "Yves R. Simon," in *The Book of Catholic Authors* (Third Series), ed. Walter Romig (Detroit: Walter Romig Company, 1945), 262–70. Recently, two accounts have been given of his life: Bernard Hubert's account of Simon's youthful years in Paris, in Hubert, "Les années parisiennes d'Yves Simon et ses premiers pas avec Jacques Maritain (1920–1929)," *Cahiers Jacques Maritain* 79 (December 2019): 51–73; and Florian Michel's of Simon's early time in the United States, in Michel, "L'américanisation d'un intellectuel français: Le cas de Yves Simon (1903–1961)," *Transatlantica* (Online), 1 (2014), https://journals.openedition.org/transatlantica/6842.

3. His thesis, his first book, was published that year: Yves R. Simon, *Introduction à l'ontologie du connnaître* (Paris: Desclée de Brouwer, 1934); English: *An Introduction to Metaphysics of Knowledge*, ed. and trans. Vukan Kuic and Richard J. Thompson (New York: Fordham University Press, 1990); 1934 also saw the publication of his second book, a complementary study of practical knowledge: Simon, *Critique de la connaissance morale* (Paris: Desclée de Brouwer, 1934). Seventy years later, this book was translated and introduced (vii–xix), by Ralph McInerny as *A Critique of Moral Knowledge* (New York: Fordham University Press, 2002).

4. It is fair to say that Maritain had three "collaborators" in his work: Raïssa, in relation to matters poetic and spiritual (and she also reviewed all his works, as he often attested); Abbé Charles Journet, and then later cardinal, in relation to matters of Scholastic theology; and Yves R. Simon, in relation to matters philosophical. For his lifelong interchanges with Journet, see the six volumes of correspondence recently published by Éditions Universitaires, Fribourg-Suisse, and Éditions Saint-Paul, Paris (1996–2009). For Maritain's almost thirty-four-year correspondence with Simon, see Florian Michel, ed., *Jacques Maritain, Yves Simon Correspondance*, Tome 1, *Les années francaises (1927–1940)* (Tours: Éditions CLD, 2008), and Tome 2, *Les années américaines (1941–1961)* (Paris: Éditions CLD, 2012). Simon says that the first lecture of Maritain he attended was on January 12, 1922, and that his personal relationship with him only began in the spring of 1924: see Simon, "My First Memories of Jacques Maritain," trans. and ed. Anthony O. Simon (Niagara, NY: Maritain Institute Series, 1985), 2 and 4. This article can also be found in *Notes et Documents*, n.s., 2–3 (April-September 1983): 106–10.

5. Waldemar Gurian, a political scientist from Europe then at the University of Notre Dame, and a friend of Maritain, had recommended Simon for his appointment at the university; see Florian Michel, "Yves Simon à la bataille de Chicago (1948–1961)," *Cahiers Jacques Maritain* 47 (December 2003): 40–56. Waldemar Gurian was an Armenian Jew by descent, Russian by birth (in 1903), German by education (from 1911), and a Catholic by conversion (in 1914). He fled Germany in 1934, came to the University of Notre Dame in 1937, and there founded *The Review of Politics*, in 1939.

6. For his connection to, and life at, the University of Chicago, see Florian Michel, "Yves Simon à la bataille de Chicago." John U. Nef would seem to have been instrumental in his appointment (see ibid., 42–43). For a listing of his twenty-six courses at the University of Chicago, see his student Vukan Kuic's list in his editor's preface to *Work, Society, and Culture* (New York: Fordham University Press, 1971), xii.

7. One should particularly single out Vukan Kuic, who edited three of Simon's posthumous volumes—*The Tradition of Natural Law: A Philosopher's Reflections* (1965); *Work, Society, and Culture* (1971); and *The Definition of Moral Virtue* (1986)—supplied an introduction to a fourth, *A General Theory of Authority* (1980), and translated and edited Simon's thesis: *An Introduction to Metaphysics of Knowledge* (1990). Also see Kuic, *Yves R Simon: Real Democracy* (Lanham, MD: Rowman and Littlefield, 1999).

8. Alfred North Whitehead's famous remark that all of Western philosophy is a "series of footnotes to Plato" is on the mark: see Whitehead, *Process and Reality: An Essay in Cosmology* (New York: Free Press, 1969), 53.

9. That Simon recognized that to know God was both the end of the entire philosophical undertaking (e.g., the goal of metaphysics) and the deepest human aspiration (as Aristotle teaches in his ethics) can be seen from the "Encyclopedia" that was Simon's final, and unfinished, philosophical project and that includes a section on "The Existence and Nature of God." This material remains in the archives of the Jacques Maritain Center at the University of Notre Dame, material that has yet to be fully mined by contemporary scholars. For a summary of what it contains, see Anthony O. Simon, "Yves R. Simon: A Definitive Bibliography, 1923–1996," 289–93. Here is a list just of those topics that have more than one folder of material devoted to them in the archives: Causality, Critique of Practical Knowledge, Ethics, Formal Logic, Metaphysics of Knowledge, Metaphysics of Love, Philosophy of Nature, Politics, Pierre-Joseph Proudhon, Psychology, Scientific Knowledge, and Work.

10. This is the concern of *A Critique of Moral Knowledge* (1934), *Foresight and Knowledge* (1944), *The Definition of Moral Virtue* (1986) (which is based on a course on the virtues that he gave at the University of Chicago in 1957), and *Practical Knowledge* (1991), a work that was put together from a series of his essays on this subject and whose outline he had already made just before his death. For full references to these and other of Simon's work cited below, see the Select Bibliography in this volume.

11. Theoretical wisdom is the concern of *An Introduction to Metaphysics of Knowledge* (1934), his foreword to *The Material Logic of John of St. Thomas* (1955), *The Great Dialogue of Nature and Space* (based mainly on a course given at the University of Chicago in 1959), and key, very late, essays in *Philosopher at Work* (1999): "On Order in Analogical Sets" (1960), "An Essay on Sensation" (1960), and "To Be and To Know" (1961).

Practical wisdom is the concern of *Freedom of Choice* (1951), *The Tradition of Natural Law* (1967) (which is based on a course given at the University of Chicago in 1958), and *Freedom and Community* (2001), half of which republishes work from 1940 and 1947, and the other half of which is based on a course titled "Political Society" given at the University of Chicago in 1955.

12. This is the concern of *Nature and Functions of Authority* (1942), *Philosophy of Democratic Government* (1951), *A General Theory of Authority* (1962) (ready for publication at his death and published the following year), and *Work, Society, and Culture* (1971), which is based on a course given at the University of

Chicago in 1958, developing ideas on work that first saw the light of day—in French—as early as 1938.

13. This is the concern of *The Ethiopian Campaign and French Political Thought* (1936), *The Road to Vichy* (1941), *The March to Liberation* (1942), and *The Community of the Free* (1945).

14. It is notable that Peter Woolf tells us (in his editor's preface to Simon, *Freedom of Choice*) that he and other scholars at the Institute for Philosophical Research had "relied greatly" on Simon's exposition of freedom of choice, in their dialectical examination of the concept (xv), and that Mortimer J. Adler (in his foreword to *Freedom of Choice*) says that it is "the perfect antidote for the errors, the misunderstandings—or worse, the ignorances—that beset the modern discussion of free choice" (xi).

15. For a brief account of the types of freedom that Adler isolates and analyzes in his monumental two-volume work *The Idea of Freedom* (Garden City, NY: Doubleday, 1958 and 1961), see Michael D. Torre, "The Freedoms of Man and Their Relation to God," in *Freedom in the Modern World: Jacques Maritain, Yves R. Simon, and Mortimer J. Adler*, ed. Michael D. Torre (Notre Dame, IN: American Maritain Association, 1989; second printing, 1990), 263–76.

16. Simon's first article was in 1923 (July). In 1924 (March), he published his fifth and sixth articles: "Les idées artistiques et littéraires de Proudhon" and "Le caractère religieux de premier socialism français" (the first part being on Saint-Simon and the Simonists, and the second part being on Buchez and Proudhon). In 1934, he published his critical "Le problème de la transcendence et le défi de Proudhon"; later translated by Charles P. O'Donnell and Vukan Kuic as "The Problem of Transcendence and Proudhon's Challenge," *Thought: A Review of Culture and Ideas* 54, no. 2 (1979): 176–85. On this point, see also Michel Fourcade, "Yves Simon entre S. Thomas et Proudhon," *Cahiers Jacques Maritain* 47 (December 2003): 4–22.

17. See *Jacques Maritain, Yves Simon Correspondance*, 2:70 (Simon letter of September 3, 1941).

18. For some examples of his important reference to, and use of, Cajetan, see some of the longer footnotes in *An Introduction to Metaphysics of Knowledge* (e.g., chap. 1, n26 and n41, and chap. 3, n19, n23, and n27). His interest in John of St. Thomas is of course evident in his introduction to, and translation of, the latter's material logic, but it can also be found in abundance in many footnotes from *An Introduction to Metaphysics of Knowledge*.

19. The *Reader* thus includes an excerpt from all of Simon's twenty books published in English to date, including *The March to Liberation*, which

is currently not in print and which cries out for a new edition to be made, as was recently done for *The Ethiopian Campaign and French Political Thought*.

20. See Donald Gallagher and Idella Gallagher, *The Achievement of Jacques and Raïssa Maritain: A Bibliography, 1906–1961* (Garden City, NY: Doubleday, 1962).

21. See Donald A. Gallagher, "Recollections of Three Thinkers: Adler, Simon, and Maritain," in Torre, ed., *Freedom in the Modern World*, 13–30, 21 and 30 (emphasis original).

22. See ibid., 20.

23. Very few corrections (mostly of punctuation only) have been made to Simon's texts.

24. Here, and throughout Simon's passages, any italicization is in his text.

CHAPTER 2

Method in Philosophy

There is something fascinating about science.
One gets such wholesale returns of conjecture
out of a trifling investment of fact.
—Mark Twain

The nature of fact, indeed the nature of science, is an issue confronted in the texts that follow. The target of Mark Twain's satirical comment may elude us, but inadvertently he tells us something about the nature of science. From one specimen of copper, it is possible to say something about the nature of copper wherever it is found. There may be aspects of the element as yet undiscovered, but it can be identified not only by its sensible properties, properties known in antiquity, but by its melting point, boiling point, specific gravity, atomic weight, and electron configuration. In short, copper has an intelligible nature, open to investigation, a nature not to be identified, as John Locke would have it, with a constellation of properties.

In the tradition of Aristotle and Aquinas, Yves R. Simon will distinguish between the sensible and the intelligible. He draws a clear line between physics, mathematics, mathematical physics, and metaphysics, identifying the material and formal object of each. Methodology, he will say, is determined by the subject matter to be investigated. The physicist, in pursuing his study of nature, must borrow interpretative principles. He is unconsciously indebted to a large intellectual climate that assumes notions such as identity, nature, substance, sufficient reason, causality, and indeed the intelligibility of nature itself. These may be called the first principles of thought and being, and, although self-evident, when challenged can be defended but not demonstrated; all demonstration presupposes them. Within the context of examining these, Simon distinguishes among fact, the intellect's assent to fact, and the role of theory in the interpretation of fact. The awareness of fact—in the language of the Scholastics, simple apprehension—is one act; an affirmation or judgment is another act, in which we assent to, or affirm, one thing said of another. Thus, truth is said to reside not in simple apprehension but in judgment. Any judgment whose referent is nature is governed by both an object of sensation and an object of intellection. Beyond the observed there is the intelligible, reached not by sense but by intellect. It is the intelligible that governs inquiry. Simon is quick to acknowledge that sense reports are not to be limited to the visually or sensorially encountered but include accounts inferred from sensory experience. Thus, we have reason to include among the observable such entities as molecules, atoms, nuclei, and electrons, but strictly speaking none has been observed. "No one doubts," he writes, "that no eye has ever seen a molecule and its different parts, but to the degree [to] which the scientific explanation of the experience is conclusive, it provides us with the equivalent of a sensation."

Simon goes on to distinguish among kinds of facts, that is, those that may be called the "facts of common experience," "scientific facts," and "philosophical facts." What one makes of the data of experience depends on the habit of mind one brings to that data. Scientific thinking is oriented in the direction of the observable and the measurable, but the scientific mind is not content with description and prediction. It seeks explanations. It attempts to understand the given in the light of its causes.

Philosophy is characterized by its propensity to seek clear definitions and intelligible language, by its habit of making distinctions, exhaustive divisions, rigorous deductions, and necessary arguments. Of its very nature, it eschews vague approximation in its movement to precise speech. Philosophy does not generate the same kind of consensus one normally finds in the natural sciences. Although capable of demonstration, its accomplishment is of a different order. By definition, philosophy is the pursuit of wisdom, speculative and practical.

Yet even so, it must be recognized that the data of common experience enjoy a priority with respect to the facts utilized by the philosopher and to a lesser extent by the scientist. Common sense includes a rudimentary philosophy, which technical philosophy will make its own. Thus, many view the philosophy of Aristotle and Aquinas as commonsense philosophy. It is the merit of the *philosophia perennis* that it carries within it a body of truth that can be passed from one generation to another. Yet the matter of philosophical experience is not entirely and exclusively provided by common experience. The history of philosophy in its relation to the development of the sciences testifies that certain scientific discoveries have affected with powerful decisiveness the course of philosophical thought. The telescopes of the astronomers and spectrum analysis have rid philosophy of the task of accounting for the stars, a problem addressed philosophically by the ancients. Similarly, advances in biology have freed Aristotle's philosophy of nature from the science of his day.

Speaking of the value of common sense and its need to be augmented by philosophy, Simon makes the point that moral debasement can affect lucidity of understanding. The commonsense man interprets his experience with the help of rudimentary concepts and principles that, although true, remain in need of defense. The philosophy of the commonsense man is a set of truths that can be obtained without any technically elaborated apparatus. But the testimony of common sense may not be equal to the power of the a priori. First, the capacity of common sense is unequal in its distribution: men possess it in varying degrees and intensity. Second, the social environment may be so saturated with error that common sense is at a disadvantage in holding its own in the face of overwhelming opposition. Experience, Simon will say, fights an unequal battle when it comes into contact with ideology. The proponents of ideology, when challenged by experience, have no reluctance in characterizing experience as nothing but an illusion. In sum, the testimony of common sense needs reinforcement, for philosophy can only be fought by philosophy.

Contributions of science to the enrichment of philosophical experience are open-ended. Philosophy does not simply incorporate into itself scientific data, but relies on it for its elaboration of and sometimes correction of common experience. For example, even though the ancients were aware of the heterogeneous parts of living beings, they regarded the inanimate individual as a homogeneous whole whose spatially distinct parts were intrinsically indistinct from one another. Modern science, of course, discloses the complex molecular structure of the inanimate and yet points to a datum of philosophical import, the unity of the heterogeneous.

If we can speak of the facts of common experience, augmented by scientific experience, we can speak of moral facts, derived from both. The kind of fact we have depends on the kind of concept involved in the formulation of the fact. Moral facts are determined by a relation of suitableness or unsuitableness to the ends of a free agent. The ethicist cannot avoid a judgment with respect to the value of an act in relation to the ends of a free agent. Moral actions are constituted by a good or bad use of our freedom. There is no mystery with respect to what adds to or subtracts from human fulfillment. Presupposed, of course, is a concept of human nature and some idea of what constitutes a properly ordered society. It is in this context that we establish moral facts. Further, in order to understand moral facts, the rectitude of one's moral judgment will have to be secured not merely by a knowledge of that which leads to fulfillment but by a habit of right action. It is not enough to know what is right and wrong in the abstract; one must be able to discern what is right and wrong in a given situation. "Thus," says Simon echoing Aristotle, "it is only the virtuous man who is qualified to understand moral facts perfectly.... That is why the development of the moralist—and the true sociologist, he too above all, is a moralist—includes a purification, an asceticism, that is not ordered only to the intellect."

Simon's treatment of methodology concludes with his reflections on Christian philosophy. He describes the position of Étienne Gilson, a historian of ideas, who, in viewing the history of philosophy from the advent of Christianity, finds ample reason to speak of the influence of

Christianity on philosophy. Gilson's view is contrasted with that of Émile Bréhier, who says that it doesn't make any more sense to speak of Christian philosophy than it does to speak of Christian mathematics or Christian physics. Simon's own reflections lead him to agree with Jacques Maritain that, given revelation, man is aware that there is something beyond a purely natural destiny and that this has to be taken into account in practical philosophy. He writes, "Revelation determines new duties, unknown to natural ethics, and whose notion makes no sense in terms of natural ethics, e.g., the duty to receive the sacraments." This recognition is in accord with a natural law ethics, as something added. It alludes to man's fallen state, something unknown to natural reason. Asceticism, for example, receives its rational foundation when the supernatural end of man is recognized. In fact, all the cardinal virtues recognized by Plato, Aristotle, and the Stoics take on new meaning in the light of man's supernatural destiny. Moral philosophy is transformed when it takes into consideration man's fallen state and his eternal destiny.

Jude P. Dougherty

The Material Logic of John of St. Thomas
("Foreword," xxii–xxiii)

From a philosophical standpoint, one major characteristic of our time is a deepened split between man's concern for mystery and the forms of scientific thought.[1] Referring to well-known propositions of Maritain in *A Preface to Metaphysics*, let us say that a question can be predominantly a problem or predominantly a mystery. A problem is a question the true answer to which leaves no room for further elaboration. Descartes was praising the handiness of problems when he pointed out that a child who has performed a multiplication according to the rules of arithmetic knows as much about the product as any mathematical genius in the world. But a mystery is a question of such a character that an answer unqualifiedly true and sound and appropriate not only admits of but also demands further inquiries into inexhaustible intelligibility. The mystery aspect predominates in religion, in metaphysics, in philosophy generally, and in human affairs. The problem aspect predominates in the disciplines called the sciences by common usage, in techniques, and generally in the fields where the pattern of positive science exercises a strong influence. Interest in philosophy, religion, theology, human sciences and humane studies is no less today than in celebrated periods of intellectual greatness. But it is impossible not to be struck by a widespread aversion to scientific forms in philosophy, theology, and human affairs—briefly, in the realms characterized by the predominance of mystery. What is most alive in the logical movement of our days is directed toward a universal and thorough problematization of science. True, the rigor achieved in the scientific handling of purely problematic questions is one glorious aspect of intellectual life in this century. At the same time a sense for mystery is not lacking. It is incomparably more profound in our contemporaries than it used to be in the golden age of rationalistic optimism—say, from the time of the Encyclopédie to the great terrors of the twentieth century. What is lacking in our relation to mystery is neither earnestness nor abundance of ideas, it is the rigor of the scientific spirit. There are things that will never be accomplished by "the tragic sentiment of life," "immersion in history," "experience of death," "aesprit de finesse," "cultural refinement," "esthetic sophistication," "our cultural heritage," etc. These things are clarity in the statement of questions and principles, firmness in inference, rational evidence of conclusions, appropriateness in predication, integral preservation of past developments, lucid order, and the unique defense against error that rational forms alone can provide. The ambition to explore scientifically the realms where mystery predominates receives little encouragement from the most up-to-date of our logicians. Some of them would say that one major merit of their work is precisely to have demonstrated the meaninglessness of metaphysical questions, and more generally of questions concerning what we call the realm of mystery.

Let it be remarked, at this point, that the scientific type borne in mind by a logician exerts influence upon the factual product called a system of logic. This does not express an essential necessity: such things happen because our energy is inexhaustible and our versatility limited. The logic of Aristotle is not exactly what it would have been if his scientific patterns had not been Greek geometry, an imperfectly disontologized mathematical knowledge, and a physics that was not disontologized at all. With the great abundance of metaphysical and theological genius which marks the work of St. Thomas and his commentators, the scientific patterns used by the logician change somewhat. Indeed, for St. Thomas and John of St. Thomas, mathematics—principally represented by Euclidean geometry—remains the best approximation to unqualifiedly scientific knowledge and consequently the pattern which the analytician bears in mind. But when logicians are so ardently interested in philosophy, they cannot omit the logical problems of particular relevance for the explorers of philosophical mysteries. Here, the logician answers a question asked by the metaphysician with burning anxiety, for the answer will decide whether metaphysical and, more generally, philosophic issues are meaningless or not. An inspiring and charming teacher, John of St. Thomas remains among us the logician who understands best the scientific ideal of the philosophers.

Foresight and Knowledge
("Foreword," 1–5)

When the literature devoted to the problem of determinism and causality by our contemporaries is examined, it is impossible not to be struck by the contrasts existing between the clear and serene simplicity that characterizes the presentation of physicists, as long as they speak as physicists, and the nervous confusion that takes hold of minds once one moves from the level of scientific exposition to that of philosophic interpretation. There is nothing astonishing in the fact that philosophical conclusions are unable, in this domain as in others, to achieve the benefits of a consensus; although philosophical certainty is of a demonstrative nature and, consequently, enjoys unlimited communicability in principle—a capability for intersubjective understanding—no philosophical doctrine, no matter how solidly established it may be, will ever be accepted in fact save by a small number of thinkers....

Numerous contemporary works in epistemology, especially those of the Vienna Circle, have shown that one of the constant characteristics of positive science is the search for a capability for intersubjective understanding in fact. In definition of his own viewpoint, the positive scientist shows a concern to exclude as much as possible any consideration apt to make the actual meeting of minds exceedingly improbable. As a consequence of that, positive science gives up viewing and stating many aspects of the world, even among those that lend themselves to the establishment of certain knowledge. But there is a willing consent to this sacrifice as the indispensable condition of the greater advantages that the capability of intersubjective understanding in fact brings in the exercise of the social functions of scientific culture. The situation of the philosopher is completely different; nothing allows him to limit his object as a function of the necessities of that capability of intersubjective understanding in fact, and all of history is there to remind him that if he wants to be the one who achieves unanimous agreement, there is nothing left for him to do but to give up philosophy....

Generally, the scientist contemptuously shrinks back from a collaborator who he knows is not of one mind with him, and he decides to construct the philosophical interpretation of science himself. But then, whether he likes it or not, he borrows his principles of interpretation from the philosophies that dominate in a diffused state the environment in which he lives, and confusion triumphs, for nothing is more confusing than a philosophical idea divested of its technical precision and misfiled in a stock of "general culture," following a journey in which it has lost all its fine points in order to preserve only a largely unconscious and mainly destructive effectiveness. Let us note the example of the notions of causality, determinism, and chance. In the lamentable state in which these notions, burdened with incoherent meanings by incompatible philosophies and simplified by the work of popularizers, reach the scientist, they are all too often only the medium cause of disorder and ambiguity....

Without the collaboration of the scientist, the philosophy of science cannot securely move beyond some statements of principle. The mutual trust between the Thomistic philosopher and the scientist is a basic condition of the progress of the Thomistic philosophy of science. Much effort has been expended with the view to establishing this mutual trust; it is appropriate to ask ourselves where we now are and what remains to be done.

A first point is established. We are present, on the side of Thomistic philosophers, at the decline of a spirit of *philosophical imperialism* which formerly was able to place the freedoms of positive philosophy in jeopardy. Maritain's work [*Degrees of Knowledge*] has definitively liquidated the *tragic misunderstanding* begun during the Galilean-Cartesian age, and no one today any longer maintains that the very possibility of an experimental and mathematico-physical science is excluded by the principles of Aristotle's philosophy....

A second point is established. Scientistic philosophy, by which I mean the mental conception that confers on positive science the characteristic of being the supreme or sovereign instance of wisdom, attributing to it a power of unappealable judgment over philosophy, conscience, and religion, has rather generally been discredited by scientists today.

A third established point is that in relation to the decline of scientism, on the one hand, and the progress in the history of ideas, on the other, the prejudice of *modernity* has lost some of its influence. In contrast to what occurred yesterday, numerous scientists today seem ready to recognize that the antiquity of a philosophy does not necessarily prove that this philosophy is worthless.

A fourth point, and this one is decisive, will be established the day when scientists will have understood to what extent Thomists share the same spirit as animates the man of science. Although Thomists are often obliged to talk like everyone else and to distinguish and even oppose the terms science and philosophy, and even though they in no way ignore the affinities that exist between and among philosophy, art, and religion, their conception of philosophy implies above all that philosophy is itself a science or, to be more precise, that the philosophic disciplines are each of them a science. We have countless occasions to notice that the scientistic conception of philosophy is what contributes most to separating us from philosophers unfamiliar with our frame of mind and from an important segment of the cultured public. There are those who will not forgive us for this perpetual criticism of the meaning of words, these distinctions, this concern for precise definition and exhaustive divisions, for rigorous deductions and necessary arguments, this horror of vague approximation. These are the admirers of what General Vouillemin [sic] so nicely called literary philosophy. But all these mental traits that we owe to the Aristotelian school—the only school in which philosophical disciplines have been brought to a degree of technical elaboration comparable to that which accounts for the prestige of the exact sciences—constitute so many bonds of kinship with genuine scientists, even if it compels us to solitude as far as literary philosophers are concerned, a solitude in which we readily find consolation. Let genuine scientists be willing to carefully read our works with enough patience to overcome the inevitable difficulties of an unusual language; they will have no difficulty in recognizing that we belong to the same breed.

The Great Dialogue of Nature and Space
("Philosophers and Facts," 144–49 and 153–60)

"Everyone has a right to his opinions, but all reasonable men should be able to agree on the facts." Such is the usual view. Rarely will anyone be suspected of dishonesty because he refuses to grant to an opinion the importance which others attribute to it; we generally and with few reservations admit that in matters of opinion we are free to judge for ourselves and can decide in one way or another, no matter how paradoxically, and that this should not be considered a sign of malice. But we admit no freedom for the mind in regard to facts; there is only a question of knowing if they were adequately established: in the presence of a well-established fact the mind can only give assent; the fact imposes itself on the mind. It is, in its own way, an absolute; as has been justly remarked, it is an "empirical absolute."

That is why relativistic critics have had to persistently attack the notion of fact; having overthrown, at least in his own estimation, the absolutes of ontology and logic, the relativist could not consider his cause won as long as the absolute, any form whatsoever of the absolute, could find a refuge in experience, or as long as science and philosophy would admit along with the common man that any mind which is proud of its creative autonomy shall find its stumbling block in facts. The dilution of the notion of fact by showing that what we call a fact is but a product of the work of the mind—which by hypothesis is free and creative—that was truly, for a relativist, to utterly ruin the last citadel of the absolute. A good deal of zeal was used up in the project.

According to the relativistic criticism, knowledge is a kind of constructive activity; what results from the work of the mind is always akin to an art object. Before attacking the absoluteness which is characteristic of facts the relativist denies that there is any essence existing independently of the mind that can impose its form on a concept. We shall not examine those postulates whose devastating gratuitousness has been so often pointed out; we shall hold firmly that the concept, to the degree that it represents a victory of the speculative intelligence, receives its characteristic from its object and not through the initiative of the subject. Thus, when we note in the formulation of what we call a fact the presence of a concept or a judgment, in a word of the results of a spiritual activity, this will involve on our part no incursion against the fundamental absolutism that the common man acknowledges to facts.

If a man has been killed on a street corner and the witnesses all agree, no doubt is permitted on that point; until the investigation establishes who the killer was and what his motives were, in all prudence we cannot yet speak of murder, for perhaps the one who struck the blow was just defending himself legitimately. But that there was a killing, that is a fact.

Suppose that a patient who had been declared tuberculous has died in a hospital and the autopsy confirms the diagnosis by discovering that the lung surfaces are greenish and pussy. The clinician notes, as a fact, the presence of caseous lesions.

The metaphysical mind, fascinated by its primary object, at first wants only to know being and nonbeing. That is why Parmenides protested that it is impossible for being to be multiple and changing, that it cannot be but unique and fixed in the immutability of its eternal identity. But Heraclitus proclaimed the fact of change, and metaphysical thinking, no matter what the cost, will have to take this fact into consideration and be flexible enough to explain it.

We have here examples of a vulgar, a scientific and a philosophical fact. In each case there is an absolute that determines the mind's attitude; in each case it is an experience that resolves the issue. But this experience is not purely and simply an experience and this absolute is not simple either.

Suppose that when a magistrate interrogates them the witnesses declare they saw one man strike another and everyone admits that they are right. Nevertheless, strictly speaking, no eye has ever seen a man; it sees only a surface that is colored in a certain way, which is the object of the sensation in its purity. Around this pure sensation there organizes itself an extremely complex system of images, memories and intellectual elements that are so intimately involved with sensation that we have no misgivings about stating, as a datum of experience, that we saw one man strike another. Let us try to distinguish the intellectual elements implied in the statement of such a fact and establish how they are related to the sensation.

Without doubt, when the man in the street declares that he has seen a man, he has in mind a rather confused representation; but one thing that is sure is that there is something there. We would make him most uncomfortable if we asked him to state precisely what he means by the term "man," but there is no doubt that he intends it to refer to something which is a definite kind of being and which can be recognized through certain unmistakable characteristics. The man in the street has only a confused concept of "man"; while the botanist has a clear concept of *Fumaria officinalis*; but just as the botanist is not afraid of confusing what he means by "that which is not" with what he means when he talks of *Fumaria officinalis*, so the man in the street is equally unafraid of confusing what he means by "that which is not" with what he means when he utters the word "man." You cannot ask just anyone the difference between identity and otherness, but everyone knows what he means when he says "this man and this other man." In the formulation of a vulgar fact then we use a concept; or better yet, two concepts are involved, to be united in a judgment: "A man struck another man," or "A man was striking another man." We do not have here a judgment in a question of essence, an affirmation of an identity whose extra-temporal character is expressed by a verb in the atemporal present, but a judgment of existence, in which the copula has a temporal character. Now, that which authorizes the one who proclaims a fact to affirm that there really exists in actuality a certain object of cognition or the union of two such objects, is the datum of sensation, around which the whole representational system enclosed in the formulation of fact has organized itself. *To formulate a fact then is to make an existential judgment under the guarantee[2] of sensation.*

In every kind of judgment we shall find these three fundamental elements: an object of sensation, an object of intellection and an object of a judgment of existence. Now, what produces the diversity of types of fact is not diversity of sensations. When the needle of a galvanometer moves, the layman and the scientist experience identical sensations, and yet the former knows only a vulgar fact and the latter knows a scientific fact. Nor is it the existential character of the factual judgment: at the sight of the same sensible phenomena both learned and ignorant persons think that *something* really exists. But for the one it is something vulgar, e.g., the movement of a mirror and of the light it reflects, produced by some unknown cause; for the other it is something scientific, e.g., the closing of an electrical circuit. In effect, within the structure of a fact the object of sensation plays only a material role; the formal side is taken care of by the object of the concept. But, all diversity of types results from a formal diversity. Thus, what distinguishes the different kinds of facts is the diversity of the concepts implied in the formulation of a fact; to a vulgar concept corresponds a vulgar fact; to a scientific concept, a scientific fact; and to a philosophic concept, a philosophical fact. The sensation calls forth the concept and the concept unites itself to the verb to be in an existential judgment whose expression constitutes the formulation of a fact. Whatever is the nature of the concept called forth, or whatever is the nature of the understanding's object that is discerned in the sensible datum, the fact that is formulated will be of the same sort. It all depends on the intellect's interpretation, what the intellect reads in the object of sensation. If the interpretation is of a vulgar type, there will be a vulgar fact; if of a scientific type, a scientific fact; if of a philosophical type, a philosophic fact.

We shall consider later on what is meant by a vulgar type of thinking. We know however what distinguishes the philosophical type of thinking from the scientific (taking scientific in its modern and restricted sense in which we oppose the natural sciences, the empiriological and empiriometric sciences, to philosophy). Scientific thinking is oriented in the direction of the observable and measurable; philosophic thinking, in the direction of being *qua* being. In the presence of a factual utterance then, to tell whether we have to do with a philosophical or a scientific fact our task will come down to establishing the characteristics of the concept implied in the formulation of the fact, which characteristics are themselves understood by referring to the term we finally end up with in the resolution of the concept.

Pulmonary tuberculosis in an advanced stage of development is characterized by the presence of caseous lesions. We call a lesion caseous when its looks remind us of that of Roquefort cheese: this is surely the most clearly empiriological concept we could cite: what we use to define and name the caseous lesion, and to distinguish it from others, is first of all a sensible sign, of such a sort that if someone did not understand why the lesions present in a tuberculous lung deserve to be called caseous, the only way to make the term and concept more clear to him would be to show him a slice of Roquefort cheese....

There is a change in the world of our experience. What is change? It is the act of a being in potency precisely inasmuch as it is in potency. Act is being which is; potency is a nonbeing which is. We are in the presence of the first object of the metaphysical mind. Being is; nonbeing is not; there is nothing else.

Thus as soon as a fact is known the orientation of one's thought, whether it be scientific or philosophical, is clearly established; as soon as a fact is formulated the options for our thought are closed. It is then impossible that the fact which philosophy incorporates into itself be the same as the fact that science incorporates into itself; even if the datum of sensation was precisely the same the fact is not the same, because the concept involved in our intellectual knowledge of the fact is not the same. Consequently, *if it is true that it is impossible to integrate into the system of philosophical thought any item borrowed from the system of scientific thought, it will be impossible to incorporate into philosophy any scientific fact*, for a scientific fact connotes a scientific mind, with its characteristics which are opposed to those of the philosophical mind....

Being exists; sensible being is multiple and subject to change; every sensible being presents a plurality of parts outside of each other; the things that fall under our senses admit of inequalities of perfection; there is order in the universe; all sensible beings are endowed with activity; there are some beings that are alive and others that are not; there are some beings that can know and some that cannot.

These facts, of inexhaustible fecundity for the philosophic mind, are not the results of any experimental technique; these fundamental philosophical facts are at the same time facts of common experience. We do not mean that they are equally evident for all men. Against anyone who would deny the existence of change we can bring up the testimony of the senses, but should anyone hold that there are not beings devoid of knowledge and that the things reputed to be such are to some degree capable of cognition and appetition, it would not suffice to invite him to open his eyes; sometimes, in opposition to a philosophical theory which denies a fact, the fact has to be philosophically established to the common man. The microscope, telescope and spectroscope would be of no help whatsoever in convincing a panpsychist of his error. Common experience furnishes us with all we can expect from the side of sensation; we have only to make precise the concepts implied in the enunciation of the fact and to show that the common data of the senses constrain us to unite these concepts in a given existential judgment. Thus, every philosophical fact from the data of common experience will not have the same dignity; those whose conceptual element represents an immediate intellectual reading of the sensible datum, previous to any technical elaboration, will enjoy a privileged condition. The first of these primary philosophical facts is the fact of the existence of being; there seems in second place to come the fact of plurality and the fact of change. An awareness of these facts imposes itself on the mind independently of all theories and it does not require the prior acceptance of any definition; the intellectual interpretation implied by their formulation results from a quite spontaneous mental functioning and if one disputes these facts, he will also have to dispute the efficacy of all mental functioning. Doubts in regard to the primary philosophical facts betoken the most advanced state of skeptical disintegration.

When we reflect on the reasons for the primacy of the philosophical facts which we call primary we understand why the philosophical facts that are based on the data of common experience themselves enjoy a priority in regards to the other facts that the philosopher will be able to use. In all rigor we can say that every essential part of the philosophical edifice is built on facts of common experience. This is because the fundamental theses of philosophy have highly general concerns and require the most perfect certitude, and it is common experience which presents us with the facts that are the most general and, by means of a correct critique, the most certain. There are no facts more general or more certain than the primary philosophical facts and it is that that confers on them their character of primary philosophical facts and makes them have, in the order of experience, a dignity analogous to that of the first principles. In varying degree every philosophical fact answering to a common experience will share in this dignity, because of its certitude and generality.

We would not however hold that every philosophical fact is at the same time a fact of common experience. There are, as we shall see, some philosophical facts which can be established only through the technical elaboration of an experience. On the other hand, we should also note that the majority of vulgar facts are not philosophical facts. We can call vulgar any fact whose conceptual element does not involve any scientific elaboration, but there are many types of vulgar facts. Limiting ourselves to what is related to our thesis and without trying for a complete catalog, we can distinguish, in the affirmations of the vulgar mind, illusory facts, which any science will reject, facts of an empiriological sort and facts of a philosophical sort. It happens that an illusory fact is born of a precipitate intellectual interpretation. Thus, for the common man who is not at all aware of the results of scientific research, it is a fact that there is above our heads a solid, motionless vault. Another source of illusory facts: it often happens that the common man unites concepts that are themselves correct in an existential judgment that is founded on an insufficient number of observations. Animal stories are filled with such so-called facts, an example of which would be the suicide of scorpions. But there are some vulgar facts of the empiriological type which science incorporates into itself with hardly no changes in their formulation: it is a vulgar fact that alcohol kills and the biologist admits that the repeated ingestion of ethyl alcohol in excessive amounts brings about organic lesions and finally the death of the animal. There are likewise vulgar facts of the philosophical type which philosophy incorporates into itself. Common sense includes a rudimentary philosophy and this philosophy formulates facts which a technical philosophy will make its own while rendering their formulation more precise.

In their desire to counteract the idea of a philosophy based on scientific facts certain thinkers have implied that the matter of philosophical experience is entirely and exclusively provided by common experience. However, the very history of philosophy in its relation to the development of science testifies that certain scientific discoveries have affected, with the powerful decisiveness proper to the *empirical absolute*, the course of philosophical thought. The clearest example is that of the theory of celestial bodies. Struck by the impossibility of discerning in the appearance of the stars any qualitative variation, the ancients professed as a fact that the celestial bodies are incorruptible and that local motion is the only kind of change to which they are subject; being above all respectful of experience, Aristotelianism saw itself constrained to add to its general theory of the hylomorphic composition a rather disgraceful appendix, very little in harmony with the rest of the structure, to make a place in it for the illusory fact of the incorruptibility of the stars. The telescopes of the astronomers and spectrum analysis have forever rid philosophy of this romanesque phase. Shall we say that a scientific fact was incorporated into philosophy? Not at all, but a new philosophical fact was, whose subject matter, being inaccessible to common experience, was provided by scientific experience.

Light emanating from the sun, when analyzed with a spectroscope, produces a double black line that occupies the precise place of the double line of sodium; from this we conclude that there exists in the sun's chromosphere a substance optically characterized by the property of emitting when incandescent a light composed of two simple radiations with wave lengths of .5896 and .5890. That is the scientific fact. What philosophy will retain is that there exists in the sun a substance of the very same species as a certain sublunary substance and that consequently it is like it subject to qualitative and substantial change. Thus, the scientific form of a scientific fact has been stripped off and its matter, a certain sensory datum, has been clothed with a conceptual form of a philosophical sort, thus making possible the formation of a philosophical fact, the only kind that can be assimilated into philosophy.

It appears that the contributions of science to the enrichment of philosophical experience are universally brought about under the condition just described. Never does philosophy incorporate into itself a scientific fact, but it does happen that a point resulting from the pure sensory intuition involved in a scientific fact has philosophical bearings and can support a conceptual apparatus of a philosophical type. Take for example the progress made by philosophy, thanks to scientific investigations, in the theory of inanimate individual things. From the simple data of common experience the philosopher can declare with certainty that this animal here or that plant there (at least if it is a question of the higher forms of plant or animal life) constitutes one single individual, but to determine what is an inanimate individual, here common experience does not furnish us with adequate indications. Is this rock a single individual or an aggregate of individuals? On the basis simply of the testimony of common experience the philosopher can no doubt give to this question only a rather weakly probative answer. If limited to the macroscopic data of common experience, the philosopher could resist only with difficulty the temptation of thinking that organization, that is, the combination of heterogeneous parts distributed according to a certain type of order, is a privilege of living beings. For the ancients an inanimate individual was a homogeneous whole whose spatially distinct parts are of the same species and do not differ except by being outside one another. Finally, if we kept only to the same macroscopic experience we could only with difficulty abstain from affirming, as did the ancients, that the parts of any individual had to be in continuity, or at least contiguity.

Contemporary research however forces us to hold, as a highly probable fact, that there exist molecules able, at least under certain conditions, of subsisting and acting in an isolated state. Science explains these molecules as complex structures of atoms that are specifically similar in the case of elemental bodies and specifically diverse in the case of mixtures; each atom is itself a complex whole composed of a central nucleus, the proton, around which gravitate one or more ions. If enlarged a hundred thousand billion times, the hydrogen atom would appear to us as a ball with a radius of two decimeters describing a circle ten kilometers in diameter around an imperceptible little body having a radius of only one tenth of a millimeter. The definitions that science gives of the molecule, the atom, the ion and the proton lack any philosophical character; consequently the fact of the reality of molecules will not be able to be retained by the philosopher in its scientific form. What the philosopher will retain is a matter of fact, which is to be found in the direction of the sensory intuition. No one doubts that no eye has ever seen a molecule and its different parts, but to the degree to which scientific explanation of the experience is conclusive, it provides us with the *equivalent of a sensation*. It is likely that if our means of observation were sufficiently strengthened we would experience sensations that would suggest to the scientist the intellectual reading expressed by the molecular theory and to the philosopher the notion of an individual composed of parts that are heterogeneous and spatially distant. It is then a probable fact that an inanimate individual, at least in certain cases, is of a size imperceptible to the senses, that it constitutes a unified whole and that its parts are not contiguous—and this fact is a philosophical one obtained by a philosophical interpretation of sensations that are correctly suggested by scientific investigation, though not actually experienced. Although it is only a probable one, this philosophical fact will permit an appreciable progress of the theory of individuality in the philosophy of nature.

In this view, the independence of philosophy vis-à-vis science is fully safeguarded. Philosophy will not have to fear being reduced to the role of a registration court, for it will have intervened from the beginning in the determination of the fact and by this initial intervention it has taken out a positive insurance against being subjected to a foreign rule. But this view also maintains the possibility of a simply unlimited contribution from scientific experience to the progress of philosophy. For as soon as the refinements of scientific experience have once or twice made it possible for the philosopher to take possession of a new philosophical fact, there is no reason to doubt that a similar success will not be repeated a thousand times. Thus the empirical concerns of philosophers will be able to find nutriment that is continually replaced without there being any risk that the course of philosophical thought will be compromised. Thus, to the degree that philosophy will add to the old philosophical facts whose subject matter was provided by common experience new philosophical facts whose subject matter will be provided by scientific experience, a new empirical philosophy in no way kindred to any form of scientism will be able to constitute itself.

In conclusion, we would like to point out what the general theory of facts suggests to us concerning the establishment of moral facts. Remember the principle we have been constantly invoking: the kind of fact we have depends on the kind of concept involved in the formulation of the fact. Whatever features the concept has, the fact will have the same ones. Now, it is enough to take a look at the features proper to moral concepts to conclude that being aware of a moral fact and formulating it will require conditions that are irreducible to the common conditions for being aware of physical facts. . . . A botanist does not distinguish useful plants from noxious herbs, because to cheer up or vex amateur gardeners does not at all help him to know the specific properties of a plant. But the one who studies moral affairs cannot dispense himself from knowing what value an act has in relation to the ends of the free agent, because moral affairs are constituted essentially by a good or bad use of our freedom. What remains of our notions of justice, temperance, theft or adultery if we abstract from the values they imply? If we forget about the idea of theft meaning an action adversely affecting a free agent in regard to the ends proper to him as a free agent and nevertheless try to think that idea, we shall have before our mind nothing but a representation denuded of any sense and capable of combining objects even more opposed than heaven and earth. There is no moral concept without a judgment of moral value and the knowledge of the fact will not be correct unless the moral judgment is itself correct.

If we can speak of facts in general, a fact is above all a certain individual reality's position as existing. In order to understand moral facts, then, the rectitude of one's moral judgment will have to be secured within the same order of individual realities; it will not be enough to know what is right and wrong in general, one must besides be able to discern the goodness or evil of a given single action. But it is *prudence* that secures a precise determination of moral values on the level of the concrete, and prudence presupposes a virtuous will. Thus, it is only the virtuous man who is qualified to understand moral facts perfectly. However, with the exception of mathematics, an awareness of the facts is the first step in scientific research. This is why the development of the moralist—and the true sociologist is, he too, above all a moralist—includes a purification, an asceticism, that is not ordered only to the intellect.

Freedom of Choice
("Freedom," 83–87 and 91–97)

Some elaboration on common sense is needed. If common sense enjoyed the essential unity of a power or function, it should be said that it did a great deal, in the scientific and philosophic domains, to deserve its bad reputation. But what the expression "common sense" designates does not enjoy any functional unity. It is an aggregate of propositions, none of which requires, in the mind that assents to it, the refinements of a special and technical training. Not all these propositions are known to all men, and it is absurd to claim that they are equally clear to all. But it is true that no man ever needed to go to school in order to be ready to assent, at least in an implicit fashion, to a common-sense proposition. A more specific formula would imply arbitrary exclusions.

In rough outline it can be said that common sense comprises three kinds of propositions: propositions of philosophic character which are the starting point of every philosophy and every science; propositions dictated by the leanings of the imagination; and propositions expressing a practical vision of the physical world. Science normally conflicts with the imagery of common sense according to which the earth is flat, people at the antipodes have their heads hanging downwards, light bodies cannot fall as fast as heavy ones, the quotient $\frac{1}{2}\pi$ does not remain constant as the radius of the circle increases, substance is something dense and hard like a desk made of oak, etc. It is only by accident that the images of common sense agree with the expressions of the scientific or philosophic mind. As to the practical vision of the world proposed by common sense, it sometimes conflicts with science: thus, for physics the earth and the feather attract each other, whereas for common sense the earth attracts the feather, though weakly, and the feather does not attract the earth at all. Sometimes science takes over the common-sense vision of the world: thus, the concept of chance occurrence as an unpredictable event is a common-sense notion accepted and modified by science. With respect to common sense as philosophy, it happens to offer to science a resistance which is limited, reducible and more apparent than real.

It is most important never to confuse the rudimentary philosophy professed by common sense with the practical vision or the imagery which are the other components of common sense. It is also important to realize that common sense as a philosophy is nothing else than philosophic reason itself, in the state of imperfect operation within which it remains confined until technical instruments have been provided by the labor of the schools. Lastly, it is necessary to distinguish, within common sense as philosophy, several sorts of propositions, several types of cognition.

(a) First, the axioms of the universal reason: the principles of identity, of noncontradiction, of the excluded middle; the principle of rationality; the principles of efficient causality, of material causality, and of final causality. Perfect accuracy would demand that these axioms be described as antecedent to all philosophy and placed above philosophy, that of common sense included.

(b) Common sense contains the statement of philosophic facts distinguished by their formal significance. The typology of objects, which is one with the typology of concepts, determines the typology of facts; the intelligible distribution of objects, within any system of interpretation, determines the intelligible distribution of facts, their rank, their hierarchical positions and their significance. Although the whole system of facts belongs to the material part of thought—for the formal part belongs to the principles—some facts are more material, and some are more formal in character. "Something exists"; "there exist, in the world of our experience, things diverse by species"; "all things perceptible to the senses are subject to motion"; these common-sense facts are the most formal among the philosophic facts.

(c) Over and above axiomatic propositions, provided with immediate and rational evidence, common sense comprises demonstrated propositions which constitute, on the level of common sense, a philosophy so called. Axioms are the principles of science rather than science itself, and facts are but the material of science: this holds for philosophic disciplines as well as for the other sciences. We shall consider two examples of such common-sense demonstrations. . . .

In the case of freedom, in order to understand that a demonstration substantially identical with that of the philosophers belongs to common sense, it suffices to remark that many persons, without having gone to the schools of philosophy or any school, consider it obvious that a man cannot be held responsible for acts committed in sleep, early childhood, delirium, insanity, and more generally in a state in which reason is not in actual use. The argument which bears out this conviction can be summed up as follows: the actual exercise of the reason is a necessary condition of the actual possession of freedom. Moreover, between reason and freedom there is an intelligible relation: one recognizes in the reason the explanatory principle or essential cause of freedom. Thus between the subject "man" and the predicate "endowed with freedom," the connection is established, according to common sense, by the mediation of the quality of rational being, and the middle term supplied by rationality is attributed a worth greater than that of a merely factual bond: it is *because* of rationality that the predicate "endowed with freedom" belongs to the subject "man." This argumentation bears all the characteristics of an *a priori* and explanatory demonstration. So far as logical essences are concerned, the philosophers do not do any better and do not do anything else. But it is their job to render the demonstration more intelligible, more powerful, more certain and more rigorous, more fruitful and more enlightening, and more certainly communicable, through processes of clarification....

We must bear all this in mind in interpreting the experience of freedom. Sheer experience would procure no more than an extremely confused assertion of existence. In order to go beyond such empirical confusion, it is necessary to philosophize, and this is what common sense hastens to do, without waiting for a technically elaborated philosophy. It is now easy to account for the accidents that the consciousness of freedom suffers both in common sense and in the philosophers. The common-sense man interprets his experience with the help of rudimentary concepts and of principles which, though not formally expressed, are strongly felt.... When the man of common sense reaches mature judgment, belief in freedom results in him from the nonsystematic but vital cooperation of an experience of consciousness and a process of rational interpretation. In order to express itself in appropriate concepts and language, this rational interpretation lacks only the technical refinements of a philosophy cultivated into a virtue of the intellect....

In philosophers the belief in freedom of choice is exposed to particularly serious dangers. At the beginning of his inquiry the philosopher finds in his consciousness the assertion of freedom.... [H]e is soon challenged to answer the question *what is freedom?* A philosopher cannot afford to be satisfied with statements of existence. He is supposed to know not confusedly but distinctly what he is talking about when he says, for instance, that free acts exist. It often happens that the mind of the philosopher is, all at once, caught by a system which *a priori* makes freedom impossible. Experience fights an unequal fight when it comes into conflicts with the hard requirements of the metaphysical, aesthetic, and moral vision of the universal order. If it is possible to change the conviction of a man who denies freedom of choice on the ground of a philosophical *a priori*, it is by destroying this *a priori*, not by stressing the persuasive power of experience. Philosophy, whenever it disagrees with experience, has no trouble to show that what is called experience is really but an illusion. Assuming that the philosopher is so happy as to escape the systematic forms of error, working out a concept of freedom remains a difficult enterprise in which occasions to err are innumerable. What happens if the inquiry issues in a poorly constructed concept? Either the philosopher keeps asserting the existence of freedom (but what he is talking of is not true freedom), or he rejects the concept of freedom as a logical monster, a product of imagination, devoid of any real meaning. As an apprentice philosopher, I hold from my inner experience the certitude of my freedom. But soon I am taught that the concept of free act involves the beginning without a cause, that of determination without a determining form, that of uncreated activity in a creature, that of absolute spontaneity, etc. By declaring that free choice does not exist, I get rid of unbearable absurdities. The violence done to experience is here the inevitable result of failure in conceptual analysis.

The fact that a great number of philosophers deny the reality of freedom can be easily explained without casting any doubt on the certitude of consciousness data. The experience of free choice is certain, but it is extremely confused. By reason of this confusion it seems that the testimony of consciousness cannot constitute a distinct argument for freedom; rather, the testimony of consciousness is the experimental point of departure of the rational inquiry designed to show all at once what free choice is and how and why and under what conditions it necessarily proceeds from the nature of reason and from the nature of will.

Practical Knowledge
("Disputed Questions: Ethics and Christian Philosophy," 88–98)

The discussions of the late 1920s and early 1930s on the subject of Christian philosophy were conducted, not exclusively but to a large extent, by philosophers known for their adherence to the doctrines of St. Thomas Aquinas. The whole sequence of those discussions started with an exposition of Étienne Gilson whose point of view was principally that of an historian of ideas. For Gilson Christian philosophy was, first of all, an historical reality, the historical reality of philosophical thoughts that, over a long period of time and under a great diversity of circumstances, existed undeveloped in close association with, and under the influence of, Christian faith. Another historian of philosophy, Émile Bréhier, not a Thomist indeed, held that Christian philosophy had no more reality than Christian mathematics or Christian physics. Father Mandonnet, who did so much over his long career for the exact knowledge of St. Thomas's work, and who certainly deserved to be considered a Thomist, was not far from upholding the paradox of Émile Bréhier. For him the immensity of the distance between the rational truths that make up philosophy and the revealed propositions that express mysteries—that is, truth that is not naturally accessible to any created or creatable intellect, but only to God Himself—ruled out the union of the two knowledges, knowledge by faith and philosophical knowledge, in any whole that could relevantly be called a Christian philosophy.

As could be expected, much confusion clouded these discussions. Maritain's book *On Christian Philosophy* provided some desirable clarification. In this work, Maritain distinguishes between the *nature* of philosophy and its state. As far as nature is concerned, philosophy is made of natural and rational knowledge, and that is all we have to say. But, by reason of its subject, this body of natural and rational knowledge admits of a variety of states. It would be nonsensical to speak of a

Christian state of mathematics or physics. But philosophy is concerned, in its own way, with God and with human destiny, and because it deals with these subjects, it admits of a Christian state. Is it in an intrinsic sense that we speak of Christian philosophy? In my opinion a consideration is not intrinsic unless it pertains to the nature being studied. Determinations pertaining not to nature but to state remain extrinsic, but extrinsic does not mean unimportant. It is extrinsically that a system of philosophy is described as Christian. But the Christian state, in which a number of philosophic systems have developed, may be of great relevance for the understanding of philosophical history and for the understanding of the conditions in which the philosophic sciences develop best in the human mind.

In *On Christian Philosophy*, Maritain made the important and often ignored point that, as far as its relation to faith is concerned, the case of practical philosophy is distinct from that of theoretical philosophy. Briefly, theoretical philosophy, like all theoretical sciences, is concerned with understanding what the things are in the necessity of their universal essences. This necessity is absolute; it is one with the necessity of the principle of identity, and cannot be altered by existential differences. On the contrary, practical knowledge, even on the high level of abstraction which is that of philosophy, is concerned with what we have to do. Accordingly, considerations pertaining to existence and state are relevant. The least that can be said is that it cannot be taken for granted that in the state of his Christian destiny man has to do exactly the same as what he would have had to do in the state of a purely natural destiny. . . .

Can there conceivably be cases in which what is declared right by the purely natural and rational knowledge of ethics would be declared wrong by an ethical position aware of what the supernatural destiny of man implies?

In the discussion of this issue let us bear in mind that there is a fundamental difference between the cases in which the mean of virtue is determined by a thing (*medium rei*) and the cases in which it is determined by an act of the reason (*medium rationis*). The situation of justice is unique, for the mean of this virtue is determined by a thing; accordingly *it is independent of changes in our existential condition*. If I have received a loan of a hundred dollars, with no interest, the sum that

I am supposed to return is exactly one hundred dollars regardless of whether the human condition is purely natural or not, and regardless of whether the last end of man is natural or supernatural. The issue is settled by a thing, and that thing is one hundred dollars, neither more nor less, under all circumstances.

The case is different when the mean is determined by an act of reason. Then a change in the last end may cause a change in the proper mean, for it is in relation to a determinate end that an action possesses the character of a proper mean. A famous example concerns temperance.... [E]xtreme forms of asceticism are considered lawful and necessary by Christian ethics in cases that may be rare. They are held immoral by natural ethics. There is nothing puzzling about such a contradiction, which originates in a more fundamental contradiction concerning the last end of man. Here also, and first of all, natural reason says that the case is such and such, and faith declares that the case is different. Let us be fully aware of such a significant opposition. At the same time, let us never lose sight of the indirect way which safeguards unity. To the question of whether extreme forms of asceticism are lawful and commendable, the answer of the moral philosopher, if it were completely unfolded, would be something like this: these extreme forms of asceticism are neither commendable nor lawful unless the last end of man is changed by a supernatural calling of which, *qua* philosopher, *qua* bearer of a purely rational habitus, the moral philosopher is not aware. The answer of the moral philosopher becomes entirely true by taking on a character of *conditionality* which is thoroughly uncongenial to practical thought, as a result of practical thought's intrinsic concern for the right and the wrong in human use and for the direction of human freedom....

Again, the case of justice is different and unique because of the settlement of issues by the *medium rei*. This should be strongly insisted upon. When the question of the collaboration of believers and unbelievers in the temporal city arises, difficulties should not be underrated; nor can it be denied that some divergences admit of no solution, except those of good will, friendship, and toleration. For example, rational ethics may accept divorce, as a practice which, provided it is held within well-defined limits, and in no way delivered to the whimsicality of desires, has a part to play in the legal forms of marriage in a certain state or at a certain level of common morality. But Christianity has placed mankind in an existential condition in which marriage should be possessed of all its dignity. When complete, the dignity of marriage implies indissolubility. In a state made up of Christians and non-Christians, it will be up to political prudence to find a means of sanctioning the full dignity of Christian marriage without imposing upon non-Christians—upon people living in the order of simple natural law—difficulties that would be neither intelligible nor manageable. We should point out that since differences in the existential condition of mankind leave matters of justice totally unmodified, matters of justice will supply a large field of complete agreement between Christians and non-Christians. When a problem is one of strict justice, there is no conceivable discrepancy between the answer of rational ethics and that of Christian ethics. Accordingly, issues concerning strict justice make up a core of complete agreement between Christians and non-Christians. The various concessions and acts of toleration which are necessary can best be conceived as taking place around the core of strict agreement made up of answers to questions of strict justice.

We have seen that a moral philosophy that cannot take into consideration the existential condition of man is unequal to its task. Several examples have shown that it gives conditional answers where unconditional ones are expected. Such a moral philosophy has been properly described by Jacques Maritain as inadequate. It is inadequate, and unequal to its object, because all it knows are essences, whereas existential conditions need to be known when there is a question of seeing the truth about the right and the wrong in human use and of directing human action....

Here, at the end of these reflections on the nature of moral philosophy, we wish to call attention to another aspect of the issue. Even though fulfillment is essential and explanation is not, and even though it is normal that the explanation of morality, as well as that of nature, should come into existence by slow progress, it is conceivable that circumstances should cause the need for explanation to be felt as a pressing one—stressing that if it is not satisfied fulfillment is endangered. Roughly, such seems to be the case with the societies of our time....

At all times and under all circumstances it is important to recall that explanation may not be considered a necessary condition for fulfillment. At all times and under all circumstances it is necessary to be ready to fulfill without understanding. Yet when the demand for explanation seems to be particularly pressing, the process of explanation should, in answer to such a demand, be carried on with particular zeal and sense of urgency. It follows that the tasks proper to the moral philosopher are particularly significant and urgent in societies such as ours.

Notes

1. [Editor's Note: I made the selection of texts for this chapter, which were subsequently approved by the contributor.]

2. [Editor's Note: Here and throughout, Simon's spelling ("guaranty") has been altered to its more familiar American usage in order not to jar the reader. ("Guaranty" is now used more narrowly, for banks and lending.) This is one of the very few occasions where I have altered his spelling.]

PART II

Knowledge

CHAPTER 3

Knowledge as Immanent Action

Yves R. Simon inquires into knowing as an activity, concluding that, more than an activity, it is the highest form of life. He arrives at this conclusion by the following steps. (1) Taking our knowledge of extramental reality as a first principle, he starts his inquiry from the premise that knowledge is objective. This means that knowing must be an activity, because pure passivity can only produce what is subjective. (2) As an activity, knowing must be immanent rather than transitive, for in cognition the act and the termination of the act are identical. (3) Because it is immanent, knowing is a self-perfecting activity, which means that it is a form of life, a way of being. (4) Since living being—that is, life or living construed as the capacity for self-actualization—is a higher form of being than nonliving being, and since the capacity for knowing confers the fullest capacity for self-actualization, it follows that the highest form of life is found in God, for whom being and knowing are identical.

On the way to the above conclusion, Simon provides an analysis of action that is as subtle as it is penetrating. Action is found in change in the sensible world and in the nonsensible world of being as being, where action and its exercise of efficient causality can occur without change: in beings whose essence and existence are not identical, their existence must be caused by an agent outside themselves, but that does not involve change, since before any came into existence there was nothing to change. Moreover, not all action produces an effect, as the distinction between transitive and intransitive activity makes clear. Transitive activity produces an effect distinct from itself, as in building a house; immanent activity, such as contemplation, produces no effect, for the activity and the end of the activity are identical. Since transitive and immanent action both belong under a transcendental definition of action, action is an analogous notion. Clarifying the analogy begins by distinguishing between activity and existence in relation to the terminal act. Existence is not a *this* or a *that*, a particular kind of thing; it is rather what causes things to be outside nothingness. Thus, every finite being has two possibilities for fulfillment, the first on the level of existence and the second on the level of nature or essence. The latter is an activity that is defined as "*the terminal act that fulfills the active nature in accordance with its specific constitution.*"

Simon identifies additional important differences between transitive and immanent action. Immanent action is a quality, a spiritual quality, a disposition, and the most perfect form of life. Producing and preserving are both transitive actions: creation *ex nihilo* and God's conservation of contingent beings in their existence are examples. Similarly, knowing, willing, and desiring are activities, for action is an emanating, terminal event. Whereas transitive action is efficiency, immanent action, even though it includes efficiency, is not efficiency, but belongs to the category of quality.

Immanent activity is a quality. It cannot be a quantity, which is homogeneous; any movement within a quantitative whole from one part to another simply passes from same to same. Nor can immanent activity depend on material functions, since the perfect identification of an activity with the termination of that activity is a purely immaterial action. It also differs from all qualities that imply potentiality, because, as a terminal act, the activity is fully actualized. This raises the possibility that, insofar as it is a quality, immanent activity is a special kind of disposition.

Immanent activity is a disposition, by which Simon means "the supreme ordering of the dynamic parts of a vital faculty in relation to its end actually possessed." This ordering is crucial, because the immanent activity of knowing unifies two mutually antagonistic characteristics. The one, a qualitative perfection that is a disposition: knowing can change the knowing faculty only by organizing its possibilities. The other characteristic, the exercise of efficiency, or active causality: not as an act distinct from itself, but in an intimate unity. Nothing in the world achieves this activity, which resembles both efficiency and quality. Simon writes: "The one who knows moves himself in his innermost depths in order to give himself over to the object and attain thereby his final perfection, which is identical with that activity that he exercises on himself."

Immanent activity is motionless activity. Unlike transitive action, which ceases its activity when the product is completed—the physician stops his treatment once the patient has been restored to health—the intellect does not cease knowing the truth once it has been discovered, nor does the heart, once it possesses its object, stop loving it. Knowing and loving are the acts of a perfect subject. With immanent activity, we have production free from change. God's creative activity does not rely in any sense on transitive activity, but instead exercises efficiency in activity that is completely immanent.

Immanent activity is vitality. In the final section of chapter 2 of *An Introduction to Metaphysics of Knowledge*, Simon completes his inquiry into the relation between cognition and activity. As the supremely perfect form of activity, cognition is thus the supremely perfect form of life. A being has life to the extent that it is self-actualizing, which is to say, self-perfecting. Cognitive beings represent a higher form of life than noncognitive beings, because knowing is a self-perfecting action. God is the supremely perfect life, because he performs no action that is not identical with his nature. His knowing, willing, loving, essence, existence, and self are identical. Thus he performs no action that does not flow from his unique selfhood. Cognition accordingly shows that a knowing being attains a level of existence that transcends the limits of its existence.

The first selection is taken from chapter 2 of his *An Introduction to Metaphysics of Knowledge* and the second is taken from Simon's essay "To Be and to Know." Both selections begin by acknowledging the difference between *to be* and *to know*, but each addresses that difference from a distinguishing viewpoint. The first focuses on the ontological basis of being seen as an activity and concludes that knowing is a becoming of the other *as other* and thus a way of being; in God, to be and to know are identical. In "To Be and to Know," Simon argues that to be and to know are not identical, but the clash between the two theses is merely apparent. From the standpoint of the objectivity of knowledge, the knower becomes the known: were a third thing to be between them, the objectivity of knowledge would collapse, because then it would not be the thing that is known, but a representation of the thing. But, from the standpoint of being, it is clear that to be and to know are not identical, for the thing *as known* has only intentional being in the intellect, which is to say, a second-order existence, while the thing itself has a physical existence all its own. As Simon writes at the start of this essay, "To know Karl Marx is one thing and to be a Marxist is something entirely different."

Raymond Dennehy

An Introduction to Metaphysics of Knowledge
("Cognition and Activity," 39–84)

Objectivity and Activity

Because in created beings to know is not the same as to be, and because creaturely knowledge is thus but a special faculty of its subject, every act of such knowledge appears necessarily to be the work of an efficient cause, the result of an activity. Nevertheless, before we turn to examine the active factors in human cognition, . . . we need to consider briefly the general question of whether each and every kind of cognition requires activity on the part of the knower. . . . What we want to know is whether the knower can be a pure recipient of the cognitive act. Can any kind of knowledge result from pure passivity on the part of the knowing subject?

Passivity is derived from potentiality, and in pure passivity potentiality rules supreme. But have we not established that potency is the negation of knowing just as it is of being? In the order of nature, all created things are subject to the law of potentiality: they are only what they can be. Beings endowed with knowledge who can become, literally, what they cannot be are the exception. It is knowledge as superexistence that triumphs over the potentiality of being and provides certain creatures with an opening upon the infinite not available to the rest of nature. Thus between the limitless scope of knowledge and the limiting function of potentiality, there is an absolute antinomy. Any form received by way of pure passivity is thereby limited to the possibilities of the receiver, subjectively trapped, as it were, and the result of pure passivity can never be more than a material union, in which the receiver becomes other than what it was, but only such as it itself could ever be. But cognition is not like that. We have already established that to know means to become the other and as one could not be. The objectivity of knowledge thus clearly presupposes activity on the part of the knower. A subject can be united objectively—not subjectively—to a form only if he actively participates in that union. This absolute exclusion of potentiality, which in God is the root of His omniscience, is imitated in the created knower by what is his most characteristic and vital activity. A knowledge resulting from pure passivity would be an absolute contradiction, a fictitious potentiality that denies itself. Cognition is action as well as existence.

But precisely because knowledge appears not only as a unique sort of existence but also as a particular activity totally without parallel in the physical world, our next step must be a thorough review of the general theory of activity....

The Fact of Change: First Definition of Action

Of all the different kinds of action, the one we recognize first and retain as the clearest is the action experienced through change. Starting with change, then, in order to arrive at the understanding of activity free from all becoming, we follow the correct procedure of empirical inquiry....

Now the facts of change attest that there are subjects with determinations that they do not possess by pure identity. What one has by identity is not acquired and cannot be lost without the annihilation of oneself. The seed is not the same as the fruit; we observe it become a fruit. And that is how the efficient cause appears to us first of all as the *source of change*. Within the limits of movable being, then, action, *the actual exercise of efficient causality*, is nothing other than change in relation to its origin, the counterpart of passion, which is change in relation to the receiver. Still, between action and passion, there is more than just a logical distinction. The gift one gives is identical to the gift the other receives, but to give a gift is not the same as to receive one. And so, in complete agreement with common sense, we are brought to the following conclusions. Action and passion, identical with change and with each other, on the analogy of a thing's remaining itself under different modalities, are really distinct from change as well as from each other precisely as a thing under one modality is really distinct from the same thing under another modality. Although the finger extended is the same finger as when bent, there is a real distinction between the finger bent and the finger extended.

Moreover, since the subject of change, *that which changes*, is the movable, the recipient of the change, and not its source, we also realize that wherever action consists in a change, the proper subject of that action is not the agent but the patient. Basically identical with the change, this action affects primarily the patient. Substantially a determination of the patient, it belongs to the agent only in a modal sense.

The object first reached by human intelligence in conjunction with the senses is the being of sensible natures making itself known by their action on the sense organs. But although joined to the sense, our intelligence succeeds by dint of an heroic effort, as it were, surmounting its natural being, in grasping from that sensible being also certain characteristics of being as being. We may say that the true life of the spirit, in which we imitate however imperfectly the spirits who have no bodies, begins at that point. As befits metaphysical thought, the meaning of causal notions is thence deepened and purified, as they are stripped of everything that the characteristics proper to sensible natures add to their essence. We have still to talk about change, but what the fact of change will teach us at this level are the laws of being as being, which are indifferent to mobility and its sensorial manifestations. Here we learn that being a source of change is only one particular form of the idea of efficient cause. Able to grasp this cause in the intimacy of its being, and consequently in its universality, we come to understand it precisely as *the source of actuality*, not only of change but also of the perfection of being. The requirements of the laws of causality remain in full force also at this level. As long as the being under consideration is not identical with its act, a source distinct from it is required, regardless of whether we are dealing with the imperfect actuality of change or with the actuality of perfection in being. And since existence itself is the one act that no finite being possesses or can possess by identity with itself, we recognize that this law of efficient causality, understood as applying precisely to being as being, extends to every finite being, regardless of whether the subject is in act by way of change or in any other way. Moreover, if action is nothing more than the actual exercise of efficient causality, then we must understand that its essence does not require us to identify it with change. There is not a trace of change in the purely conserving action by which God keeps the creature in existence, the just soul in the state of grace, and generally maintains realities united to one another that are not one by identity. What happens at the beginning of things, at the very instant when the nature that does not possess existence by itself arises out of nothingness? Well, here not only is action unaccompanied by any change, which clearly presupposes an existent that would change, but it is also unaccompanied by any kind of reception, there being nothing to receive it. And that is how we learn that the idea of efficient action is expressed most excellently in the act of creation. No longer involving either change or reception, action here becomes pure production, that is, efficiency elevated to unconditioned freedom....

The Notion of Immanent Activity

At this point, however, a doubt arises: Do we have to say that the end of every agent is some kind of product? Or are there not also agents that go about their business without producing any effect? In response to this doubt and in order to show that the act is the end of potency in every kind of activity, Aristotle, without using these very terms, is led here to distinguish between two kinds of activity, immanent and transitive....

The distinctive feature of immanent action, defined in a wholly negative but perfectly clear way by Aristotle is precisely never to consist in the production of anything, never to be a way of leading to a term distinct from itself. Thus immanent action is not and can never be an exercise of efficient causality, and our first definition of action given above does not cover it. To see or to contemplate is not to produce anything. But do we have to say, then, that seeing and contemplating are not really acting? Ordinary language says that they are, but reluctantly. Though we speak spontaneously of acts of seeing and thought, and of minds ever on the alert, we also tend to set the contemplative and the active in opposition to each other, as if only what manifests itself in external effects deserves the name of real action. These hesitations of language give us a warning. If realities as remote from each other as transitive and immanent action are to be brought together under some general, transcendental definition of action, it will have to be by way of analogy. . . .

A Second (Transcendental) Definition of Action

And so we come to understand how activity and existence are to be distinguished with the notion of the terminal act. Existence is not *this* or *that*, a particular kind of thing; it is what causes things to be outside of nothingness. This does not mean, of course, that the existence of one particular species is the same as that of any other. They all *are* different. But we must realize that these differences, even as they affect it, come not from the act of existence itself but rather from the *things* that are. Of itself, existence is indifferent to the kind of nature that it causes to be, provided any intrinsic repugnance to being, namely self-contradiction, is excluded. But given this condition, the only potency that existence fulfills in its subject is this potency to be, common to all things that do not imply contradiction. This point cannot be made too strongly: the potency stemming from the internal relations of their specific characteristics is a property common to all things possible and in no sense involves what is original in each species. If existence completes essence, it does so *in the universal order of being*, not on the level of specific constitutions. This is why an affirmative answer to the question of whether a thing exists (*an sit res*) tells us nothing about its nature. The certainty that a particular object of thought really exists assures us only that we are dealing with a real object of thought, i.e., with a possible thing; it does not give us even a hint about what kind of thing it is (*quid sit res*).

In order to know what a thing is, we look at its activity. For minds that do not grasp essences directly and intuitively, that is the only way. But it is also a perfectly safe way, because if it is true that activity (at least in created beings) is a terminal act really distinct from existence, a thing's action fulfills it precisely on the plane of specific nature, the essence, or quiddity. Thus from the characteristics of the action observed, our mind spontaneously infers the characteristics of the acting nature, and metaphysical deduction establishes the legitimacy of this inference. This entire procedure may be summarized as follows. Proceeding analytically, first we recognize two kinds of apparently irreducible realities that reveal the characteristics of the terminal act—existence and action. Then, proceeding synthetically from the primary object of metaphysical thought, namely, being as being, we also recognize that every finite being, because of the duality of the principles that it includes, has two possibilities of fulfillment: one of them opens on the act of being; the other is deployed on the level of essences. The first is accomplished in existence; the second, in activity, which we are now able to define more precisely as *the terminal act that fulfills the active nature in accordance with its specific constitution.*

Third (Transcendental) Definition of Action

But there is more to be said. The above formula, rather than clarifying its proper nature, gives us no more than a basis for constructing a comprehensive notion of action. To arrive at a truly general definition of action, we need to return once again to the analysis of ordinary thought as it arises spontaneously from experience.

As already pointed out, of all the realities that may be called actions, common sense and ordinary language are most willing to consider as unquestionably such the transitive actions identified with change. We call the political leader who is introducing many important reforms a man of action; if he then becomes satisfied just to keep the system going, we say that he is now preserving rather than acting. Yet to preserve is also to exercise efficient causality, to engage in transitive action. How are we to account for this difference in interpretation? . . .

Just think of the common distinction of psychological facts under the headings of knowledge, affection, and activity. Though it would be wrong to insist that this represents an ontological division of the powers of the soul, this classification rests on sound observations, which make it quite useful in contexts other than the ontological. For instance, willing is an immanent activity, and if it looks more like action than either knowing or desiring does, it is not only because willing is closer to transitive activity commanding as it does the most important of our external acts. Willing is for us the same as acting, because in free volition the self is in a special way the principle from which its determination issues. When our intellect confronts its object, it is not up to us to recognize or not to recognize that object; nor is it up to us to cause or withhold attraction in our sense appetite in the presence of things desirable. But in free volition, the person is the master of his determination, and in it we all experience a uniquely intense feeling of *activity*.

But let us note that even though there is no freedom of choice in cognitive processes, we can and do speak of them as being active or passive. For instance, when a student is satisfied simply to accept what his teacher or textbooks tell him, we call him passive. But when a student makes an effort to review the evidence of the demonstrations on his own, so that the judgment in which his intellectual labor terminates issues truly and profoundly from himself, we honor and praise him for his "active mind."

Thus whether in transitive or in immanent activities, the idea of activity is intimately linked to the recognition of the origin, of the derivation, emanation, or processing, of something. The notion of activity becomes clearer and is accompanied by more intense emotional certainty as that activity is recognized more clearly as an emanation. Therefore, born in the womb of the acting nature, action may be said to be an *emanating terminal act*, standing in an "AB" (from) relation to the potency which it fulfills.

By contrast, existence does not proceed in any way from the nature that it brings into being. The non-existent nature is but a shadow of reality in nothingness, and of itself it can do nothing to become incarnate. Being, the spouse of nature, so to speak, always comes to their encounter from the outside. Therefore, received from without, existence may be said to be the terminal act that fulfills any nature through a special "IN" (in) relation.

Fourth (Transcendental) Definition of Action

What we have to do now, however, is to examine more carefully the nature of the emanation implied in all activity to decide whether this emanation is realized in the same way in immanent and in transitive activity....

[A] relation of efficient causality seems implicated in every activity. And the best way to understand what that means is to examine the problem of the efficient cause of action itself.

The two realities that emanate or can emanate from the terminal act of the efficient cause are effect and action. The effect proceeds from its cause *by means of* a transitive action, which is the intermediary through which the effect flows from its source to its term. The transitive action itself, however, proceeds immediately from its cause, for if the subject acting produced its action by another distinct action, we would have an infinite regression of intermediary actions between the cause and its action. Moreover, action by any created efficient cause cannot be attributed in its entirety to the created efficient cause from which it so proceeds without any intermediary. As a reality distinct from the subject acting, to which it does not belong by identity, action can be joined to it only by a separate cause. Therefore, to explain the union of any created cause with its action, we have to call upon a higher cause whose causality is exercised unconditionally and whose action belongs to it by pure identity. This is how we establish the theory of physical premotion and recognize its connection with the theory of creation. For just as the thing distinguishable from its actual existence cannot, of itself, place itself in existence or preserve itself there, so the being that does not have its action by identity cannot, by itself, join itself to its action. It is just as impossible to claim that an agent really distinct from its action can act without the divine concurrence as it is to claim that a contingent being can exist without being created.

In the purity of its conception, immanent action implies no term distinct from itself. Here there is only a single emanating reality, namely, action, and the efficient cause of this reality can be none other than the acting subject. Immanent action proceeds really from its subject, on which it depends and to which it is bound by what we have called an "AB" relation. But what that dependence, direct emanation, and "AB" relation amount to is precisely a case of efficient causality. The efficient act by which the agent produces its immanent action is incorporated in the latter without constituting it in its specificity. Thus what acts of thought or of volition may be said to "produce" is something that is basically indistinguishable from those acts themselves.

In view of all this, then, activity may finally be defined as *a terminal act emanating by way of an efficiency with which it is identified without being necessarily absorbed in it*. It is a definition that nicely confirms the insights of common-sense thought revealed in the ordinary use of language. We reserve the term *active* for those whose life is spent in producing external effects precisely because transitive action alone qualifies as efficiency formally considered. But we also speak of *acts* of thought and of will because these immanent activities, too, are produced by efficient causality. Moreover, we attribute the character of activity more readily to making decisions than to acquiring knowledge or having desires precisely because in the act of free choice the soul is the efficient cause of its determination not once but twice: first by nature, and a second time by reason of its freedom. Finally, we can see how even in matters of cognition we distinguish between active behavior and passive behavior as a kind of shorthand for distinguishing degrees of involvement. For there is no doubt that the soul is the efficient cause of its cognitive determinations in proportion to the alertness of its faculties and the functioning of the will that moves the intellect.

Though the idea of efficient causality is thus common to both these kinds of action, their unity is imperfect and analogical. For there is no generic unity between an efficient act whose entire essence consists in efficiency and another efficient act whose specific character consists rather in immanent perfection. It is true that both transitive and immanent actions emanate from the subject that performs them as terminal acts of an efficient cause; that is what they have in common. But this common element is, in the two cases, affected by irreducible differences. In the case of transitive action, the terminal act of the efficient cause does what efficiency is supposed to do: lead to a term distinct from itself. In immanent action, that does not happen. Hence, it is *in* itself and in *its essential idea* that this common element is modified, and this intrinsic differentiation between these two kinds of action absolutely rules out the formation of a univocal concept. Transitive action is efficiency. But even though it includes efficiency, immanent action is not efficiency; it belongs to the category of quality. . . .

Action and Quality

The two elements that constitute the corporeal subject, form and prime matter, show their characteristics in its internal attributes, namely, its quantity and quality. Quantity is uniformity, homogeneity; when we move from one part of the quantitative whole to another part, remaining strictly within the order of quantity, we pass from the same to the same. The reason for this is that quantity is related to a substance not on account of its particular form but on account of its matter, which, despite all its determinations, shares in the uniform clay of which all lower things are made. By contrast, the parts of a qualitative whole are all different from each other. The powers of the soul form a whole, but the will does not resemble the sense of touch; courage does not resemble mercy. Just as the specific form is what, in the order of substance, causes a being to be this or that, so quality proceeding from the primary form is what, in the order of accident, causes a being to be precisely such and such. The broader use of the term quality, which is often applied to whole species, confirms this analogy....

The category of quality, however, includes several very different kinds of realities that need to be distinguished from one another. As far as immanent activity is concerned, two things are certain. Because of its spiritual character, immanent activity differs from all those qualities that for whatever reason require material support. And because its nature is that of a terminal act, immanent activity also differs from all those qualities that in any way imply potentiality. These exclusions suggest that as a quality immanent activity may be a special kind of disposition....

[W]e understand by disposition any order, systematization, arrangement, or organization of the parts of a whole. It is not just any sort of distribution, as might result from some kind of casual gesture; it is a purposeful distribution, set out with a view to an end. We judge the arrangement of the fruit at the fruit stand with regard to whether the display is more or less likely to attract buyers. Thus every disposition of the parts of a whole is either good or bad precisely because disposition is relative to an end, whether the parts involved are fruits displayed in a stall or divisions of an army deployed in battle....

But the metaphysical notion of disposition applies to all kinds of wholes with parts. It is relevant to the understanding of a whole that it is substantially one, such as the living body, and it is relevant to the understanding of a dynamic whole, in which the plurality of the parts does not imply the location of the parts outside each other. For instance, considered in its natural state, so to speak, before any acquisition of knowledge or moral qualities, a particular faculty of the human mind presents a plurality of possibilities or dynamic parts which, because they are not yet reduced to unity by a disposition, constitute an interior obstacle to the perfection of the faculty. Thus the will may prefer either material goods or spiritual goods, may make either lust or friendship prevail within itself.... And so, for the good of the faculty, a disposition must intervene to put these dynamic parts in order, just as the commander-in-chief organizes and deploys his divisions with a view to winning the battle. The possibilities inherent in the intellect having to do with theoretical knowledge, with moral activity, and with material production are put in order through the stable dispositions we call science, prudence, and art. By overcoming the initial plurality of possibilities that blocked from the inside the pursuit of its ends, these dispositions enable the intellect to perform its acts with ease and joy. The moral virtues of temperance, courage, and justice do the same for the will.

These habitual dispositions of the active faculties are not, however, ultimate determinations. The scientist not actually thinking about what he knows, or the just man not at the moment rendering someone his due, remain, in relation to the act of scientific thought, or in relation to the just act of the will, in a state of potency. Thus, although its dynamic parts have been perfectly disposed and reduced to unity as far as is possible without going beyond the limits of potency, a particular faculty falls short of being a fully united whole until it executes its terminal act. The scientist who relaxes his mind by playing bridge has the potency to think of an infinity of objects; his intellect, disposed for theorizing, remains open to a multitude of possibilities; and this multitude of dynamic parts will be reduced to unity only by his turning his mind to a particular scientific object. And if it is true that this act is a quality, we have to think of it as a disposition, as *the supreme ordering of the dynamic parts of a vital faculty in relation to its end actually possessed.*

The conclusion to which we are driven by this analysis is that the immanent activity of knowing combines in a wondrous union two antinomic characteristics. On the one hand, it is a qualitative perfection consisting simply in a disposition. To know modifies the knowing faculty only by an arrangement of its possibilities; beyond this disposition there is present in cognition only the intentional object, which neither alters nor is altered by the faculty. One cannot conceive anything more delicate or more intimate than the modification of the subject in the act of knowing. While nothing could be farther from alteration by way of a contrary, there is yet no contact more radical and penetrating than that of a knowing mind with its object. Because its delicacy and depth are so perfect, the quality of knowing is a masterpiece of interiority. On the other hand, does not cognition imply more than just efficiency, or active causality, which we usually associate with things exterior? The answer is that "to know" includes this efficiency, not as a reality presupposed and distinct from itself, but in the supremely intimate bond of absence of real distinction. The importance of the insight opened by this notion of an activity that resembles both efficiency and quality, so clearly separated in the rest of the world, cannot be overemphasized. The one who knows moves himself in his innermost depths in order to give himself over to the object and attain thereby his final perfection, which is identical with that activity that he exercises on himself.

Motionless Activity

The theory of immanent activity allows us to understand better the problem of the relations between activity and change. First of all, we note that although efficiency does not necessarily imply mobility, change appears by contrast to be an essential property of transitive action. The subject of transitive action, as the receiver of its effect rather than its producer, is an imperfect being that has to wait for its completion until the transitive action exercised upon it is ended. And when this happens, the action belongs to the past. Work is done only upon what is incomplete, considered precisely in its incompleteness and to the extent that it is imperfect—which is the very definition of change.

Immanent action, on the other hand, is essentially resistant to any kind of mobility. Once a truth has been discovered, the intellect does not cease knowing it, as the workman must stop working when a particular job is done; nor does the heart, in possession of its object, stop loving it. Contemplation and joy are above time, because they are above change. Of course, it is true that human intelligence proceeds by way of discourse and that human desire involves *effort*. But the discourse of our reason and the striving of our will—spiritual images, as it were, of mobility—share in their nature of becoming not as immanent activities but rather because our knowledge is insufficient; we desire the good only because we do not fully possess it. Stripped of these accidental imperfections, knowing is the act of a perfect subject and so also is loving. . . .

Finally, concerning production unaccompanied by change, such as God's creative and conserving activity, we need to understand that what it involves has nothing to do with transitive action but represents rather efficiency wrapped up in wholly immanent activity. Every divine action is identical with the being of God and is consequently immanent in the highest degree. The universe is simply the result of divine superabundance and adds nothing to the creative action that is God. His activity in the first six days is identical in God with His rest on the seventh. . . .

Vitality

Thus the notion of life, which arises first of all at the sight of a local movement by a being that moves itself, extends generally also to all changes completed within the subject from which they are understood to proceed. But when, on the metaphysical level, we replace the notion of change with that of *actuality*—change being only one kind of actuality—we arrive at a more comprehensive understanding of life as being the power to confer upon oneself some kind of actuality, to act upon oneself, or to give oneself one's appropriate perfection.

The indispensable metaphysical minimum that permits us to speak of life is, then, the non-fortuitous coincidence of the efficient and of the material or receptive causality in the same individual subject. But if the efficient causality of a particular living subject produces not only the effects that remain with it but also the *predeterminations of its actions*, then what we have is not just life but the realization of a superior degree of vitality.

Every efficient cause that is not identical with its action has to be predetermined with reference to that action. . . . And that is why before any action can be performed, not only must it have an object but the form of that object must be present in the agent. In the case of transitive action, the object is pursued as an effect; in the case of immanent action, it is something to be contemplated or loved; in either case, for the object to be specified properly, its form must in some way pre-exist in the agent. What this requirement for an objective determination, which covers every kind of action, expresses, then, is precisely the need for any agent to be predetermined formally with regard to its action, the need for an idea to direct the activity. . . .

Over and above the idea of the object that provides its *formal predetermination*, the efficient cause that is really distinct from its action and that brings about the action also needs an *existential predetermination* provided by the desire for an end. An action without a formal object could never appear in existence because of the lack of any kind of form; but without a final cause, an action would still not make it into existence, because there would be no reason for it to appear rather than not to appear. At the term of every action, there is an object and an end; at its beginning, an idea and a tendency. . . .

What needs to be recognized at this point is that the two predeterminations of the agent, the need for which we have just established, can also be separated in such a way that one of them springs from the initiative of the agent while the other is decided by nature. Take, for instance, an automatic reflex action in response to some sense stimulus. What the agent will do, the form of that reaction, has been knowingly predetermined by the agent himself; but when the occasion arises, it is nature alone that triggers it by joining to the idea of the object the further note of suitability or goodness. But both predeterminations can also belong to the agent himself, and what we have then is a free agent. The power of deciding that a particular object knowingly proposed by the agent himself is good or bad, the power of joining or separating the formal and the existential predeterminations of one's actions, of giving one's self a goal to be reached by one's own power—that is what we call liberty. Thus the mind alone, we learn, is the cause of its perfection in every order of causality, and only beings who have minds can be said to be fully alive.

Still, no created minds can realize the notion of life in its fullness, since no creature is the sufficient or ultimate cause of what it causes, except in the order of material causality, that is, in the order of passivity. Thus even though all natural beings are characterized by spontaneity that is lacking in our machines—and the living things show more spontaneity than the nonliving, the animal more than the plant, man more than the animal, and angel more than man—still no created being enjoys an absolute spontaneity. Thus whatever the role played by the created efficient cause in making ready its action, the performance of that action requires divine premotion. The created mind may be the knowing cause of its formal determination, but it is never the ultimate cause of it. The birth of thought in the human intellect is not entirely free, for it presupposes an influence exercised on our senses by external objects. And as for pure spirits, if it is true that their ideas in no way depend on things, it is also true that they do not possess them by identity but have received them from God. Similarly, the created intelligent being cannot be the ultimate cause of his own actual development, for it is the weight of his nature, received by the grace of Him Who created him, that inclines him toward his final end. If he is free to choose among particular ends, it is only within the limits of the general end to which he is inclined by his nature.

Thus the idea of life, originally derived from the observation of material nature, appears to leave behind the whole created world to acquire a unique meaning in God. Actually, however, what we learn when we thus reach the summit of the hierarchy of life is that our idea of life, already turned metaphysical and analogical, must undergo a further purification based on an even more profound analogy. The first of living beings offers no grip to the notion of a causality that turns back on itself. God is not the cause of His perfections, since His perfections are not really distinct from his being. To give expression to its first and supreme analogate, then, we need to rework our idea of life. If to live means to bring about change in oneself, or to confer upon oneself some kind of actuality, then, we come to realize, it is He Who possesses every actuality by identity with His own being, activity, and goodness Who is Life itself, and everything else is by comparison as if it were dead.

Every immanent activity, since it remains as well as originates in the agent himself, deserves the name of vital activity. But the converse is not necessarily true. . . . In the vegetative life, what is immanent is only the effect of the activity, which makes this activity not immanence but production. . . .

Vegetative activity, like the activity of inanimate beings, takes place completely within the order of physical existence and, as a direct function of nature, is limited by that nature. By contrast, cognition presupposes that the being endowed with it has access to an order of existence transcending the limits set to its existential capacity by its constitutive idea. And this access gives birth, with the appearance of understanding, to something marvelously resembling divine infinity.

Philosopher at Work
("To Be and To Know," 173–92)

The metaphysics of knowledge begins with the experience of the diversity between to be and to know....

The diversity of to be and to know is expressed, first of all, by the contrast between the amplitude of to know and the narrowness of to be....

The contrast between the narrowness of what we are and the amplitude of what we know has been adequately expressed by the philosophers. "To sum up what has been said about the soul, let us say again that the soul is in a way all existing things" (Aristotle, *On the Soul*, 3.8, 431b20). In reference to this text, St. Thomas writes that "what distinguishes things endowed with, from things devoid of, the power of knowing is that whereas the non-knowing things have but their own form, the knowing things are designed to have also the form of other beings.... Thus, it is clear that the nature of the non-knowing thing is more restricted and limited, and the nature of things possessed of knowledge has greater amplitude" (Thomas Aquinas, *Summa Theologiae* I, 14, 1). Elsewhere, St. Thomas shows that even in purely spiritual creatures to understand and to be are necessarily diverse; if they were identical, the being of a creature would have to be infinite like its understanding....

When a subject and a form unite in such a way as to result in a third thing, in a compound within which each is modified, the union is of the matter-form description, whether it takes place in things material or in things of another order. When the union leaves untouched the identity of the things united, results in no compound, preserves the possibility of indefinitely many other such unions, and makes for unrestricted amplitude, then the union is of the objective type: it may take place in the intellect or in the sense, but this is only of secondary relevance. "Science is, in a certain way, the scientifically known objects, and sensation, the objects known sensorially...." (*On the Soul*, 3.4.431b22).

When the union is of the matter-form type and involves the bringing about of a compound, it never can be said that the receiver has become identical with the received or that it is the received. If we are particularly impressed by the genuinely Marxian character of a Marxist's attitudes in the most diverse situations, we may happen to say that this gentleman is the essence of Marxism, but we know that we are speaking metaphorically. Likewise, it is in a metaphorical way that we say of a man who remains just at any cost that he is the essence of justice. The matter does not become the form, and it is not possible under any circumstances (except by metaphor) that the matter is the form. On the contrary, it is Aristotle's contention that the soul is, in a way, all things, that the scientific intellect is the universe of the things known scientifically, and that the sense is all sensible things. The matter cannot be said to be the form, it only can be said to be informed, and to make up a whole with the form that it has received. But the knowing power and the object do not merge into any whole and this makes it possible for the knower to be the object that he knows. Knowing is just another way of being, free from the conditions that restrict every created thing to a genus or a species. In its more familiar forms, knowing is being the other qua other. The amplitude that primarily distinguishes *to know* from *to be* is traceable to the particularities of the *objective* way of existence....

The object of knowledge is a *pure object*; this may be the best approximation to a definition of knowledge. To be united with a pure object is to be one with a formal cause that is extrinsic and that comprises, by association with other features, that of a term. To be united with such an object is to be this object. Knowing is a way of being. But it is not the common way of being, according to which things are restricted to what they are and possess no forms except those with which they achieve matter-form unions. The analysis of "objective union" and of "pure object" has explained the Aristotelian formula, "the soul is in a way all things," both with regard to the identification of to be and to know ("is") and with regard to the qualification of their identity ("in a way")....

The understanding of ideas would be easier if it were not that things also do exercise the function of representations and images....

A photograph is, in a certain way, a double-sided reality. It primarily is a thing made of such material as paper and chemicals, and in the capacity of thing it terminates a definite act of cognition. Its first function pertains to the order of physical existence—the order in which unions are of the matter-form type. Any relation it has to objective existence and objective union is but secondary. In the whole theory of knowledge, there may not be any problem more significant, doctrinally and historically, than this: are ideas representative things, like photographs, paintings, and sculptures, or are they a distinct kind of entities, defined by the primacy [of] representing, defined by the primacy of objectivity, defined by the primary function of bringing about objective rather than matter-form unions, defined, in short, by the primacy of objective over natural existence? . . .

In our endeavor to explain the relation between things and ideas, many useful lessons can be derived from the history of idealism. The philosophy of Descartes is not unqualifiedly idealistic. It does not hold that the "to be" of material things is reducible to their being perceived; correspondingly, the distinction between things and ideas remains fundamental. But in Descartes, *what* is known first is not the thing; it is the idea, and the whole problem of true knowledge is to determine the dependable ways of proceeding from the idea to the thing. . . .

Thus the root of idealism, in its modern versions at least, would be the postulate that between the idea and the thing the relation is one of causality. In its attempt to identify the trustworthy representations, Cartesian idealism, paradoxically, may not have taken full advantage of the feature that distinguishes the genus of being called ideas from the genus of being called things. A bridge has to be built, and the principle of causality is entrusted with guaranteeing the resemblance of the idea to the thing represented. (In case causality does not suffice, divine veracity, parallelism, and pre-established harmony are at hand.) Indeed, it is causality that makes it possible to know, through the footprint, the presence of an animal at a certain place and time. But in the case of a footprint, as much as in that of the deer or the bear that the footprint represents, the first existential function is to exist. It is but in secondary fashion that a footprint represents and signifies. As remarked in the foregoing,[1] a two-sided entity may still be a thing. What determines an entity's belonging to the genus of being called, in the words of Cajetan, "the intentions of things, their sensible or intelligible forms," is not its two-sidedness; it is a certain primacy of the existential order. In terms of existence, an idea is not first of all a distinct kind of being; it primarily is one with the thing that it represents; it has not being of its own save as needed for its representative function.

Note

1. [Editor's note: Simon is here referring to his earlier discussion of Cajetan's *Commentary of the Soul*, 2.11 (in which his words quoted here can be found).]

CHAPTER 4

The Distinction of Thing and Object

Ordinarily, "thing" and "object" are equivalent. In epistemology, "object" is opposed to a conscious "subject." A thing need not be an object, nor an object a thing. A thing is considered an object insofar as it is known or knowable. Being an object involves a relation to consciousness; an object is that with which a cognitive state is concerned. Our cognition being partial, there is also a more precise epistemic use of "object": whatever of a thing is made manifest to knowledge.[1]

In our first selection below, Simon uses the distinction between things and objects to answer, for the only time in the history of philosophy, two fundamental questions concerning truth. First, if truth is conformity of the mind with what is outside the mind, how can we ever know truth? We cannot compare the known to the unknown, so we can only compare what is "in the mind" to what is "in the mind."

The truth of affirmative propositions requires that the same thing(s) is made an object in different ways. We can grasp the truth of "Socrates is a philosopher" because we are already aware of a thing made object by the name "Socrates" and of a thing made object by the predicate "philosopher." So each of these objects must, to begin with, be known to be identical with something that is not just an *object*, not just something related to a knowing subject in this way or that, but an (actual or possible) mind-independent *thing*, and thus something potentially objectified in more than one way. Grasping the truth of the mental constructs called propositions results not from directly comparing the mind with reality, but from comparing one object already known not just as an object but as a transobjective thing with another object already known as a transobjective thing. (We can call mind-independent things "transobjective" only after the mind's reflection on itself gives us the concept of "object," but that reflection itself could not occur unless we were already aware of what we can after reflection call the transobjective: features pertaining to things as things.)

In comparing thing with thing, we are aware that the thing has been diversely objectified; if it was not diversely objectified, we could not compare it to itself. So awareness of truth also requires an at least implicit reflection of the mind on its own acts of objectification, and the awareness of the identity of objects as things that give us knowledge of truth is also awareness of the mind's conformity with things.

This leads to the answer to the second question: What is the epistemological purpose of forming propositions when we are already aware of things by means of concepts and sensations? The mind forms propositions in order to express to itself an alleged—there can be falsehood—identity of distinct objects with the same thing, an identity that the mind can know to hold only by comparing the known to the known, for example, comparing what is objectified by the name "Socrates" and what is objectified by the predicate "philosopher." Propositional comparisons of the known to the known can express the truth about what exists "outside the mind," because each of the compared objects is already known to be identical with an, at least putatively, possible thing: what is objectified by "Socrates" is known as one entity and no other; what is objectified by "philosopher" is known as an entity possessing certain characteristics that are independent of the knower's mind. Simon hypothesizes the existence of "exhaustive" angelic knowledge as a foil in contrast to our knowledge. The validity of his argument does not require belief in angels.

The same object, then, unites values pertaining to things as things, such as being this entity and no other, or being a philosopher, and values pertaining to things as objects, such as being named "Socrates," or being in the extension of "philosopher." The latter are "beings of reason," which can have no existence (no status) other than that of being objects (being in apprehension). In particular, they are *logical* beings of reason, secondary features that pertain to prior objects of rational knowledge only as objects, that is, only as a result of, and for the sake of, our knowing those prior objects: being a subject or a predicate, being the middle term of a syllogism, and so on. The distinction between what pertains to objects as objects and what pertains to objects as things, which Simon explains in our second selection below, provides the way out of some perennial philosophical traps.

First, there is the false dichotomy that logic must be either a branch of psychology or the study of abstract objects. Logic is not about laws of *thought*. Logic's laws govern *objects* of (rational) thought as objects, because they govern, and result from the nature of, the beings of reason that are properties pertaining to objects of reason as objects of reason. Second, the distinction between the features of objects as objects that make the laws of logic true and the features that make statements about things as things true shows the fallacy of trying to model ontology on logical properties of our knowledge of the real. The correspondence that makes statements about things as things true cannot be between things and *logical* characteristics belonging to things only as objects of concepts and propositions. With respect to the logical order, thing and object must differ, since truth requires that thing and object be at least logically distinct, but only logically, not really, distinct.

The thing/object identity analysis of truth is not Frege's "identity theory of truth." The truth condition of a proposition is not identity between a proposition and a state of affairs, which would require that states of affairs share a logical structure with propositions. The truth condition is a prior identity between each of the diverse objects compared in the proposition and the same actual or possible thing(s). Nor is the thing/object identity analysis of truth based on an interpretation of the verb "to be"; in particular it is not an interpretation of "is" as an identity sign. The awareness of the identity of an object with a thing that is prior to the awareness of truth is also prior to the awareness of the function that "to be" has in propositions.

Simon clearly preferred the subject-copula-predicate way of expressing propositions. But the thing/object analysis itself does not commit him to the existence of such things as the true "logical form" of statements or of their true "logical subjects and predicates." Being able to fall back on an analysis of propositions from the point of view of their essential *epistemological* purpose, he would be free to say that, as long as that purpose was served, different *logical* purposes could be legitimately served by different logical syntaxes, purposes such as using calculational methods as tools of logic. It has been shown that the function-argument syntax is as consistent with the thing/object identity analysis of truth as is the subject-copula-predicate syntax.

John C. Cahalan

An Introduction to Metaphysics of Knowledge
("Experience and Thought," 137–54)

We possess the truth of knowledge only in the act of judging.[2] In sensation, the sense is assimilated to the object sensed, but whether it is truly conformed or whether, owing to some accidental failing, it falls short, the sense itself cannot tell. Likewise, and barring accidents, in simple intellectual perception all that happens is that the intellect conforms to its object. But in judgment this conformity of thought and thing becomes itself an object of thought. Here the intellect compares what exists inside itself with what exists outside itself; it compares the idea in which the thing exists intentionally with the thing as it exists physically; and in doing so, the intellect can recognize whether its knowledge, in producing the thing in intentional existence, has preserved the thing's identity with itself.

Indeed, this is what judgment seems to be in essence: an act of knowledge that by simply declaring a thing to be such and such bears directly on the relation of knowledge with the extramental real. A synthesis or composition when affirmative, and a division when negative, what judgment primarily deals with are not, as a superficial analysis might lead one to believe, mere ideas. Judgment composes or divides the intramental and the extramental; it compares knowing and being. And so even as it necessarily deals with the association and comparison of ideas, the syntheses and divisions exercised by judgment are those of the mind that has become one with a thing existing outside the mind....

To understand exactly why our knowledge of truth requires a complex act, a judicative synthesis [judgment], it is necessary to be maximally precise on the relation of the notions of *thing* and of *object*. If we understand by "thing" the concrete reality whose act is extramental being, made up of an essence joined to its properties, its contingencies, and finally its existence (actual or possible), and by "object" whatever of that thing is made manifest in knowledge, we have to say, *first*, that there is no sense in which the object and the thing make two—as if the object could be something other than the thing—but also, *second*, that the thing and the object do not necessarily coincide totally. Total coincidence of object and thing is found only in an exhaustive knowledge, in which the entire thing is constituted as an object. The object is always identical with the thing, but this identity may be only partial, and in every knowledge that is not exhaustive, there is more in the thing than in the object. Now, it is this lack of total coincidence between the object and the thing, wherever such is the case, that gives rise to the problem of the identity of the thing and the object in our knowledge. Not that this identity can be purely and simply unknown; it is the essence of the object to represent the thing or, better, to be the thing as it manifests itself in knowledge. Thus the skeptical position, which despairs of knowing whether there is, beyond the phenomenal object, some reality identical with what is perceived, goes contrary to the natural movement of the intellect, and can be refuted by reduction to absurdity. In fact, it is worth noting that despite the most systematic determination to contradict the spontaneous certitudes of the intellect, skeptical doubt concerning the identity of the object and the thing—of the phenomenal object and the thing itself—has never been extended to the phenomenal object considered in its phenomenality. The skeptic gives up on knowing the truth because he does not know where to go from there; namely, how to verify that the object is identical with the thing. And so even though truth consists in the relation of conformity between thought and reality, rather than in the identity between the object and the thing, and even though that identity is never *unknown*—it can only be *disregarded* at the price of an arbitrary forcing—knowing the truth certainly involves acknowledging expressly that identity, which a simple grasping of the object does not always provide. For how could the mind expressly recognize its conformity to reality if it did not expressly recognize that its object is identical with the real? And if the mind sees its object as identical with the real, how could it not see that it itself conforms to reality? The act of knowing the conformity of the mind to reality and the act of recognizing the identity of the object and the thing must go hand in hand. When simple perception of the object includes knowledge of truth, it is because that perception is sufficient for knowing expressly that the object is identical with a thing. When in addition to simple perception a further act is required for knowing the conformity of the mind with the real, it is because the identity of the object and the thing is not adequately expressed by simple perception.

In an exhaustive knowledge, the identity of the object and the thing is as fully manifest as the object itself. For a mind sufficiently penetrating to grasp immediately and without any remainder everything knowable in the thing, leaving no transobjective element, the recognition of the identity of the object and the thing does not require a distinct act, because such a mind knows that thing fully at the same time as it knows the object. There is no skepticism among the angels; the skeptical doubt that the human intellect cannot really live with cannot even be feigned by the angelic intellect. Regardless of the state of his will, an angel can no more feign doubt about the object–thing than the skeptic can feign doubt about the object–phenomenon, and for the same reason: the thing known exhaustively has entered wholly the order of phenomenality.

But in knowledge that is not exhaustive, the identity of the thing and the object, even though never in doubt, cannot be expressed by the mind to itself except through comparing the object with the thing. And this is where the skeptical doubt comes in. Because the thing extends beyond the perceived object, if our human, less than exhaustive perception is unable to express their identity, how, then, are we to get hold of the thing to compare it with the object and its idea? To the extent that it exceeds the object, the thing in itself, by itself, is something unknown. Therefore, comparing the object with the thing that does not totally coincide with the object would mean comparing the known with the unknown, which is something evidently impossible.

And yet it has to be done. We have to be able to compare the object with the transobjective thing in order to verify not only their identity but also the conformity of our thought to reality. But because one cannot compare the known with the unknown, and since the object of the non-exhaustive perception is presented to the mind surrounded by an area of the unknown, somehow the object must be made to refer to what it does not express. We must find a way to use the certainty of its presence to get beyond it and to penetrate the transobjective thing in its very transobjectivity. And there seems only one way to do this.

Comparing the limited object with the thing, clearly absurd if it is a matter of comparing the known and the unknown, is possible by means of a comparison of two objects, which would tell us what goes on in the transobjectivity of the thing and make that transobjectivity, so to speak, pass into objectivity.

This is the roundabout way, unknown to the skeptic, that an intellectual realism has found to solve the paradoxical problem of comparing the object and the thing. We compare one object with another object, the known with the known, and if either rational analysis or experience reveals the need to identify them, the problem is solved. That need posits an identity that is not realized in the phenomenality of the object—otherwise the two objects would be one—and can only be in the transobjectivity of the thing. For instance, the object *Socrates* is not identical with the object *man*. So, if I have to say that Socrates is a man, this can be only because of their identity in the transobjective realm. The thing that is Socrates, and that manifests itself in the object of thought "Socrates," is the same thing that is man, and that manifests itself in the object of thought "man." But when I thus verify the identity of these objects in the transobjective realm, by an operation that is strictly the work of my own mind, I know at the same time that my mind conforms to the real thing.

It is in this way that we come to understand the role of the enunciative synthesis [proposition], how necessary it is for the preparation of the judicative synthesis, and in what essential way the latter differs from it.[3] Judgment consists in saying *Yes* or *No*. Yes, the thing is just as the thought presents it; no, it is different. An exhaustive perception requires no comparison between the mind and the real, since it testifies directly to the mind that the thing is just as it reveals itself. But lacking an exhaustive perception, we carry out the necessary comparison between our thought and the real by way of the enunciative synthesis, in which the mind both reflects upon itself and transcends objectivity to attain reality in its most distinctive otherness. . . .

By "reasons for judgment" I mean the light that compels the mind to assent to the identity in a transobject of objects of thought that are not identical in their being as objects. As we have seen in the preceding, although the identity of an object and a thing is acknowledged only in judgment, it is never unknown. The identity of object and thing is present when an object is first attained. From the first instant of knowledge, that identity possesses an obscure efficacy and power to make itself known. What compels the mind to identify two objects of thought cannot arise from the transobjectivity of the thing, which at that moment is not yet penetrated by the mind, nor from the characteristics belonging to the object considered in its status as object. For those characteristics of the object prevent it from being identified with a distinct object; from this point of view the Megarians were right. And what that means is that this call for interobjective identification can come only from the objects themselves not as objects but strictly as they are *manifestations of the thing*. In other words, what gives any object of thought, non-exhaustive as it may be, the power to reveal to us its transobjective connections with some other aspect of reality is nothing else but its real identity with the thing.

Sometimes it is the objective content of the concept that reveals its need to be joined in the mind to the objective content of another concept, and the judgment so determined is what we call a rational judgment. At other times, when their contents do not reveal the need for such an association, it is experience that shows us the need to associate one particular object with another. For example, although there is nothing in the concept of this man and in the concept of a flute player that compels my mind to assent to the proposition "This man is a flute player," I do so because I see and hear this man playing the flute.

The Great Dialogue of Nature and Space
("The Real and the Ideal in Nature," 94–106)

A being of reason is an object, which neither does nor can exist except in the mind in the capacity of object. You have in this definition all you need in order never to do what has been done by so many people: to confuse a being of reason with a psychological reality. That is the ambiguity of the expression "being of reason," but the Latin *ens rationis* is just as bad. Ignoramuses may take it to designate psychological realities, but a psychological reality is an *ens reale*, a real being of a particular kind that is just as real as anything else. Take a man with plenty of happy memories who is unfortunately involved in a head-on collision, so that as a result of brain injuries his memory is gone. A certain facility that he had to remember what he did as a child and as a young man is gone. Something real is gone. We may elaborate indefinitely on the nature of such psychological realities, our sensations, our images, our recollections, our acts of understanding, our acts of reasoning, our concepts and so forth and so on; that these are real things is not questionable. You may say that they are reducible to movements of particles if you are a very staunch materialist after the fashion of a hundred years ago—that is one way to see things. Then psychological realities would ultimately be of the same nature as the so-called physical realities. Real they are anyway, whether you interpret them materialistically or not. A being of reason is that which neither does nor can exist except in the mind and in *the capacity of object*. This is the distinguishing part, the differentiating part of the definition. "In the capacity of object," not in the capacity of disposition, not in the capacity of habit, not in the capacity of memory or image or concept but in the capacity of object.

Let us consider some examples. Beings of reason are found in several domains. There is one where they are overwhelming because they are alone. It is logic. Logical properties are beings of reason. That is the first thing to get in order to define logic and to distinguish it from its unscrupulous neighbors. Logic is surrounded by neighbors that have absolutely no scruples, for instance, the psychology of the intellect, the critique of knowledge and, worst of all, the ethics of thought. These neighbors of logic are always ready to swallow it up. There are on the market indefinitely many books of logic, especially perhaps since the beginning of the nineteenth century, where there is a little logic and much that may be very good in itself but is not logic. However, what is very good in itself and is not logic becomes vicious when it is called logic. What we have to understand here is exceedingly simple. Just take a little fact such as an incident in the jungle. A beast of prey, a lion, devours a deer. That is a real event that does not belong to the logical world; it belongs to the real world. When you have observed a number of the same such facts you are perfectly entitled to generalize and to say that the lion is a carnivorous animal. Here you are no longer considering an individual, real event, but a general property. I would even say an essential one. We approach very clumsily, imperfectly and unclearly such essences as that of lion. If you ask me exactly where this species of lion begins and exactly where it ends, you know that we do not know those things. Opinions on it change from generation to generation of zoologists. Though we are very uncertain about those things, when I say a lion and a deer, I am sure that I speak of two different things, things that have different natures. Without being able to ascertain their natures with much clarity, when I say "lion" I circumscribe one thing, and when I say "deer" I circumscribe something else. A lion is carnivorous so that if there are too many deer in a jungle it is a good thing to let the lions do their job. And a deer is herbivorous so that if you grow corn it is better to destroy a deer. All that is clear. We are talking about the real world all the time. We start with individual happenings, then we consider, no matter how clumsily, universal types. We speak of the real world all the time. Then a day comes when I consider the proposition: "The lion is carnivorous." That proposition refers to the real world but I may reflect upon the proposition and say, "In the proposition, 'the lion is carnivorous,' 'lion' is subject and 'carnivorous' is predicate." But there are no subjects or predicates in the jungle. Those objects exist in the mind alone. It is as simple as that in principle. The development of those principles may involve tremendous difficulties. In principle it is as simple as that: a lion belongs to the real world, the devouring of a deer by a lion belongs to the real world, the lion's property of being a carnivorous animal belongs to the real world, and when I stop to think that I understand those properties in arrangements of objects my understanding belongs to the real world too. But as I arrange those objects in such a way as to understand them, what happens to those objects in this mental arrangement? They acquire properties that they never have in the jungle or in the desert. We can put it in a slightly different way. The lion and the deer exist twice, in the jungle and as objects in the mind. As a result of the second existence that they enjoy in the mind, they acquire new properties that depend on their first existence but that follow in part too from the distinguishing characteristics of this second existence. That is the difference between the logical and the real world. It is these new properties that are the object of logic. You can think of indefinitely many examples of them. To be a subject, to be a predicate, to be a major term, to be a minor term, to be a middle term, to be a middle term in a syllogism of the first figure; these are so many logical properties that belong to things, not in their real but in their objective existence.

We ought then to try to rule out the confusion of beings of reason and psychological realities. I understand the lion through a disposition of my psyche (call it a concept if you please), which is something real, a psychological reality. A memory of a lion, which is simply an image by which I remember it and which can be destroyed if a hammer is suddenly applied on my skull—that is a psychological reality. I understand subject, predicate, middle term, and so on, also through psychological dispositions which are realities, just as real as anything else. The relevant point here concerns not that through which I understand but the object understood, Lion: real; deer: real; devouring: real; carnivorous: real; subject in the proposition "The lion is a carnivorous animal": that is a logical property. You see that it does not exist in the jungle. And it cannot exist anywhere else than in the mind in the capacity of object. Why? Because it is a property that things acquire as a result of the peculiarities of the second existence that they enjoy as objects of consideration, as objects of knowledge. It should be clear, then, why the possibility of making real a being of reason, a logical property, is excluded. These are properties that result from existence as objects. So, in the real world it is simply contradictory to fancy that they may exist. Those logical properties are not contradictory in themselves. There is nothing contradictory about a predicate or a subject. What would be contradictory would be the realization of a predicate. The day will never come when you can tell me, "I shook hands with a predicate in the street." That is impossible because it is a strict contradiction.

It is obvious that we have here a linguistic and almost a social problem concerning the word "object." A young friend of mine who taught logic to freshmen told me that they all come to college with the interpretation of "object" as the thing that you aim at, an end, a goal, an aim. That is not astonishing at all because they are practical boys. And the object of practice and of the arts has the character of an end. So it is no wonder if object and end are lumped together in the mind of freshmen. When they are so in the mind of philosophers too it is less excusable, and it is too bad that it should happen. On the other hand, there is something much more serious, which is the identification of object with thing. Many people tell you, "This table exists objectively," meaning thereby that if I cut my throat and go out of existence and you also and all men, the table will still exist. Now, pay attention to the role of object in all theory of knowledge, including the theory of knowledge that you are using every day, and you will see that far from meaning real, "object" means almost the opposite. For instance, there are objects in a dream, represented objects. Do they exist objectively? It is even the only way they exist. They do not exist as things, but they do exist as objects. We just have to reflect upon those things and upon our spontaneous use of words to see the difference between real existence and objective existence. I beg you to pay attention to that. Words have an awfully tyrannical power and can pervert anything.

When speaking of beings of reason, the first domain to consider is obviously that of logic. Logic could be defined as the science whose object is constituted exclusively by beings of reason. Does this mean that any consideration of reality is out of place in a book of logic? That is another question. Just remember the example of the lion and the deer and it is clear enough that the logical beings of reason are grounded in reality. It is because the lion actually devours the deer that in the proposition, "The lion is a carnivorous animal," "carnivorous" is predicate. You see how the logical is grounded in the real. So far as I can see, in order to be understood, in order to be intelligible, the logician should be constantly considering the real foundation of logical properties. So, even if a book of logic is supposed to give you an understanding of logical objects, do not be surprised if it is filled with considerations relative to the real world, under either its physical, metaphysical or psychological aspects. For example, in his treatise *On Interpretation*, Aristotle considers the logical division of propositions into contingent and necessary. That involves a physics and a metaphysics of contingency and necessity. In a philosophy like that of Spinoza, if Spinoza could be absolutely consistent, *non datur contingens in natura rerum*, there is nothing contingent in realty. That is a motto of Spinoza. How consistently he lives up to that, I do not know. Suppose that a philosopher is absolutely consistent in developing a philosophy of universal and absolute necessity; for him the division of propositions into propositions whose matter is contingent and propositions whose matter is necessary would make no sense. Aristotle, however, is quite normally led apropos of this logical division to expound his philosophy of contingency, so that if you want to write a paper on contingency in Aristotle, you will have to consult not only the physical and the metaphysical writings but also his logical works. Wherever he is concerned with the division of propositions into necessary and contingent, you are likely to find some remark on necessity and contingency in the real world because that is where the logical properties of these propositions are grounded. . . .

In logic all objects are beings of reason by strict necessity. What about mathematics? Here, there are two points to be made. First of all, a mathematical entity always *may* be a being of reason in the sense that it is just as good if it is a being of reason as it is if it is not. As you know, the symbol "i" in algebra means the square root of –1. Is it a being of reason? By all means. By all definitions of number and of multiplication, the square root of a negative number, an imaginary number, is a thing not only impossible but contradictory. It is contradictory by the definition of multiplication. If you multiply 1 by +1, you get +1. And if you multiply –1 by –1, again, you get +1. So that the square root of –1 is a thing which does not and cannot exist actually, and yet it can and does exist in the capacity of object, in which capacity it plays a considerable part in mathematics. . . .

The second remark is more fundamental. If a mathematical entity is not purely and simply a being of reason, it still implies a condition of reason. What is decisive here is to understand the character of mathematical abstraction, as a result of which if and when a mathematical entity is not purely and simply a being of reason, it still implies a condition of reason. Consider a simple example. I have already mentioned it. The word "triangle" designates a gadget that you can buy in an office supply shop. It is a physical thing. If the house burns down, a triangle made of plastic will burn. If it is made of celluloid, it may even help the house to burn down. If it is made of metal, it will melt, or at least, be distorted. However, "triangle" also designates a geometrical entity, which cannot be destroyed by fire. This entity, though relative to things capable of existence, involves a condition of reason which makes it invulnerable to fire, acid and any physical agent. So, if I think of the mathematical triangle, can I realize that thought of mine? I can take a piece of paper and cut it with a pair of scissors, but the result will be a physical triangular thing made of paper, it will not be a mathematical triangle. I think we have a lot of what we need to understand the relation of mathematics to the real world if we keep in mind two considerations. When a mathematical entity is closest to the real world, it still involves a condition of reason which makes it incapable of real existence; so, to realize a mathematical triangle is impossible because as soon as it exists otherwise than in the capacity of object, it loses its mathematical condition and acquires a physical one. A mathematical object, even as close to the real world as a sphere or triangle, simply cannot be realized. Following upon this basic characteristic of mathematical abstraction, it is always possible for a mathematical entity to be purely and simply a being of reason, as in the case of the square root of a negative number, to be what is called an imaginary number. . . .

We have remarked that in mathematics we have always at least a condition of reason, and we can even have an outright being of reason as in the case of the square root of a negative number. But in both common thought and in all the sciences of the real we use not only negations and privations but also relations which are of reason. For instance, if I say that a cat may look at a Queen, I imply that a Queen may be looked at by a cat. Now, consider the relation of the cat who is looking at the Queen and the Queen who is being looked at by the cat. The relation is real in the cat but it is not so in the Queen. A cat who looks at a Queen does not bring about a reality in the Queen. The change, the new reality is entirely in the cat. That is why a cat may look at a Queen. But to understand what is happening we are not afraid to say that the Queen is being looked at by the cat, and the relation of being looked at is a *relatio rationis*, a relation of reason. So you see that we find beings of reason everywhere, even in the most realistic interpretation of knowledge.

Notes

1. [Editor's Note: Simon refers his readers on this matter to L. M. Regis, *Epistemology* (New York: Macmillan, 1959), esp. 175–252.]

2. [Editor's Note: To maintain and fully bring out Simon's subtle thoughts on the distinction between thing and object, the contributor revised Vukan Kuic's translation of *An Introduction to Metaphysics of Knowledge*.]

3. [Editor's note: The difference between an "enunciative synthesis" and a "judicative synthesis" may be clarified by several of Simon's earlier notes in this text. In particular, he notes (146n69) Maritain's distinction between enunciation and judgment in his *Petite Logique* (108n3); see his *Oeuvres Complètes*, Vol. 2, *1920–1923* (Fribourg/Paris: Éditions Universitaires Fribourg/Éditions Saint-Paul, 1987), 402. In the first, the copula ("is") unites two mental terms, but in the second it relates them to the extramental thing: "Socrates is a man" ("a" is united to "b") and "it is true, Socrates is a man." In the same note (p. 147), Simon goes on to praise Franz Brentano (in his *The Origin of Our Knowledge of Right and Wrong* [Westminster: Constable, 1902], 15), quoting him on a similar point: "We may combine and relate presentations at will—as we do when we think of a green tree, or a golden mountain, or a father of a hundred children, or a friend of science—but if we have combined and related, we have made no judgment. . . . What then is distinctive about judgment? It is this: in addition to there being an idea or representation of a certain object, there is a second intentional relation that is directed upon that object."]

CHAPTER 5

Analogy and Metaphysical Knowledge

The passages to follow highlight the metaphysical perspicacity, profundity, clarity, and literary elegance of Yves R. Simon. With respect to the nature of analogy, very few essays can be mentioned in the same breath with Simon's work "On Order in Analogical Sets." To perceive the value of this essay, it helps to understand the reasons owing to which one might be reluctant to concede that the analogy of being is an analogy of proper proportionality.

Some have thought that this analogy is too abstract, too close to some sort of univocity, and indeed—as is suggested by its very name—that it is almost too mathematical in its abstraction, too quantitative, as is in a way suggested by the language of "proportionality." After all, the form of proportionality is to be found in 2:4 as 4:8, yet this reduces to 1/2, for 2:4 = 1/2 and 4:8 = 1/2, and 1/2 is fully equivalent to 1/2. More univocal than this one will not get (but—of course—while the form of proportionality is here, this is decidedly not the *analogy* of proper proportionality, precisely because it reduces to one univocal meaning). Perhaps more importantly, in the analogies of attribution—in which one thing is denominated as being "x" because it is a sign of "x," or a cause of "x"—there is clearly causal *order*, as is likewise the case in analogy of metaphor. But some have thought that the element of abstractness in analogy of proper proportionality is such as to suppress order. In analogy of extrinsic attribution, or of metaphor, a thing is only denominated analogically to be thus and so because of some causal relation to something extrinsic. For example, a good complexion is not properly speaking "healthy," but may be said to be healthy by analogy of extrinsic attribution insofar as it is a *sign* and an *effect* of health. Likewise, if one says that a leader is a "roaring lion," this is only because there is something in the leader that brings to mind properties of courage and conspicuous forcefulness reminiscent of the powerful boldness of the roaring lion—again, an extrinsic relation.

But, in analogy of proper proportionality, every analogate is subject to the analogy properly and intrinsically—for example, as light is to the eye, so is truth to the mind; or as the creature is to its being, so is God to his being. The relation of light to the eye is one sort of perfecting relation, and the relation of truth to the mind is a very different sort of perfecting relation. Both are perfecting relations. Nor is the perfection merely one thing, a unitary meaning; rather, we have two very different perfectings, a likeness of diverse *rationes*. Similarly, as the creature is to its *esse*, so is God to his *esse*—that is, in each case, *esse* denominates a pure perfection (albeit in the one instance limited by potency and in the other not); yet the perfection is different in each case. Nothing could be clearer than that we do not have merely one unitary meaning, but a likeness of differing proportions. The analogue is found in each case intrinsically and not merely by extrinsic denomination: when we say that as the creature is to its being, so is God to his being, being is affirmed of each (although it is the full perfection of being that is in God, and a different, and in each case, limited perfection of being that is in every creature).

Simon insists that in analogy either abstraction is not to be found at all (as with analogies of extrinsic attribution and of metaphor), or it is to be found (as it is in analogy of proper proportionality) but "uses ways that are not its own." For example, in the metaphysical analogy of proper proportionality, each thing is said *to be*, and both the differentiating and the common features are equally included within the "common ground" of *being*. Being is not a genus—there is no merely generic element indifferent to various specific determinations/actualizations and awaiting these. Rather, the differences are included (they exist) *within* the analogy itself, within the "common ground" of the analogue. Hence, analogical abstraction here occurs by "fusing together" the analogical members, literally by "confusion"—not combining in a nominalistic heap, but *fusing together*.

Or, as he puts it elsewhere in "On Order in Analogical Sets," "To question that every analogical set, even in proper proportionality—where predication is intrinsic in all cases—is an orderly one, would be to question that to be comes before not to be." Thus, there *is* order in analogical proportionality—as becomes prominent in the expressions that intellect is in man, compounded with potency, and that intellect is also in God, purely and infinitely and not compounded with or limited by potency. In man, we have a mixture of assertion and negation with respect to the pure perfection of intellect, as compared with the pure case of unbounded Intellect in God. The common ground—the "fusing together" of the analogy of proper proportionality—includes both the similar and the different. Inasmuch as differentiation emerges within being by the contraction of analogical perfection by potency, one sees that priority and posteriority naturally and necessarily arise within the analogy of proper proportionality.

The metaphysical analogy of proper proportionality *is* abstract. Yet it involves an abstraction that "uses ways that are not its own," and necessarily articulates the *ratio* or order *intrinsic* to the analogates as members of *this* analogical set or community. It cannot avoid doing so, because it is only by the assertions and negations within the common ground of the analogy that the differentiations internal to the analogy occur. Hence, in "On Order in Analogical Sets," Simon masterfully showcases the metaphysical profundity of the analogy of proper proportionality. This metaphysical profundity is also well illustrated in the passage that follows from "Liberty and Authority," wherein he depicts the analogicity of the transcendental perfections—according to proper proportionality—whereby discourse regarding God is rendered possible.

The material derived from "To Be and To Know" touches an issue of first importance for metaphysics (and one central to Aquinas's *De ente et essentia*). This issue is that of the status of the idea and of objective union whereby the same nature that exists physically in a thing is said to exist differently, immaterially, and intentionally, in our knowledge. Here, again, where the ontology of knowledge intersects with metaphysics, Simon highlights the fashion in which "through the method of analogical abstraction, metaphysics transcends the world of our experience without ceasing to be experimental. Physical reality, here represented by the ways of knowing proper to animals and man, becomes the first member of an analogical set comprising created spirits and God." He also brilliantly points out the primacy of the existential order, and of the *actus essendi*, in determining that something belongs to the intentional order—that is, that the idea "has no being of its own save as needed for its representative function" and that "the features of the idea are determined by a proportion to the act of existing objectively."

The passages that follow from Simon's great book *The Tradition of Natural Law* converge on the diverse ways in which the natural law is natural and is law, and on the crucial importance for natural law of the identity of "to be" and "to act" and "to think" in God. They articulate the profound insight that the normativity of the natural law finally reposes not with subintelligible nature but with the superintelligible divine Wisdom—the ordering wisdom of God.

The reader who is unfamiliar with the metaphysical penetration and profundity of Simon, or who has never savored his pellucid reasoning and style, will find in all the passages of this chapter a cornucopic introduction. But those who know his work, and perceive its proper and eminent dignity, will also find these passages on analogy and metaphysical knowledge remarkably revelatory in their rational power, penetration, and profundity. For anyone seeking clarity and profound penetration into the subject of analogy and metaphysical knowledge, the selections here given—most especially those from "On Order in Analogical Sets"—should be prime objects of study. They merit careful attention, and assiduous contemplation.

Steven A. Long

Philosopher at Work
("On Order in Analogical Sets," 140–64)

Analogical Abstraction

The understanding of analogy begins when we realize that between likeness and difference there is, in analogy, such a link, such an essential relation of interdependence that if the differential is removed, the like is removed also and nothing is left. This is tantamount to saying that the unity of the analogical term is not one of abstraction properly so-called. Etymology, here, is dependable: to abstract is to pull out, to pull something out of a complex to which it originally belongs. In the analysis of a species, a generic component is pulled out of the complex in which it combines with a differential component. Because the generic can be pulled out of the complex constituted by species *a*, and out of the complex constituted by species *b*, and out of the complex constituted by species *c*, its unity can be pulled out of the multiplicity constituted by *a*, *b*, and *c*. This is what "to abstract" means, and when it is purely and simply impossible to pull a component out of a complex and a unity out of a multiplicity, it is necessary to confess that abstraction unqualifiedly understood is impossible. True, it is not always easy to know if a meaning that belongs intrinsically to *a*, *b*, and *c* enjoys a unity of univocity or merely one of analogy. To decide this issue, the appropriate method is to attempt abstracting this meaning from the differential components with which it associates. The most convincing example of the failure to abstract that follows upon the irreducible plurality of the analogue is supplied by the concept of being as predicated of the diverse categories. Being is predicable in intrinsic fashion of substance, and of quantity, and of quality, and of relation, etc. Let us imagine this operation: pulling the component common to all beings out of the complex constituted by its association with the differential component that distinguishes substance, and out of the complex constituted by its association with the differential component that distinguishes quantity, etc., and consequently out of the multiplicity constituted by the diverse genera of being. Obviously, being is no less predicable of the differential than of the common, and as we try to pull the common out of its association with the differential, the whole thing is pulled, the differential no less certainly than the common, and nothing is pulled *out*. Nothing is abstracted. We have seen that there is, purely and simply, no abstraction in the analogies of attribution and of metaphor. In the case of proper proportionality, the least that can be said is that *unqualified* abstraction is impossible.

Since diversity of meanings proves irreducible in every analogical set, since no abstraction can drive into a state of pure potency the differential components of each and every meaning, since the differences remain in act, it is reasonable to ask whether the unity of an analogical set is anything else than that of a collection. . . .

But John of St. Thomas also warns against the nominalistic interpretation according to which "what corresponds to the analogical concept of being is the whole collection of beings in a certain state of confusion." Answering the nominalists, he says, "This noun 'being' is not a collective noun: what it signifies is not an aggregate of all its inferiors but their kinship in an analogical notion."[1]

The unity of the universal concept qua universal is one of abstraction. It is in virtue of abstraction and of the unity resulting from it that the universal is predicable of its parts. This law holds, of course, for the universal concepts of collective realities. "Deliberating assembly" is a universal whose subjective parts are senate, house, city council, etc. The relevant comparison is not between the divisive and collective universals but between the method of unity proper to the universal concept—whether it be divisive or collective—and the method of unity proper to the thing that the collective concept signifies, namely, the collection itself. The latter method of unity entirely pertains to the order of concrete existence. Antecedently, to any abstraction and, more profoundly, to any work of the mind, a number of gentlemen are gathered in a deliberating assembly. The causes of their collective unity are (a) in the capacity of final cause, the good of deliberation by several, (b) in the capacity of formal cause, the constitution, (c) in the capacity of efficient cause, the body politic acting according to the constitution, (d) in the capacity of material cause, the hall where they convene, and various circumstances.

To say that an analogical set, for example, being, is a mere collection, would be to say that the unity of being, as object of metaphysical consideration, is entirely traceable to the real causes of the things that are beings in one capacity or another. That such is not the case is established by the universal predictability of being. Of any thing that is, or admits of existence, it is possible to say that it is a being, whereas it is not possible to say of a senator that he is the Senate or that he is senate. The collection is not predicable of any of its parts. But the analogue (in proper proportionality) is predicable properly of each and every analogate. Its being predicable of many demonstrates its being abstracted from many. Besides unqualified abstraction, which pertains to the univocal alone, there is such a thing as an analogical abstraction, although, in this expression, the adjective weakens the signification of the noun. Objects abstracted according to the analogical method remain diverse in act and consequently the analogue is not, in strict propriety of language, a universal. To say that it is a collection would be to ignore the essential part played by abstraction in the constitution of its unity. To call it a set excludes neither the role of abstraction nor the actuality of the differences. The expression "analogical set" is vindicated both in the case of attribution and metaphor, where there is no abstraction, and in that of proper proportionality, where abstraction, though genuine, is held in check by irreducible plurality....

It is easy to find historically significant examples of the tendency to eliminate the analogy of proper proportionality and the mysteries that fill every space where this analogy is allowed to penetrate. Thus, in the issue of the divine names, the proposition, "Being, one, good, just, loving, and all terms expressing absolute perfections are predicated analogically of God and of creatures," can be dispensed with either by the agnostic method or through a pious annihilation of the world. In all varieties of agnosticism, an affirmative proposition of which "God" is the subject is described as devoid of meaning. On the other hand, many metaphysicians and religious thinkers are driven, more or less consciously and consistently, by the tendency to believe that being, goodness, and the other absolute perfections belong to God in such an exclusive fashion that they can never be predicated of a creature in an intrinsic way. The created world disappears into a vacuum and it seems that God's infinite perfection is fittingly exalted. All of our metaphysical troubles are over. But not for long, since any such experience as that of pain or love or duty causes us again to touch the universe of finite perfection. It is the glory of Aquinas to have understood that the world of creatures, though caused out of nothing, ready to disappear into inexistence, and truly akin to nothingness, is full of reality, full of activity, full of life, and full of liberty. All mystics proclaim that God is He who is, and that I am the one who is not; but these mystical expressions of God's infinity and of the creature's wretchedness are balanced by equally mystical expressions of a sense for what is real and great in this most wretched of all creatures, myself, and a time comes when this is what St. John of the Cross has to say: "Mine are the heavens and mine is the earth. Mine are the nations; the just are mine and mine are the sinners. The angels are mine, and mine is the Mother of God, and all things are mine. And God Himself is mine . . ."[2] Another familiar example concerns the problem of evil. The Stoics and many others endeavored to drive physical evil out of reality as if moral evil were the only thing of which evil can be predicated intrinsically. Thus, we would not have to bother about the analogy of proper proportionality in which evil is predicated of moral and of physical evil. Yet disease is present, and children die every day.

To sum up, let us survey the methods of unity used in the four cases of univocity, attribution, metaphor, and proper proportionality. When a term is univocal its unity is, unqualifiedly, the work of abstraction. In the kind of analogy exemplified by "healthy" or "cheerful," the unity of irreducibly diverse meanings is brought about by relating an effect to its proper cause or a cause to its proper effect. In metaphor, the method of unity is, according to etymology, the transfer of the name designating a thing to another thing that it cannot designate properly so long as it retains in act the character of a transferred name. In proper proportionality, the method of unity is abstraction indeed, but it is an abstraction *by way of confusion*. It is an incomplete, weak, partial abstraction that does not go so far as to drive the differences into a state of potentiality. An analogical set is made of meanings that remain actually diverse; accordingly, an analogue is a set rather than a universal. But inasmuch as the set is said to be analogical by *proper proportionality*, its unity is traced to an operation of the mind. Regardless of what real causes do or do not do for unity, the parts of the analogical set, considered as analogical, are held together, relatively and in such a way as to let actual diversity subsist, by a sort of abstraction. Because this abstraction is incomplete, and the unity that it brings about relative, attributing the name of the set to each of its members will always be accompanied by the restricting clause: in its own way. This clause brings forth the actuality of the multiple in the analogical set. Inasmuch as the analogue (for example, being) contains its inferiors in act, an analogical set is like a forest that owes whatever unity it enjoys to its real causes. But inasmuch as an analogical set possesses in some way, no matter how qualified, a unity of abstraction, the comparison with the forest proves deficient: from the top of the hill it remains altogether impossible to say that a tree *is* a forest. . . .

Order and Abstraction

Considering the way in which the nature of the triangle is specified by the particularities of the isosceles and those of the scalene, it is impossible to say that the generic nature is, in any sense whatever, asserted by one system of particularities and denied by the other. But in analogy that which is common and determined elicits its differences and determinations out of its own ground, and *this cannot be done except by assertion and negation.* Let us analyze several examples.

Take the division of being into infinite and finite: to obtain the differentiating factor of the infinite, nothing is needed except an unqualified assertion of being—an assertion that is not held in check by any negation. But in order to obtain the differential factor of the finite, being has to elicit a limitation of itself. It cannot be said that being is indifferent to infinity and limitation as triangle is indifferent to the particularities of its species. Infinite being, never-ending being, expresses being infinitely more genuinely and faithfully than being that is limited and circumscribed by an area of nonbeing. In comparison with the infinite being, finite things disclose mostly their kinship with nothingness. That the limitation of being is itself a way of being that is derived from being and from nothing else, is a paradox indeed. But let us be aware that a similar paradox is involved, more or less noticeably, in every analogy of proper proportionality.

The analogical set of the "ways of life" can now supply information that was inaccessible to the preceding analyses. The differential factor of animal life is derived from the common ground by a definite assertion, namely, that of self-motion in the order of formal causality, and the differential factor of vegetative life is derived from the same ground by the negation of this particular excellence in self-motion. What brings forth the differential feature of life by motionless activity is the assertion of a definite fullness, namely, the fullness that pertains to the act of a subject in act. What brings forth the differential feature of life by self-motion is a negative clause negative, I mean, in relation to the concept of life itself—for an agent that lives by way of motion is one for which vital operations remain the acts of a subject in potency, that is, of a subject that is *not* in act. And when, finally, we compare life by way of self-actuation (whether motion be involved or not) with life by way of absolute actuality, it is an all-embracing assertion, exclusive of every negation, that expresses the supreme form of life. But finite life is expressed by denying, in the case of all the living except God, the plenitude constituted by the absolute identity of essence, existence, and activity....

A transcendental relation is a mixed relation. It is a relative thing that, by reason of identity with itself, contains a relation. There is nothing in it that is not relative, and yet its *esse* is not just an *esse ad*. Even though the whole of its being is relative, relation does not constitute the whole of its being. What distinguishes the transcendental from the predicamental relation is that in the transcendental the assertion of the common ground, analogically expressed by the word "relation," is associated with the assertion of an essence, such as quality, which is something else than relation, no matter how thoroughly relative it may be.

To sum up: whereas the concept of the double or the half is entirely and exclusively constituted by a relation, the concept of a transcendentally relative thing implies, together with relation itself, an essence (for example, quality) that, so far as its distinguishing features are concerned, simply is not a relation. Thus, the division of relation into predicamental and transcendental is effected by pure assertion in the case of predicamental—indeed, a *pure* relation—and by assertion coupled with a negation in the case of transcendental—indeed, a *mixed* relation. This division is brought about by the opposition of the "yes" on one side and the togetherness of the "yes" and the "no" on the other side. Both the "yes" and the "no" and the togetherness of the "yes" and the "no" concern the common ground: if they did not, there would be univocity, not analogy. And thus we now can express with more precision than in the foregoing the criterion by which, in difficult cases, it can be decided whether a concept is univocal or analogical. This decision is safely obtained if only we answer the question, "Where do the 'yes' and the 'no' belong?" If in the common ground (for example, being as divided into substance and accident, or life as divided by the ways of self-motion and those of motionless activity, or evil as divided into physical and moral, or relation as divided into predicamental and transcendental), then the common ground is analogical. If in differences added to the common ground and specificative of its potency, the common ground is univocal and its character of community is unqualified.

At this point it is possible to explain the paradox of a confusion in which an order is implied. So long as abstraction uses the ways of its own, it does not, all by itself, establish any kind of order. It effects a unity of universality and says nothing about priority and posteriority among the things of which the universal is predicable. When the concept of tree has been disengaged from the complexes that constitute the oak, the maple, and the pine, we know nothing about what comes before and what comes after among the species of tree. But, in analogy, abstraction uses ways that are not its own, for the obvious reason that the differentiating features exist in the common ground as actually as the common features. These differentiating features cannot be expressed except by assertion and negation of the common ground, and thus order is brought into logical existence, for assertion comes before negation and pure assertion comes before any complex in which negation plays a part. Analogical abstraction proceeds by "fusing together" the members of a set. But such "fusing together" involves assertions and negations that define priorities and posteriorities; if these assertions and negations were ignored, there would no longer be "confusion": rather, there would be substitution of the ways of abstraction for ways that abstraction cannot recognize as its own, and a fallacious imposition of univocity upon subjects [that] exclude all unity except that of analogy.

Let it be noticed, further, that within the analogy of proper proportionality the obviousness and the significance of order increase as the possibilities of abstraction decrease. It is in varying degree that analogical sets admit of the qualified abstraction that expresses, together with irreducible diversity of meanings, the distinctive attribute of proper proportionality, namely, intrinsicality in every instance. "Good," as predicated of a healthy condition and of a human action makes up a set subject to the law of qualified abstraction. But what about "good" as predicated of a creature and of God? Here, infinite distance between the analogates exalts order as it cuts to a minimum the possibilities of abstraction. Many would hesitate to say which comes before which in the set of "accident" as predicated of the nine genera listed by Aristotle, but whenever a term is predicated of God and creatures, order between its meanings comes forth with splendor. So far as nature and intelligibility are concerned, divine names—being, knowledge, love, justice, mercy—belong by priority to God and by posteriority to creatures, although they belong by priority to creatures in the development of our knowledge. It may well be that no two analogical sets admit of abstraction in the same degree; if such turns out to be the case, we may expect order to assume necessity and obviousness in indefinitely many degrees, for the function of order, in all sorts of analogy, is to procure whatever unity is not procured by abstraction....

Proportionality and Order

Thus, every analogical term conveys the togetherness of resemblance and difference, affirmation and negation, though in a variety of ways. (As often remarked, the concept of analogy is itself analogical.) It can be called, with equal accuracy, "the principle of essential causality" and "the principle of resemblance between cause and effect." Owing to this resemblance, an effect is explained by being traced to its essential cause. The accidental cause has no power of explanation. To question that every analogical set, even in proper proportionality—where predication is intrinsic in all cases—is an orderly one, would be to question that to be comes before not to be. Indeed, priority and posteriority can be found in univocal meanings, but there they do not concern the common ground, they concern only the differentiations that it contains in potency. In the language of St. Thomas, the expression "by priority and posteriority" (*per prius et posterius*) is synonymous with "analogically" (*analogice*). No doubt, this synonymity holds in proper proportionality, independently of any combination with another type of analogy, because here also, despite intrinsicality in all cases, what is asserted of one analogate is denied of another.

Freedom and Community
("Liberty and Authority," 33–34)

Yet, all the teaching of St. Thomas shows that liberty is an absolute perfection, *perfectio simpliciter simplex*, which can be attributed to God in a formal sense. Recall the highly intelligible distinction made by metaphysicians between the perfections of being whose concept necessarily implies some imperfection (here *perfectiones mixtae*, mixed perfections) and those perfections whose concept does not imply any imperfection. The world of our experience, empirically considered, does not show anything but imperfect realizations of the perfections of being. Just as our biological life, which involves all the imperfections bound up with materiality, so our intellect is an essentially imperfect thing, a power doomed to acquire painstakingly and step by step limited cognitions whose possession always remains precarious. The difference will not become manifest unless the analogical insight of metaphysics is substituted for the short-sightedness of the empirical consideration. From a metaphysical point of view, things of the observable world have in themselves, at the core of their imperfect entity, perfections that can be abstracted from any imperfect realization without their essential constitution being impaired in any way. An idea like that of biological life is not capable of such a treatment; forcibly abstracted from the imperfections that it connotes, it disappears altogether. If I consider, on the contrary, such a thing as the intellect of man, I recognize in it the transcendent essence of the intellect, which essence, far from being necessarily bound up with the limitations of its human realization, aspires to a condition where it could get rid of them and assert itself completely. I understand that the intellect is infinitely more truly an intellect without the limitations imposed on it by material existence, or, more generally, created existence. In the same way, the truth that human knowledge is capable of is partial and precarious, the justice that the human heart is capable of is a poor justice, ceaselessly jeopardized by opposite forces. But I understand that truth and justice are infinitely more identical with themselves, realize more genuinely and more formally their idea, in an infinite existence. The intellect, truth, justice, are absolute perfections of being and divine names.

Philosopher at Work
("To Be and To Know," 183–86, 191–92)

In self-consciousness, the self is itself again, but according to a way of being which is open to an unlimited multiplicity of forms and perfections, for the objective union of the self with itself involves none of the restrictions that are necessarily implied by any union of the matter-form type. This remark may prove of decisive significance when the consideration of knowledge attains the extension and profundity that are distinctive of metaphysics. Through the world of analogical abstraction, metaphysics transcends the world of our experience without ceasing to be experimental. Physical reality, here represented by the ways of knowing proper to animals and man, becomes the first member of an analogical set comprising created spirits and God. By the law of analogical order, all we can know about the non-physical ways of knowing will have to be reached through those ways of knowing which, being present in our experience, come first in the genesis of our cognitions. But the analogical set with which we are dealing is the subject of a double order. In such a set what comes first in the genesis of our cognitions comes last in intrinsic perfection, genuineness, and absolute intelligibility. Through the understanding of what is first in our cognitions, we achieve a glance, no matter how imperfect, at what is first absolutely. Then a fruitful reconsideration of the former takes place in the light of the latter. To know how being and knowledge are related in God, we need to consider first their relation in the world of our experience. But it is the relation of to be and to know in God which, no matter how inadequately attained by a merely analogical approach, will supply the deeper understanding of what the diversity of to be and to know signifies in man and other finite beings.

Some of the worst difficulties commonly encountered in the theory of knowledge result from our failure to assert, in all relevant connections, the intelligible primacy of *to be* over *that which is*, and of existential ways over forms of being. We are aware that beside the universe of the things there exists a universe of entities for which we have no handy name, and whose relation to things is obscured both by extreme familiarity and by the ambiguities of our expressions....

To designate those entities which are that by which things are known, a generic name would be very useful. There does not seem to be any felicitous one in any language. As far as English is concerned, there is no choice. In spite of difficulties which will have to be dealt with in the unlimited variety of particular contexts, the only word that can be set in contrast to the word thing in the sense in which "memory," a disposition of the psyche, is set in contrast to "memory," a remembered event, is the word idea....

In terms of existence, an idea is not first of all a distinct kind of being; it primarily is one with the thing it represents; it has no being of its own save as needed for its representative function. A memory is both the event remembered and a psychological disposition. But this psychological disposition is not just a thing representative of another being. *Primacy, here belongs to the objective way of existing which is that of the event remembered.* No bridge has to be built, for the memory, as disposition of the psyche, is not known first: what is known first is the remembered event. The disposition of the psyche is a means rather than an object of knowledge, except in the secondary process of psychological reflection. All this, and much more, is contained in the basic proposition that the features of the idea are determined by a proportion to the act of existing objectively, just as features of the thing are determined by a proportion to natural existence. In either case "'to be' is the actuality of all acts and the perfection of all perfections, and nothing is more formal than to be." (St. Thomas, *On the Power of God*, 7.2 ad 9.)

The Tradition of Natural Law
("Natural Law," 138–39 and 143–45)

It is not by accident that in the history of natural law (with the possible exception of Aristotle) the problem of the relation of nature to God is generally answered by the consideration that God is the author of human nature as well as of physical nature. In the eighteenth-century deism, for instance, there are rough formulas, metaphysically not very rich but retaining at least this much metaphysics: so long as God is there one does not have to be afraid that feathers will become heavy and lead light, that heavy bodies will go up and light bodies come down; the laws of nature are guaranteed by the divine stability. And by analogy from the physical nature, order and stability in the human universe, in the moral world, also are guaranteed by "Nature's God." There is at the root of all things, human as well as physical, an intellect and a will which offers an ultimate guarantee. Ultimately the order belongs to the rational. In this scheme we have the following three stages. First, natural law exists in our minds as a proposition. For instance, "Cheating in the execution of a contract is wrong by nature." But saying "by nature" we imply that natural law, before it is apprehended by the intellect, exists embodied in things; that is the second stage in the order of discovery. In the third stage, we are led to the recognition of an "author of nature" (this eighteenth-century expression, freed from its psychological, moral, political, and religious connections, is perfectly acceptable metaphysically) who is the legislator of nature. And thus the law which, *in the order of discovery*, exists first as a proposition in our minds, secondly as a way of being, thirdly and ultimately exists in the divine mind, where it takes on the name of divine law. There are a hundred reasons for opposition to natural law, but this is one of them and at certain times it may be the strongest: obligation in natural law does not hold unless the natural law exists in a state which is actually prior, but which is ultimate in the order of discovery—"this law is an aspect of God"....

With regard to my natural being I am restricted in a hundred ways, especially in regard to duration, to power, to versatility. But by thought there is something limitless, intrinsically infinite in me; by thought I can comprehend, I can be, in some ways, all things (Aristotle, *De Anima* 3.8.431b21). And so we understand that in the Supreme Being, in the Being where "what it is" and "to be" are one, there is identity of "to be" and "to know." The infinity which is characteristic of "to know" becomes ontological in the Supreme Being. If there were such a thing as a definition of God, this would be a good one. Of course, that is not a definition in any strict logical sense, but as we have to use substitutes for a definition of God this is perhaps the most profound of all: Being in whom "to be" and "to know" are one and the same in all possible respects. One can make a valid distinction between the understanding of God and the will of God, between His understanding and His love. It is not a real distinction, but it is a valid distinction of reason, just as there is a valid distinction of reason between twice six eggs and one dozen eggs and the square root of 144 eggs. Those three are the same thing but we have diverse aspects grounding a valid distinction in our understanding. Mathematics would not exist if there were no valid distinction between twice six and twelve. Likewise, there is a valid distinction between the understanding and the love of God. But between the "to be" of God and the "to think" of God there is no distinction whatsoever; it is like two names designating exactly the same thing. And it is this identity of being and knowing that stops the regression to infinity in our search for the ground of obligation under natural law....

We have to stop at a thing which is directing by nature; so why not this thing, this organ, this planet, this universe? Since we have to stop somewhere, why should we not stop where we are and be satisfied with a design without a designing intellect? Answer: for the simple reason that in the things of nature—sulphuric acid, a plant of corn, Earth, universe, all behaving with remarkable regularity—there is no identity of "to be" and "to think" and no identity of "to be" and "to act." The privilege of the First Cause, the reason why there is no regression to infinity and why there is an intelligible stop—no matter how many phases we may have between the second and the third stages in our cognition of natural law—the privilege of the First Cause is the identity of "to be" and "to act" and "to think" which cannot be had anywhere else. The author of the article insisted that we must end with a thing which is designing by nature. Why place it outside the world and thus get lost in infinity? Why not place it, instead, in the world? Because, in order to place it in the world, we would have to support in that thing an identity of "to be" and "to act" and "to think," i.e., the predicates of God which, by clear evidence, are not realized in things of nature. These are mutable, multiple, stretched in space, subject to accidents, etc. Here we see how reasoning about finality in nature and reasoning about obligation ultimately converge. The ways are slightly different, but the logical structure and the end are the same. The facts of order in the universe and the facts of obligation under natural law, i.e., that our reason bows before things, both require rationally a transcendent First Being in whom "to be" and "to act" and "to think" are one and the same.

Notes

1. John of St. Thomas, *Ars Logica*, P. II, Q. III, a. 2; *Material Logic of John of St. Thomas*, translated and edited by Yves R. Simon, John G. Glanville, and G. Donald Hollenhorst (Chicago: University of Chicago Press, 1955), p. 97.

2. John of the Cross, *Oracion del alma enamorada*, in *Vida y Obras de San Juan de la Cruz* (Madrid: Editorial Catolica, 1950), p. 1281.

CHAPTER 6

Sensation and Physical Knowledge

The discussion of the object of physical knowledge, dealing as it does with "the whole of sciences whether philosophic or positive," leaves aside the important division of physical knowledge into empiriological and ontological analysis that constitutes two species of the same genus. This significant division is examined by Simon in his early work *Foresight and Knowledge* (1944). He there contrasts science, which concerns only what is necessary, and the contingent singulars of ordinary experience.

Physical knowledge concerns *ens mobile*, *ens materiale*, and *ens sensibile*: mobile, material, and sensible being. Let us note that the attempt to indicate the equivalence of the three terms, the main subject of that work, also involves a number of distinctions that Simon will develop at much greater length in "An Essay on Sensation" (1960). I refer to the distinction between what is inherently sensible and what is not, between pure sensation and perception, and the distinction between the proper and the common sensibles. Such distinctions are used in his earlier work to clarify the problems of sensation, and to provide some answers to them. In that work, Simon also points out that physical knowledge verifies its findings by a return to the sensible (*conversio ad sensibilia*). The judgments of physics have to be verified, or falsified, in sensible experience itself. Thus, the sensible provides both the starting point of physical knowledge and its terminus.

The first stage in his later inquiry here included is to identify exactly what kind of operation sensation is. To achieve this, he examines a number of oppositions: that between autonomic and heteronomic passion, that between immanent and transient [transitive] activity, and that between objective and subjective unions. What kind of a union is involved in sense knowledge? He concludes this first stage when he identifies sense knowledge as an autonomic passion, an immanent action, and an objective union.

Second, he asks about the process by which sensation occurs, given its characteristics. This leads into an examination of the Epicurean explanation of sensation by the simulacra, and of the Aristotelian and Thomistic accounts. Although he generally endorses the Thomistic account, he observes that for Thomas and his follower John of Saint Thomas, "the 'species' are entrusted with tasks which really belong to things." We are indebted to "the refined methods of scientific experience for a correction of these earlier errors."

Then Simon confronts the widely held belief regarding the unreliability of sense experience. No doubt we can recall physics courses in which the instructor emphasized various ways in which the senses lead us to errors and fallacies. However, these expositions tend to be superficial, for if they were radical they would undermine the very notion of a physical science. Simon thinks that objections to the truthfulness of the senses do not originate in the development of modern science, but are much older and of philosophical provenance, traceable to ancient skepticism. Nevertheless, modern thinkers did introduce certain approaches that eventually led to a philosophical crisis.

Cartesian dualism—that is, the division between thinking and extended substance—has a number of implications for the treatment of sensation. Activity, if it is not a movement, and hence a mode of extension, must be a mode of thought. Hence sensation is identified with a thinking substance. On the assumption that only clear and distinct ideas can be true, sensation fails the test, for it is far from clear, and confused.

Simon recognizes what the mechanistic method has contributed to science, but he shows that, by dint of quantifying all data, it is incapable of accounting for qualitative diversity. Now, not only did Descartes leave us with a negative assessment of sense experience, but he came to the conclusion that there is no physical science, only a mathematical treatment of physical reality and no more.

Simon does not underestimate the difficulties concerning the truthfulness of the senses. There are the conditions under which sensation takes place. There are subjective conditions, such as color blindness, that explain certain errors. Truth in an exact sense is to be found in the intellectual judgment composing and dividing. So, if there are errors about sense experience, they have to be explained in terms of the extent to which the senses are reliable and the extent to which they are not. A judgment based solely on the apparent convergence of railroad tracks in the distance will be erroneous unless aided by other perceptions. The statement that the external senses are trustworthy with regard to their proper objects dispels some of the long-standing objections to sensation based on a failure to distinguish between proper and common sensibles.

Ever since Aristotle broke with the opinion of Cratylus and Plato that the world of sense experience as fluctuating could not provide the object that science required and he defended the existence of physical knowledge, there have been periodic attempts to deny any physical knowledge, because we only discover physical regularities amid the process of chance in the world of sense experience.

Finally, Simon examines the work of three theorists important in the philosophy of science with regard to sense experience and physical knowledge. Pierre Duhem is known for his conception of science as saving the appearances. Auguste Comte, as the primal positivist, identified explanation with generalization. Science is about general facts. Max Planck saw an ontology inside science. The question about the conformity of sense experience to reality has no meaning for Comtean positivism, but it does for the positions advanced by Duhem and Planck. If the task of science is to save the appearances, according to Duhem, this perspective presupposes a certain truthfulness in the senses. The same is true of Planck's position. So Simon asserts that, through sense experience, we attain the experimental absolute, for if there is no truthfulness at the beginning of our quest for physical knowledge, how can there be any truth possible in its later elaboration?

Ralph Nelson

Philosopher at Work
("An Essay on Sensation," 57–111)

The worst difficulties of the present subject originate in our inability to achieve the experience of a sensation free from association with images, instinctive judgments, memories, and thoughts.[1] If it were possible for us to suspend, no matter how briefly, all such associated representations and processes, if it were possible to elicit pure sensations and yet to watch ourselves sensing, the understanding of sensation would, no doubt, be greatly facilitated. But sensation is the center of a complex, and from this complex it cannot be extracted, except by rational analysis. Experientially considered, sensations always exist in the vital unity of wholes....

In Aristotle's words the more determinate sense of the expression "to be acted upon" refers to the destruction of one contrary by the other: this remark is strikingly borne out by the fact that in various languages the words meaning passivity generally connote suffering. But the passion in sensing is not a destruction; rather, it is the maintenance, the progress, the salvation of the passive subject under the influence of a friendly agent which resembles the patient as act resembles the ability to be in act. When the sense opens to the world of physical appearances, what it receives is its own actualization, its own perfection, its own fulfillment according to its own law. Think of a blind person who recovers sight: his sense is acted upon, indeed, by a host of colored spots; thanks to this welcome invasion, a subject naturally able to be in act of vision, but accidentally prevented from exercising his natural ability, becomes what his nature wants him to be. The possibility of being acted upon by the colors and shapes and the other visible properties of the world gives him a chance to be what he is. In this distinguished way of being acted upon, the passive subject is changed into itself. St. Thomas uses the expression "passion properly so-called" to designate the "being acted upon" which implies a complex change, a displacement of form by form and a destruction. He uses the expression "passion improperly so-called" to designate the "being acted upon" which consists in a simple accomplishment and a pure progress. The passion properly so-called may also be described as heteronomic, and the passion improperly so called as *autonomic*.

The first tenet of Aristotle's doctrine on the senses is that sensation is an *autonomic passion*. To ascertain this proposition, good method demands that inquiry be focused on the most difficult cases, namely on situations where a passion of the heteronomic type asserts itself conspicuously and seems to constitute the whole state of affairs. Near the fireplace, colds hands and feet soon become warm, and whichever way we interpret such notions as those of cold and heat, it is clear that a state has been displaced by another state. The presence of a heteronomic passion is obvious, but the relevant question is whether this passion constitutes sensation. Just consider that the same heteronomic passion takes place in the garment, in the dead leather of the shoes, in the dead wood of the chair, and would take place in a corpse. *Sensation begins where heteronomic passion ends.* . . .

Sensation produces nothing that could be likened to a concept, although it leaves behind itself a variety of effects, the most obvious of which is the lasting impression that we call image or memory. But sensation does not *consist in* the production of an impression capable of being activated later; it is an activity by itself and independent of what it leaves behind it. If, contrary to general opinion, there existed sensations unproductive of any image or memory, these would still be as genuine as any others, even though their function in animal and human life would be quite different. . . . Sensation, no matter how significant its traces may be, is not exhausted and is not intelligibly constituted by the production of traces. It has a nature of its own and a worth of its own as a qualitative accomplishment which is the fundamental actualization of animal life.

Inasmuch as it does not consist in the production of a change, the immanent act of sensing is an instance of motionless activity. No doubt, sensation is surrounded with, and entirely dependent upon, change: its organ is modified by the action of the stimuli, the sensorial environment is ceaselessly changing, and a forcible attempt at immobility impairs sensing. Yet, if only we bear in mind the characteristics of activities by way of motion, it is easy to understand that sensation, no matter how imperfectly, exists in a condition of rest.

To shape wood into a chair is absolutely nothing else than to bring about definite changes in a definite matter. The act of the carpenter, which coincides with the becoming of his work, is, by essence, a thing fluent and unfinished which belongs to the past as soon as it is completed, as soon as what was intended is obtained. When the chair is finished, the carpenter may start working toward another chair, or do something else, or be idle; the thing that he cannot do is to keep bringing about changes in a thing that is assumed to be completed. Or, to use the most simple example, it is impossible to carry a thing to a certain place when the thing is already in that place. Neither is it possible to discourse toward a conclusion when the conclusion is already established, nor to keep striving toward an object of desire when this object is present and actually enjoyed. But contemplation implies the actual grasp of truth, and joy the actual possession of the good, whereas it is possible to love both things present and things absent. Love exists both in movement and in rest; contemplation and joy are, by essence, above movement. Shaping, walking, learning, building are acts of imperfect subjects, i.e., acts of subjects which have not yet attained their ends. But suppose that we want to see what there is on the other side of a hill: when we have climbed up to the vantage point we may stay there and contemplate the scenery as leisurely as we please. The fact that we have been seeing this scenery for a while in no way excludes the possibility of looking at it for another while. But having climbed up to the vantage point, we no longer can be climbing toward the same point. Such is the difference between movement and sensation. Unlike movement, sensation is an activity by way of rest. It is the first image of eternal life.

In order to understand how autonomic passivity and immanent activity are related in sensation, let us now consider the character of presence which, as recalled, distinguishes so sharply the object of sensation from such objects as those of imagination and memory. A familiar example will help to clarify the meaning of this issue.

At night and in a silent place a friend is walking away. For a while we can hear the sound of his steps, but the time soon comes when we no longer know whether we are still hearing these sounds or only imagining and remembering them. Until he comes back, and perhaps throughout our life, we shall remember our listening to these steps, remember this last experience of a presence that nothing can replace. Again, we never knew exactly when presence and experience came to an end; it is true that a weak sensation and an image may be, on their borderline, empirically undistinguishable. Yet, there is a world of qualitative difference between them. It is also true that vivid images convey a feeling of presence. Dreams are sometimes cherished as the only things that can bring relief to the sufferings of prolonged separation. What they procure is a soothing illusion. The vivid image of dream may imitate successfully the intuitiveness of sensation. But, far from blurring the distinction between sensation and its imaginative likeness, acquaintance with illusion is of help in understanding that the object of sense experience is characterized by a unique sort of presence, by a presence unqualifiedly asserted.

The notion of presence admits of degrees, and an object may be said to be present in a variety of ways. Let us survey the main kinds of presence, beginning with the weakest, the most qualified. An object devoid of real existence, devoid of real possibility and afflicted with internal contradiction, may be said to be present to the mind, and, in this weakest of all kinds of presence, it may significantly contribute to the establishment of truth. To understand, for example, that the "best possible world" is a contradictory fiction is a valuable step in the theory of evil. Next to such contradictions come the beings of reason whose constitution is in no way contradictory, even though it would be contradictory to represent them as capable of real existence. Such are the second intentions that make up the object of logic. There is nothing contradictory about the notions of subject, predicate, and middle term, but attributing a real existence to the property of being a middle term would imply contradiction, for such properties accrue to things by reason of the second existence they assume as objects of intelligent consideration. Next to the beings of reason come various conceptions and constructions whose possibility cannot be determinately negated although their existence cannot be established. Many can be found in the hypotheses of physical science. Then come the things—for example, dinosaurs—whose real possibility is certain, although they are out of actual existence. Then come the things whose actual existence is known with certainty, but indirectly, that is, through an inference or a testimony. But actual existence would not admit of indirect ascertainment; it could not be inferred or believed in, if it had not first been grasped directly. At the basis of all our cognition of things existent, possible or fictitious, there is an act that implies in essential manner the physical presence of its object....

From all this it follows that sensation is an incomplete form of immanent action. The immanent act of the sensorial power strictly coincides with the transitive action exercised by the stimuli and the objects upon the senses and their organs. It is one and the same act that is immanent on the part of the sense and transitive on the part of the thing that is sensed. To interpret these as distinct acts would be to deprive the sensed object of the characteristics of physical presence and of physical activity that constitute the hard core of our experience. An immanent act of sensing that would not be at the same time a transitive action of the thing sensed would no longer be an experience; it would become the most suspicious of all abstractive processes. Abstraction is an operation validly exercised upon the data of antecedent experience, but if the immanent act of sensing did not coincide with the transitive action of a physically present thing, sensation would disappear into the fictitious entity of an abstraction exercised on no previous experimental data.

Let us now focus our inquiry on sensation considered as the *union* of a thing alive with some aspect of its environment. We have described a contrast between the passivity of the sense and the common ways of being passive, and another contrast between the act of sensing and the common ways of being active. These descriptions suggest that it is worth determining whether there is a corresponding contrast between the union of the sense with its object and the common ways in which a subject unites with a state or quality....

What distinguishes knowing from being is that whereas the known object retains its otherness and the knowing subject its identity, a subject that requires a state of quality in the world of sheer existence becomes other than it was. An Englishman who becomes a Spanish scholar does not thereby lose any of the English ways, nor does he necessarily acquire any Spanish manners. In his scholarly progress, which is one of pure knowledge, he remains what he is, and the thing that he comes to know remains something else than what he is. There is union between the scholar and the object of his scholarship, but it is an altogether objective union. Quite different is the case of an Englishman who settles in a Spanish country, changes his language, and undergoes assimilation to the Spanish environment. Here, a certain identity is replaced by another identity, and union with the thing that is such and such affects the subject in its subjectivity. What used to be an Englishman has become a Spaniard. This is a *subjective* union. Since it is a kind of union which characterizes the relation of form and matter, it is most precisely described as a matter-form union. What we want to know is whether sensation is a matter-form union or, like understanding, a union of the objective type....

The hand exposed to the heat of the fireplace becomes hot, and the hand that holds a golf ball is shaped by the pressure of the hard thing inside it. These are obvious instances of matter-form union, in strict coincidence with the alterations, the heteronomic passions described in the foregoing. But the relevant fact is that the matter-form union, though a voluminous and conspicuous concomitant of sensation, is not sensation itself. The hard ball causes the hollow of the hand, and this is a matter-form union, but the hand senses the round of the ball, and this is a union of the objective type. The bad thing with anesthesia, that is the suppression of sensation, is that it allows matter-form unions which may be detrimental—for example, in the case of burning heat or crushing pressure—to go unnoticed. Sensation, which begins where heteronomic passion ends, also begins (from a slightly different standpoint) where the union is no longer of the matter-form type: this holds as certainly in the case of touch and smell as in the case of hearing and sight. There is objectivity, union of the objective type, wherever there is sensation....

The questions asked in the introduction to this paper now have received an answer: inasmuch as sensation is an autonomic passion, an immanent action, and an objective union, it is a psychical, not a merely physical process. Its being an objective union further determines that it is a cognition rather than an affection. Finally, the physical presence and the transitivity that belong to the sense object demonstrate that sensation has a distinct nature as a cognition and cannot be reduced to any kind of thought or abstract representation....

The entities which we designate by such words as images, memories, ideas, etc. are two-sided. Their two-sidedness may be instrumental in producing endless illusion. What do we mean, for instance, when we speak of a memory? We may be designating a mode of the psyche, a psychological reality engaged in a context of psychological existence where it can be affected by such psychological occurrences as emotions, or by physiological accidents, such as brain injuries. Under the impact of a sudden and extreme sorrow, I may lose irretrievably the memory of an event: this has nothing to do with the reality of the event itself, which either has or has not taken place, regardless of what happens in the brain or the emotions of the witnesses. But "memory" may also designate the event that is remembered, as when I say that the destruction of my father's machine shop by fire is the earliest of all my dated memories. The destruction of a machine shop is not a psychological reality; it is the object represented by the psychological reality designated as a memory. True, we never hesitate to call memories events that no one, with the exception of the most radical among the idealists, ever thought of placing in the psyche. A big fire is said to *be* my first dated memory, and I like to describe as one of my happiest memories the meeting of a person who became a dear friend. Such is the double-sided character of memories, images, concepts, etc. Inasmuch as these entities have a subjective side, they are modes of the psyche and pertain to psychology, but by their objective side they are one with their object. An objective concept, that is, a concept objectively understood, is an object of concept; it is that aspect of a thing which the mental reality, also called a concept, discloses and represents. If a physics teacher says, "Today, gentlemen, we are going to study the concept of energy," if a teacher of literature declares that he is going to work out the concept of classical tragedy, no one will suspect that these gentlemen have turned psychologists: clearly, they are using "concept" in the objective sense and what they intend to define is the object which is energy and the object which is classical tragedy. But if you are skillful at substituting the mental side of the concept for its objective side and vice versa at the appropriate moment, the proposition that thought never goes beyond its own concepts—understood, this time, in the subjective and psychological sense—assumes some degree of plausibility. The purpose of these remarks is to explain the great division of entities into things and ideas. A thing may represent something else than itself; yet, what it does primarily is to exist, and representing is but, for a thing, a secondary and super-added function. In the words of an artist "a painting, prior to its being... any kind of anecdote, is essentially a plane surface covered by colors assembled in a certain order." Before it exercises representation, a thing is a way of being; in this capacity, it enjoys an intelligibility of its own. But, for the idea, the function of representing is primary. An idea, considered psychologically, i.e., as distinct from the object itself, enjoys no intelligibility except in relation to the object that it stands for. The idea of energy makes no sense unless it is referred to energy, and the idea of classical tragedy is equally nonsensical if it is not referred to classical tragedy.

Within a great diversity of interpretations, most philosophers have asserted the existence of ideas in the intellect, where they are called ideas, notions, and concepts; in the imagination, where they are called images or representations; and in the memory, where they are called memories. Describing the development of mental life, from elementary sense impressions to the most abstract concepts and arrangements of concepts, is a job that has been done with brilliancy by several philosophical psychologists. Strikingly, quite a few of them take the sense impression for granted, and their skillful analyses begin with the evolution which leads from the data of sensation to images capable of entering into a multiplicity of combinations. *But how did the sense impression get there?* This is a question that many like to dodge. How is communication primarily established between the mind and physical nature? As soon as a content has been provided by sense experience, a plausible description of the mind's development, up to the loftiest ways of thought, can be worked out in a system that claims to be nothing but empiricism. Yet the sense impressions have to be taken for granted, the communication between the mind and physical nature is left unexplained, and few are so frank as to say, like Bourdon, that it is unexplainable. Working toward an explanation of what is absolutely initial in mental development, working toward an intelligible interpretation of the first relationship between the mind and physical nature, is the most indispensable, as well as the most difficult part of the philosophy of sensation....

Aristotelianism is the philosophy that places ideas not only in the intellect, the memory, and the imagination, but also in external senses. It is the philosophy that explains sensation by the daring theory that the first ideas are not generated in any part of the soul but in physical nature. It is the philosophy that bridges the gap between nature and mind by holding that some qualities of the natural world can assume, inside the senses, the capacity of ideas. . . . As soon as the division of entities into things and ideas is understood, the expression "sensorial idea" is no longer paradoxical. The ειδοσ of Aristotle, the *species sensibilis* of the Schoolmen, is an idea that is to sense experience what an image is to an act of imagination, a memory to an act of remembrance, and an intellectual representation to an act of understanding. . . . [J]ust as remembrance is made possible by two-sided realities that are called memories, so sensation is made possible by another instance of those two-sided realities whose primary function is not to be but to represent, and which are in one way states of the psyche and in another way the objects that they stand for. . . .

Back to the example used at the beginning of this discussion, let it be said that when the hands placed near a heater get warm and feel the heat, this double effect calls for a double system of influence. Inasmuch as a thing that was cold becomes warm, there is production in it of a quality that is, itself, a kind of thing. But the autonomic passion of the senses, its immanent action, and its objective union with the sensed imply that the sensible quality is there not only in state and capacity of the thing but also in the state and capacity of idea. . . .

Let us consider *together* (a) the features that distinguish sensation from the common processes of nature—most of all, the character of *objective* union—and (b) the *experimentality*, the relation to a physically present and active object, that distinguishes sensation from other autonomic passions, immanent actions, and objective unions. When the mind achieves an objective union with a thing absent, as in memory, the problem of causality does not concern directly the thing objectively united with the mind. In the recollection, say, of the destruction of a building by fire, the problem of causality is contained within the mind and its organs. The fire itself is not directly involved. The past sense impression is taken for granted. But a building, fire, smoke, fire trucks, and firemen are directly involved when the problem is to account for that which is antecedent to memory, namely the sensations themselves. To sum up: when it is essential for an object to be physically present, and when its physical presence is procured by its transitive action, the means of objective union, that is, the idea, must itself be produced by the physically present object. The "sense impression" cannot be taken for granted. The familiar ways of physical causation account for the alteration of an organ by stimuli, but the thing that acts as stimulus also plays the part of object: the problem is to determine by what ways physical things, in the exercise of their presence and of their transitive action, bring about *the means of objective unions that involve the physical presence of the things objectively united with the senses*....

So far as the validity of sense experience is concerned, the case of the accidentally sensible objects is expressed by one simple law: the sensorial nature supplies no guarantee of truthfulness in the apprehension of objects that are related to the sense in a merely accidental way. A frightened lady hears heavy steps in the attic, and it turns out to be a rat: if we please to call this an illusion of sense, let us, at least, be aware that no defect of the sensorial nature is involved. Such species as man and rat are not objects of sensation except by accident, that is, by reason of their being associated with objects of sense experience....

The essentially sensible objects are those that make an impression upon the sense and its organ. They comprise, first, all the sense qualities and, second, modes that pertain, in a variety of ways, to quantity.... Between the sense qualities themselves and their quantitative modifications the primary difference is that each kind of sense quality belongs exclusively to one sensorial power, whereas movement, number, etc., can be apprehended by more than one sense.... Sense qualities cannot be defined except by direct appeal to experience, and this method yields only a low grade of intelligibility. But no matter how limited our ability to define color or sound and their varieties, it cannot be doubted that sight is essentially relative to color and hearing to sound....

Here is a particularly vexing aspect of the problem of sensation. All other experience ultimately rests upon a firm basis of natural determination that is nothing else than the relation of each sense to its proper object. But because our understanding of sense qualities remains obscure, the critique of sense experience and, in a way, the whole critique of human knowledge terminate in a system marked by obscurity. No wonder that mechanistic science exerts never-ending fascination; among many other feats, it performs the invaluable service of substituting for an obscure reference to ill-defined qualities—for example, the red and the green—a reference to nonqualitative entities—for example, wavelengths—which admit of precise and easily communicable definitions. But, when all the enlightenment procured by mechanistic methods is duly acknowledged, the philosophical problem of the sense qualities remains as inescapable as ever.

To sum up: an essential relation to a particular genus of quality—color, sound, etc.—pertains to the constitution of each particular sense. This relation is a matter of natural determinism. Here, in the relation of the sensorial power to its proper object, we find a natural guarantee of normality, of soundness, of regularity, of truthfulness. This guarantee does not extend to the common sensibles. And by this the bulk of the literature about the deceptiveness of sense experience is disposed of. Two straight lines that are declared equal by precise measurement happen to look unequal. Why should they not? Even though magnitude modifies every spot of color, it does not pertain to the proper object of sight, and consequently the correct perception of relations in magnitude is not guaranteed by the natural determinism that controls sight sensations. The correct perception of the common sensibles, as well as that of the accidentally sensible objects, demands a training and remains subject to deception....

All these examples suggest that sense experience can be falsified if certain conditions of neutrality are not realized both on the part of the organ and on that of the medium. The significant issue is whether such falsifications should be understood in a merely pragmatic way, or should be said also to bear meaning in relation to a truth independent of human purpose. In the first interpretation, the blue color of the curtain material under artificial light would be just as true as the green color under natural light; more exactly, the question "which one is the true color of this material?" would be meaningless except in relation to practice. The privilege of natural light would be due to practical and social circumstances. For one thing, curtain material is more often looked at under natural than under artificial light, and for another, there is a silent convention that when we communicate about colors and other sense qualities, we refer to conditions deserving to be called standard by reason of their frequency....

The external sense can be said to judge, for it distinguishes between a shape and another shape, a color and another color. The failure of the sensorial judgment may constitute—as in the case of the color blind—an error of sense in relation to its proper object. This remark leads to an important specification of the principle that the truthfulness of the senses, so long as the proper objects alone are involved, is guaranteed by nature. Here, as in any domain of mutable reality, essential determination does not exclude accidental failure. It is only in fewer cases that senses err concerning their proper objects—that is, fail to apprehend such distinctions as that of the red and the green....

The relation of the sensorial powers to their proper objects taken with the modes of their action constitutes the nucleus of all certainty in sense experience and, ultimately, of all certainty in human knowledge. Again, this indefectible truthfulness does not suffice to ensure truthful judgment, that is, successful distinction, even on the strictly sensorial level, when the power of the sense is impaired by an abnormal disposition of the organ or a particular state of the medium. No doubt, there is a constant possibility of accidental error in the judgment of the sense about its most proper object, and such error has to be corrected by various factors involving conditions more complex and elaborate than those of immediate experience. Thus, the color blind know, from the almost unanimous testimony of their fellow men, that they cannot trust themselves with traffic lights and that they should watch the behavior of drivers and pedestrians. The housewife comes to know, through trial and error, that she cannot safely distinguish the rather blue from the rather green under artificial light and that she should go shopping for curtains in the daytime....

We have been insisting on the fluidity and relativity of all that pertains to sensory life. Inasmuch as the absolute involves necessity and eternity, it is clear that sense is not the faculty of the absolute. These views must be supplemented by the consideration that the senses possess, in their own way, a power of ultimate decision. A classical exercise for beginners in philosophy is to analyze a "scientific fact" into its components—a great many of which belong to theoretical constructs and often to highly elaborate ones. Yet, all the interpretations and constructs involved in the constitution and expression of a scientific fact are, either directly or indirectly—perhaps most indirectly, but to be sure, ultimately—centered about the data of sense intuition. These data answer by yes or no questions that cannot be eluded without the deductive system losing all its relation to physical reality. There is something absolute about the thing that, ultimately, depends upon the sense and its truthfulness. With due allowance for the voluminous parts played by interpretations and constructions, the analysis of scientific facts brings forth a core of existential decisiveness by reason of which the fact can be called *the experimental absolute*. . . . Without a minimum of strictly experimental determinations, a deductive system, if it is essentially designed to save physical appearances, utterly fails in its design for it no longer is an approach to nature. . . .

Many difficulties encountered in the philosophic study of sensation seem to follow upon this basic paradox: a certain absolute, namely, the experimental absolute, the fact, the thing by reason of which we make the difference between to be and not to be, is primarily delivered to us in an act that relativity and fluidity characterize. By going more deeply into the contrasted meanings of the experimental absolute and of the flux in which it is attained, much could be learned about sensation, and also about human nature, for the definition of man implies, among other things, that it is in the flux of a relation to sense qualities that he achieves his first acquaintance with the absolute.

Note

1. [Editor's Note: I selected most of the texts, expanding on indications the contributor made before his death.]

CHAPTER 7

Knowledge of Persons and Society

The problem posed in "From the Science of Nature to the Science of Society" may be one of the most persistent and vexing challenges in modern philosophy. Upon the demise of medieval Aristotelianism, the seams of nature were sundered and unbridgeable gaps emerged between nature, man, and society. How do we account for the distinctiveness of the human and the political and avoid the attractive pull of reductionism? In the context of modern science most attempts have failed, falling either into reductionism, as did Thomas Hobbes in his series *De corpore*, *De homine*, and *De cive*, or into dualism, as we see in Descartes through later attempts at "Geistwissenschaft." We still find such a standoff between Edward Wilson and Richard Rorty, as one now reduces man and society to scientific terms, and the other resists and deconstructs any certain knowledge of man and society. Many working within the tradition of St. Thomas Aquinas often prefer not to encumber their ethical reflections with philosophy of nature or metaphysics. This is not so with Yves R. Simon. Through his overall project of the recovery of nature, and recovering Aristotle's account of it, Simon attempts to establish the differences of man and society within the similarities and formalities of nature.

Simon in the readings we have in this chapter elaborates three fundamental theses: (1) psychology, both positive and philosophical, is part of the study of nature; (2) nature must be properly understood in terms of "natures" and "finalities"; (3) the "right use" of natural capacities and finalities constitutes the distinct order of intelligibility for ethics and politics. As such, "the science of society," that is, ethics/politics, must encounter the freedom and moral character of man, and, therefore, it must be a "practical" science oriented to action and the good.

But the capacities and finalities of being human are known through nature. Simon resists the temptation to begin psychology free of nature, to jump-start it through metaphysics or mind untethered; instead, he begins in a thorough grasp of soul in nature, specifically of the human sensible powers and appetites, and the emerging intellect and will as form of the body. He thereby envisions two poles of human psychology, the "positive" and the "philosophical," along the lines of a philosophical or "general science of nature" open to further empirical determination and differentiation by specific scientific inquiry. The good for human beings is known on this "scientific" side of the divide. Simon finds of crucial importance the sketch by Thomas Aquinas of the three levels of being in *Summa Theologiae* I-II, 94.2 (referenced in our second selection), and the corresponding inclinations in man to preservation, procreation, and rational perfection in truth and fellowship, and ultimately in God.

Modern psychology and ethics are in a bind because they ignore or nullify these natural finalities. Following the pattern of modern science, the sciences of man and society seek intelligibility and explanation in the mathematical, and therefore they must be nonteleological. These sciences must be readily communicable and directly useful. In other words, we still must understand the triumph and tragedy of Cartesianism. Modern science is intrinsically connected to technology. Simon defines technique as "a rational discipline designed to assure the mastery of man over physical nature through the application of scientifically determined laws."[1] Technology is not primarily the assemblage of things and equipment. It is a rational discipline, which may well entail external things, but technique, as rational discipline, may also involve the use of the body, cognitive powers, the will, and sense appetite. Simon sees the dangers of what he calls "psycho-technology" and "social engineering."

They are "substitutes for virtue" that ride the crest of technological success in the mathematical sciences of nature. Technical mastery is shorn from ethical knowledge, but, in order to use the technique well, "a sound knowledge of human finalities is necessary." Through the heritage of Descartes, the mantle of authority comes to rest upon the value-free or neutral "experts" and "managers." And the hopes for mastery of nature and the relief of the human condition rooted in early modern philosophy now appear to be realizable. Simon says that dominion over nature is part of man's "vocation," but the danger derives from the nullification of human finalities, and most of all from the failure to recognize the limits of mastery in a science of society because of human freedom and the mystery of evil. Simon observes that "the pattern supplied by almost infallibly operating techniques exalts the rule of expertness. The mystery characteristic of human affairs becomes more and more bewildering and uncongenial.... The rationalism born of technological pride hates human liberty both on account of its excellence and on account of its wretchedness." The wider significance of the passage from the "knowledge of nature to knowledge of society" is to be found in Simon's love of political freedom and concern for the democratic regime, now threatened from within by the sophistry of social engineering. For "the training of free men," it is imperative that we follow Simon in the recovery of nature and restore the knowledge of the soul and its powers to their proper place. Natural law requires a prior understanding of human nature through its inclinations and finalities.

The comprehensive science of society, then, stems from a general science of nature and man, but emerges through the mystery of human freedom and character. It finds its proper focus on the question of "right use." The moral problem is "essentially the problem of good human use both of things and of one's powers in relation to oneself as well as other people."[2] Thus, this science must culminate in ethical judgment, ethical action, and political prudence. In our pivotal selections, we can see how Simon has begun the work of healing the scission of nature, man, and society.

John P. Hittinger

Foresight and Knowledge
("Knowledge of the Soul," 117–25)

Generally it is admitted that there are two theoretical sciences of the soul. One of them is akin to philosophy; the other, to positive science. To teach the first we prefer a man of philosophical background who has read Plato, Aristotle, Lucretius, Saint Thomas, Descartes, Leibniz, Kant, J. S. Mill, and Renouvier. To teach the second, we prefer a man who has spent some time in laboratories and psychiatric hospitals. Current ideas hardly admit of a more precise division. The terminology is changing and confused. Metaphysics, metaphysical psychology, rational psychology, speculative psychology, philosophy of mind are the expressions most often used to designate this so badly defined science of the soul, regarding which there is a vague agreement to acknowledge it as especially a matter for philosophers. Psychology (without a modifier), experimental psychology, positive psychology, scientific psychology are so many expressions serving to designate this science of the soul to which we attribute in a confused way the honorific title of positive science, without bothering too much as to what this last expression exactly means.

Concerning the theoretical form of the knowledge of the soul, the problem of psychology is only a particular case, but a particularly difficult one, of the relationship between positive science and the philosophy of nature. Recent transformations occurring in the structure of physics have reminded us that the oldest established positive sciences have not yet succeeded in achieving the conquest of their autonomy. A positive psychology exists; it is recently established. Numerous researchers have enthusiastically pursued the ideal of a fully positive psychology, as independent of philosophy as chemistry and biology are; some of them have become discouraged. During the last fifty years, many psychologists have come to admit, with or without sadness, that a state of confused association with philosophy could well be the permanent condition of so-called positive psychology.

This resignation appears to us to be an unhealthy thing, as is every attitude destined to perpetuate disorder in the system of our knowledge. No doubt, there is no essential reason prohibiting the science of the soul from putting on an entirely positive form, but different accidental reasons abundantly explain the failures suffered by positive psychologies in their endeavors at autonomous system-building, without implying that these failures are definitive. Let us briefly indicate some of these reasons.

1. Unlike what occurs in physics, chemistry, and biology, psychological facts are for the most part familiar to common sense. Now, common sense, when it does not become absorbed in practical preoccupations or deceived by the figments of the imagination, is much more inclined toward a philosophical than a positive interpretation. It follows that the elaboration of a positive concept in psychology often consists in the recasting of a philosophical concept. Such a recasting requires an extremely vigilant critical sense and is effected only through trial and error. In the case of protracted failure, the autonomy of the positive synthesis becomes compromised by the violent and, moreover, generally unconscious incorporation of a philosophical concept.

2. It has often been remarked that positive science is the work of a sagacious reason, capable of controlling the ardor of its natural penchant for the being of things. This remark is particularly relevant for the knowledge of the soul. The rational appetite for the being of things makes itself felt with a particular vehemence when the thing to be known is the very principle of our life and the subject of our destiny. Unless he is a pure empiricist gone astray in theoretical science, the positive psychologist must fight without letup against the ontological enthusiasm that threatens at any moment to change the epistemological nature of his interpretations.

3. In the investigation of sub-human nature, few facts lend themselves to an ontological interpretation. The frequent and evident failures of attempts at a philosophical explanation effectively protect positive reason against the interventions of philosophy. In things of the soul, on the contrary, especially when higher functions are at issue, a considerable proportion of facts entail an ontological interpretation.

The philosophical mind has more occasions to become conscious of its possibilities and fewer occasions to recognize its limitations.

4. Finally, it is appropriate to remark that the success of a scientific systematization is conditioned by the possibility of exploring the set of facts whose systematic expression is at issue in an ongoing way. If the positive datum presents numerous gaps, it is very difficult, and maybe impossible, to achieve a satisfactory systematization through the use of positive principles alone. In case of failure, it is necessary either to give up the advantages of the systematic form or to borrow the principles of systematization from philosophy....

In regard to that science of the soul which is part of philosophy, or, more precisely, a part of the philosophy of nature, the simplest expression is also the most adequate: we shall call it *philosophical psychology*. Not only is the expression "metaphysical psychology" inexact, it is contradictory, for the soul, *psyche*, is not beyond nature but in nature; it belongs not to the metaphysical but to the physical world. It is unquestionably possible to carry on a metaphysical study of knowledge, appetition, intellect, and will, but to take this metaphysical study for a psychological study is simply to ignore the peculiarities that affect the perfections of being when they are involved in the world of mobility; it is to ignore the animating role of the soul. The expression "rational psychology" is equivocal and disturbing; it suggests a bad sort of apriorism. The expression "speculative psychology" has a definite meaning only in contrast with the expression "practical psychology"; hence, it implies that any nonphilosophical science of the soul is a practical science, and that is false. The expression "philosophy of mind" reduces the realm of philosophical psychology in an arbitrary way by suggesting that only the rational part of the soul is susceptible to philosophical analysis.

Concerning the positive science of psychic facts, the only correct expression is *positive psychology*. The expression "experimental psychology" is too narrow and, strictly speaking, designates only research carried out by means of experiments, excluding research carried out by observing non-induced phenomena. The expression "general psychology" is devoid of any exact meaning; the expression "scientific psychology" inconveniently suggests that philosophical psychology has nothing scientific about it and belongs to literature, a fantastic conception that many positive psychologists are only too willing to accept.

Most of the positive sciences generate a technology. Let us call *applied psychology* the technique or set of techniques that derive from positive psychology. So, in addition to theoretical psychologies, two practical psychologies exist: moral psychology and applied psychology. The big question is to understand rightly in what way they are to be distinguished, under the same heading of practical sciences.

Each of them sets out to know man in order to act upon him, to foresee his conduct in order to direct it. Now, two causal systems exist in the human soul: the system of determined causality and the system of free causality. Each of these systems provides a distinctive mode of interpretation, foresight, and influence. It is possible to understand a man's free acts by relating them to the dispositions of his free will; it is possible to predict his free reactions with varying degrees of probability; it is possible to affect his free behavior by modifying the dispositions of his freedom. It is possible to understand his determined reactions by relating them to their determining causes, to foresee them sometimes with a high degree of confidence, and to modify them by transforming their determining causes. The first mode of interpretation, foresight, and influence is that of moral psychology; the second is that of applied psychology.

If we deny the existence of free choice, we find ourselves obliged to transfer the functions of moral psychology to applied psychology, and man is surrendered to a technique whose primary task is to achieve the suppression of freedom by any means whether crude or subtle. In fact, as long as freedom refuses to be suppressed, the technical knowledge of human action will suffer numerous setbacks in its imperialistic endeavors. Countless minds are obsessed by the ambition of a technical knowledge extended to all the spheres of human action and absorbing the knowledge of moral man for its own benefit. This constitutes an exceptionally serious threat. It is a threat all the more formidable since it is often hard to draw a line of demarcation between the realm of determined causality and that of free causality, between the possibilities of technical knowledge and those of moral knowledge. We will try to show by several clear examples how it is possible to draw distinctions between these two realms in typical cases. A distinction based on the certitude of typical cases may still guide thought in the obscurity of confusing situations.

1. A witness states before a court that he has seen a woman wearing a red dress in an unlighted alley at 6 o'clock at night. It is sufficient to apply a simple law of positive psychology to know that the testimony is substantially false; the human eye cannot distinguish red from black in the dark. But the judge needs to know something else. It is necessary that he know whether the witness is an honest person fooled by his imagination or if he is trying to fool the court. To verify the sincerity of a witness is a problem in moral psychology.

2. A public transportation company is involved in hiring drivers to serve a particularly dangerous route. The first thing to do in examining the candidates is to test the state of their sensory and sensory-motor functions, which are determined functions. Several rules of applied psychology will allow one to recognize the candidates who should be considered unfit regardless of their good will: the color-blind, the myopic, subjects whose reaction time varies greatly or who show themselves incapable of sustained attention will be eliminated without any more ado. As to the subjects considered fit, one will not entrust them with the driving of a bus without being assured that they possess certain dispositions such as temperance, discipline, habits of regularity, and a sense of responsibility. This second part of the investigation is a matter of moral psychology.

3. In the preceding examples, the respective roles of applied psychology and moral psychology are so sharply distinct that they can be conveniently separated. It is not necessary that the technician assigned to measure reaction time be a psychologist in the ordinary sense of the word, an expert in the human heart. It is enough that he knows how to operate an apparatus and make a calculation. On the contrary, sometimes the problems of applied psychology and those of moral psychology are so mixed together that their borders are practically indiscernible.

The progress achieved by applied psychology in recent generations has conferred a new attraction to the most daring of scientistic ambitions: thanks to the positive science of the human soul—or if one prefers, of human behavior—the utopia of mankind's exercising a control over itself analogous to that which it exercises with an ever-increasing success over irrational nature. This utopia requires the suppression of free choice; that does not mean that it is completely unrealizable. To the extent to which it is possible to suppress man's inner freedom, applied psychology promises potentates a power that no industrial science would have given them; souls themselves are placed at their mercy.

In fact, that is what the tragic experiences of our time have taught us: psychological techniques, which can be exercised only on determined causes, have the power to create the subject on which they want to practice. In fact the tyrannies of the past had only physical means as instruments of constraint; today's tyrannies have *psychic constraint* at their disposal.

By considering what has been accomplished by totalitarian states, we can form a rather exact idea of what mankind claiming to guarantee control over its destiny by means of a technology of human phenomena would be like. In order to ensure the triumph of this technology *extended to man*, one would have to have an absolute and irresistible power, capable of suppressing any dissenting opinion. In the silence of an unbounded despotism, a gigantic scientific mechanism of psychic constraint would complete the annihilation of inner freedoms and would endeavor to remake human desires according to a model dictated to psychologists by their employers. Let us be aware that this utopia has already received important initiatives toward its realization.

Practical Knowledge
("From the Science of Nature to the Science of Society," 115–20 and 123–32)

THE EMERGENCE OF SOCIAL SCIENCE

The concept of social science, as it is commonly interpreted, is something comparatively new. It would be presumptuous to assign the date of its first appearance; yet it can be said that it did not enjoy popularity until late in the eighteenth century.

From then on it accomplishes quick progress; by 1830 it has won a position of overwhelming importance. Such success is explained to a large extent by an obvious and loudly proclaimed relation between the newly shaped theory of social science and the theory of physics which had been firmly established for some time. In order to know what we are talking about when we speak of social science, we must keep in mind the pattern after which it was first constructed. What are the characteristics of the physical system in which the founders of social science saw the archetype of all scientific treatment?

1. Physical science, such as the early social researchers saw it, is related more to a demiurgical ambition than to a contemplative ideal. Clearly, our knowledge of nature admits of two directions. It may be so conceived as to find its end in itself, in its own perfection, in the glory of truth. And it may be so conceived as to give man greater power over nature through the prediction of events. The ways determined by these two purposes do not necessarily coincide, and history shows that they often diverge.

At the dawn of Greek culture, the story of Thales illustrates the theoretical or contemplative ideal which was to prevail among the Greeks. Thales, a philosopher and astronomer, was despised by business-minded neighbors because, they said, a man of science cannot gain much wealth. But astronomical observation gave him a chance to let his detractors learn more about what science can do. He foresaw a large crop of olives and rented all the olive-presses of the region. When harvest time came, farmers had to accept the monopoly prices that he exacted of them for subletting the presses. Thus, he was in a good position to maintain that a physicist can make money if only he cares to.

The contemplative ideal exalted by the Greeks remains predominant throughout the Middle Ages. It is at the time of the Renaissance that demiurgical ambitions take hold of scientific minds. Such ambitions are expressed by Bacon and by Descartes in terms never forgotten. They pervade the modern science of nature.

2. The system used as a pattern for the science of society is a mathematical interpretation of nature. Among the many implications of this epistemological feature, one is of particular relevance to the present inquiry: if nature is treated mathematically, finality is excluded, more or less consistently, from its interpretation. There are no final causes in mathematics. Things that have been processed by mathematical abstraction are not desirable, no matter how desirable their knowledge may be. Nature, as read by mathematicians, is deprived of goodness and of love....

The demiurgical character of our physical science and its privilege of steady communicability combine in such a way as to produce an unprecedented relation between man and the physical world. The description of an example, which may well afford to be imaginary, may constitute a sufficient exposition of this combined operation and of the resulting state of affairs.

In spite of the good work done by our physicians, surgeons, biologists, and chemists, we cannot yet say that we know how to treat many forms of cancer. Now, so much good work has been done in the last generations for the treatment of the most stubborn diseases that we shall not be surprised if within a short time we hear that methods for the treatment of cancer have been used with complete success in an impressive number of cases. We all hope to see the day when a few hypodermic or intravenous injections suffice in most instances to free a human organism from such a dreaded disease. This happy day may come soon, it may come late, and it may never come. What matters for the present discussion is that we are able to set forth definite connections between the discovery of a specific remedy for cancer and happenings of great human significance.

If the discovery is genuine, it will quickly gain general recognition; within a few months or at most a few years it will obtain the unanimous assent of medical men all over the civilized world. Such a process of communication could not conceivably be prevented, postponed, or slowed down except by some great disaster. A second step will take place with almost equal inevitability: as soon as the medical authorities of the world are convinced that cancer can be effectively treated (or prevented) by the use of existent medicines, these medicines will be produced in amounts proportionate to the need. With the possible exception of a few remote islands, they will be available wherever wanted. Application will follow upon availability, and cancer will decline as did smallpox, yellow fever, and tuberculosis. Thus, in the relation of man to a common disease we perceive a factual link between knowledge and these developments: communication of scientific propositions, application of technical formulas to physical nature, and actual transformation of the world. It is not contended that these connections happen infallibly; in order that they be of high significance it suffices that they should hold in many or in most cases. Tuberculosis no longer is a major concern in technically advanced societies. Likewise, we shall no longer be badly worried about cancer when we know that it often can be healed or prevented by a few shots. Roughly: discovering the significant relation is all we need to ensure the actual promotion of human welfare. As soon as a new fragment of applicable science is available, society takes care of the application. True, there have been sad cases in which, for a long time, only a small part of mankind enjoyed the beneficial effects of a scientific progress. But, as society becomes more technological in its structure and its habits, the world-transforming decisions contained in the newly established formulas of natural science are enforced more speedily and more thoroughly. In a number of cases it can safely be said that major difficulties are over as soon as the phase of scientific discovery has been successfully concluded. Nothing so closely similar to salvation through knowledge alone has ever been experienced.

Unfortunately the salvation procured by the science of nature is so incomplete that disappointment is a constant experience for the scientific man. Is there a way out of a persistent wretchedness which is made more intolerable by its co-existence with inebriating success?

Here, the image of a science of society patterned after the science of nature could enter the scene. The domain of salvation through knowledge would then comprise, over and above our relation to physical things, the whole universe of social relations. Servitude, exploitation, destitution, and war would fall under the power of science. Hope for the end of exploitation would have as good a foundation as hope for the end of cancer. A good part of the problem of evil would be virtually solved. Such a vision attained a climax of intensity about a century ago; the best proof that social thinkers are still haunted by it is the resentment that fills their souls. We often read in works of popular philosophy as well as in scholarly journals that our mechanical engineers have done their duty and that our social engineers have not done theirs. The social engineer is a gentleman in charge of transforming society through the application of scientific formulas. As compared with those colleagues of his who deal with mechanics, he finds himself at a disadvantage. It is not enough to say that his task is more difficult.

Between physical and social causality the difference is such that the concept of engineer simply does not admit of being transferred from the physical to the social order. The undine, the zombie, and the social engineer are so many beings of reason with no foundation in the real world. All this is granted by many who still fail to see what a deep reconsideration the concept of science calls for when we move from the world of nature to the world of society.

The concept of social engineering, whatever its relation to reality may be, seems a safe approach to the kind of scientific form that social objects require. A social engineer would be possible if it were not for the particular features of social causality. Now, these features matter not only in the phase of application (engineering) but also in the phase of understanding. If social engineering is impossible, so is any science which postulates that a natural system of causality controls social relations. . . .

Practical Knowledge of Social Science

If we use our intelligence to interpret regularities, circumscribe essences, penetrate them—no matter how exhaustively—observe adjustment, adaptations, successes and failures, the idealistic construct of the value-judgment fades away. A seed of corn grows into an adult plant of corn with remarkable regularity; is it so hard to understand that this is not just a matter of chance, and that you could not expect a seed of wheat, or a gold coin, to grow into a plant of corn with anything like the regularity displayed by corn seeds in spite of larvae, birds, floods, and dry weather? If we are able to understand that there are natures in nature, that natures are tendencies and that human nature is no exception, it should not be so extremely difficult to realize that the observation of men's behavior can teach us a few things about the tendencies of human nature and about what is good for man. Shall we speak of human nature? This expression, provided it is free from idealistic implications, is legitimate and necessary. In the celebrated passage in which he shows what principles should be followed in the division of the natural law, St. Thomas gives a simple and convincing demonstration of a transition from facts, metempirically considered, to values realistically understood. To set in order the multiple precepts contained in the unity of the natural law, let us watch human tendencies to discover, if we can, their relations of anteriority and posteriority. "The order," he says, "of the precepts of the natural law corresponds to the order of human inclinations." There are tendencies that man has in common with all things, such as the tendency to keep existing, to persevere in being. Suicide is contrary to natural law in the deepest and most radical sense. It goes against a tendency that springs from what is deepest in man and in all things, being.

"For there is in man, first of all, an inclination to good in accordance with the nature which he has in common with all substances, inasmuch, namely, as every substance seeks the preservation of its own being, according to its nature; and by reason of this inclination, whatever is a means of preserving human life, and of warding off its obstacles, belongs to the natural law."

Then there are tendencies that man has in common with other animals, such as those relative to generation.

"Secondly, there is in man an inclination to things that pertain to him more specially, according to that nature which he has in common with other animals; and in virtue of this inclination those things are said to belong to the natural law which nature has taught to all animals, such as sexual intercourse, the care of the offspring and so forth."

Finally some tendencies pertain to what is distinctively human in man, the life of reason.

"Thirdly, there is in man an inclination to good according to the nature of his reason, which nature is proper to him. Thus man has a natural inclination to know the truth about God, and to live in society; and in this respect, whatever pertains to this inclination belongs to the natural law: e.g., to shun ignorance, to avoid offering offense to those among whom one has to live, and other such things."

Let us dare to suggest that the needed information of social science may require, as an antecedent step, the reconsideration of physical knowledge itself. The first object of our understanding is the intelligibility of nature, and every intellection, no matter how abstract, remains in some way connected with the things that were understood first. Nature supplies our intellect with a universal pattern of intelligible reality. Correspondingly, the science of nature remains, in a way, the pattern after which we conceive all sciences or at least all sciences of the real world. The mathematical interpretation of nature, with all its beauty and all its utility, supplies our knowledge of the real with a deceitful pattern if it is erected into what it is not, viz., a philosophy of physical reality. A new effort to ascertain the principles of physical science may be the first thing required for the needed reinterpretation of the science whose object is human society. . . .

Nature and Use in Social Science

There is a context in which the consideration of acts, in order to be intelligent, needs to be interpretative in terms of right and wrong. The question now is whether social science exercises its acts in a context of this nature. Seen from a certain angle, human facts present such an objective constitution that the perception of their relation to the right and the wrong is essential to their understanding. Does social science consider things from this angle? The theory of ethical neutrality holds that it does not. What we need is a criterion for the identification of those contexts in which the intelligibility of facts includes a reference to human values.

Our suggestion is that the key to the answer lies in the relation between the concept of nature and the concept of use. As long as we are concerned with natures—human nature not being excluded—the consideration of the ethically right and wrong is plainly irrelevant. But when the human use of natures pertains intrinsically to the intelligible constitution of the object, the principle of ethical neutrality, contrary to the claims of its upholders, conflicts with the requirements of objectivity....

As long as the intelligible structure which is being considered is that of a nature, use remains extrinsic, moral quality remains incidental, and the principle of ethical neutrality holds. In the works of Aristotle psychology is nothing else than the upper part of natural science. It is conversant with the nature of the soul, of its powers and operations; it has nothing to do with the good or bad use that men make of their senses, their memory, their imagination, their intellect, and their will. If it ever considers a question of integrity, the integrity considered amounts merely to the entirety or plentitude of a nature. Psychology, a part of the science of nature, ignores the unique kind of plenitude which consists of conformity between the freedom of man and the rule of his action. On the contrary, the studies of facts which, as recalled, play a great part in ethics and in political philosophy center in the use that men make of things and of themselves. The principle of ethical neutrality holds in psychology. (Thus, insights into the right and wrong use of memory are entirely extrinsic and altogether obnoxious in a psychological study of memory.) The principle of ethical neutrality does not hold in the factual investigations pursued by the moralist and the political philosopher. (Thus, a moralist who studies memory does not abstract from the good or bad use that man makes or is likely to make of it. From his standpoint, memory appears as the power of realizing the wretchedness of an existence that cannot endure without entering into the unknown and disappearing into nothingness; such a power demands to be healed and strengthened by the virtue of hope.) Does the social scientist resemble the theoretical philosopher and like him consider natures and natural integrity? Or does he resemble the moralist, who, even when he deals with facts and utters no "ought," remains intrinsically concerned with human use? This may be the decisive statement of the problem.

To increase the chances of finding the answer, we must clarify our notions concerning the causes of social events. But in such a connection epistemological inquiry is commonly hampered by prevailing ideas about causality. We all received from our early philosophic education the notion that causality implies the qualitative and existential relations which define a deterministic scheme in natural science. Any process at variance with the laws of a deterministic scheme is uncritically deemed to evidence a lack of causality; it is interpreted in terms of contingency and chance, and its incompletely "causal" character is traced to some deficiency, some inachievement, some lack of determination. The consequences are obvious: since there is no science of the accident, we cannot even hope for the constitution of a social science without postulating that social processes are brought about according to the laws of a so-called deterministic system. It follows that the science of society is held to be a study of natures, of natural events, of natural growth and decrease, and of natural plenitude. Such a science is unconcerned with use and consequently requires an attitude of ethical neutrality. The whole question was begged when it was granted, perhaps carelessly, that a process at variance with the deterministic pattern is necessarily marked by a lack of causal determination. The basic mistake was our willingness to be satisfied with cheap postulates about the issue of freedom. The whole framework of the epistemological problem changes when we come to realize, in spite of common prejudice, that the free will is not less but more of a cause than the univocally determinate nature; that freedom originates in an excess rather than in a lack of natural necessity; that a free process is superdeterminate rather than indeterminate; that freedom is an intense, excellent, and overflowingly powerful mode of causality; that it is not accident or chance, and that the mystery of free events, in spite of appearances, is opposite in character to the mystery of chance. As soon as the theory of freedom is cleared of indeterministic misinterpretations it becomes possible to consider coldly the question whether the object of social science comprises, over and above facts pertaining to natural determination, some facts pertaining to the use that human freedom makes of itself and of the natural powers subjected to it. . . .

From Social Science to the Philosophy of Society

If a fact belongs to the order of use—as distinct from the order of nature—its statement implies a minimum of interpretation in terms of the kind of plenitude, the kind of entirety, the kind of integrity that are proper to human use. But moral good is nothing else than this plenitude, and moral evil is nothing else than the corresponding privation. When the thing or event whose existence is asserted pertains to the order of use, the statement of fact normally contains some amount of interpretation in terms of right and wrong. . . .

Facts pertaining to the life of human society seem to be of such character that a philosophy of man is necessarily at work in the reading of their intelligibility.

Notes

1. [Editor's note: All of the quotations in this paragraph are taken from "On Technological Society," a section in the last chapter of Simon's *Philosophy of Democratic Government* (Chicago: University of Chicago Press, 1951), 267–78. His final reference in this paragraph to "the training of good men" is to the title of the second-to-last section of that chapter (296).]

2. [Editor's note: Hittinger is here quoting from *The Definition of Moral Virtue*, 37.]

CHAPTER 8

Moral Knowledge

One of the advantages of philosophizing within a tradition is that one is unlikely to be swept off his feet by the fads and fashions of the day. When one considers what Yves R. Simon had to say on moral knowledge and then think of the Anglo-American moral philosophy contemporary with him, the contrast could not be greater. Under the baleful influence of the *soi-disant* naturalistic fallacy, bequeathed to Anglophone philosophy by G. E. Moore, philosophers were giving accounts of moral language that departed ever more swiftly from the common sense that Moore had once had the common sense to defend. It was more or less agreed that moral language is not expressive of any knowledge, and positions ran from the claim that moral judgments were meaningless, and thus neither true nor false, to what became the ultimate and common position, that moral judgments express the subjective feelings of the speaker and make no common cognitive claim on others.

In the manner of much modern philosophy, this is the dismissal of the common knowledge of the race in moral matters. Philosophers might agree among themselves that "good" and "bad" did not derive their meaning from any features of the thing called good or bad and that, effectively, anything, whatever its features, might be called good. But no nonphilosopher is likely to stand still for such nonsense when he is buying a used car, for example. Or even a used philosophy book.

Of course, it was not simply his good fortune to be a Thomist that enabled Simon to escape from this, and from Continental versions of it that were no better.

I have a vivid memory of an evening in South Bend when John and Jean Oesterle were entertaining and among the guests were Yves R. Simon and Charles De Koninck. The two men had figured in a controversy over Maritain a few years previously, and it might have been an edgy evening. *Au contraire*. Soon the two men were vying with one another, each determined to establish his peasant credentials. Few peasants could have followed the conversation that night at the Oesterles, but this was not an instance of radical chic before the term. Both Thomists would have counted it a fundamental failing if they could not have made themselves intelligible to any peasant of your choice.

Of course, this is a feature of the philosophy of Thomas that Simon embraced. To become a Thomist was not to be introduced to a jargon, some scholarly Esperanto that enabled you to fool your friends. Rather, it was anchored in and moved off of that which everybody knew and it never lost linkage with that origin. Everyone knows what it is like to put his mind to the task of doing or making. A few examples suffice to establish this. So what are we doing when we take thought and then act upon it? To say we are engaged in practical thought is simply to spin one's wheels, to give a name to what has already been described. So be it, so long as the label is applied to something obvious.

Under the tutelage of Thomas, and guided by his own reflections, Simon discerned the stages and levels that practical knowledge can exhibit. Furthermore, he was in this matter influenced by Jacques Maritain, and he undertook to defend an innovation of Maritain's that had come under criticism: practically practical knowledge. But that is a refinement within a framework that it is important to stress.

Human knowledge is at first vague and general and only gradually becomes precise. Children begin by calling all women mommies and all men daddies; these particular terms have a range they gradually lose as the females who are mothers and the males who are fathers are separated out, often the subsets in one-to-one correspondence. It is the knowledge, not the terminology, that is general and vague before it is precise. Something like this is to be seen in reflecting on practical knowledge. As we anticipate what we are going to do, we bring the possible deed under a very general category, the good. Whatever we aim to do will be thought of as a good, as fulfilling or perfective of us. But not all acts are good in the same way. To be fair to others, to be truthful, not to seduce the wife of another and to be true to one's own, to eat and drink in a manner befitting a human agent . . . the human good thus exfoliates and reveals itself in a congeries of guidelines. It is at this most general level of practical thinking that those principles or starting points called natural law are to be found.

Practical thinking thus involves general principles, and it is possible for us to reflect on them in their generality, which is pretty much what we do in moral and political philosophy. But the neuralgic point of practical thinking is where all this is brought to bear on the here-and-now circumstances in which the agent finds himself. One need not be good in order to grasp the truth of general practical principles, but only the virtuous agent can successfully see his circumstances in the light of the virtuous ideal and act accordingly. For this, he must be appetitively disposed to the good that is cognitively recognized. Hence the talk of connatural knowledge, the knowledge that reveals the affinity between the agent and the good.

The following passages have been selected from different works of Simon to illustrate some of these introductory points. But of course the passages should eventually be restored to the books from which they are drawn, for only then will the reader get the full effect of the wisdom of Yves R. Simon.

Ralph McInerny

A Critique of Moral Knowledge
(Selections: 9–13, 17–21, 41, 48–49, and 53)

Art is defined as the exact rational determination of things to be made, and prudence (or *practical wisdom*) as the exact rational determination of moral acts to be performed, which leads us immediately into some of the most instructive difficulties.[1] Since their function is to measure an action that ultimately depends on us, art and prudence clearly have the contingent for their objects. How, then, can we include "exact rational determination" in their definitions? Is there such a thing as rational determination of the contingent, of that which by definition can be otherwise than it is? Thus, there are many who do not think that our prudential acts can ever possess the unqualified certitude of rational determination. Yet look where such a denial leads. If there were no rational determination in prudence, the prudent man would be incapable of distinguishing between the false and the true. Or, to put it another way, we would have to say, quite simply, that the human mind is made by nature to be defective in its practical function.

The response of Aristotle's school to this difficulty is well known: the truth of moral intelligence is not a speculative truth at all, but a practical truth. Whereas speculative truth consists in a relationship of conformity between judgment and reality, practical truth consists in a relationship of conformity of judgment with the movement of desire—if the movement of desire itself is as it ought to be. There is conformity between judgment and movement of desire when to the positive movement of desire with regard to a certain object (tendency, attraction, love) there corresponds in the mind, with regard to the same object, the act of affirmation, or to the negative movement of desire (repugnance, aversion, hate), an act of negation....

Thus, what is properly called true, when we say of practical knowledge that it is true practically, is not the formal cause introduced into the soul by knowledge, but the pure relation of this formal cause to the final cause intended by a just will. It remains possible that there could be error from the point of view of knowledge, speculative error; that the formal cause constituted by practical judgment could be inadequate to its object. But as long as the formal cause is in conformity with the inclination of a virtuous will, the prudent man will be assured that, with respect to the end pursued and all the circumstances, it is indeed the formal cause that ought to direct his actions and this practical judgment that he should embrace....

The clearest example of affective knowledge is the practical judgment of prudence. In the order of scientific thought, judgment derives its justification from an anterior knowledge. But in the prudential decision the cause and justifying principle of judgment is the inclination of desire. Intelligence here becomes the pupil of love. One who acts out of the instinct of virtue, knowing nothing of moral science, senses that it is repugnant to his nature to act otherwise, and this is sufficient for him....

There is sympathy between two persons when they are disposed to have the same feelings when confronted by the same stimulus. We extend to a bereaved family our sympathy; that is to say, the event that saddens them causes sadness in us as well. There is sympathy between desire and the object of judgment when the passions of desire correspond to the passions of the objects, in such a way that to the objective demand of an affirmative judgment, desire reacts with a positive tendency, and to the objective demand of a judgment of negation, with repugnance. But for this sympathy to exist, desire must in some way have *become* the object of which intelligence must judge in conformity with the movements of desire.[2]

The virtuous man, in order to judge well what concerns virtue, can do no better than follow the inclination of his heart. This is because virtue is established in him as an active force: the regulative law of his desire is the very law of virtue. Equally, a soul divinized by the intimate presence of God takes no risk in judging divine things according to its own inclinations, for God Himself, present in it, incites and measures the movement of its love. Or, to put it in another way, the certitude of affective knowledge requires the establishment of the object to be known in the heart of the knowing subject. Whenever the object to be known has not been so introduced within us as to regulate the movements of our desire in the way the constitutive form of a nature regulates the tendencies deriving from that nature, the docility of judgment to the inclination of the heart will run the risk of being the source of delusion.

This is why it is so important to distinguish with utmost care knowledge by intellectual connaturality, whose contribution in establishing speculative truth is by no means negligible, and knowledge *by affective connaturality*, which plays its proper role in practical thought and in mystical experience. It often happens that, prior to any determination, a scholar sees flashing before him wrapped in peculiar familiarity the answer that he was looking for and of which he is now completely certain. Still, unable formally to justify what he sees, that is, to attach this new truth to those previously acquired, our scholar is apt to speak of intuition and to admit that he owes his discovery not to his mind but to his heart. But he is mistaken, for the heart he listens to is only *the heart of his mind*. The inclination he follows is the natural tendency of the mind toward the true, which is the object of intelligence and its good....

When we move from the self-evident principles formulated by the moral sense to their first scientific determination, our knowledge changes in kind, as natural and immediate knowledge gives way to demonstrative knowledge, acquired by an effort of mind. Similarly, when we move from the last practical judgment in universal matter to a practical judgment in singular matter, our scientific knowledge, whose justification depends on anterior knowledge, gives way to prudential knowledge, justified by the inclination of the virtuous will, or *affective connaturality*....

The danger of theory or speculative science encroaching upon issues that can be settled only by prudential judgment is virtually eliminated from moral philosophy precisely to the degree that it adapts to its motivating role. A moral philosophy that takes its role to be not only to try to define essences and finalities but also to inspire interest in the good will never forget that the end toward which it is directed is not for it to reach in concrete action. And so, instead of pushing for application of general *a priori* rules, this philosophy will openly recognize that its maxims are true only in most cases and will therefore carefully surround them with appropriate reservations, restrictions, and exceptions as befits general rules of human action.

Again, if moral philosophy were totally without a motivating role, it would be rather incongruous to claim rationality for human conduct. To act fully as human beings, we need a practical light emanating from the intelligible depth of things. And provided that we understand what its motivating role implies, there is little danger that universal-practical thought should stifle the free development of those additional qualities of character upon which singular-practical thought depends exclusively for correct decisions in concrete actions.

Finally, since we really cannot live without philosophy altogether, if we denied the practical and motivating character to moral philosophy, we would have to turn for general rules for our actions to some sort of completely speculative science of human finalities. But such a science is not organized along an axis that allows it to descend from metaphysical abstraction to the level of concrete action; nor has any such science any use for the synthetic method which makes sense of practical discourse in real life. . . .

The moral philosopher cannot escape the law of analysis which dissociates *what* the natures envisaged *are* from *what they are not*, even when he is committed to the higher law of synthesis, that is, of putting together *all* the factors necessary for the integrity of the moral act. Thus, it is inevitable that, in the descent of practical thought toward the absolute concrete, a moment comes when the demands of the proximate guidance of action becomes totally incompatible with those of ontological analysis, and that is when the role of the philosopher is finished. Under no pretext can he as philosopher renounce speculative analysis, which alone can resolve concepts into the idea of being, the condition of the philosophical character of thought. And so, just as in speculative science the philosopher gives way to the scientist when going further into the detail of sensible things calls for the renunciation of definitions resoluble into the idea of being, so in practical science when it becomes impossible to satisfy the demands of direction without renouncing the use of ontologically exact definitions, the moral philosopher gives way to the moral practitioner.

Practical Knowledge
("The Ultimate Practical Judgment," 1–5, 15–16, 21–23, and "On Moral Philosophy," 53–61, 65–66, 71–74)

Our inquiry will be centered on an example, and the chosen example will be complex enough to exclude the illusions that simplicity might produce. Here is a true story: two geographers, who were also men of wisdom, had just heard of an accident in which several mountain climbers had died. Having no professional interest in the exploration of mountains, I somewhat shyly remarked that it was perhaps unlawful to expose one's life to such dangers for no other purpose than those served by the climbing of a peak. To my surprise the geographers blamed as plainly unethical the recklessness of mountain climbers.

Let us imagine a dialogue on this moral issue, and follow the track of practical thought all the way down to action itself. One character in the dialogue says that the immorality of extreme risk is particularly obvious when a man is in charge of a family. This occasions the remark that even a bachelor is not master and possessor of his own life. At this point someone declares that, after all, every human action or abstention involves risks; the important thing is that the seriousness of the risk should never be out of proportion to the worthiness of the cause. Then the conversation turns to the purposes of mountain climbing.

To accept danger in the service of science is better than lawful, especially if the benefit expected for theoretical and applied knowledge is great. Thus, mountain climbers, before they decide to go on an expedition, have a duty to weigh the probability of gathering useful information. Here it is pointed out that many times, in the history of science, discoveries resulted from investigations that looked unpromising; thus it would be good and desirable to climb mountains even without any definite expectation. But someone holds that the balance of wisdom is being disrupted, and says, with a bit of indignation, that you cannot endanger your life unless there is a strong indication that significant results are at hand. Tired of such insistence on the service of science, another person shrugs his shoulders: mountain climbers care little for the improvement of knowledge but enjoy the thrill of danger and the intoxication of accomplishment. An austere moralist stresses that such is the case indeed, and, in an impassioned tone, censures the lightheartedness that drives people to early death for the sake of what is no more than vainglory.

However, is there not something to be said in favor of the attraction that dangerous life often exerts on generous natures? For the service of society, it is all important that many persons, especially among the young, should face the supreme sacrifice with cheerful readiness. Dangers that look absurd, like those incurred by jockeys and car racers, by mountain climbers and circus performers, are socially beneficial inasmuch as they keep alive, in young people especially, a readiness to die without which society would suffer every day from softness and cowardice, and be exposed to betrayal in times of crisis. But it is replied that great inconvenience attaches to any practice suggesting that human life is little valued. Bullfights have a bad reputation in this respect; they are said to foster disregard for man as well as cruelty toward animals.

The dialogue may go on for a long time without ceasing to be reasonable. Idle talk is not yet in sight. All that has been said so far is true, and more truth can be relevantly voiced on the ethical problem raised by the dangers of mountain climbing. The statements made conflict with one another, yet this does not mean that any of them is false. They express contrasting aspects of the issue: precisely, a wise deliberation gives keen attention to contrasts, and the most important task of wisdom often is to preserve a multiplicity of goods in spite of their opposition.

So far, all the rules brought in are general in character and lie at a great distance from action. But consider the problem of a sportsman who has just been invited to join a team determined to ascend a challenging peak. For his deliberation to be faultless, all the propositions of the preceding dialogue must play a role—though, perhaps, in merely virtual and implicit fashion. And many more particular questions are of essential relevance: granted that it is lawful to take some risk for the service of science and the glory of sportsmanship, what about the particularities of this individual case? Is the moment properly chosen? Whether we are or are not in the season of avalanches makes all the difference between foolishness and reasonableness. What about the guide? Is he experienced, serious-minded, temperate? How was his reputation established? By reliable witness or by hearsay? A conclusion is reached when and only when full assent is given to a judgment which, whether by affirmation or negation, immediately touches action. Let us suppose that this judgment is affirmative. The sportsman is equipped, walks toward his companions, and says, "Everything looks fine, fellows, I'll go with you." And off they go.

We were already definitely within the system of practical thought when we were pondering, at a rather high level of abstraction, such general duties as those concerning the preservation of one's life and the necessary readiness to accept death for a worthy cause. But the practical character of thought has obviously increased with the transition to more concrete subjects and to questions closer to the final decision. The ultimate degree of practicality is attained by the judgment which, except in the case of interference by some external force, cannot not be followed by action. Such is the *command* that a sportsman gives himself when he walks toward his companions and declares that he is ready to go. It is by the study of the ultimate and ultimately practical judgment that we propose to establish the fundamentals of the theory of practical wisdom.

This judgment, metaphorically described as touching action immediately, is, in a direct and proper, and unqualified sense, the *form of action*. Therefore, it is as practical as action itself.

The notion of form, though primarily relative to the explanation of physical change, here retains all its signification. Within a complex reality, the form is the component by reason of which the complex is what it is rather than anything else, by reason of which it belongs to a genus and a species rather than to any other genus and species. The act of determinately willing to do this—e.g., of willing to go on a mountain climbing expedition, not hypothetically, but factually and here and now—is what it is, is constituted in its identity, is distinguished from whatever it is not, by the ultimate practical judgment. A practical judgment is ultimate inasmuch as, all hypothetical considerations being transcended, it has the character of a command. Action and the judgment that commands it are no more external to each another than the marble statue and the shape by reason of which it is a statue of Hercules rather than one of Apollo....

All practical judgments belong to the order of practical thought, but the ultimate one, and it alone among judgments, belongs also, intrinsically and necessarily, to the order of action. The ultimate practical judgment is the form of action and the final expression of thought in its practical function. Through it principles come to exist in the world of action....

What is unique in the synthesis that the last practical judgment involves is its decisive *weight*, the actuality of the tendency it conveys, the drive by which it carries a "that" toward the action of existing, in short the unconditional fashion in which it unites the formal cause and the final cause, the object of cognition and the object of appetition. Let this synthesis be called the *synthesis of realization*, and let us remark that it determines, all the way down from the highest principles of the practical order, a synthetic behavior in sharp contrast with the ways of theoretical thought....

The uncertainty of our prudences appears frightful as we consider the great variety of factors that can adversely affect the relation of practical judgment to reality. Involuntary ignorance in a leader does not result only from failure to get information that, next time, can be procured by consulting the proper memorandum or the proper man. On a deeper level, it may result from such deficiencies as lack of memory for names, faces, or traits of individual character; slow associations and slow processes of thought; inadequacy in the complex of abilities that we confusedly but meaningfully call instinct, knack, intuitive craft, practical sense; cold temperament, entailing privations of the warnings and suggestions that emotional intuition alone can procure; exposure to disturbances by irrational inclinations and aversions.

Concerning this last factor, one might be tempted to say that right desire should procure immunity to such disturbances, but in order for this remark to hold, the rightness that is spoken of should pertain not only to desire but also to the conditions and instruments involved in its operation. In fact, one may be a man of good will and right desire and yet suffer from significant imperfection with respect to these conditions and instruments. Likewise, a violin player may be a great artist and yet give a poor performance because of defects in the material conditions and in the instrument of his art. This famous virtuoso may not do so [*sic*: as] well as expected because he has been tired by a long trip, or because the only available violin is a relatively poor thing or because the physical circumstances of the auditorium adversely affect the working of the instrument. A man of right desire will strive to protect his judgment against all emotional disturbances, but to expect that he will be entirely successful is as illusory as to hope that both the virtuoso and his instrument will always be in perfect shape. In fact, it is much easier to keep a virtuoso in shape and a violin in tune than to keep a man of excellent will free from deceitful emotions, and free from the blind spots that may result from a lack of emotions. . . .

The system of good inclinations required for the virtuous steadiness of the prudent judgment is a *complete* one. This implies, first, that nothing short of virtue properly so called can procure the needed rightness of the desire; good dispositions which have not yet attained the status of virtue do not suffice. It implies, second, that all moral virtues are needed to guarantee prudent judgment in any domain of morality. It would be pleasant to imagine that in order to judge prudently in matters of justice it suffices to be just. But assuming—fictitiously—that it is possible to possess justice without possessing the other moral virtues, let us see what would be the condition of judgment about problems of justice in a soul deprived of courage and temperance. So long as the benefit to be derived from unjust choice is not very great, the weight of covetousness and cowardice is not too badly felt and lucid judgment is not impossible. A man temperamentally inclined toward the just, but afflicted with disorderly passions, can be expected to distinguish the just from the unjust when the matter does not arouse his greed and his fear, in other words, when the matter is of insignificant weight. But when the right choice entails heavy sacrifice, lust and fear cause the confusion of judgment and color the unjust with an appearance of justice. . . .

Notice, however, that prudence can be genuine without all moral virtues being possessed in an equal degree of excellence. There is no justice without fortitude, but a man may be excellently just without having more fortitude than is needed to avoid grave acts of cowardice: his justice can be distinguished in spite of his fortitude's being merely sufficient. . . .

Altogether, the good moral quality which does not have the firmness of virtue is valuable in three respects. (1) Considered in itself, such a disposition procures a frequency of good actions under average circumstances, and this is much better than complete casualness. (2) A frequency of good action is of immense importance for society. Inasmuch as it contributes to the stable good of the community, the unstable good of these dispositions is, so to speak, lifted above its own capacity. (3) With regard to the individual agent, the imperfection of these dispositions is normally a way to virtue. It is only by accident that complete moral debasement favors conversion to ethical excellence more than dispositions to virtue would....

Moral philosophy does not pretend to be totally practical. Nor could it be without dealing with contingencies that are so many restrictions on intelligibility. The primary purpose of moral philosophy is to understand moral essences. This implies that the said essences are abstracted from, pulled out of, the contingent aggregates in which they are generally engaged in immediate experience. Thus, insofar as analysis means explanation, i.e., the tracing of an effect to its proper cause, moral philosophy is analytical. And insofar as analysis means the decomposition of an accidental whole into the essences that make it up, again, moral philosophy is analytical.

Let us now ask whether moral philosophy retains in any way the synthetic procedures that characterize practical thought. In chapter 1, when practical thought was considered at the peak of its practicality, we said that the synthesis of a certain "this" and the act of existing essentially pertains to it. Now, from the very fact that moral philosophy is concerned with use, it is concerned with this synthesis. To say that such and such a use of our powers is right is to say that such and such a use must come to exist, must be united with the act of existence under the proper circumstances. To say that fortitude is a virtue is to say, among other things, that one must *be* courageous, that fortitude must be united with the act of existence. To say that stealing is wrong is to say that this particular essence, stealing, should not be united with the act of existing. Thus, as far as the synthesis of a certain "this" and the act of existing is concerned, moral philosophy involves the synthetic way characteristic of practical thought....

We can now approximate the sense in which moral philosophy can be said to *direct* human action. By the very fact that it is concerned with the right and the wrong use of our powers, moral philosophy says that human action ought to be such and such. And this is an act of direction. However, direction is obviously incomplete when the action to be elicited is considered apart from the contingencies that are a part of it when the "this" under consideration is joined with the act of existing. To say that moral philosophy directs human action *from a distance* is to use a well-grounded metaphor. In fact, the distance is often great. . . .

Things may be done the way they should be done as an effect of virtue and prudence. Under these happy circumstances, we still find it necessary to philosophize. It is true that, all things being equal, philosophy procures a better mode of fulfillment, but this is not the problem. The problem is for us to understand why we are supposed to act the way we do. Assuming a state of ideal completeness in fulfillment, we still would want to understand why such and such laws ought to be fulfilled, and it is precisely for the sake of such understanding, for the sake of explanation, that, even without hoping for more complete fulfillment, we want to philosophize. It is entirely clear that the primary purpose of ethical philosophy is not fulfillment but explanation. From this it follows that moral philosophy is principally analytical. . . .

The ways of a discipline that treats ethical subjects as Aristotle, Augustine, and Aquinas treat the subject of virtue are theoretical. No matter how practical it may be in other respects, moral philosophy is a theoretical science as far as its fundamental ways are concerned. Its own way of being practical is a theoretical one. It is a *theoretically practical science*. . . .

With regard to the contrast of analysis and synthesis as basic expressions of the theoretical and the practical ways, let it be said that the first and indispensable synthesis distinguishing the practical from the theoretical is the putting together of nature and use. Prior to this synthesis it is impossible to speak of practical thought except in an improper, accidental, and subjective way—as if we say that geometry is, for a particular student, an altogether practical subject, meaning thereby that he is interested only insofar as acquaintance with geometry leads to diplomas and positions. But as soon as the particular synthesis constituted by the putting together of nature and use is essential, science is practical in an intrinsic way. . . .

The essential character of the consideration of use in moral philosophy entails a logical and epistemological feature of utmost significance. In moral philosophy, as well as in any way of thinking that is practical in a proper sense, *judgment enjoys priority over concept*. . . .

It must be said that every concept—I mean every formally practical concept—exists in dependence upon some antecedent judgment. The concept of assassination presupposes the judgment that innocent people ought not to be put to death. That is so clear that the word "assassination" would be considered to involve falsehood and defamation if killing was lawful and perhaps obligatory, as it is in self-defense. The concept of theft presupposes the judgments that things can be appropriated and that they ought not to be taken away from their lawful proprietor. The concept of matrimony supposes the judgment that the relations between man and woman cannot be entirely delivered to the control of individual and transient inclination, but should, to some extent, be regulated by society and contained within the dignity of a social status. The concept of faithfulness presupposes the judgment that one should live up to one's pledges, promises and contracts. The concept of perjury depends upon the judgment that it is particularly bad to lie under oath. It is unnecessary to multiply examples. The relevant thing to see is that these two propositions, "In moral philosophy, the consideration of human use is essential" and "In moral philosophy—and more generally in practical thought—judgment is antecedent to concept," convey most closely related meanings. *It is because moral philosophy considers not only natures but also human use that it implies a priority of judgment over concept*. . . .

The most striking, if not the most profound, contrast between prudence and moral philosophy involves the incommunicability of knowledge. Once more, what is really decisive, the final factor of certainty in prudence, is incommunicable. What we communicate when we succeed, as it frequently happens, in convincing our neighbor that our prudential decision was right is a host of inconclusive considerations; these are plausible enough to cause persuasion, as long as there is no particularly strong ground of opposition, but these plausible considerations did not cause the certainty of our conclusion. Its certainty was caused by agreement with right inclination, and this is a cause of certainty that no discourse can communicate. Whoever has had to discharge duties of moral leadership knows that, although much can be done by sheer power of faith and example, there comes a time when, in order to cause in others adherence to what we know to be right and aversion to what we know to be wrong, we depend on the power of demonstration and communicable knowledge. This is precisely where moral philosophy begins. . . .

Although all moral errors, no matter how monstrous, have always been lavishly represented both in the actions and in the thoughts of men, it is possible to point to periods—to avoid arbitrariness and empty talk we would have to be very particular about the subjects, the societies, and the periods under consideration—when some sort of consensus, sufficient for many social purposes, existed by way of affective communion about such matters as the evil of infanticide (unborn infants not excluded), the evil of murdering incurably sick people, the preferability of matrimony to free union, the prohibition of incest and homosexuality, etc. Since the nineteenth century it has become necessary, and it will remain necessary forever, to explain to an ever-growing number of people why those things are wrong. The working out of these explanations may be tragically difficult. But we know that we have no choice. The times of exclusive dependence upon judgment by inclination are gone forever. The realization of an historic need does not imply any underestimation of the value and the irreplaceable power of knowledge by inclination. But it seems that the very preservation of knowledge by inclination demands that something be done along the line of explanation. Again, the risk is tragic: it is a great disaster to replace a virtuous instinct by a mere rudiment of science. Yet no matter how great the risk, we often feel that we have no choice, that the urge toward understanding is rendered irresistible by the forces of history, and that some sort of progress toward explanation has become necessary for the preservation of what is left of virtuous instinct and correct judgment by inclination.

The Tradition of Natural Law
("On the Knowledge of Natural Law," 125–36)

Henceforth natural law means what we understood it to mean from the beginning of the inquiry: the natural law of the moral world. How do we know it? That is the problem and it is not an easy one. Objections and difficulties with regard to the very statement of the question are great and must immediately be recognized. Among them the following is the best known: if there is such a thing as a natural right or things right by nature, this right or these things should be recognized and known by everybody. Strange mores are observed in the Pacific islands, the Amazon jungle, the four corners of the world, and throughout the history of mankind. Moreover, even among ourselves some would judge a thing purely and simply good, while others would condemn it absolutely. Take, for instance, a subject like euthanasia. In our society one finds people having tea, playing bridge, and doing more important things together, being good friends. And yet some of them think that killing a patient who has incurable cancer is murder, while others think it is the charitable thing to do. A man is gone anyway, he has no possibility of accomplishment or enjoyment; he is in this world for a few more weeks or months, with no prospect but to stand terrible suffering; give him a pill of morphine and let that be the end of it for him and everybody around him; it is better that way. Now that is certainly a problem of natural law under the first heading above: should the inclination of being to keep existing be respected in the case of the miserable patient with no hope of recovery? Only a few more weeks or months of terrible suffering.... What is the right thing to do, right by nature? Not only Greeks and Barbarians, Londoners and Fiji Islanders are divided on the issue; people belonging to the same circles in a rather homogeneous society also disagree. Clearly the question, "How do we know natural law?" is not an easy one to answer or even approach....

Many judgments are determined by way of inclination. To all kinds of propositions I say "yes" rather than "no," or "no" rather than "yes" as a result of an inclination. Is that arbitrary, a kind of wishful thinking? It certainly is if it is applied in domains where judgment by cognition is available and in all cases where wishes are not what they are supposed to be. But if the inclinations are sound, the judgment which is assented to because of an agreement with an inclination is perfectly certain in its own way. In fact, this is the only way to ascertain practical judgments when they are considered concretely. . . .

When moral problems are considered concretely—in all their concreteness and individuality—the last word belongs always to sound inclination. There are no exceptions. There is always some aspect of the entirely concrete, circumstantiated issue—individual, unique, unprecedented, unrenewable—some aspect that can be decided only by inclination. There is a true theory that in case of extreme necessity I may help myself or help my baby with some food that does not belong to me. Yes, but who is going to decide whether or not I am in the condition of extreme necessity? That depends on and varies greatly with circumstances. In Wisconsin in September, if I were hungry, I would not have to feel terribly hungry to pick an ear of corn in the immensity of that field of corn. But in Greece in 1945–46, when all babies were short of milk, to take or not to take a bottle of milk belonging to someone else was a much harder problem for a mother. Only the inclination of the honest heart provides here the right answer. When moral problems are considered on the completely concrete, practical level, on the level of the last word, as it were, that last word belongs to inclination.

But law is a premise; it is the work of the reason having the character of premise. And among laws, the natural laws have the character more of premises than positive laws; they are prior premises. What has been said concerning ultimate conclusions in moral problems does not answer the questions concerning those premises, including the first premises which are called natural law. How are they known? By way of cognition or by way of inclination, or in both ways? One way is not necessarily exclusive of the other. There are cases in which a man spontaneously exclaims: "Oh no. I won't do that. I don't do things like that!" He judges by way of inclination. Pressed for an explanation, the man ponders and finally says, "Yes, I can tell you why." And then we have a judgment by way of cognition. The explanation, the connection with antecedent cognitions, is established. But the example again bears upon an ultimate practical conclusion. What about the premises themselves? What about natural law? . . .

Aristotle maintains that "there really is, as everyone to some extent divines, a natural justice and injustice.". . . No doubt Aristotle in this passage maintains that natural law is known by inclination. There is knowledge by inclination of what is naturally just and what is naturally unjust. Does knowledge by inclination exclude knowledge by rational evidence? Certainly not; it precedes it. Natural law is known by way of inclination before it is known by way of cognition.

Let us take a simple example. What do you think of cheating in the execution of a contract? . . . We all find it disgusting. How do we know that? By an inclination? Certainly. The proposition is, "let us cheat in the execution of this contract," and we feel a repugnance. It is good that we should feel that way. Here is something unjust by nature, unright by nature. It is identified by way of inclination; or rather, the conflict of a certain rule of action with an inclination warns us that this is not right, that it is wrong. Wrong by reason of what? No doubt, by reason of nature. To be sure, it is by human enactment, by free choice that the contract was made; the situation is obviously man-made. And yet, we know by unmistakable inclination that it is wrong to cheat in the execution of a contract. We could say that that is clear, except that the word "clear" is ambiguous in this context. Knowledge by inclination is not clear; it may be certain, but is not clear. In fact, it is incommunicable. It is perfectly sufficient for the fulfillment of an obligation, but it is not enough in order to understand. A virtuous inclination and a repugnance to do otherwise are sufficient for fulfillment, but one cannot teach an inclination or repugnance. Rhetoric and example are ways of influencing people, but they do not amount to rational communication. Again, fulfillment without understanding is very often all we can do, but the nature of human fulfillment demands that there be a tendency toward as much understanding as possible. Not only from a theoretical point of view, which is obvious, but also from a practical point of view it is relevant to have as much understanding as possible. It matters from the very standpoint of fulfillment that there be understanding of what is being fulfilled.

Now notice that in our example the judgment is not merely one by inclination; it is also judgment by rational apprehension. The language of the contract is clear; there was bargaining and deliberation, the signing was free from duress. Anyone recognizes, therefore, the essence of the wrong in the proposition, "Let us cheat in the execution of this contract." The judgment "Cheating in the execution of a contract is wrong," is known to be true both by inclination and by rational apprehension. One perceives, one apprehends, one recognizes the essence of the wrong in the subject "cheating in the execution of a contract." It is an immediate proposition. It is not only rational, it has the character of an absolute premise, which does not have to be demonstrated by an antecedent premise....

In the proposition, "Cheating in the execution of a contract is wrong," the predicate is of the essence of the subject. There is no middle term, there is no demonstration. It may be used as a premise to demonstrate some conclusions, but it is itself not a conclusion in any sense. It is a formula of natural law.... It is, indeed, quite normal that we should distinguish the right from the wrong by inclination before we are able to apprehend the essence of the right or of the wrong in such and such a subject. Psychoanalysis has given the word "rationalization" a bad sense, but we may use it is this context in its extreme analytical meaning, namely of grasping rationally that which so far has been grasped indeed but not yet rationally. The rationalization of what has already been grasped by inclination is a perfectly normal aspect of our progress in the natural law. There are domains of human action where rationalization so understood does not seem to involve extreme difficulties. For instance, in matters of exchange the rule of justice is awfully clear: an exchange is just if, and only if, the values exchanged are equal. All the problem—not necessarily always easy—is to ascertain their equality, and improvement in the evaluation of things in exchange will normally advance our apprehension of justice. But the field of justice in exchange is rather simple. Its admitted difficulties appear quite manageable compared, for instance, with the problems of marriage, sex, and related subjects, which are immensely more mysterious and refractory to rationalization. Consequently, in these matters judgment by way of inclination assumes an almost unique importance.

The Definition of Moral Virtue
("How Do We Know Right From Wrong?," 109–11)

Let us take another, more difficult and complicated case. We shall assume that adultery is wrong, and that it is better not to commit adultery than to commit it. Ordinarily, there should be no problem here, because people know whom they are married to and whom they are not married to. But I remember a story from the last big war in which these things got somewhat mixed up. A man on the notorious Burma Road was reported killed, and after a decent interval his wife, in perfect good faith, married another man. Shortly thereafter, however, rumors began to spread that the man was not dead after all but was a prisoner of war. Now, in times of wars and revolutions all sorts of stories and rumors are constantly circulated, and it is not easy to know what deserves to be taken seriously. So what are our couple to do? If the first husband is actually alive, the only decent thing to do would be to separate immediately. But if the story of his being a prisoner is not true, going through the heartbreak as well as the hardship of a separation would definitely be wrong also. The couple would certainly want to investigate the rumor, but that might take quite a long time, and the question is what they are going to do in the meanwhile. Now this is plainly one of those contingent situations in which nothing can be done by pure logic, where the determination of the right choice cannot be effected by any derivation from rational principles. The decision has to be made by prudence, and only a man of practical wisdom will be able to make the right choice.

Does that mean that in the situation we have just described there should be only one objective answer? I do not think so, and I do not think that Aristotle would think so. . . . The choice would depend on who these people are, for as Aristotle would point out, the mean, albeit determined by a rational principle (adultery is wrong), is relative to them and them alone. So with the apparently same amount and the same kind of information on hand, one couple could conceivably separate immediately, while another couple stayed together until they found out more about the rumor. Now, clearly there is great temptation here to jump to the conclusion that what it all finally boils down to in "morality" are strictly subjective judgments. This temptation is not without a ground, because the ultimate moral decision *is* determined by the disposition of the subject. . . . Think again of the honest businessman who flatly turns down a fabulous deal in which he himself can find no fault—except that "it stinks." His decision is determined by subjective disposition, as are all judgments by inclination. But this disposition, while belonging indeed to this man, this subject, has been built up from a consistent practice of honesty in business dealings over a long period of time and may therefore be said to have grown objective in matters of justice. In other words, the disposition of this particular subject inclines him toward justice in such a way that even without being able to tell what is wrong with it, a crooked deal causes in him a strong feeling of repugnance. So we can think about it as follows. In knowledge by inclination, subjectivity—that is, the constitution of a subject—works *as a way of judgment* in all cases, including the case of correct, right, good judgment. And then we, too, can say with Kierkegaard that "in der Subjektivität liegt die Wahrheit."

Notes

1. [Editor's Note: At the contributor's request, I selected the texts from a given range and in relation to his introduction; his death prevented him from being able to confirm the selection.]

2. "Amor transit in conditionem objecti," John of St. Thomas, *Cursus Theologicus, IaIIae*, disp. 18, a. 4 (Vivès, VI, p. 638). [Editor's Note: This is the first time Simon quotes this favored passage from John of St. Thomas, one that he quotes throughout his oeuvre.]

PART III

Freedom

CHAPTER 9

Human Freedom

We are free "by [virtue of] a living relation to the comprehensive good." In short, our freedom is more response than initiation; its engine is not ourselves but the good that draws us. So what most of us identify with freedom itself—the need and the opportunity to choose among alternatives—cannot be identified with freedom itself, but follows as a corollary from what Yves R. Simon calls our "superdetermination" to the "comprehensive good." It follows that when the choices we make succeed in aligning us with that overriding good, we can be said to be free. In that sense, freedom is a *habitus*, inclining us to act so as to align ourselves with the very good to which we are ineluctably oriented. And we need that virtue, since there are so many other pulls on us, which effectively enslave us to contrary inclinations, also endemic to ourselves, yet leading contrary to our authentic good.

What Simon fails to specify, of course, is the origin of this *superdetermination*. It could be a simple fact, but as a prime constituent of what it is to be human, it must be more than simple fact. That is, this orientation is closer to a principle of being human than a feature, which is to say that it must be a necessary feature or (in Aristotle's sense of the word) a *property*, such as a sense of humor. It is more like "hunger for the good" than an otherwise contingent feature. It is the *desire* that Aristotle identifies at the outset of the *Metaphysics*: "All human beings desire to know." Yet where does this grounding orientation of our affect come from? The only plausible answer has to be that we are so constituted. Aquinas capitalized on this pervasive orientation to an end, with which everything in Aristotle's universe is imbued, to argue (in his fifth of five "ways" to ascertaining the existence of a creator-God) that only an intelligent creator could have so endowed things with an orientation that itself bespeaks intelligence (*Summa Theologiae* 1.2.3).

Yet the prospect of *good* that ineluctably moves the affective dimension of mind, the heart (or will), is not to know something but to become that very one we are called to become. What *will* must appropriate, to become free, is the end or goal to which human beings are called *as* human beings. That very orientation is not something about which we have a choice—hence the "superdetermination"—although we can, it seems, refuse it. And therein lies a most radical freedom of the sort that we usually associate with free choice, yet it proves to be destructive of the very self that we are enjoined to use our freedom to help flourish. It is this paradox that should motivate us to look to someone like Simon, rather than untutored "libertarians," as a guide into the reaches of human freedom. For, without such an analysis, denizens of a capitalist society will simply presume that being free means "doing what I wanna do." Yet it does not take a Socrates to remind us that such a policy will soon reveal that our wants are chained to gratifications that need not lead to our flourishing and may even contribute to our destruction. And one can insist, of course, on the "right" to make destructive choices, yet it is difficult to think of them as anything other than freedom gone awry.

What underlies this sixth sense is the standing conviction (limned in Plato's *Republic*) that we will not be able to be free except as participants in a body politic, where the shape of that society can at once enhance and distort our freedom. Enhance it by offering us ways to escape the bondage endemic to a conflicted self, or distort it by seducing us into conformity with dysfunctional social structures. Simon's *Philosophy of Democratic Government* will remind us how Aristotle echoes Plato's grounding conviction by presenting ethics as a subtext of politics. Both self and society must find ways to acknowledge this indisputable orientation to the "comprehensive good" while leaving room for human pilgrims to find the way toward it that suits their individual gifts. That is the secret of child-rearing and of the friendships that form the warp and woof of any living society. These practices help to shape our personal freedom by orienting it to choices that will move us closer to that "comprehensive good." Indeed, it is through such choices, made in response to the siren call of "the good," that we are led to what piecemeal knowledge we can gain of "the good." However sinuous the path may be, looking back will allow us to discern the good proper to each one of us, and so celebrate the freedom by which we have in some measure attained it.

David B. Burrell, CSC

Freedom of Choice
(Introduction, 3–15; "The Will," 18–24 and 44–65; "Freedom," 144–58)

The dialectic of the whole issue [of freedom] is often biased from the beginning by the postulate of a conflict between order and freedom.[1] For those fascinated by order, the treatment of freedom consists, at most, of reluctant concessions. But the lover of freedom claims that any excess in the administration of order destroys both freedom and life. Thus, on either side, freedom is interpreted as something disorderly, exuberant, lavish, inventive, creative, and insane, which gives all things color and warmth but carries the threat of universal chaos.

The proposition that disorder, or a tendency to bring about disorder, pertains to the essence of freedom is often expressed or understood in the treatment of moral, political, and pedagogical issues; it also appears very often in the less impassioned discussions of the physicists and philosophers of nature. Most scientists hold that freedom, if tolerated anywhere, would jeopardize the orderliness of the scientific universe. Aversion to disorder is the real motive of their faith in unqualified determinism. Indeed, according to the dictates of our imagination, *a free act is an event without cause, an exception to the law of causality* and to the principle of uniformity in natural occurrences (*principe de legalité, Grundsatz der Gesetzlichkeit*). Such a thing cannot exist. Thus, at the end of a long inquiry, Sir James Jeans declares that freedom is but the unconscious determination of a man's action by his character and his personal history....

The Epicurean theory constitutes a daring pattern for all philosophies that identify freedom with causal indetermination, or at least place the beginning of freedom in the indetermination of natural events. Epicurus is a moralist who needs a certain vision of physical nature in order to carry out a moral reformation aimed at peace of mind and heart.... Democritean physics had to be modified on the subject of necessity. Epicurus conceives the world as made of unlimited empty space and of infinitely many atoms, falling like drops of rain in parallel lines. By itself, this construct says that things happen according to predetermined patterns and inflexible directions. In order that the fear of fate may be removed, events must be allowed some flexibility. The implacable picture of fall along vertical paths must be softened by unpredictable deviations. What Lucretius calls *clinamen*, swerve, is the atom's ability to deviate, unpredictably and uncausally, from the straight line....

The physics of Epicurus is a hypothetical and deductive system finally vindicated, in terms of absolute truth, by its moral adequacy. Whereas a pure physicist may be satisfied with the constructions from which observable regularities can be logically derived, the Epicurean philosopher needs constructs which not only infer physical phenomena but also bear out definite insights on the good life of man....

The Epicurean swerve is a thing contingent in an absolute sense. It springs from nowhere and holds natural necessity in check. With regard to the theory of freedom, Epicureanism enjoys a unique significance inasmuch as it places the principle of all free choice in an act of contingency boldly conceived apart from any cause, any nature, and any intelligible ground.

This interpretation of freedom in terms of radical contingency combines with a materialistic system of explanation.... Materialism is best defined by the set purpose of giving precedence to explanations through material causes. Indeed, there is nothing materialistic about vividly realizing the significance of material causality in nature, in human affairs, in metaphysics, and in logic. What characterizes the materialistic spirit is a stubborn resolution to use material causes regardless of the cost, i.e., even when parsimony points to causes of another order.... The Epicureans disregard without examination or mention the theory that the principle of freedom should be sought on the level of wholes and organisms rather than on the level of elements. They take for granted that freedom, if there is such a thing, must derive from the primary components of things.... When modern physicists came to attribute to the behavior of particles a character of indeterminacy, men of science, philosophers, and cultured readers alike felt that freedom was at last given a chance. A. S. Eddington suggested humorously that, though for a physicist it had never made sense until 1927, it was making sense for the first time. In classical mechanics the path of every particle was strictly determined; there was no room for choice in a world where elementary processes followed lines subject to increasingly precise calculation. For the problem of freedom to make sense, determinism had to be challenged in the pathways of primary particles. *Yet there is nothing absurd about relating freedom to forms, wholes, and organisms rather than to primary components.*

The use of a materialistic method in the search for freedom begs the question of freedom's nature. If freedom is, by set purpose, sought out on the material side of things; if freedom is basically conceived after the pattern of material properties; if freedom is intelligibly traced to the material properties; if freedom is intelligibly traced to the material cause of things, to "that out of which" things are made, freedom is necessarily conceived as indetermination, absence of determination, formlessness, causelessness, groundlessness, and irrationality. The swerve of the Epicureans is the uninhibited expression of a philosophy that we shall recognize wherever freedom or its principle is sought on the part of the material cause. . . .

Of all the grounds that can tentatively be assigned to freedom, voluntariness is the most obvious suggested by experience. Let us, accordingly, compare two acts outwardly similar, of which one, however, is considered by common interpretation of experience to be voluntary, and the other one involuntary. Such a comparative description should bring forth the distinguishing features of the voluntary act and make it possible to decide whether voluntariness constitutes a ground for freedom.

Here are some homely examples. A motorist is driving on a winding and dangerous road. He has been driving for several hours; he is tired and drowsy. He made a mistake in not stopping at the last town for a rest and a cup of coffee. Now he must go on in spite of fatigue. Suddenly a beautiful dog steps onto the roadway a few feet ahead of the car. It is too late to stop, and on the left side another car is approaching at high speed. The driver turns right and the car falls into a ravine. He survives.

In the same setting another driver perceives at a distance a group of children walking on the shoulder of the road. They are safe and there is no reason why he should slow down. But one of the children drops a rubber ball which rolls across the roadway. The child runs after the ball. In a split second the driver realizes the situation. Sometimes it does not take much time to achieve perfect attention and go through a complete deliberation. It is too late to stop and on the left side a car is approaching fast. The driver must run over the child or expose himself to almost certain death. He crashes into the ravine but survives.

In the hospital the two men owe some explanation to their friends and relatives. The first confesses that he did not act reasonably, but he does not like to be blamed for having acted absurdly. True, he was unreasonable an hour earlier when he needed to rest but yielded to his desire to get home, and drove on. To the question "Did you really mean to lay down your life in order to save that of a dog?" he answers that he did not mean anything. He did not act for a purpose. He would like to say that he did not *act* at all but rather *was driven*—precisely the thing which should never happen to a driver. He did not ask what was the greater good. He did not think of the better and the worse. He was nearly napping. He did not know where he was going. He did not know what he was doing. He felt that this beautiful animal should not be run over. He just saw the dog and turned the wheel.

No matter how modest, the second driver must confess that he knew where he was going and what he was doing when he boldly exposed his life to preserve that of a child. He was not drowsy, he was awake and attentive, and very much aware of what was happening. It did not take him more than a very small fraction of a second to realize that he had to choose between going to almost certain death, or being for the rest of his life the man who had run over a child. He was not eager to die, but the prospect of this horror seemed unacceptable: every day and night, perhaps for half a century and more, to be the man who, in order not to die, consented to be instrumental in a child's death. It was too much and he felt that he hated the death of the child more than his own death. He was as fond of life as any sound and hopeful young man; but under the circumstances he simply found it good to go to death. Saving the child at the cost of his own life was what he considered good under circumstances that he had not chosen. The facts being what they were, it was good to drive into the ravine.

The conduct of the second driver exemplifies ethical excellence: here is a man who voluntarily does what is morally good—nay, delivers himself to the requirements of heroic perfection. In this example the excellence of virtue serves to emphasize the voluntariness of action, but voluntariness may be found also, and no less certainly, in a course of action morally inferior or definitely bad. If the question concerns voluntariness as opposed to involuntariness, the consideration of virtue and vice is altogether accidental. The voluntary action is essentially relative to the good, but not necessarily to what is morally good. In any situation I may find it good to observe the rule of morality but I may, just as well, find it good to procure an advantage incompatible with this rule. What matters is the connection between my action and my judgment that it is good, for some reason or other, to elicit this action. The first driver did not act voluntarily because he was too drowsy to recognize the good, to place the good in one thing or in another, in action or in abstention. He feels that his friends should not ask him whether he really meant to sacrifice his life for a dog: this question ignores the circumstances of his drowsiness. He saw the dog and turned the wheel and that is all there is to the story. He never thought that it was good to lay down his life for a dog. He was too tired to think. If his power of thinking had not been suspended, he certainly would have found it good to save his life, he would have placed the good in the preservation of his own life. He does not want to be blamed or teased for an action altogether involuntary. Rather, he would accept the blame for not having stopped and rested when he felt that uninterrupted driving involved an absurd danger. It takes some will power to stop a car when you are far from your home, and still more when you are close to it. He was too lazy to stop. His laziness made him find it good to keep going, although he knew he was acting unreasonably.

As to the man confronted by the risk of running over a child, he may, as in our story, judge that it is good to sacrifice his own life. He may just as well consider that it is good to remain alive regardless of what happens to a child who, after all, was not supposed to be playing on the roadway. There also may be in the back seat a person whose life must be preserved, for the sake of the common good, even at the cost of a very painful sacrifice. The driver on the winding road may be responsible for the commander in chief of an army engaged in just action, or for half a dozen children entrusted to his care: in either case, he would rightly judge that it is good, under the circumstances, not to drive into a ravine.

The good to which voluntary action is relative is not restricted to the genus of morality or to any other genus. It is not particular in any sense whatsoever. It is *the* nonparticular good. It transcends all its embodiments and, though engaged in every thing that is good, it is not circumscribed by any of the things in which it is embodied. It is at work, so to say, in all pursuits and all enjoyments. It is immense, it is present in rest and in motion, in contemplation and in action, in study and in business, in pleasure and in austerity, in the gratification of the senses and in those of the spirit, in the ways of justice and in those of crime. It is present in revolt and blasphemy, in the delight of breaking the law, of doing wrong with full awareness of right and wrong. It has the character of a form with regard to all the particular things or actions in which it is realized.

To designate the good, considered as form of all the things good and as the distinguishing object of the will, St. Thomas and his followers use the words *bonum in communi*. This expression will be easily misunderstood unless it is firmly set in opposition to *bonum in particulari*; it is merely designed to bring forth the nonparticularity of the good regarded by voluntary actions, its inexhaustible ability to transcend the things in which it materializes. Let the words *in communi* never be allowed to bring into the picture conditions of abstraction—worst of all, conditions of univocal abstraction—which would sharply conflict with the nature of volition, and, more generally, with that of appetite. Such phrases as "the good so understood as to comprehend all goods" or "the all-embracing nature of the good" would convey rather exactly the meaning of *bonum in communi*. The expression "the comprehensive good" can be used as a substitute for these heavy phrases....

The relation of voluntary life to the good has often been expressed in the more homely language of a desire for happiness. The proposition that all men seek happiness naturally and necessarily is common, in varying degrees of explicitness, to Platonists, Aristotelians, Stoics, Augustinians, Thomists, and Humanists. It seems to have been more challenged in the last two centuries than in any period in the past. "I do not strive toward my happiness," Zarathustra says, "I strive toward my work."[2] In trends of great moral significance, happiness seems to be replaced, as object of human striving, by the fulfillment of duty, the achievement of power, the control of man over nature, cultural refinement, etc. True, it makes sense to say that these substitutions do not reach the heart of the matter, and that whoever strives toward his work rather than his happiness has actually placed his happiness in his work. Yet anyone familiar with the social and historical significance of moral ideas would not perceive any redundance in the view that it is the distinction of humanistic civilizations to place happiness in happiness, the end of man in the happiness of man. We are here confronted by a contrast, both parts of which are certain in terms of moral experience. Of an artist who sacrifices his fortune, his health, his love, his honor, and his soul to his creation, it can be said relevantly that he has placed his happiness in his creation. But he can also relevantly reply that for the sake of his work, he has surrendered all claim to happiness. From the study of this contrast much can be learned about the meaning and conditions of harmony in human desire.

The happiness that all men desire by nature and necessity has the character of a form capable of inadequate embodiment in indefinitely many matters. Whatever satisfies a tendency is a thing in which the form of happiness can be placed. In this basic and transcendental sense, Zarathustra deceives himself as he cherishes the belief that he has overcome the common striving of men for happiness and replaced it by something more distinguished and sophisticated, such as the striving for one's work.

But among things in which happiness is actually placed by men, some unite harmoniously with the form of happiness and some behave as if they could not undergo this form without suffering some sort of violence. We do not only mean that there is such a thing as true happiness and such a thing as false happiness. We do not only mean that the form of happiness can be placed in the proper and in the wrong subject, according as order is observed or not in the accomplishment of human tendencies. Induction shows that things in harmonious relation to happiness are characterized by their agreement with nature, their interiority to man, their being enjoyable in peace and their being enjoyable in common. With regard to the first and most basic of these features, let it be said that contemporary literature presents striking examples of human attitudes held and cherished precisely because of their being at variance with nature. An artist who considers that the duty of art is to give the lie to nature and who has dedicated his own substance to the embodiment of his artistic ideal, would be very willing to say that he does not strive toward his happiness but rather towards his art. No doubt, he is deceiving himself, and his art is actually the thing in which he has placed his happiness. Yet, the contrast is meaningful, though not ultimate. It is possible indeed to place happiness in aversion to nature, but if we inquire into *true* happiness, into the thing in which the form of happiness demands to be placed, one of the very first features that we shall find, one of the features closest to the very form of happiness, is agreement with nature. The artist dedicated to giving nature the lie in his art, and in a life shaped after the pattern of a work of art, can indulge in some meaningful way the claim to be seeking not happiness but something else. The claim is made meaningful by the absence of one of the most formal features of the thing in which the form of happiness truly consents to reside. There is, or there can be, an order inside a material cause; among the components of a "bearer," one may be close to, and the other remote from, the form. What is, within a bearer, closer to the form has itself the character of a form in relation to more remote components. In short, when Zarathustra declares: "I do not strive toward my happiness, I strive toward my work," the proposition is rendered meaningful not by the absence of the form of happiness, but by the absence of one or several of the most formal features of the subject in which happiness can be placed truly.

To sum up: the proposition that all men want to be happy is not properly understood unless it refers to happiness in such a purely formal way as to be fully compatible with the extremely significant fact that many men are aware of seeking something else than happiness.

To understand properly the notion of happiness as the end of voluntary action, it is necessary, further, to bear in mind the relation between real achievement and pleasure. An organism in need of water attests to a state of real achievement when its normal ratio of water is restored; if this organism is endowed with consciousness, the state of need is normally notified by a particular feeling and the state of real achievement normally causes the experience of pleasure. We call real achievement the state of affairs constituted by the union of a natural tendency with its object. Just as an organism endowed with intelligence naturally tends toward the possession of truth, and just as the satisfaction of a biological need procures a pleasure, so the satisfaction of the urge toward truth brings about the joy of knowing.

In our daily interpretation of happiness we sometimes refer to real achievement, and sometimes to pleasure and joy, and sometimes we refer unanalytically to the real achievement and to the pleasure that follows it. We say, for instance, that a man of lofty character is really happy in a situation marked by acute suffering. Such language is readily understood, and yet it conveys a paradox. To say that the just is really happy in his suffering makes sense, inasmuch as justice is a real achievement of excellent rank; but inasmuch as there is suffering instead of joy, order is upset and the happiness of which we speak is but relative and qualified. We happen, on the other hand, to remark that some people find happiness in crime. We express ourselves, on such a subject, with significant hesitations; some would say that no one should worry about these people since they feel perfectly happy; others would say that the greatest of all misfortunes is precisely the coincidence of evil and joy which, by suppressing the warnings of pain, dims the prospect of restoration to real goodness. Clearly, when evil and joy coincide, happiness is understood in a strongly qualified sense. Unqualified happiness, happiness properly so called, involves both real achievement and the pleasure or joy normally following upon it.

True, the separation of real achievement and pleasure, which is a matter of very common experience, raises a problem. If pleasure is a conscious effect of real achievement, it is hard to see how real achievement can be accompanied by a state of pain and how pleasure can be accompanied by destruction. The problem would not arise, the normal concomitance of real achievements and pleasure would be realized with perfect regularity, if the human dynamism were not made of a multiplicity of tendencies. Such multiplicity involves a possibility of interference and entails a demand for order. Again, the problem would not arise if nature assured this order invariably; but, by obvious experience, this is not the case. Whenever a tendency is satisfied without the requirements of order being met, there is pleasure, by reason of accomplishment, and destruction by reason of disorder. Consider for instance the case of a man dedicated to a passion for learning: to this passion he sacrifices his wealth, his health, his social life, his most sacred duties, and his soul. He is not really happy, although he enjoys this kind of life. We say that he is not really happy because the sacrifices following upon his passion involve disorder and a destruction for his person considered as a whole. Yet his illusionary happiness results from a real achievement, viz., from the real perfection of his intellect, won at the cost of disorderly sacrifice.

Again, the satisfaction of any tendency in a pluralistic system such as the human dynamism demands balance, equilibrium, harmony, and a hierarchic distribution of accomplishments. It is important to distinguish, in this connection, what pertains to the essence of multitude and what pertains to the particular character of pluralistic dynamism in the case of man. Let it be said, roughly, that the demand for order pertains to the metaphysical nature of multitude, whereas the need for sacrifice corresponds to the particularities of multitudinous dynamism in things natural and material. Any dynamic whole demands that order should obtain in the satisfaction of the tendencies which make it up; but it is not necessary that the satisfaction of one tendency should conflict with that of another; accordingly, it is not by metaphysical necessity that order involves sacrifice. Order comes to involve sacrifice when and only when there is some sort of contrariety among the tendencies which make up the whole, so that the satisfaction of one tendency—say, toward good health—is incompatible with that of another tendency—say, toward universal knowledge. The law of contrariety, i.e., of the compatibility of forms, originates in matter and, within the complex unity of man, centers on material conditions; but the effect of these conditions extends to all parts and functions of human life.

At this point it is necessary to ask in what sense, or senses, the notion of happiness implies totality of satisfaction, plenitude of accomplishment and joy, the saturation of desire, and should be declared incompatible with any residuum of unsatisfied tendency. Let this question be divided into two phases. Consider, first, the total set of tendencies which make up the human dynamism. To the question whether happiness implies the satisfaction of each and all of these tendencies, the answer obviously is in the affirmative. So long as something remains to be desired our happiness is qualified and from this it is readily inferred that the only happiness attainable in the connatural condition of the human nature is a strongly qualified happiness. Within this condition at least one component of happiness will be missing, viz., everlasting enjoyment. The antinomy involved in a so-called happiness doomed to termination and constantly threatened with violent extinction is an inexhaustible commonplace of human complaint.

This consideration of infinity in duration leads to the second phase of the question, which can be most clearly described by way of a contrast with the first. In the first phase, a set of desires is considered precisely as a set, i.e., as a whole made up of members, and what matters is whether the concept of happiness allows any member of this set to be left unsatisfied. Let us now consider, with regard to amplitude and comprehensiveness, the objects of the desires which make up the human dynamism. What matters, in this connection, is whether the objects of human desires are contained within limits or extend to infinity. Let us consider here those desires which proceed from the rational grasp of the good and pertain to voluntary life. Clearly these desires extend in unlimited manner to the whole universe of being and its perfections.

Humanistic and human studies disclose the restless heart described by St. Augustine. Exploration into the heart of man often leads to the discovery of God via the infinity of human desire. To put an end to restlessness and force the human heart into the pattern of positivistic peace, Auguste Comte multiplied the warnings of his patronizing serenity against the ever recurring abuses of "idle curiosity." In consistent manner he was led to impose drastic restrictions on scientific progress, and soon he was obliged to isolate himself from what was going on in the contemporary scientific movement. Thus, the scientific movement of the nineteenth century would have quickly ended in failure if Comte had been taken seriously by physicists and mathematicians. Even in disciplines of nonontological character, the spirit of science is driven by an eagerness which, through definite methods, regards an unlimited universe of truth. The infinite eagerness of the scientific spirit establishes, in spite of all valid boundaries, a sort of continuity between the positive sciences and the philosophy of human action, metaphysics and theology. Positivism is probably the most consistent effort ever made to hold in check the human urge toward infinite accomplishment. This effort was intelligently centered on the very source and soul of infinity in man, viz., the intellect, and on what is most firm and most ambitious in intellectual life, viz., science. The positivistic attempt has been and remains favored by a unique set of historical circumstances. Because of the location of positivism in the nature and in the history of the human mind, the adventures of positivism are extraordinarily informative. All aspects of resistance to positivism—in religion, in ethics, in art, in the interpretation of history, in metaphysics, in the philosophy of nature, in positive science itself, in industrial life, in medical and psychiatric technique—express an aspect of man's adherence to infinity.

The distinctive feature of the voluntary act, which has been described as relation to the good and as relation to happiness, can also be described, from a slightly different standpoint, as a relation to the final end. It is by the same constitutive necessity that every voluntary act involves adherence to the good, adherence to happiness, and adherence to the final end. The first description is properly relative to the independence, unconditionality, and transcendence of the good; in the second description, the good was considered in the capacity of happiness, i.e., in the ability to procure the total well-being of a rational nature. Again, let us now consider the good as the term of means and of anything that participates in the nature of means.

Acts of men are related to a last end in proportion as they are rational. Recall the explanations given to friends and relatives by the driver who avoided hitting a dog by running into a ravine: his struggles to make them understand that he never decided to lay down his life *in order that* the life of a dog be preserved. If he had understood what the problem was, the dog would have been run over. There is indeed something obviously teleological about the behavior of a driver who sees a dog and turns the wheel; but such teleology pertains to nature and instinct, not to voluntariness. True, the character of a purpose attaches to the preservation of the life of a dog, but in rational discourse such a purpose is not allowed to act as if it were final. The drowsy motorist was a victim of the shortsightedness of instinct. Had he been more alert he would have looked beyond the good of protecting the life of a dog; this good would have been considered against the background of more basic purposes. Suppose that these are also of a nonterminal character; suppose, for instance that the nearly slumbering driver is a very ardent huntsman and that he is generous enough to think of how other huntsmen feel about their own dogs. In contrast to the case in the foregoing story, he did not just see the dog and turn the wheel; he saw the dog, recognized is as a pointer with a distinguished pedigree, thought of how sad and angry its owner would be, and then turned the wheel. Rationality goes on for part of the way, but irrationality soon gains control. In this new version of the case, the driver friendly to the dog's species still must emphasize his drowsiness to avoid being blamed for his foolishness. To spare the feelings of the dog's owner is a thing desirable indeed but not unconditionally. Reason demands that it be considered against a background of more fundamental purposes. If these purposes are not, themselves, terminal, either they will be related to still more fundamental purposes or again blame will be put on the incompleteness of rational consideration, as a result of drowsiness, intoxication, distraction, or some other factor. Unless the discourse of reason is cut short by some interfering power, the teleological process goes on until it reaches a thing that has unqualifiedly the character of a term, and this thing is what is called the final end.

To remain in the same circle of examples and images, imagine a driver on the winding and dangerous road who coldly runs over a child in order not to expose his own life to any bad chance. He is not drowsy, not intoxicated, and not absentminded. By saying that he knows very well what he is doing and where he is going, we mean that his consideration of the end is not restricted to any interfering factor and does not fall short of its term. The final end is not involved in the act of a sleepy driver who sees a dog and turns the wheel; neither is it involved in the incompletely rational behavior of the driver who does not turn the wheel until he has realized how sad and angry the dog's owner would be. In both of these cases, something that falls short of complete rationality—call it nature or instinct, or what you will—has taken care of the situation. Such behavior is described as involuntary. An act is not unqualifiedly voluntary unless it proceeds from a judgment which declares, in terminal manner, that it is good to act precisely in this way. Now, to declare in terminal, final, ultimate manner that it is good to do this or to refrain from doing it is precisely to involve the last end.

The difficulties which may be found in this description arise principally from interference by images of concreteness. To say that voluntary action naturally adheres to the last end does not mean that it naturally adheres to the thing which, in truth and reality and wisdom, constitutes the last end. Here, as well as in the case of the closely related notions of the good and happiness, the object of necessary and natural adherence has the character of a form. Every voluntary action is determinately related to a thing which possesses, for the agent at the time of the action, the character of a final end. Every voluntary action is determinedly relative to the final end, although, as experience shows, there is in mankind much disagreement and inconsistency as to the thing in which the character of last end should be placed. For some the last end consists in wealth, for others in power, for others in glory, for others in pleasure, for others in culture, and for others in God. Within the same day of the same man the last end may be placed first in God, then in some created good—say, pleasure—then in another created good—say, honor—and in God again.

In order to understand the meaning of the last end formally understood, it is necessary to refer to some aspects of the general theory of finality. Recall, first, that the opposite and related concepts of means and end admit of combination in all degrees. Let us never think that whatever is a means is thereby entirely denied the character of an end, or that whatever has the character of an end is thereby denied the character of a means. A pure means is a thing that has absolutely no desirability of its own and cannot be desired except as a way leading to a thing desirable. Few things or operations are entirely pure means. On the other hand many things desirable in themselves are held desirable in subordination to greater goods. Physical and mental health are not mere means: these are things desirable in their own right; but from this it does not follow that the goods of virtue, in case of conflict, should be sacrificed to good health, and that the physician or the psychiatrist should tell me, with scientific definitiveness, what use I should make of my faculties. The means which is but a means and the end which is but an end are the extremities of a series whose intermediary members combine the character of means and the character of end. Understandably, our mind inclines toward notions marked by simplicity. A complex and antinomic notion, like that of intermediary end, is constantly threatened by the neighboring notions which are free from antinomy, viz., those of mere means and final end.

Attention should be called, further, to an enlightening relation between the orders of formal and final causality. Let the formal cause be defined as that by reason of which a thing is *what* it is. In relation to the composite, matter is describable as that *out of which* a thing is made; but in relation to the form itself, matter should be described as that *in which* the form resides and that which owes its own determination, its own being such and such, its own whatness, to the form. Clearly, a relation of matter to form obtains, within the order of final causality, between the means and the end. Every means, as such,[3] derives from the end its being what it is, its desirability, its goodness, its intelligibility as a thing in the order of final causality. The end is the form of the means; the ulterior end, which is more of an end, is the form of the inferior end, which is more of a means.

There is, within the last end itself, a duality which, in order to be well understood, must be interpreted both in terms of formal causality and in terms of final causality—or, to put it in entirely precise language, in terms of the kind of formal causality which belongs to the end in relation to the means. Take, for instance, the case of a man who places his last end in what his community calls honor. Respect for the law of God never prevented him from fighting a duel when the code of honor demanded that a duel be fought. Then a day comes when the appeal of pleasure outweighs the power of habitual adherence to honor; this brave man, who so many times risked his life in order to keep his honor clean, lays down honor for the sake of pleasure. It may be a temporary accident and it may be the beginning of hopeless decadence. Clearly, the form of last end, first placed in honor, is now placed in pleasure. But in the order of final causality the end and the end alone has the character of a form. Whatever has the character of a matter is means. The duality of form and matter discloses, within the last end itself, a duality of means and end. If I place my end in honor I thereby choose honor as supreme means to my last end. That in which the form of last end is placed has, inasmuch as it is bearer of such a form, the character of a means. At this point, it is impossible not to ask the question whether the duality of form and matter in the ultimate end is forever irreducible. The form of the last end can be placed in honor, and from honor be transferred to pleasure, and from creature [i.e., from a created good] be transferred to God, and from God be transferred, again, to pleasure or honor: such is the uncertainty of our pathways. The natural philosopher is in no position to deny the possibility of a final reduction to unity. But if there exists a situation establishing absolute coincidence between the form of last end and the thing in which this form is placed, this situation is not given in the experience of the natural philosopher.

So far we have been considering operations of a certain kind, viz., voluntary operations, and their specific character. Only operations fall under our experience; the permanent principle which accounts for the stability of their specific feature can be known only *a posteriori*. We have reached the point where the consideration of the power should supplement that of the operations. The distinctive feature of voluntary acts makes it possible to describe the nature of the will. Only a nominalistic prejudice incompatible with the essence of philosophic analysis would see anything adventurous in the exploration of a power by which man elicits actions characterized by voluntariness. When the prejudice against the powers of the soul does not originate in sheer nominalism, it proceeds from the fear of accidents which, apparently, have occurred often enough to occasion a stubborn attitude of diffidence. These accidents are: (a) the illusion that the powers of the soul are the object of a distinct experience, as if each of us could see by introspection the nature of his understanding or of his will, in the way in which man, according to Descartes, intuitively perceives the thinking nature of his substance; (b) the weight of language seems often to have inclined philosophers to treat the powers of the soul as so many substantial wholes communicating with one another; (c) the notion of operative power is philosophic and ontological; this does not mean that it has no part to play in nonphilosophic disciplines; in fact the least philosophically minded of psychologists are not afraid to speak of sight or hearing or memory or imagination. But, like every ontological notion transferred to a field of nonontological science, the notion of power of the soul needs to be reconsidered and reshaped according to the requirements of the new epistemological context. If by mistake such reconsideration has been omitted, there occurs the kind of disorder to which the scientific spirit is most sensitive, for its very principles are at stake.

The preceding descriptions and analyses can be summed up by saying that voluntary operations are essentially relative to an object describable, from slightly different points of view, as the comprehensive good—happiness and the last end. Through the voluntary operations, this relation belongs in essential fashion to the permanent principle by which man elicits the so-called voluntary operations, the will....

The will is pictured as drawn by motives of unequal force. Is it free to choose between them? Let us suppose that it chooses the weaker one. There is more actuality in the stronger motive, in the greater good, than the weaker motive and the lesser good. If the weaker motive prevails, the will acts according to the line of less actuality. There is, no doubt, goodness and actuality on both sides, but if the side of less actuality and more potentiality prevails, is it not necessary to say that the agent acts *according as he is in potentiality*? Let us take as an example a man who, in order to assuage his hatred, commits a crime. He does not believe that he has any chance of escaping punishment. Thus, having to choose between a moment of satisfaction at the price of perpetual imprisonment and a normal and happy life at the price of an effort (painful, no doubt, but, after all, very limited), he chooses the moment of hateful satisfaction. Considering the things in themselves, the good chosen is the lesser good. But was it not the greater good for this man, if account is taken of his character and all the good reasons which he has for hating, and for revenging himself? Freedom thus would be reduced to the power of being ourselves in our desires. Our individual being would have the property of coloring the situation in such a fashion that a good could be greater for us, by reason of the accidents of our history, in spite of the nature of the things and natural finalities. Thus conceived, freedom would only escape from the necessity of essential determinations in order to be identified with the necessity of accomplished facts and collections of facts. It would be brought back to an individual and gloriously anarchic spontaneity, but it would be totally deprived of that mastery in which we have recognized the essence of free will. The theory of the determination by the strongest motive, even if it makes a great deal of room for individual history in the constitution of this motive and is accompanied with all sorts of subtleties designed to enhance the distinction of unique actions, will never be anything except a variety of determinism.

And yet, to say that a motive *prevails* is to say that in a certain sense—to be defined with extreme care—this motive is the strongest. To say that a good is in fact chosen is to say that it gets the better of rival goods; to say that it gets the better of them is to say that, in some sense, it is greater and more powerful. The question is how to know if the good chosen possesses the greater power anteriorly to the choice and independently of the act of choosing, or if it acquires it through the effect of choice and does not possess it until the moment when it is chosen. It is only a question, when all is said and done, of knowing if the will can confer on a good (can give it, as one gives a gift to a friend, i.e., gratuitously), by the exercise of its mastery, that character of being the greatest. And all the difficulty consists in the appearance of a conflict between such a gratuitous gift and the principle of the actuality of a cause.

I suppose that in the course of a conversation I feel the desire to tell a story that is not very charitable. Matters contrary to charity can be very amusing and in that way constitute a good; but an aspect of non-goodness clearly accompanies this particular good. To comply with charity by remaining silent is a good action which also presents an aspect of non-goodness since it is contrary to certain of my desires. If I speak, I shall give myself a moment of lively pleasure at the price of a very great injury, perhaps infinitely great. If I am silent, I shall live according to charity: there is nothing better. The particular goods to which these two judgments are related ("It is good to tell this story" and "It is good not to tell this story") are immensely unequal and I am fully conscious of this. I know that I would be ridiculous to prefer a moment of malicious pleasure to the good of charity. And nevertheless it happens to us that we tell uncharitable stories in full recognition of the case. I shall tell the story and choose the lesser of two particular goods, if I put my happiness in an instant of malicious pleasure.

Sometimes a spontaneous expression of ordinary language makes a philosophic thought stand out with admirable neatness. We must believe that common sense has a profound understanding of freedom, when it uses the expression "put my happiness in . . ."; no philosopher could have found one more adequate. To put one's happiness in a particular good is to give to a particular good the additional quantity of goodness it needs in order to make it desirable, absolutely speaking, to the rational appetite. But whence do I draw the power of adding to the goodness of things, to their desirability? In technical language, I draw this from my adherence to the universal essence of good. In more familiar language, the question would be "how does it happen that I can put my happiness where I want?" and the answer is "I can put my happiness where I will *because I will to be happy.*" If it is true, in other words, that the will desires happiness necessarily, and if it is true that all concrete goods that are presented to it are particular goods mixed with non-goodness, then it follows that the voluntary agent has the power of putting his happiness where he pleases—or, what comes to the same thing, of adding to the desirability of a particular good to the point of making it into an absolutely desirable good.

In producing this surplus of goodness, the will brings it about that the judgment relative to such a particular good is the last judgment. Every difficulty is gathered together in this crucial act by which the will brings it about that a certain practical judgment terminates the deliberation and constitutes the decision. This operation cannot be without foundation, without reason; it is impossible that it be a product of indetermination, an absurdity, a causal emanation not according to act but according to potency. It is necessary then to designate the force or energy which makes this operation possible.

We want to know how the principle of the actuality of the cause is verified in the act by which the will brings it about that the last practical judgment is the last. What then is the actuality according to which it acts here? Where do we find that reserve of actuality, of energy, which the will can use in order to accomplish this act that is imperceptibly and, in a most proper sense of the word, decisive to bring it about that a certain judgment be last? If it comes from the side of the particular object, it seems, at first sight, that determination by the greatest good or by the most powerful motive follows inevitably. But there is here an illusion due to an improper statement of the problem. The determination of the greatest good does not follow. Nothing follows. Nothing happens. Deliberation is prolonged indefinitely. Neither the greatest nor the least good, since both are mixed with non-good, attracts the will determinately. The true question is "under what condition does a particular good become unconditionally desirable for a rational creature?" This condition is the same for the greatest good and for the least good. It is no less necessary in the case of the greatest good than in the case of the least good, and its realization does not present any more difficulties in the case of the least good than in the case of the greatest good. In both cases equally it is in the will that we find the energy which the object lacks. In stopping the deliberation, in bringing it about that such a judgment is last, the will acts according to the actuality which its adherence to the universal essence of the good confers on it. The use of this actuality is no less necessary in the case of the greatest good than in the case of a good incomparably smaller. It is in virtue of this actuality that the will is free to act or not to act with regard to a very small good or with regard to a very great good. Because of its natural determination it possesses enough actuality to add to the least of particular goods all the surplus of goodness which it needs in order to be found constituted of absolutely desirable good. Its natural determination makes the will capable of practicing, with regard to all particular goods, its policy of the gratuitous gift, wherein is verified the principle of the actuality of the cause according to the mode that is proper to the free choice.[4]

Obstinately, the initial question recurs. We know that the will possesses all the actuality necessary in order to make this or that determinately desirable. One wants to assign a reason to this preference, one demands *why* the choice is made one way rather than another, and one does not perceive that this restless question contains a *petitio principii*. What does this *why* signify? (a) One could mean that it relates to a cause sufficiently characterized by alterity, actuality, and resemblance to the effect: the free cause is not excluded, if it presents all these characteristics.

If the question is thus understood, it receives the answer: "the will insofar as it adheres to the universal essence of the good and to the practical judgment of its choice is a cause presenting these characteristics and it is free." (b) One can mean that the question *why* relates inflexibly to a cause provided with univocal determination. Any discussion framed within such a *petitio principii* is superfluous.

It is useful, however, to understand how the begging of principle is here produced. Efficient causality is divided into free causality and determined causality. The first part of this division constitutes, without doubt, the most intelligible case in itself. But determined causality is less mysterious and, despite certain appearances, more familiarly known than free causality. The begging of the question of which we speak recalls that it is difficult to surmount the influence of a familiar model. It serves to recall that the understanding of freedom demands a new effort and a fresh mind. A little while ago, tired minds only understood "classical determinism"; nowadays, many among them show preferences for an indeterministic vision that is borrowed from physics according to procedures of doubtful logic.

Few thinkers ever awoke to the theory that freedom is superdetermination rather than indetermination, and that its principle is more highly and more certainly *formed* than that of determinate causality; freedom proceeds, not from any weakness, any imperfection, any feature of potentiality on the part of the agent but, on the contrary, from a particular excellence in power, from a plenitude of being and an abundance of determination, from an ability to achieve mastery over diverse possibilities, from a strength of constitution which makes it possible to attain one's end in a variety of ways. In short, freedom is an active and dominating indifference. Whereas the line of spontaneity or "from-withinness" leads to the notion of the voluntary, it is the line of *actuality in causal power* which leads to the notion of free choice.

Whether or not it is possible to express the principle of causality in a single formula, a plurality of expressions effectively helps to secure an exact understanding of this principle. For one thing, the notion of cause is primarily relative to the world of change which constitutes the first object of our intellect; accordingly, the primary expression of the principle of causality is relative to becoming, and describes the cause necessary to the existence of any change, of any event, of any thing that comes into existence. By reason of this essential reference to change, such an expression of cause and of the principle of causality remains physical, and belongs to the philosophy of nature rather than to metaphysics. It is only in an ulterior phase of elaboration that cause and the principle of causality are expressed in terms of being *qua* being and refer to accomplished existence as well as to the process of coming into being. Without the duality of the physical and the metaphysical formulas, cause and the principle of causality would never be the subject of a metaphysical consideration—or if they were, their metaphysical treatment would ignore the law of order in analogical sets which alone can insure the experimental foundation of metaphysics, and makes the difference between metaphysical science and the questionable products of metaphysical imagination. Moreover, whether causality is considered physically or metaphysically, the diverse aspects of cause and its relation to effect are best expressed by a diversity of formulas. After having asserted that every union of things really diverse, as well as every event, demands a cause, the notion of cause and the relation of cause to effect are specified in terms of actuality, in terms of resemblance, and in terms of otherness. "Every agent acts according as it is in act" traditionally expresses the principle of the actuality of the cause; "every agent produces a thing similar to itself" expresses the principle of resemblance between cause and effect, which can also be termed principle of essential causality, for it holds in the case of the essential cause and by no means in a relation of accidental causality; "whatever is in motion is moved by something else" expresses the principle of the otherness of the cause. Of these three, the principle of actuality is the first and the most fundamental. True, the human mind, in its primary endeavor to explain change, is led to efficient causality by the insufficiency of the material cause, by the insufficiency of the thing potential, by the impossibility of deriving change, without further ado, from the ability of a bearer to stand a succession of forms, or from the permanence of that which proves able to be formed in diverse ways and to enter a diversity of composites. When a lump of clay becomes a work of art, the process can be traced, indeed, to the potency of the clay, but not without further ado. What the principle of efficient causality primarily says is that change requires, no less certainly than the potency of whatever is in change, a being in act, a thing which, just as matter causes change by way of potency, should cause change by way of act and account for the difference between the actuality of change and the mere ability to change—a difference in which the metaphysician recognizes a particular case of the contrast between "to be" and "not to be."

Every agent acts according as it is in act; no agent ever acts according as it is in potency, but the actuality of the cause admits of degrees. The actuality by reason of which an agent acts may be more or less of an actuality, it may be more or less complete, more or less intense, it may cover more or less ground, it may include a smaller or a larger multitude of virtualities; in short, it may be characterized either by relative poverty or by plenitude. The center of the problem of freedom lies precisely here. The decisive issue is whether freedom results from particularly weak or from particularly strong actuality on the part of the cause. In a remarkable variety of contexts—philosophic, theological, moral, scientific, psychological, and literary—it has been held that the poorer the actuality of the cause, the better its chance to act freely. A person ready to do wrong as well as to do right would enjoy a distinguished degree of freedom, far superior to whatever freedom, if any, is enjoyed by the souls that have been simple enough to let themselves be confined within the limits of virtue. Indeed, many people fear that if they become stabilized in the good their freedom will be curtailed, and such curtailment they hate so much that to assert and maintain what they consider their freedom they choose to commit, once upon a while, wrong actions in which they are not particularly interested. The "gratuitous act" so popular in modern literature—e.g., to throw out of the window of a train a gentleman whom you have never seen before—is a striking literary expression of a theory also represented in domains where fancy is supposed not to be tolerated. From the consideration that a causal or deterministic process is predictable, it is commonly inferred that unpredictability is the measure of freedom. Such a view has been applied to the whole hierarchy of nature: there would be more freedom in a dog than in a chemical because, within our ability to define the circumstances, the behavior of a chemical can be predicted with incomparably more certitude than that of a dog. When this approach is applied to human affairs, it entails the puzzling consideration that the most free of men are also the most unpredictable, from which anyone can infer that, for the smooth operation of our business, there should not be too many free men among our associates. In close relation to these views, let us recall the theory, so common among social scientists, that if social science were complete and ignorance totally routed, liberty would disappear together with our hesitancies, our trials and errors, and our arbitrariness. More than one social scientist, having remained intuitively, emotionally, and morally dedicated to liberty, wishes, at the bottom of his heart, that social science should always be so imperfect as to leave plenty of room for trials and errors and for the arbitrariness of individual preference.

In the language of moral psychology, indetermination is termed irresolution or perplexity. To apprehend the true relation of freedom to causality, it is helpful to ask this simple question: "where do we find the most unmistakable examples of whatever we call freedom, free choice, free will, liberty?" Do we find these distinguished examples in perplexed, irresolute, weak-willed and highly suggestible people? Or should we consider as the most certain exemplifications of the free man persons in firm control of their images and emotions, persons who know what they want and who will not be deterred from their goals by accidents of imagination or affectivity, pressure or lure, disease or poverty; persons who, at the summit of human energy, hold that death itself is an accident which cannot affect their relation to the really important ends of human life?

Notes

1. [Editor's Note: Because of a duplication in texts some contributors chose, a different set of texts than had first been suggested was finally chosen to fit the introduction to this section; the contributor reviewed and approved the texts.]

2. Friedrich Nietzsche, *Thus Spake Zarathustra*, in *Complete Works of Friedrich Nietzsche*, ed. Oscar Levy (New York: Russell and Russell, 1964), Vol. XI, LXXX—"The Sign," pp. 401–2.

3. This reduplication should be strongly emphasized. The thing which is a means is never exclusively constituted by its being means. Insofar as, independently of its being means, it is a thing, it involves the determination of its own which even may exclude the relation to the end in which there is a question

of placing it. In the physical order an example of such a situation would be that of a surgical operation too dangerous to be worth performing. In the moral order, there is the case of placing a morally wrong means at the service of a worthy end. The ethically wrong means does not actually lead to a worthy end considered in its ethical worthiness. It is but seemingly that there is a relation of means to end. Some light is shed on this appearance by considering the means in its matter-to-form relation to the end. Not any matter can stand any form: there is necessarily a proportion between form and matter. This proportion is lacking in the case of the morally wrong means believed to be subservient to a morally worthy end. Just as a child would believe that a motor can be made out of wooden parts, so many people who should have an adult conscience believe that the welfare of the civil community can be furthered by perjury, character assassination, etc. Such intrinsically evil actions are matters that cannot bear such a form as the service to the community. All the trouble comes from our failure to realize what this form actually implies.

[Editor's Note: Simon will make the related point that considering an only apparent but not true means to an end does not widen the scope of our choice, but distracts it from being made between true means to our end. As here, a morally evil choice is not an expansion of, but a limit on, our freedom, one that represents a *failure* to use our free powers well. (He makes this point most forcibly in his essay "On the Foreseeability of Free Acts": see the Select Bibliography for a full reference.) We find Simon making this same point in the text from *The Community of the Free* that V. Bradley Lewis references in chapter 13 (selection "Freedom in Daily Life") on intellectual freedom.]

4. Jacques Maritain, *A Preface to Metaphysics: Seven Lectures in* [sic: on] *Being* (New York: Sheed and Ward, 1948), fifth lecture, p. 103: "To this potentiality in all creatures and therefore in all created goods corresponds the dominating influence of the will. The will is specified by good as such, that is to say that it is unable as soon as it comes into operation to will anything without first tending to a good chosen as absolute. It thus of its own fiat renders efficacious the particular good which the understanding presents to it, and which determines it. For it pours out upon that particular good, of itself wholly incapable of determining it, the superabundant determination it receives from its necessary object, good as such. It gratuitously makes that good purely and simply good for itself—the subject—in virtue, to put it so, of the fullness of intelligible determination with which it overflows. Thus the principle of sufficient reason plays no more magnificent part than its part in making possible the freedom of the will."

CHAPTER 10

Human Reason and Will

The common sense of "many persons" with little or no schooling, Simon argues, recognizes that moral responsibility presupposes freedom and rationality. But a philosophic thinker is required to spell out and clarify the arguments that bear out the convictions of common sense, for example, "the actual exercise of reason is a necessary condition of the actual possession of freedom." And a psychology is required that does not treat different powers of the same agent, say, appetition and cognition, judgment and desire, as separate substances, but rather as mutually interpenetrating powers.

The judgment of the will, of rational appetite, that designates something as good or bad is not a free judgment (and, consequently, a free will) if the judgment and will are uniquely and necessarily determined "as fire burns and the liver secretes bile." If there is to be freedom of the will, a certain practical indifference, indifference of judgment, that liberates the human agent from necessitous and nonfree determination, is presupposed.

The cause of any *free* practical indifference, free indifference of judgment, Simon argues, is not any cognitive insufficiency, but rather the positive, natural, and necessary adherence of the will to the *comprehensive* good, in comparison with which any particular good, any non-comprehensively good thing, reveals some deficiency, some element of non-goodness. The least element of goodness attracts, the least element of non-goodness causes aversion: "The mixed character of the particular good guarantees the indifference of the judgment—provided however that the mind turns around the partially good thing and considers both its goodness and its non-goodness." This turning around is what is usually called deliberation.

Simon speaks of the indifference of practical judgment as originating "in the natural *superdetermination* of the rational appetite." "Superdetermination" would seem to be an abundance of determination, an ability to master diverse possibilities, a power of the will (intellectual appetite) to choose or reject any particular good by virtue of its understood compatibility or incompatibility with the comprehensive or universal good (see St. Thomas Aquinas, *Summa theologiae* I-II, q. 9, a.3, and I, q. 83).

There are many particular practical judgments that are devoid of indifference, that is, determinate judgments, like judgments of sense or instinct that issue in natural, but nonfree, movements that we call passions or emotions, also practical judgments of fact. The fundamental condition for indifference of practical judgment "is the perception of the discrepancy between the particular good and the comprehensive good." The level or degree of freedom in any act depends on the clarity or confusion with which this discrepancy is perceived.

Throughout *Freedom of Choice* Simon patiently but indefatigably criticizes and refutes those images and arguments that link freedom with irresolution, indecision, perplexity, willful irrationality, and *empty* indifference. But why, he asks, are those arguments and images so obstinate that it becomes necessary to remove them again and again? There are, he explains, two kinds of indifference, largely opposed, but "connected by the thin thread of an analogous resemblance which warrants the use of a common term in spite of a danger of confusion." The deluding confusion arises from the failure to perceive the difference between the *active* indifference of freedom and the *passive* indifference of empty indetermination. As indifferences, both are opposed to uniqueness of determination. Multiplicity is opposed to uniqueness. Their similarity consists in their opening their subjects to multiplicity, but to multiplicities of very different kinds: the active indifference of freedom "consists in a power to produce a multiplicity of effects," the passive indifference of empty indetermination "consists in an ability to receive a multiplicity of influences." The first arises from abundance, the second from deficiency. The will, through the perception of the discrepancy between particular goods and the comprehensive good, comes to determine which of its own possible operations is more or less attractive; as Simon put it, it "consists in the domination that it exercises over the attractive power of its own operations.... Freedom is not only active indifference: it is dominating indifference."

At the very beginning of the voluntary process, indifference of judgment is not yet present; it is preceded by a determinate judgment of desirability or undesirability, an attraction that is "merely undergone precedes the attraction which is freely chosen." For many of us, if not most of us, for most of our actions, mixtures of motives "merely undergone" and motives shaped by the indifferent judgments of freedom control our actions, and we are more or less free: more to the extent that we are clearly conscious of our motives, and that our attractions are formed by that consciousness; less to the degree that we are moved by attractions merely undergone. More free is clearly better, but it would be a mistake for rational *animals* to despise any condition that is not perfectly free.

So far this discussion has properly concerned itself with what takes place within the psyches of individuals, but there is one dramatic place (the last paragraph of our selection) where Simon points to some of the political and social implications of his analysis. It is the dream of every tyranny to give society, the group, such a power over the nonrational powers of all its members that practical judgments contrary to collective imperatives become impossible. Tyrannies aim at arousing and manipulating hosts of images and emotions (especially the emotion of fear) so as to destroy "the deep center of all freedom, viz., the indifference of practical judgment." One is reminded of Plato's *Republic*, where justice is spoken of both as an order between the parts of the souls of individuals and as an order of different kinds of persons within the whole of political society. These two orders are shown to be mutually interdependent. *Freedom of Choice* and *Philosophy of Democratic Government* go together.

Laurence Berns

Freedom of Choice
("Freedom," 97–127)

FREEDOM OF CHOICE AS FREEDOM OF JUDGMENT

Such is the contrast between cognition and appetition that we often fail to see how intimately the will remains united, in all its activities, with the acts of the understanding.[1] It is misleadingly convenient to imagine the understanding and the will after the fashion of two biological individuals. Treating distinct powers of the same agent as if they were separate substances is a naive blunder which commonly renders the so-called "faculty psychology" suspect to minds possessed of a keen sense for the features of active unity and interpenetration of the parts by one another which characterize living things and particularly things endowed with a psychological life. According to the construct of imagination, the will, once it is brought into existence, would elicit its operation autonomously, like an adult individual which no longer depends upon its generator. Considering that every act of the will proceeds from a judgment which expresses the desirability of a thing, it is all-important to realize that the dependence of the will upon the practical judgment holds not only in the order of finality but also in that of formal causality.

Clearly, the judgment which declares that a thing is desirable plays an essential role in the order of final causality. The practical judgment causes the act of the will not only by proposing an end for it but also by constituting its form. The practical judgment is the formal cause of the appetition that follows upon it. The final cause is an extensive cause, but the formal cause is intensive. The act of the will owes to the practical judgment the entirety of its specific being—of its being such and such, of its structure, of its way of existing—just as a machine owes to the nature and arrangement of its parts the entirety of its determination as such and such a machine. Accordingly, necessity and liberty, which are formal modes of the act of willing, are primarily modes of judgment. They belong to judgment before they belong to the will. There is no freedom of the will without freedom of judgment. There is no freedom in the appetite if the form from which the appetition proceeds is uniquely determined. *Liberum arbitrium* is free judgment. Unless judgment is free, the will exercises its operations in a uniquely determined way, as fire burns and the liver secretes bile. The problem is to designate the conditions under which a judgment escapes the necessity of unique determination.

From the standpoint defined by the purpose of this inquiry we may represent the activities of the intellect as a multiplicity set in order by a polar opposition. Judgments relative to essential, intelligible, evident, and necessary truths make up one of the poles. Here, demonstrated propositions—i.e., propositions brought to a state of evidence through the labor of the mind—center on immediately evident premises. Here, the highest function of the mind, i.e., the ability to perceive the necessity of the first principles, gathers around itself what is best, most finished, and most scientific in the sciences. Here, an absolute necessity obtains not only on the part of the object but also on the part of the judgment; for the mind, when confronted with an obvious proposition, elicits its assent with the spontaneity and the inflexible necessity of a natural process. Here, everything would be luminous and actual if it were not that our intelligence is bound, in all its phases and domains, by a law of gradual accomplishment and never-ending progress. Let this extremity of our intellectual structure be called *the pole of rational determination*.

Propositions capable of determining the assent of the mind with unqualified necessity are but a small part of the material that our mind has to deal with. Scientific disciplines, as they are understood in academic courses and treatises, comprise only a small nucleus of certainties hard enough to remove all wavering and all contingency from assent. In its effort to achieve science, the human mind has actually constructed systems comprising a broad and changing set of beliefs and opinions more or less successfully ordered by axiomatic premises and fully demonstrated conclusions. Some propositions are held as no more than probable, some are treated as altogether provisional tools of research, and many propositions are guaranteed only by the good faith of a colleague whose experiments and computations have not been repeated by anyone. Thus, some sections of scientific disciplines are placed at a great distance from the pole of rational determination. Yet they constantly undergo its attraction; if they did not, they would soon drop out of the synthesis animated by the principles and achievements of science.

But when there is a question of human action, choice plays an essentially different role in the causation of assent. In scientific disciplines the countless circumstances which make it necessary to deliberate, and to work out opinions on the basis of unsatisfactory data, are defective and uncongenial to the spirit of theoretical truth. On the contrary, a man of action sees nothing abnormal in the choices that action ceaselessly demands of him. He hates incertitude, ambiguous information, incomplete files, answers which wander away from the questions, decisions made on insufficient data, careless collaborators, and late trains: all these are defective circumstances which prevent the principles of action from asserting themselves and give the will no chance to exercise its mastery, for they do not leave it much of a choice.

To understand the true character of action and practical intelligence, one must consider the felicitous and by no means exceptional circumstances in which we are aware of possessing all the data required for a wise decision. Let it be supposed, further, that the instruments of our action are so dependable that there is no danger of missing our end. Our decision retains the character of a choice; no objective obviousness imposes itself upon our mind with the unique determination of an axiomatic premise or a demonstrated conclusion. At the upper limit of this judicative system, all admixture of hesitancy has disappeared; choice is made in full light and attains the climax of its intelligibility. Hesitancy is contrary to the dynamism of choice, for what makes us hesitate is the fear of erring, of missing our goal, of choosing an illusory means—in one word, of having only the appearance of a choice. Thus there exists in our mind, independently of all ignorances and absurdities, a principle whose proper effect is the indifference of judgment. *A pole of practical indifference* is set in opposition to the pole of rational determination. Again, in scientific matters, the inability of the object to cause a uniquely determined judgment always results from some insufficiency on the part of the mind: such is not the case at the pole of practical indifference and in the area in which its attraction obtains. Here, it is a positive reality, not a privation or limitation which causes the indifference of the judgment. It is a force, not a lack of force, and this force is a thing normal and good—witness the feelings of joy, of expansion, of orderly and fruitful life by which its operation is accompanied when there is no interference by any factor of perplexity.

The force which holds in check the determining power of the practical object has been described in Chapter 2 of this book: it is the spontaneous, natural, necessary, and nonvoluntary[2] adherence of the will to the comprehensive good; it is the natural desire for happiness; it is the necessary volition of the last end. By reason of its being a living relation to the comprehensive good, the will invalidates the claim of any particular good to bring about a determinate judgment of desirability. At the instant when the attraction of a thing good in some respect inclines the mind to utter the proposition "this is good for me," the infinite ambition of the will reverses the perspective. The thing which is good only in a certain respect discloses uncongenial aspects, and the proposition "this is not good for me" fights with its contradictory for the assent of the mind.

A simple comparison may help to understand how the necessary appetition of the good causes indifferent judgment in relation to particular goods. Let us imagine persons traveling, in a night without moon and without stars, toward a house in the midst of a forest. One window is lighted but as soon as the travelers have seen it, a capricious pathway makes them lose sight of it. They are near their goal but are not coming closer to it. The lighted window guides them for a short while—then disappears, reappears, and disappears again. The travelers understand that the path turns around the house. When they are on one of the three dark sides there is nothing to direct them. If they want to arrive before daybreak, they will walk straight toward the light, through bushes and ditches, as soon as they perceive it again.

A particular good is to the power of willing what a partially lighted thing is to the power of seeing. The particular good is able to act upon the will by bringing about the proposition "this is good for me." This proposition would be definitively assented to, and the act of the will would follow with necessity if, of all aspects of the particular good, only the desirable one were perceived. Likewise the travelers would not wander away from their goal if they remained on the lighted side of the house. But just as three sides of the house fail to act upon sight, so some aspects of the particular good fail to attract the will. At this point the analogy proves deficient: the non-lighted aspect of a partially lighted thing does not bring about any act in the power of seeing, but the non-desirable aspect of the partially desirable thing is of such nature as to cause a negative act, a movement of aversion whose form is the proposition "this is not good for me." Whether the desirable and the detestable nearly balance each other or whether one of the two greatly outweighs the other is but of accidental significance. The least element of goodness suffices to cause the affirmative practical proposition and the movement of attraction; the least element of non-goodness suffices to cause the negative practical proposition and the movement of aversion. The mixed character of the particular good guarantees the indifference of the judgment—provided however that the mind turns around the partially good thing and considers both its goodness and its non-goodness.

The center of the problem is now at hand. We have to determine how and under what conditions the necessary adherence of the will to the comprehensive good entails the indifference of the practical judgment. The travelers, having understood that they are indefinitely turning around their goal and, every time they see it, soon lose sight of it again, think of the legends in which a bewitched horse takes his rider through unknown lands and long spaces of time. Everything happens as if a magic force constrained them to turn in a circle instead of advancing. Inasmuch as the will is dedicated to the good, i.e., to a good free from qualifications and desirable in all respects, the very presence of the will in act reveals an infinite distance between particular goods and the comprehensive good. The proposition "this is good for me," loses its impetus against the unlimited demands of the rational nature. A practical proposition, if it is affirmative, cannot be true in an absolute sense unless it regards the very object of the will. Accordingly the negative practical proposition has already appeared. Under the determining impulse of the will, itself determined by its natural object, the intellect has turned about the partially desirable and partially detestable thing. Neither the desirable nor the detestable is strong enough to impose itself upon the mind. Both are limited. The practical intellect considers the goodness of things in relation to the requirements of the will, which requirements admit of no limit. The will is naturally too determined; it is naturally determined by too great and too strong an object for any particular goodness to coincide determinately with its desire. *The indifference of the practical judgment does not originate in any indetermination of intellect or will, it originates in the natural superdetermination of the rational appetite.*

But what conditions must be satisfied for this cause of indifference to operate actually? In order to answer this question, we propose to examine some typical examples of causal relations, beginning with the cases in which determinism is most obvious.

1. An event of nature such as the action of an acid upon organic matter is, by general agreement, a perfectly determinate thing. If someone claims that he can place his hand in concentrated sulphuric acid without suffering any damage, and performs a demonstration before witnesses, we shall make the following hypotheses: (a) in spite of appearance, the liquid is not concentrated sulphuric acid; (b) the demonstrator has not actually placed his hand in the acid, but his skin was covered with a protective substance. If neither of these hypotheses stands the examination of the facts, we shall try other hypotheses of the same kind. We may have to confess that we do not know what actually happened. We may even go so far as to consider the possibility of a supernatural intervention. But we shall never adopt the theory of an acid's indifference to cause or not to cause the destruction of a definite matter. Such a theory is too absurd. There are many things that we do not know, but we are absolutely sure that a chemical reaction, when all its conditions are realized, takes place necessarily. Its form is the very nature of the chemicals involved, its mover is their natural tendency to act and react according to their nature; this tendency is really identical with their nature. If a reaction did not take place when all its conditions are satisfied, things would not be as they are. They would both be and not be. If some primitives attribute to natural energies a character of caprice and indifference, it is either because they conceive them after the patterns of free wills or because they postulate frequent supernatural interventions capable of invisibly suppressing a condition required for the production of an event.

2. If an event of nature depends upon a complex system of conditions, as is the case with the development of an organism, determinism

is less obvious but we know that it is no less real. In order that this maple seed, which just fell on the ground, should become an adult plant, it must escape innumerable factors of destruction; it is necessary, further, that all the surrounding natures should give it positive cooperation by supplying food, an appropriate amount of heat and light, etc. We shall refrain from unconditional prediction because we have no way to make sure that all necessary conditions are and will be realized.

But we shall not hesitate to utter a conditional prediction: if all the conditions required for the development of the seed and the young plant are realized, this seed will one day become an adult plant, according to its species. To question it we would have, as in the simpler case of a laboratory reaction, to imagine that things both are and are not what they are.

3. With regard to operations regulated by cognition, anthropomorphic imagination, which is famous for the tricks it plays on the primitives, plays also very ugly tricks on civilized people. It obstinately suggests that the bird which jumps from branch to branch, in entirely unpredictable fashion, masters its movements and inclinations. The best way to overcome anthropomorphism in these matters is to know ourselves better and to understand how things happen in the nonrational part of our activity.

Let us consider in the first place reflex actions. Some of them—e.g., the contractions of the digestive tract—are purely biological processes where cognition does not play any role. Others depend formally on sensations. As an example of the second genus consider the graphic reflex described by Georges Dwelshauvers.[3] The subject is directed to hold a pencil motionless on the surface of a recorder. He watches a swinging pendulum or listens to the beating of a metronome, or closes his eyes and imagines an oscillating object. The curve records the movements—conscious in some, unconscious in others, but described by all as entirely involuntary, which mark the rhythm of the pendulum, the metronome, or the imagined oscillating object.

It is hard to define philosophically the way in which the perception of the image causes movement in this case. But it is beyond doubt that between the perception or the image and the movement there is strict correspondence, and that cognition plays, in regard to movement, the part of a uniquely determined form, which admits of no contrary.

4. The movements resulting from habit take place in proximity to reflex action. I enter an apartment building which I recently left after having lived in it for a long time. Here is the mail box which used to be mine: I examine it as if it could still contain my mail. Letters addressed to an unknown person make me understand that my action was absurd. The movement was elicited because the idea of not eliciting it came too late. Until I read the unknown name, the imperative representation of the habitual movement was in control of my imagination, and my reason was busy elsewhere. As there was no conflict, the representation has stimulated in a determined and determining way the motor tendency born of habit.

5. In order to find an example of instinctive judgment not seriously modified by rational activity let us turn to the broad area of the infelicitous reaction of instinct. It often happens that the line of behavior suggested by instinct is disapproved by reason as soon as rational control is restored. A fire suddenly breaks out in a theatre: several persons are killed in a panic. By the next day, it is well established that there would have been no casualties if the audience had not been panic-stricken; if the audience had remained cool-headed and had understood that slow motion was much less dangerous than a rush toward a narrow exit. But no one remained cool-headed, which is the same as to say that the working of reason was suspended in everyone. At the sight of the flames, the instinct of self-preservation alone acted, and the speech uttered by this instinct, "You must run away quickly," was not held in check by any opposite speech. The determinate judgment gave birth to an equally determinate desire and an equally determinate act.

6. By "animal intelligence" we generally designate the principle of nonrational estimations which bear the mark of individual experience and which are ceaselessly transformed by the acquisitions of experience. Whereas the behavior of insects is mostly instinctive, that of the higher vertebrates is remarkably capable of adjustment to the circumstances. If the question of animal intelligence is so poorly known, it is probably because it is very difficult to separate, even incompletely, the processes pertaining to animal intelligence [in us] from the rational processes which penetrate them intimately. Yet the cases in which the judgment of animal intelligence conflicts with that of reason clearly disclose the nonrational essence of our animal intelligence.

Two men are about to undergo the same minor operation. Both are aware that the dangers involved are hardly greater than those present in the circumstances of daily life. One of the men considers that whoever drives a car and works in a factory should be able to undergo this minor operation without being particularly moved. He no longer thinks about it. In him the nonrational sense of safety and danger works in harmony with reason.

The other man makes the same reasoning and waits for the day of the operation with increasing anxiety. True, his reason tells him that he is not more likely to die that day than the day he has his horseback ride, but the nonrational sense of safety and danger—one of the functions of animal intelligence—fills his mind with terrifying visions: a distraction of the anesthetist may cause death by asphyxiation; a loose thread may result in a fatal hemorrhage; an accident in aseptic precautions may entail a fatal infection. If the control of the reason weakens, the nonrational judgment of danger fills the soul with a fear which will not disappear until all danger is removed. It may even outlast the period of danger.

7. Thus, nonrational processes, whether they be physical or psychic, relatively simple or particularly complex, never admit, on the part of the *active form*, of the indifference which makes the act of choosing possible. A judgment of animal intelligence affects the appetite in a uniquely determined way, just as a chemical reaction is caused, with unique determination, by the nature of the chemicals involved. Differences are very great if we consider the observable regularity of events, the possibility of prediction and control, the part of contingency and chance, but they are null if one considers the only thing relevant for the theory of freedom—viz., the relation between the appetite and the formal cause of its action.

When the formal cause is a judgment of reason it sometimes is determinate and sometimes indifferent. In the first case the act of the will is merely natural; in the second case it is free.

Clearly, there is no indifference in the judgment by which the intellect presents to the will, as absolutely desirable, the comprehensive good. Many particular practical judgments are also devoid of indifference. In the course of a scientific reading my attention is attracted by a beautiful theory: I like the truth that it sketches. This love and this desire are experienced in the way proper to passions, although they are acts of the will. I have the power to suspend the exercise of these acts, but I cannot substitute contrary acts for them. I could have stopped my reading at the preceding page, but having actually pursued it until the theory was outlined, my intellect has recognized its good in the foreshadowed truth and has uttered a determinate judgment of desirability. Suppose that I persist in my design to know this theory. As I consider its difficulties, I go through phases of discouragement; but the remembrance of past difficulties which were overcome, indeed, stirs in me feelings of hope. It is in my power to yield to discouragement or to make hope prevail in my soul, but it is not in my power to undergo or not to undergo a phase of discouragement when the difficulty appears. It is not in my power to undergo or not to undergo a movement of hope when the remembrance of past difficulties gives me a reason to hope. The judgment which brings forth the difficulty of the enterprise and the judgment which brings forth my chances to succeed appear determinately in my mind according as the course of my thoughts brings to the foreground the difficulty to be overcome or the energies which make it possible for me to overcome it. I shall go through phases of audacity when I consider how beautiful it is to solve a difficulty, and phases of fear as I consider the possibility of failure. In case of final failure it will not be in my power to experience or not to experience a feeling of sadness and irritation. In case of final success, it will not be in my power to experience or not to experience a feeling of joy. Just as the judgments of sense, instinct and animal intelligence, which are always determinate and never indifferent, bring about in the animal appetite nonfree movements that are called passions or emotions, so the judgments of reason bring about in the will sentiments which are natural acts, not free acts, so long as the conditions of the indifferent judgment are not realized.

It is commonly said that deliberation is a necessary condition of indifference in practical judgment and of freedom in choice. This proposition certainly holds in the most frequent cases, which are also the clearest, and the most significant in terms of human interest. What the indifference of practical judgment requires as its proper condition is the perception of the discrepancy between the particular good and the comprehensive good. The least that can be said is that in most cases this perception takes place in and through the complex process of deliberation. Without a phase of indecision and deliberation, no matter how short we please to imagine it, the discrepancy between the particular good and the comprehensive good is not perceived or is perceived in a confused and merely incipient way: consequently, the act which follows is not free, or possesses merely a low degree of freedom. This is indeed how things happen within the limit of ordinary experience.

The problem is to determine the nature of the necessity by reason of which indeliberate judgments, or most of them, are deprived of indifference. One thing is sure: this necessity is not metaphysical. Yet deliberation, which is a discursive process, and the phase of indetermination in which the deliberative discourse takes place, are made necessary only by the factor of potentiality which affects the intellect and the will of man. This factor of potentiality is an obstacle to freedom rather than a cause of freedom.

Let us raise the question: is deliberation necessary to the indifference of the judgment? The question has two aspects: (a) Deliberation is a way to achieve the perception of the discrepancy between the particular good and the comprehensive good. The thing necessary for the indifference of the judgment is this advertence. If advertence, which plainly can be achieved through deliberation, can also be achieved through some other method, then deliberation is not necessary to the indifference of the judgment, and an indeliberate action can be free. (b) The need for deliberation, whenever actually experienced, is traceable to potentiality in the human mind and will.

In the first chapter of this treatise we recalled that the idea of freedom is commonly accompanied by images of disorder. Then we tried to show that the principle of freedom resides in the necessary constitution of the will, and that freedom results from a state of superdetermination, not from a lack of determination. We have been removing indefatigably the images which lump together freedom and chance, freedom and non-rationality, freedom and disorder, freedom and ontological deficiency. But why should such images be so obstinate that it should be necessary to remove them again and again? Why is it that so many authors, not all of whom are insignificant, express themselves about freedom in terms of contingency, of indetermination, of doubt, of hesitancy and wavering, as if it were conceivable that the principle of freedom should reside in the weakness, the deficiency, the inachievement of the will, as if it were conceivable that the free determination should be less than the unique determination? The time has come to consider the background of such general and stubborn illusions, the aspect of truth which causes these errors to look plausible and attractive.

Freedom of choice properly consists in the indifference of practical judgment. Now, there are two kinds of indifference, which are opposed in many respects, and yet are connected by the thin thread of an analogous resemblance which warrants the use of a common term in spite of a danger of confusion. One indifference results from abundance and another from deficiency. There is the indifference of the rich man, who feels sure that he will not lack anything, and that of the poor fellow, for whom all is good, because he has nothing; that of the strong, who feels invulnerable, and that of the weak, who feels incapable of any resistance. There is the indifference of things which are hard, which force their way through any environment without damage, and there is the indifference of things which are soft, which change form at every contact and take on all imprints. One indifference consists in a power to produce a multiplicity of effects, and the other indifference consists in an ability to receive a multiplicity of influences. One kind of indifference is grounded in the accomplishment of being—its perfection, the integrality of its determination, its actuality, and its activity. The other kind of indifference is grounded in the incompleteness of being—its imperfection, its indetermination, its passivity, its potentiality. Briefly: there is such a thing as an active indifference, and there is such a thing as a passive indifference. The amount of passive indifference is inversely proportional to the ontological level of the thing. It reaches its maximum in prime matter—in matter in an absolute sense—which of itself is "neither substance nor quantity nor quality...," which is ready for any form because of itself it is formless. Active indifference reaches its maximum in the will. Freedom is a distinguished case of active indifference.

Cognitive powers are actively indifferent inasmuch as they are able to exercise, within the limits of their distinctive object, acts of an indefinite qualitative diversity. Thus, sight reacts to the unceasing changes of the sensorial environment by sensations which always are, in some degree, things new and unprecedented. But with regard to the very attraction of the act to be accomplished, cognitive powers do not enjoy any indifference; they undergo in necessary fashion the desirability of their own acts. I cannot not see when it is clear and my eyes are open.

But the will, at the term of deliberation, is able to will and not to will. Its privilege among the actively indifferent causes consists in the domination that it exercises over the attractive power of its own operations: ultimately the attractiveness of the will's operations, as well as the attractiveness of their object, comes from the will itself. Freedom is not only active indifference: it is dominating indifference.

Yet, not all is determination, actuality, activity, energy, and power in the will of man. Opposite the active and dominating indifference which results from its necessary determination and constitutes its freedom, our will contains a passive indifference which results from its weakness, from its relative indetermination, from the aspect of potentiality that its nature implies. This passive indifference is an obstacle to freedom, but by reason of the analogical connection mentioned in the foregoing, there is here a deceptive resemblance between the power which is supposed to overcome the obstacle and the obstacle that the power is supposed to overcome. By dominating indifference the human will is an image of God; by passive indifference it is rather an image of prime matter. Aquinas mentions a philosopher who "most foolishly" thought that God was the prime matter. Without going so far many people handle analogical intellection so clumsily that they confuse free choice with the passive indifference of the will.

Yet, in order to remove the danger of such a confusion, it suffices to think of what the predominance of passive indifference means in terms of concrete psychology. Passive indifference is to the will what doubt is to the intellect, and just as firm judgment implies the elimination of doubt by knowledge, so every decision implies that passive indifference is defeated by active indifference. If passive indifference resists, the will remains in a state of suspense. The passive indifference of the will is known to all under the familiar names of irresolution, perplexity and indecision. In Hamlet, thought is constantly busy feeding the resistance of irresolution. Morbidly maintained and expanded, passive indifference kills action and kills freedom. The prodigal child of André Gide, who on his return to the house of his father regrets the good time when he shared the food of the pigs, would have few admirers if his speeches did not appeal to a tendency secretly present in the heart of all men. As a result of the analogy which connects, in spite of all contrasts, the two kinds of indifference, the charms of indetermination are often mistaken for those of freedom. As soon as man yields to the lure of decadence, he is tempted to substitute the delectations of a state of availability for the strong but costly joys of the mastery of one's self. In the heroes and the saints the sense for freedom is accompanied by a sense of the unique worth of irrevocable decisions. The literary characters who seek mobility in order to avoid decisions do almost exactly the contrary of what the heroes and saints do. They would be without prestige and without imitators if the cultivation of passive indifference did not procure a cheap substitute of freedom to intellectuals who no longer have the sense of freedom.

To sum up: the discursive act of deliberation is the form commonly assumed by the perception of the discrepancy between the particular good and the comprehensive good. Yet the necessity of deliberation, precisely considered as a discursive act, does not pertain to the essential causes of freedom. Consequently it is impossible to say that freedom never exists in any degree without deliberation. It can be said, indeed, that there is no human freedom without deliberation if, and only if, it is established that deliberation is the method that advertence necessarily assumes in man. An indeliberate practical judgment is capable of indifference if and insofar as it is possible to perceive without deliberation the relation of the particular good to the absolute good. Under ordinary circumstances such a perception is not possible, or if it is possible it is too incomplete to bring about a fully indifferent judgment and a fully free act.

With this specification, it must be said that the conditions of the indifferent judgment are not realized at the starting point of the voluntary process. The indifferent judgment is preceded by a determinate judgment, and an attraction which is merely undergone precedes the attraction which is freely chosen.

The reading of a scientific book has brought forth to my mind the consideration that it would be good to study a certain theory, and through that theory to know a certain truth. This consideration has given birth to a desire. Then and only then do indifferent judgment and free choice become possible. This particular desire is infinitely far from coinciding with the only desire that I experience unconditionally, viz., that of a good which exhausts the universality of the good: already, the practical judgment, which initially was determinate, is suspended by a contrary practical judgment. Deliberation has begun. The disadvantages of the undertaking appear. A thorough study of this theory will take much time, at the expense of my other studies, of my business and of my pleasures; it will demand much night work at the expense of my health; it will make it necessary for me to do some reading for which I am poorly prepared, and so on. The initial desire will be confirmed and followed by execution only if it stands the test of the period of indifference. True, it is easy to consider a great number of cases in which no phase of indifference takes place, in which the desire does not undergo any test, in which the execution follows immediately the determinate judgment and the determinate desire. This is what happens whenever some factor prevents the construction of a judgment opposed to the initial judgment and renders deliberation impossible. This inhibiting factor may be the lack of time, as it happens when a sudden danger makes it necessary to define our conduct in a split second; it may also be a haunting image or an exclusive passion, as it happens in some mentally diseased people and in many people whose health is excellent.

Thus, the broad genus of the acts devoid of freedom, or at least not capable of unqualified freedom, comprises, besides the operations in which the reason plays no part, the initial acts of the will and all the subsequent developments thereof if any lasting obstacle prevents the judgment from having complete access to the state of indifference. Among the inhibiting forces which oppose the indifference of the judgment, the best known pertain to the pathology of the nervous system.[4] The theorist of free choice may have failed to recognize the significance of sociological factors. There are some ways of being bound by the social whole and in the social whole—in other words, some forms of sociability—which give the group such a power over the nonrational faculties that a practical judgment contrary to the collective imperatives becomes physically impossible: a host of images and emotions keeps a watch on the threshold of consciousness in order to prevent the construction of such a judgment. The dream of every tyranny is to systematize this form of sociability and to establish in the soul of everyone a praetorian guard over nonrational forces in order to assure the safety of the regime and its smooth operation by destroying the deep center of all freedom, viz., the indifference of the practical judgment.

Notes

1. [Editor's Note: The texts are substantially based, but somewhat expanded, on those the contributor selected. Occasionally, a text he had selected was removed, to avoid overlap with the text selection of other contributors. The contributor's death prevented his being able to approve of the changes finally required.]

2. [Editor's Note: Simon explains his use of "nonvoluntary" in the original French version of this work, in *Traité du libre arbitre* (Paris: Librarie Philosophique Jules Vrin, 1952), 75; it is so named "because it is more radical than any voluntary act" (elle est plus radical qu'aucun acte volontaire). Thus, we might say this act is more voluntary, rather than less so, "super-voluntary" rather than "in-voluntary." He has just described this "adherence" in our chapter here referred to: "Adherence to the comprehensive good intuitively and intelligently grasped is the most voluntary, the least constrained, the least coerced, the most spontaneous of all action. Yet this supremely voluntary action involves no choice and accordingly no freedom" (27).]

3. Georges Dwelshauvers, *Traité de psychologie*, second edition (Paris: Payot, 1934), pp. 274–275.

4. The exploration of subconscious and unconscious motivations, pursued with so much success by psychologists of the twentieth century, has cast a doubt in many minds on the reality of free will, or at least on the frequency of free acts. I am conscious of having freely chosen a certain line of conduct for a certain reason. But a day arrives when analysis reveals that the reason avowed by consciousness did not have any influence on my choice; my true reason was altogether different. Drawn by motives of which we are not conscious, are we then free? It seems that the discussion of this very important and good question could be organized by the following principles:

(a) An authentic process does not lose any authenticity just because it may be imitated. To use the famous example of Bergson's, a fool may pretend that he is Napoleon. Napoleon pretended the same thing. Their declarations do not have precisely the same value, but the fact that the authentic process can be imitated can always pose problems of identification, sometimes difficult and sometimes impossible to solve. We know with surety that such a sick person, who believes himself to be Napoleon, is not; we are very much less categorical when it is a question of persons in whom one believes to recognize the son of Louis XVI or Czar Alexander. These risks of uncertainty are inseparable from our destiny as intelligent beings constrained to seek nourishment in a world of contingency.

(b) There is no doubt that in the ideally perfect exercise of free will the motivation would be entirely conscious. It can hardly be contested that without perfect coincidence between the motive of which I am conscious and the motive which really is effective, liberty is lessened somewhat. It does not follow at all that it is abolished. The plurality of motives and the indefinite multiplicity of degrees of consciousness make it necessary to conceive of a vast zone of actions of which all one can say is that they are free to a certain degree and that they would be more so if, all other things being equal, their true motives had been more clearly conscious.

(c) Must we then say that in the extreme cases the unconscious motive suppresses freedom? Without doubt. Such would seem to be the case of the man who executes a post-hypnotic suggestion: he finds good reasons for his actions and is totally ignorant that the true reason is the influence to which he is subject without apparently having any consciousness of it. It is possible that here the consciousness of freedom might be totally illusory. Similar phenomena can be observed in dreams.

(d) The frequency of fully free acts is a subject that is bound to remain mysterious until the end of time. We have only very imperfect means for knowing our own life of freedom. We know even much less well the life of others. This situation entails difficulties in the life of society, especially in the administration of justice, which man must, without letup, work to surmount. The sciences and the humanities could render great services to justice by improving our means of understanding the concrete life of freedom. On the other hand we should note that in a great number of circumstances, and in many respects, it is not important, it is not even desirable, that I know my life of freedom or that of my brother: it suffices that these things are known to God.

(e) Finally, against the deterministic prejudices, which the popularization of the psychological sciences spreads actively among our contemporaries, it is well to recall that the clarity of our consciousness and the risk of being deprived—whether a little or a lot—of our freedom by unconscious forces are matters subject, in considerable measure, to our free decisions. There are bad habits and vices which favor ignorance of what happens within us. And there are virtues which make it happen that souls can clearly see into themselves, and there are sciences which, when well understood, place into the hands of these virtues instruments that are more and more effective.

CHAPTER 11

Good Use and *Habitus*

In this very enlightening discussion, Simon examines Aristotle's definition of virtue, "a stable state of character concerned with choice." The issue of use arises as he questions some of the modern substitutes for virtue, such as psychotherapy. He argues that, given that psychotherapy may be very helpful in many situations, its limitations rest with its inability to address meaningfully the problem of "good *human* use." What he means is that psychotherapy largely leaves the evaluation of right and wrong out of the picture. So, though psychotherapy may in fact help a person overcome a phobia or an addiction, it may not promote virtue.

To make this point clear he distinguishes three components of the concept of good "use." First is the good use of the thing itself, where its own nature is important. Second is the thing in its "particular use" by an agent. Third is the thing in its "human or moral use." A piano can be in itself good or bad according to its ability to fulfill its function and that, to some extent, influences the possibilities of its good and/or bad use. The piano can be played well or badly by a particular agent. Finally, that playing, either good or bad, can have moral implications, for example, someone playing loudly in the middle of the night, disturbing the neighbors.

He next examines the relationship between the nature of a thing and its good or bad moral or human use. In general, it seems there is no clear connection between the good nature of a thing and its good use. A good thing can be used both well and badly. However, the bad condition of a thing may tend it toward bad use, for example, bad brakes on a car. This suggests that things in bad condition may lead to bad human use because they place people at risk for harm.

Next he moves to the relation between the natural condition of various powers of the human soul. Memory, he argues, seems to be neutral in regard to its use. A good memory can be used badly to remember insults and slights; a bad memory can be used well to remember accomplishments and compliments. Weakness of will and diseased emotions are quite different, however. He argues that a weak will simply cannot support dependable virtuous action. The problem, then, would be to try to repair it. Here, psychotherapy may help one develop a stronger will, still open to misuse. However, the *possibility* of good moral use is at least open.

Diseased emotions, such as a "murderous tendency" can, of course, never be used well. The best one can hope for is the ability, which includes strength of will, to control them. He suggests that a "lofty moral situation" is where a person has experienced such control. Note that this person would not be Aristotle's virtuous man, who has no such bad tendencies, but rather is the "morally strong" man, who overcomes such tendencies (*Nicomachean Ethics*, bk. 7, 1146a15). Simon ends this discussion by arguing that "right human use" of things tends toward an improvement of their natural condition and misuse or disuse tends toward a destruction of that natural condition. Thus, good human use of one's memory or one's tendency to charitable actions tends to strengthen such tendencies, whereas a failure to develop one's memory or to exercise one's intellect tends toward its dissolution.

Concluding his discussion of psychotherapy as a substitute for virtue, and armed with the ideas developed in his discussion of good human use, Simon turns to a discussion of the kind of steady disposition of character that is the necessary ground of virtue. We often think of this as a "habit" of acting that allows one to be characterized as "virtuous." The use of the term "habit" here, however, is misleading. Simon sees three important characteristics of a habit. Habit (1) is a disposition to act in a certain way, (2) is developed by repetition, (3) whose necessity is subjective. That is, it arises from within the nature of the habituated being. The tendency to take the same route to school arises from within one's human tendencies in a similar way as the tendency of a rope long coiled to return to its coiled position arises from within its nature.

The steady disposition of character to act virtuously is quite different! This difference is so important to our understanding of virtue that Simon argues it is necessary to resist any temptation to translate the Latin word *habitus* with the word "habit." Thus, he uses the term *habitus* to speak of this particular type of steady disposition to act. What makes *habitus* different is that it is *objectively*, rather than subjectively, determined. Actions from *habitus* are the result of the good human use of a kind of habit, such that we are dependably ready to act thoughtfully and voluntarily to achieve a good human goal. Acts arising from *habitus* are thoughtfully and freely chosen precisely because they will help achieve a virtuous goal. Simon argues that although actions that arise from habit are never completely free from thought and volition, they are often significantly thoughtless and not what we might have wished. Thus, the habit of taking the same route each day is such that on occasion after turning onto one of the streets along our normal route as we head for the bank, we may "end up" at school because we were "lost" in thought. Habits lead to repeated, somewhat thoughtless, somewhat involuntary actions.

The stable disposition of character found in virtue is precisely not involuntary, but rather is the result of repeated, carefully chosen, thoughtful actions that were designed to achieve the goal of good personal action. This disposition to act is never very far from immediate thoughtful direction guided by its objective goal, good *human* action. For example, when we desire to drive safely, we develop a variety of specific techniques to support that goal. That goal of safe driving and our thoughtful attention to it are never far from any particular act of driving. We may be thinking about other things, but the presence of children in an unfenced yard playing ball will be enough to bring us to immediate full attention and action that lessens the possibility of disaster. Such stable disposition to act is freely chosen and fully voluntary and is objective, since it is rationally directed to good human action. This goal of good human action is objective from both an ontological and an epistemological point of view. Much of what is good for individual persons is directed to their *human* nature and the presence of that good is open to verification by others. *Habitus*, then, is the good human use of our natural tendency toward habitual action.

Catherine Green

The Definition of Moral Virtue
(Nature and Use: 19–29, and *Habitus*: 55–61)

Nature and Use

To elaborate on this distinction, let us again proceed by way of examples and common understanding of experience. And because our inquiry cannot do without it, I propose that we consider first of all the notion of "use." Consulting the dictionary, we find the following meanings for the verb "to use": to employ for some purpose, put into service, make use of, to avail oneself of, to practice habitually or customarily. Correspondingly, the meaning of the noun "use" is: act of employing or using, or putting into service, e.g., *the use of tools*; state of being employed or used, e.g., *this book is in use*; an instance or way of employing or using something, e.g., *each successive use of the tool*. It is all rather plain. But for our purposes we need to go a little deeper in order to bring out several tacit assumptions behind these common meanings of the notion of "use."

For instance, we all take it for granted that a thing—any thing—in the power of an agent does not have to be always in use. And from this it follows that there are actually three distinct components of the concept of "use." First, there is this thing that can play a role in an operation; second, that thing is understood to be in the power of an agent; and third, there is this thing actually playing a role in an operation. Notice that I am using, quite deliberately, the most indetermined expression available in this context, namely, "a role." The thing we are talking about may play this role in the capacity of a formal cause, or in the capacity of an instrument. We leave that open, for we are here interested in the broadest definition of use on which we can all agree. I suggest the following: use is the application of a thing to an operation. The special advantage of this definition is that since, clearly, such an application may or may not be successful, everyone also understands that the notion of use embraces the distinction between right and wrong use.

A very simple example would be "playing the piano," and I draw your attention to the three aspects of the case. First, of course, there is the piano itself, which can be either a good or a bad piano, say, a cheap piano well tuned, or an expensive piano out of tune, etc. This has as yet nothing to do with the use of this piano, being simply a condition of its "nature," so to speak. We say that it is a poor piano if some of its keys are missing, or if it does not sound right. It is a good piano if everything is in order, and it has an especially clear sound. Second, and assuming that ours is an excellent piano, there is the question of how well, or poorly, one can play it. For clearly "playing the piano" means "using it" in relation to the specific, particular purpose of the piano player, in which the skill of the artist is matched to the nature of the instrument. If he knows how to play well, we say he is a good piano player. We are talking about the artist's art, not his character. If he uses the piano as a piano player is supposed to, he is a good piano player. Is he also a good man? I do not know. And so we come to the third aspect of the case. First, there was the question of the condition or the "nature" of the piano; second, the question of its particular use by the artist as a piano player. But there is also a third question, in which piano playing is referred to what I shall call its human use. For instance, a great artist might play a beautiful but loud piece on his concert piano long past midnight, when his neighbors have a right to peace and quiet. This would be a clear example of a virtuoso putting a splendid instrument to a questionable human use. There is nothing wrong with his grand piano, and he plays it to perfection; but this artist is keeping people awake who want to sleep, and who have a right to rest.

In considering the notion of use, then, let us try to keep the nature of a thing, its particular use, and its human use separate. Even though these things, and especially "human use," are very hard to define formally, for the time being we shall know what we are talking about if we remember (1) that the piano may be in good or bad shape; (2) that a person may know how to play it well, or wretchedly, or not at all; and (3) that, knowing how to play the piano beautifully, a person may still make wrong human use of it. Suppose a death had occurred in the apartment next door, and the artist plays light, cheerful music all night long. This would be a bad human use of a good instrument of which the man knows how to make good particular use.

Plato never tired of stressing this contrast—between being good at a particular skill and being good absolutely speaking as a human being (see *Apology* 22D, *Euthydemus* 288D and *Gorgias* 448B).[1] But the difference is still not appreciated by all, and among those who do not seem to grasp it fully, we find some fine minds. For instance, Charles Sanders Peirce, reputedly the founder of American pragmatism and a truly deep thinker, seems to have actually believed that Logic is subordinate to Ethics. He did not exactly say that Logic is a branch of Ethics, but he came close to it. He said that Logic should come under the direction of Ethics, because Logic has a definite end and Ethics is the general science of ends. What do you think of that? The distinction on which Plato worked so hard is here completely ignored. Of course Logic is concerned with an end, and I feel safe in defining Logic as the art of valid and demonstrative reasoning. No doubt, that is its end, that is what it is for. Logic thus has its own specific, particular end just like any other art, and the only sense in which it could be said to be "subordinated to Ethics" is the sense in which also carpentry or piano playing could be said to be so subordinated—namely, with reference to its human, not its particular use. One can play the piano very well and at the same time do something humanly wrong, if one plays at two o'clock in the morning when other people want to sleep. Similarly, while engaged in valid demonstrative reasoning one could be doing something humanly wrong, if one continued to argue in the presence of a person desperately in need of help at that very moment. But that is the only sense in which Logic could be said to be "subordinated to Ethics."

Next let us ask whether a good condition of nature which by itself is clearly never sufficient to guarantee good use, may nevertheless favor good human use, and conversely, whether a bad condition of nature might not favor bad human use of a thing. This is an everlasting human and philosophical problem, but modern psychotherapists have, in my opinion, shed some new light on it. Moralists who expect even emotionally sick people to act always according to the rules of Ethics are wrong. Before a person can be given moral advice, he or she needs to be emotionally sound. The psycho-technicians definitely have a point here. But the whole issue is rather complicated, and we had better proceed in several steps.

The first step is to identify the four general possibilities in the use of things. Any thing in good shape can be put both to good and to bad human use, and the same holds true for things that are not in such good shape. Take, for instance, the automobile. Whether I own a new car or an old jalopy, I can still help my neighbor get where he needs to go; but I can also wreak havoc on the highway with either a new or an old car. The general possibilities are definitely four, and only fifteen years ago I would have said that that was the end of the story. Actually, it is only the beginning.

What I have come to appreciate more keenly during these years is that in some cases a thing in good condition may involve something like a tendency toward good human use, and that, conversely, a thing in poor condition may involve something like a tendency toward wrong human use of it. We can see these additional possibilities already in the use of external, material things like the automobile. A jalopy is a respectable thing as long as its brakes hold. But if its brakes are completely gone, a car, whether old or new, should not be kept in the driveway. One cannot keep it there in good conscience, because a car totally without brakes can hardly be put to any good use. Perhaps under most exceptional circumstances, in some kind of emergency, one could take a sick person to the hospital in it, driving carefully in the first gear. But under ordinary circumstances, driving a car without brakes is plainly wrong from the point of human use. That is quite significant: to use a thing in a poor condition is often humanly wrong in itself, and the four possibilities identified above may thus not be all equal. If my car has no heater, I can still make good use of it; if it does not have blinkers, I can put out my hand to indicate the turns. But if its brakes do not work, I had better not use the car. I should either have it repaired or junk it. I should not keep it in the driveway, for I might be tempted to use it, even though its use would be humanly wrong.

Turning now to the use of internal things such as the powers of the human soul, let us first consider memory. A person's memory can be excellent, it can be pitiful, and it can be anywhere in between. Can we say that a poor memory involves a tendency to make wrong human use of it? I would not say so. I think we have here a thing quite neutral with regard to its human use. I can use my poor memory to remember all the unpleasant things my neighbor did to me and remain resentful for the rest of my life, which certainly is not a very good human use of memory. But I can do the same with a good memory too. Conversely, whether my memory is poor or good, I can always try to remember birthdays, anniversaries, and such, which makes people so happy. The condition of one's memory thus seems to be neutral with regard to its human uses. But what about the will power, another internal power of the human soul? Most psychiatrists and psychologists as well as moralists firmly hold that a will is naturally in good shape if it is strong and in poor shape if it is weak. The moralists moreover recognize also the difference between a strong and a good will. For there are, unfortunately, many strong-willed people who are not good at all. We can think of any number of historical or contemporary examples of people who in their public careers have given definite proof of their extraordinary will power, but who have put this will power to literally criminal use. In fact, most really famous criminals seem to be endowed with powerful wills. Does this mean that having a strong will necessarily involves a tendency to make bad use of it? Of course not. On the contrary, it is the opposite which is the worrisome case. For example, a time comes when a man becomes conscious of himself and of his destiny (this may occur around fifteen years of age at the earliest, with no upper limit), and he realizes that he has a weak will. Well, from a moral point of view, that is a serious handicap, because a weak will cannot really support virtuous, dependable conduct. A weak will is somewhat like a car without brakes, except that the urgency of having it repaired is far greater. One simply cannot avoid making use of whatever will one has, and if it is weak—if the brakes do not work, as it were—all sorts of accidents become exceedingly probable.

Finally, in addition to such things as memory and will power, we need to consider also the tendencies which make up our emotional life. Among the powers of the soul, they may well be the most interesting in the present context. We all know that even perfectly normal tendencies—say, ambition to excel, enjoyment of pleasure, sex drive, or high spirits—all need to be disciplined to make sure that they will serve only good ends. What, then, can we say about abnormal tendencies? I do not mean just idiosyncratic preferences, "kinky" or "weird" impulses, but definitely abnormal, destructive tendencies—say, obsession with dominating people, or literally murderous sexual desires. Clearly, what we have here is something of which no good human use can be made. In fact, these things are far worse than a car whose brakes do not work. For not only could I, under exceptional circumstances, put such a car to some good use; I can also leave it alone. By contrast, even though incapable of good human use a diseased emotion also refuses to stay quiet. Being a tendency, it demands, it insists on realization, on being satisfied. And that is why, in the theory of virtues, this is the decisive case. When it comes to emotional tendencies, their condition can never be neutral with regard to their use. To make good human use of emotions, they must be sound. Nevertheless, we may still distinguish two kinds of cases. A destructive emotional tendency may be of such intensity as to suspend completely any rational control. Then we have a case for the asylum; the poor fellow cannot be punished for what he has done, because he is not responsible. He has to be put away for his own protection as well as the protection of society. I do not know just how numerous such cases of absolutely irresistible destructive tendencies are, and I do not think that the available statistics of populations in state hospitals are necessarily indicative of their incidence. It is not easy to tell who is completely insane. But assuming that the destructive tendency is truly beyond a person's control, it is best to leave the case entirely with psychiatric experts.

The other kind of case is, I believe, more frequent. Though the destructive tendency may have its origin outside a person's will, its intensity may not be such as to suspend all rational control. And if that control is successfully exercised, we have a case of a lofty moral situation. Think of a person who has lived, say, fifty years without ever indulging a tendency of which no right human use can be made. More than likely, controlling that tendency involved a great deal of effort and brought that person considerable suffering. Therefore, if such tendencies could be eradicated once and for all by psychological techniques, that would be immensely desirable. But that is not always possible, and we have to realize that there are people who have to spend their lives fighting against all sorts of tendencies which simply do not admit of any good human use. Each of us probably knows several such people, whose secret we do not even suspect, because having succeeded in repressing their urges through the efforts of an enlightened strong will, they lead entirely normal personal and social lives.

The complex relationship between "nature" and "use" reviewed above may, then, be summed up as follows. First of all, we understand that we can make either good or bad use of certain things, like our car or our memory, regardless of their own condition. But secondly, we have also seen that a poor natural condition of a thing may sometimes result in its wrong human use. Thus one should not drive a car whose brakes are gone, and if one happens to have a weak will, one definitely should do something about it. And finally, we have also established that as far as emotional tendencies are concerned, their healthy condition is an absolute prerequisite for good human use. Diseased emotions simply do not admit of good human use; we are lucky when they can be controlled.

Keeping all this in mind, let us now ask another question of decisive importance for any theory of ethics. Does the tendency toward right human use involve a tendency toward improvement of the natural condition of the things we use? To explore this interesting question, it is perhaps best to start with what seems neutral as regards its human use, for instance, our memory. Suppose a man has poor memory for names, like myself. I am better now, but for a while it was really terrible. I antagonized many good people, because I could never remember their names. For a philosopher and a teacher, that is very annoying. But it is the same for men of action, say, a business leader or an army officer; not to be able to remember names is for them, too, a crushing defect. Therefore, I suspect that in all such cases a sincere desire for its good human use is quite likely to elicit an effort to improve the natural condition of one's memory.

Here again "phycho-technology" [*sic*: psycho-] may be very helpful, for there are fairly reliable methods of learning how to remember names—and match them to faces, which is the really difficult part. At the time of William James, about three quarters of a century ago, there was a great controversy among psychologists as to whether or not memory could be improved. James held that it could not. But he conceded that methods of learning could be improved, which in a way amounts to the same thing, especially for a pragmatist.[2] At any rate, if you have a poor memory, and you are in a social position in which it is important to remember names—you are a dedicated kindergarten teacher, industrial leader, or naval officer—and if you want to do the right thing, you would definitely want to improve your memory.

The importance of this example can hardly be overstated. In the beginning, we established that the good in human use and the good in natural conditions of things are two totally separate cases. But now we see that they are not so completely unrelated, which has all sorts of wide-reaching implications. For instance, we often meet people who tell us that they have no gift for public speaking, or for writing, especially for letter writing, and so on. To me it sometimes sounds as if these people are bragging about their limitations. Do not ask me to do things I simply cannot do! they say. But perhaps they could, if they tried harder. And it seems to me that they would do so, if the tendency toward the right use of whatever abilities they have is strong enough.

Think of a person to whom writing letters is nothing short of an ordeal and of another person who loves to write pages upon pages that, even though not always dealing with important things, are pleasant to read. In both cases, the disposition involved is most likely natural (even though we suspect that in the latter case it is strengthened by long practice). Moreover, if the reluctant letter-writer is forty years old or older, he is probably set in his ways, and we cannot realistically expect him to change. Still, there are letters that need to be written, not only about one's business affairs (which are important from an ethical point of view too), but also to people who are sick, disturbed, lonely, unhappy, in mourning, etc., and a person who is fully aware of such human needs should be able to overcome his letter-writer's cramp.

Notice how this brings us right back to Plato's distinction between a good man and a good carpenter, albeit in a slightly different perspective. We now suspect that a disposition toward right human use may well encourage improvement in the conditions of things we *use*. Does that mean that a disposition toward wrong human use may lead to their deterioration?

In my experience as an educator, I have seen the following problem come up fairly regularly. Here is a young man of average intelligence but extremely strong good will; and here is another young man of unquestionable brilliance but with a considerably weaker, somewhat disorderly will. The immediate practical question between them may be the last available fellowship, but this is clearly tied to a deeper issue, namely, which one can be expected eventually to do better in his chosen field? On the basis of my own observations, I am inclined to favor the young man with the strong will over the one with the brilliant mind, which may well be his by accident, so to speak. A brilliant mind at the mercy of an unstable will is something rather disquieting; the average intelligence supported by a disciplined will seems to me much more promising.

While these things are, of course, hard to ascertain, I do know a few people who used to be intelligent, but who have made themselves idiotic—at least in my opinion—just by bad human use of their intelligence. And their examples go for me a long way in clarifying the relation between human use of things and their natural condition. Do you see what the connection is? Let us take a hypothetical case of two philosophy students, to illustrate it. The smarter but less disciplined one is easily tempted to do a few things in philosophy to show off, to satisfy his pride, to prove that he is indeed brilliant. In doing this, he is clearly not putting his excellent mind to the best *human* use. But notice also that he is not making proper *particular* use of philosophy either. The specific purpose of philosophy, its proper end, is definitely not to satisfy one's craving for applause. And by using it wrongly in this technical sense, the poor fellow may well end by making a fool of himself professionally. By contrast, the other student possessing average intelligence but plenty of good will can be expected, to begin with, to be more inclined to trust his teachers, which is very important in philosophy. There are mathematicians of genius at sixteen; but philosophers of genius below the age of forty are extremely rare. In philosophy, being able to do things entirely on one's own takes a long time and remains forever difficult. Thus simply by remaining teachable, this second student is more likely to become professionally competent and, eventually, perhaps, not such a bad teacher of philosophy himself.

What, then, is the connecting link between the tendency to good human use and the improvement of the conditions of things we use? It is nothing else than their specific, technical, particular use. Rebellious rejection of fundamental rules of doing things, be that driving a car or studying philosophy, may well lead to the deterioration of the "natural" conditions of the things used, be that a person's intelligence or his car. By contrast, deliberate acceptance of proper particular use of things, supported by a strong tendency toward good human use, may well lead to their improvement, especially when these "things" happen to be the internal powers of the human soul. If there is a secret at the bottom of the question about the relation between "nature" and "use," in my opinion, this is it.

My reservations about "psycho-technology" should also be clearer now. Its main fault is that it tends to ignore the notion of use, which is crucial in any realistic understanding of human dependability. Again, modern psychology has made great strides both in treating diseased emotions and in assertive training, that is, in methods for strengthening the will. Yet over and above what psychology can do for the powers of the soul, there looms the vast world of human action proper, consisting of the human use of these powers, for whose problems psychology has no answers....

HABITUS

Our first problem here is clearly one of vocabulary. While the lack of just the right word, accepted in common usage, has cramped philosophical progress often enough, the case of *habitus* may well be one of the most interesting in all the history of philosophy. For the last thirty years or so, I have tried to do something about it, and I keep trying, because *habitus* is a very important philosophical term. The notion it stands for is useful in several philosophical contexts and absolutely indispensable in a realistic theory of ethics....

It is the conventional translation of the Latin *habitus* as "habit," however, that creates the worse problem. For if instead of "state of character" Aristotle's four moral virtues—temperance, fortitude, justice, and prudence—are called "habits," his whole theory of ethics quickly dissolves into nonsense. I feel rather strongly about this, and some years ago I really had it out with a fellow member of the academy. I had reviewed for a popular journal *The Basic Writings of Thomas Aquinas*, newly edited by Anton C. Pegis, then President of the Pontifical Institute of Mediaeval Studies of Toronto [*Commonweal* 42, no. 13 (1945): 313–14]. I welcomed the publication of the volume, and I praised its selections and their organization. But I did point out also that, throughout the text, *habitus* was consistently and wrongly translated by "habit." And so, Professor Pegis and I became involved in a protracted correspondence, which gradually became less and less polite. As I remember it, toward the end he accused me of being ignorant of the history of philosophy, but probably only after I had suggested that by insisting on "habit" as an acceptable translation of *habitus*, he proved that he did not quite understand St. Thomas. Then we simply stopped writing. But a few weeks later, something happened that led to our final exchange. A student in one of my courses, who had been reading the *Basic Writings* put it to me as follows: "An act done out of habit is involuntary, isn't it?" To which I replied: "Yes, sure, insofar as it is done out of habit. It may not be done purely out of habit. But if it is done purely out of habit, I don't see how it could be otherwise." And then came her next decisive question: "Virtue is a habit, is it not?" I did not know whether to laugh or to cry, jump for joy or faint. But as soon as I got back to my office, I took pen in hand and wrote Professor Pegis another letter. "The matter between us," I wrote, "is now settled." Then I told him exactly what this unusually intelligent student had asked me after reading the assigned texts. *Habitus* translated by "habit," I said again, forces readers to conclude that for Aquinas acts proceeding from virtues are done involuntarily, which is totally absurd. I really did not expect a reply, but I got one. And what is more, Professor Pegis finally conceded that, if there was a valid objection to translating *habitus* by "habit," that was exactly it, namely, that it makes the reader wonder whether a virtuous act might not, after all, be involuntary.

To me this objection is decisive, because for Aquinas as well as for Aristotle moral virtues are paragons of voluntariness, and thus the very opposite of habits. But there are other objections to translating *habitus* by "habit." In the Aristotelian-Thomistic tradition we also have four so-called "intellectual virtues," understanding, art, science, and philosophical wisdom, which are neither states of character nor habits. In

Latin, they are called *habitus*. But if we call them habit in English, we cannot even get close to explaining their nature. I thought about this problem for a long time, and this is what I finally came up with. Since there is no modern name for these qualities, discarded in the philosophical revolutions of the seventeenth century, I have decided that the best thing to do is to adopt habitus in the vernacular and explain its meaning as needed. . . .

Now to explain here what habitus is, we may begin by contrasting its main features with those of our habits. Thus while both may be described as stable dispositions established through repetition of acts, with regard to necessity no two things could be more different. As we have seen, the necessity present in our habits is strictly subjective necessity. Moreover, for Hume and James, among others, that is all there is even in the seemingly most certain of our cognitions and reasoning about the world. Of course, one wonders about that, because if scientific knowledge is nothing but a collection of mental habits, it is not so easy to explain the historical development of science and especially its great breakthroughs. Are not habits notoriously hard to change? Yet modern science takes great pride in its virtually continuous development. Besides, how many modern scientists as they go about their business in biology, chemistry, physics, or astronomy really believe that they are just cultivating mental habits? Today's scientists may be reluctant to philosophize about "reality," but they are far less alienated from the living world than some modern philosophers of science.[3] The practicing scientists may hedge about some ultimate meaning of "objectivity," but they are not so eager to concede that their knowledge, in whatever field, is only intersubjective, let alone strictly personal. Thus one may say that, whether they know it or not, most of them tend to think of their science as a habitus, that is, a quality or disposition which, in contrast to habit, is grounded in objective necessity.

This may perhaps best be illustrated by the example of mathematics, which serves today perhaps even more than in Plato's time as the model for all intellectual disciplines. Now, it is true that in view of the fantastic developments in the last hundred years or so, mathematicians no longer seem sure what mathematics is all about. Legendre's supreme confidence inspired by the vision of the Euclidean system as perfect and complete is gone forever. But that does not mean that modern mathematicians, even as they roam their imaginary worlds of many dimensions, no longer recognize objective necessity in their science. For instance, I have heard the famous mathematician André Weil suggest that in view of their great proliferation, mathematical theories should perhaps be evaluated from now on by aesthetic standards. For him, a mathematical theory to be interesting not only must be free from contradiction but must also "look good." Thus not all non-Euclidean geometries are equally acceptable, because some are much more elegant than others. And therefore, Weil said, what the mathematicians perhaps need most now is a strong sense of beauty. I think that an excellent idea, because any intellectual discipline is bound to be enriched by such consideration. But what is equally important is that Weil, despite his subjectivist overtones, leaves no doubt that he takes mathematics to be a habitus grounded in objective necessity. If there was no necessity in it, could mathematics be beautiful? Plato did not think so, and I suspect neither do modern mathematicians.[4]

Being grounded in objective necessity, however, is not the only way in which we can tell habitus from habit. What we may call their operations are also quite different. For while, as we have seen, even as they serve specific ends, habits operate automatically or mechanically, the operation of habitus is characterized by unmistakable vitality. Habit relieves us of the need to think; but habitus makes us think creatively. Among many examples, the following seems especially fitting. As students, we have all known two types of teachers, the pedantic and the inspiring. The former have a definite method and operate according to well-established habits; the latter need neither, because they know their subject through and through. Indeed, we may say that teaching methods, which generate subjective habits, are but poor substitutes for the kind of objective intimacy with the subject matter to be taught, which we call habitus. Now, it is true that teachers relying on their habitus rather than a given method are not always easy to follow. They tend to experiment with unrefined concepts, they use metaphors, and they even jump to conclusions; their thought seems forever to run ahead of their power of expression and demonstration. But at least the better students seldom mind, because such teaching is an invitation to master, not just a procedure, but a subject. Compared to habit, habitus represents thought that is truly alive. As Weil's favorite mathematician,

David Hilbert, explained it, "A branch of science is full of life only as long as it offers an abundance of problems" [ibid., 306]. To ask the right kind of questions is as much part of creative work in science as to find answers to them. And if, as Hilbert holds, "the indissoluble union of the parts is a necessary condition" for the vitality of mathematics, we can say again that mastering a science means grasping the objective necessity in its object. He who has attained that grasp possesses habitus: *he has it*.

As some notorious cases show, however, this does not mean that we can never mistake a mental habit for a habitus. For instance, how long had people believed that the earth was flat? How long did they believe that the earth was at the center of the universe, and that the sun revolved around the earth? Things seem to be that way, and there is nothing like daily experience to turn appearances into most stubborn mental habits! I am sure you remember having some difficulty as a child trying to imagine the people in the southern hemisphere walking around upside down. But notice that for reasons that are very practical, architects and builders continue to this day to treat the earth as flat by assuming that all verticals are parallel. The case of the belief that the sun moves around the earth is not much different. Not only had people observed the sun move daily across the sky for eons on end, but they had also eventually found in the Ptolemaic system a fairly rational explanation for such phenomena as seasons and eclipses. The acceptance of the Copernican system thus required breaking some truly formidable mental habits. In fact, I suspect that Galileo's theory was condemned by ecclesiastical authorities as much for challenging what appeared as uncontrovertible empirical evidence as for allegedly challenging the teaching of the Scriptures. As the record shows, Galileo could have avoided his famous trial had he been willing to concede that his theory was of the kind that "saved the appearances," that is, accounted for the phenomena without claiming to be really, objectively true. But that is not what Galileo thought of his theory, and he did not want to buy peace at that price. His theory, Galileo was convinced, did not just explain the appearances; it explained real relations between the sun and the planets. In other words, when he muttered "Eppur si muove," Galileo struck a blow against one of the most stubborn habits of the human mind in favor of science conceived as habitus.

Notes

1. [Editor's Note: This reference, as the next three, was originally in a footnote. It seems the editor of this posthumous work, Vukan Kuic, included these references because he found them in Simon's "work-up" of the text that he then published. The other three notes here, being longer, have been kept as footnotes. It seems fair to say that, of all Simon's editors, Vukan Kuic was best placed to footnote him appropriately.]

2. "*One's native retentiveness in unchangeable. It will now appear clear that all improvement of the memory lies in the line of ELABORATING THE ASSOCIATES of each of the several things to be remembered. No amount of culture would seem capable of modifying a man's GENERAL retentiveness.* This is a psychological quality, given once for all with his organization, and which he can never hope to change: (emphasis in the original)." William James, *Psychology* (New York: Harper Torchbooks, 1961), p. 163. This book was originally published by Holt in 1892.

3. Doing Descartes one better, one of them has written: "We have no conclusive evidence that there is a physical world, and we have no absolutely conclusive evidence either that we exist." Hans Reichenbach, *The Rise of Scientific Philosophy* (Berkeley: University of California Press, 1951), p. 268.

4. "It is certain," Weil writes, "that few men of our times are as completely free as the mathematicians in the exercise of their intellectual activity," and that while "others have to have recourse to the muddy streams of a sordid reality," the mathematician is assured that "the very sources of knowledge will always continue to pour forth, pure and abundant." But he also quotes with unqualified approval from a lecture given in 1900 by "the great mathematician" David Hilbert, who concluded by asserting that "mathematics is an organism for whose vital strength the indissoluble union of the parts is a necessary condition." André Weil, "The Future of Mathematics," *American Mathematical Monthly*, 57 (1950): 296, 304.

CHAPTER 12

The Definition of Moral Virtue

Ancient philosophers took for granted that the primary subject matter of ethics was virtue, its nature and variety. The central task for ethics, then, was to formulate and defend a definition of virtue. In modern ethics, it is, of course, otherwise. In early modern philosophy, virtue was displaced from the heart of ethical theory (and from the heart of the moral life itself) in favor of notions of law and consequence that have increasingly dominated modern moral philosophy. Contemporary advocates of "virtue ethics," as it has come to be called in its recent revival, thus have to argue, first, that virtue deserves a central place in ethical thought before proceeding to the traditional task of giving a definition of it. Yves R. Simon's discussion of the definition of virtue does not conform, however, completely to this pattern. His most extended discussion of the definition of moral virtue is found in his 1957 lectures at the University of Chicago on "Virtues" (*The Definition of Moral Virtue*, ed. Vukan Kuic, Fordham University Press, 1986). Although this course of lectures is a comprehensive discussion of the virtues, the question of the definition of virtue is at its heart. Simon clearly believes that the best defense of a broadly Aristotelian/Thomistic approach to ethics, which puts virtue at center stage, is to articulate clearly what virtue is and to defend the claims of the virtues, as traditionally understood, against modern substitutes for them.

Simon initiates his discussion of virtue by attending to what he argues is its "common understanding" as "unconditional dependability." The virtuous person, above all, "can be depended upon to abide by what is right regardless of circumstances." The cardinal virtues operate in different areas of our practical life and shape practical decisions in distinctive ways, but they all share the property of making their possessors unconditionally dependable in doing the right thing. For Simon, everyone must recognize the necessity of this dependability if social harmony and personal fulfillment are to be achieved. The central question for contemporary ethics is whether this dependability is to be achieved by making men virtuous or by adopting one of the modern substitutes for virtue.

Simon argues that modern philosophers have proposed and defended three distinct and culturally influential substitutes for virtue. The first, *natural spontaneity*, finds its classical statement in Rousseau and claims that dependability in acting correctly is best secured in human life by "liberating the natural goodness of man," which is achieved by insulating persons from the unhealthy influence of society. The second modern substitute for virtue, *social engineering*, takes an opposite tack in achieving dependability. Instead of liberating men from social influence, Marx, Fourier, and other advocates of the social engineering model sought to redesign the basic structure of society in order to mold agents in ways that would ensure dependable right action. Finally, Freud and other modern proponents of psychoanalysis have adopted therapeutic techniques for enforcing dependability, relying on what Simon calls the model of *psycho-technology*.

Simon is careful to recognize the partial truth to be found in these various modern substitutes for virtue, but he argues that no one of them can guarantee the kind of dependability in acting rightly that we would require of any adequate substitute for virtue. They at most produce habit, but never *habitus*.

The negative part of Simon's account of the definition of virtue is found in his rejection of the three modern substitutes for virtue; the positive component lies in his attempt to resurrect and state in modern terminology the traditional definition of moral virtue found in book 2 of Aristotle's *Nicomachean Ethics*.

For Simon, the key to articulating the notion of moral virtue for moderns is to locate it correctly with relation to habits and knowledge (i.e., Aristotelian science). He insists that we must resist the temptation to identify virtue with knowledge, as Socrates seemed to do, or with mere habit, as many moderns have. Though virtue shares many properties with habits and states of knowledge, it cannot be identified with either. In distinguishing virtue from mere habit, Simon labors mightily to resuscitate the concept of *habitus* (which he argues resists any translation into modern European languages). Whereas habits are involuntary, subjectively determined, and mechanically observed, *habitus* involves voluntary action that is objectively determined and creatively deployed. In distinguishing virtue from knowledge, he draws on a more abstract distinction between qualitative readiness (e.g., the readiness of a well-trained mathematician to solve a mathematical problem within the range of his abilities) and existential readiness (e.g., the readiness of a fully just person to perform a just act). The mathematician's qualitative readiness means he is *prepared* to solve a difficult mathematical problem, but he may choose not to do so for any number of different motives. The just man's existential readiness to perform just actions is not, however, in this way optional. Existential readiness is not a matter of mere preparation or skill, as is qualitative readiness. It requires, in addition, an unconditional motivational element. Knowledge embodies only qualitative readiness, but virtue requires both qualitative readiness and existential readiness. Hence, Socrates was wrong to identify virtue and knowledge.

Having clarified the notion of *habitus* and defended it against modern distortions, Simon finally turns to Aristotle's classic definition of moral virtue as "a state of character (*habitus*) concerned with choice, lying in a mean, i.e., the mean relative to us, this being determined by a rational principle, and by that principle by which the man of practical wisdom would determine it." His earlier discussion prepares him to accept this definition, but he notes that there is "a serious gap" in Aristotle's ethical theory in that he fails to delineate fully an appropriate set of moral axioms that would determine "what makes men good or bad." One may doubt, I believe, whether it is the job of general ethical theory, as opposed to the phronetic judgment of virtuous agents, to provide such axioms, but, even if it were, this is hardly a problem for the *definition* of moral virtue. It is at most a difficulty for the theory as a whole. Simon, as others before him, believes this "gap" is best filled with a broadly Thomistic account of natural law.

At the time in 1957 when Simon lectured so brilliantly on the definition of moral virtue, the question of virtue was not even on the agenda of mainstream academic moral philosophy. He could hardly have foreseen that within a year of his lectures Elizabeth Anscombe's enormously influential article "Modern Moral Philosophy" would initiate a revolution in moral philosophy that would return the concept of virtue to center stage. As a result of that revolution, scores of books on virtue have been published in the last few decades, but few have measured up to the interpretive richness or insightful engagement with the modern enemies of virtue of Simon's careful discussion.

W. David Solomon

The Definition of Moral Virtue
(Selections: 1, 15–16, 69–87, 91–92, 106–8, 116–19, and 127–30)

There is nothing worse from a pedagogical point of view than to begin a discourse with a ready definition unrelated to the reader's personal experience and thoughts.[1] The place to begin a discussion of a subject is always its common understanding. Now, some may think that virtue is very hard to define, while others may think that they have a definition at hand. It does not matter. What matters is that everyone recognizes the difference between people who are really dependable and those who are not. For instance, there are people who are very gracious and kind, provided all is well with them, and they feel happy. But there are also people who are gracious and kind regardless of circumstances, and regardless of whether they are happy or not. It is these people I call virtuous, because the good disposition of those others is only conditional. Think of an honest man who is honest only as long as he is not exposed to great temptations. He will not steal fifty dollars from anybody, but if he had a chance to steal fifty thousand, without much risk of being caught, he might do it. Likewise, it is not so rare for people to be truthful as long as they are free from pressure. But put under pressure, many will break their word and tell lies. Such conditional behavior is not exactly what one would call virtuous, even though it is better than nothing and quite useful in social relations. In fact, relative honesty and truthfulness may well be all that can be expected from most people most of the time. But the virtue of justice is not like that, for a just man can be depended upon to abide by what is right regardless of the circumstances. And that is also what virtue means in the common understanding, which is the first thing we need to begin our discussion. . . .

The difficulties encountered today in trying to explain the meaning of virtue, however, include also some more or less conscious attempts to deny any need for it by offering substitutes alleged to work much better. I have considered three of these, natural spontaneity, social engineering, and psycho-technology, and I have not tried to conceal my opinion that none of them, nor all of them together, would solve our problems. But that does not mean that I do not recognize how these ideas contribute to our understanding of the human condition.

Take, for instance, the Romantic invocation of native spontaneity. While its extreme advocacy may have caused some harm, both intellectual and moral, the notion itself is by no means illusory. Especially in education, or, better still, in the up-bringing of young people, reliance on spontaneity, I think, is very important. It was not Rousseau who first had this idea, it was Montaigne. In his *Essays*, Montaigne denounces the harsh teaching methods used in the sixteenth century and proposes instead that teachers engage the spontaneous, natural interest of the student. He learned Latin so well, Montaigne says, because nobody tried to force it upon him. Rousseau thinks along the same lines, as do most contemporary educators. Parents do not always like this kind of pedagogy, and once in a while we do hear some rather amusing stories about the consequences of permissive methods in progressive schools. Nevertheless, the continual revival of this approach to education over the centuries convinces me that there is something to it. Thus I definitely do not hold that reliance on "natural spontaneity" is an empty theory. I only maintain that it is not an adequate substitute for the theory of virtue.

The same goes for "social engineering." In fact, I cannot think of a social philosopher or political theorist starting with Plato who does not take it for granted that specific social institutional arrangements affect people's behavior. But again, the question here is one of the degree to which the social environment can be relied upon to shape individual characters or, as in the case of Fourier, accommodate all conceivable human tastes and tendencies. While we are definitely social beings, we are also individuals, and without conscious development of character I doubt that anyone can attain the full status of a human person.

Finally, with regard to "psycho-technology," I can truly say that I admire both its technical approach and its achievements in the treatment of emotional disturbances. But I still do not think that modern psychology has the answer to all human problems. For we all know perfectly well that a person can be in excellent health, physically and emotionally, and still do wrong, harming himself or herself as well as others. The good, healthy condition of a person's natural qualities by no means guarantees that this person will *use* these qualities in the right way. To be of sound mind and body does not mean to be also honest, reliable, charitable, truthful, courageous, just, or in a word, virtuous. And that is why I insist that, over and above what psychological techniques can do for diseased emotions and the maintenance of sound dispositions, the only way to assure human dependability is by acquisition of virtues....

We may never know exactly what Socrates meant when he concluded that virtue is a form of scientific knowledge, but the quickest way out of the confusion generated by this suggestion is to reverse his query. Is science a virtue? I suspect that even Socrates would want to deny it, precisely because scientific knowledge as such clearly does not incorporate the kind of human reliability that is expected of virtue. With science, as with art, one can do as one pleases. One may use any science, or art, against even its own particular or technical purpose. In the famous example of Aristotle, the grammarian may, if he wants to, use his knowledge of grammar to make a grammatical mistake....

To elaborate on the contrast between science and virtue, or scientific and moral habitus, I wish to draw your attention to two distinct kinds of readiness, which I shall call qualitative and existential. Both science and art embody qualitative readiness, but in virtue there is also existential readiness. For instance, don't you know someone who, in your opinion, is wasting his or her talents, whatever these may be? A scientist perhaps, or a writer, or a musician, who has not done anything worthwhile for a long time? There is no doubt in your mind that he can do it, but he is not doing it. Why? Perhaps he has become lazy; perhaps he does not care anymore; or perhaps he is rich and does not have to work to support himself. There are people like that in every walk of life, in every science, in every art. While indubitably qualified, they do not use their qualifications. They can do good research, or make beautiful music; but they may not want to do it, and their science or art cannot change that. For me, this is an example of qualitative readiness without existential readiness.

By contrast, if you have a friend distinguished by his prudence, or temperance, or courage, or sense of justice, you are not worried that he may waste his virtues. You confidently expect your friend always to do the right thing at the right time, which is also why, if you have a moral problem, he is the person to whom you will go for advice. He may not tell you exactly what to do, for only you can solve your own moral problems, but you do not have the slightest doubt that, if he tells you what he would do in your situation, he would indeed do it. This is not like the story some writer may tell about the great American novel he will write one day. A just man cannot postpone his justice. His readiness is both qualitative and existential.

Now, because I coined it myself not so long ago, this expression "existential readiness" may not be familiar to you. But the concept it stands for is both familiar and important in philosophy.... It means the same as "finality," though of course I did not invent this new name for it just to be different. Rather, I was looking for ways to get around the accumulated difficulties and confusion that the notion of finality brings to discussions between philosophers of different schools as well as to those between philosophers and scientists....

Whenever we think of finality, we inevitably think of the good. For example, when we ask about the purpose of an organ, we are in effect asking what it is good for. What is the function of the pancreas, the liver, the gall bladder? These are clearly teleological questions, related to the good of the whole body, and try as he may no biologist can here get away from at least an operational use of the concept of finality. Thus it is not by accident that those who believe that finality is not totally irrelevant to our efforts to know the world invariably support their arguments with examples from the world of the living. Yet finality may not be the exclusive property of living things, and I rather think that there is finality wherever there is movement or process. The only trouble is that we do not know and may never know what most movements and processes in nature are good for. And that is why in all such cases it makes much more sense to speak of "existential readiness" rather than "finality."

Again, the good, or goodness of a process—which is its finality—is most easily perceived in and among living things. For instance, because vital processes in our bodies continually produce substances which have the character of poisons, we could not live long without our kidneys' doing their job, performing their function, serving their purpose. There is thus no mystery about what the kidneys are good for, since the functions of the parts of a living body are all plainly related to the good of the whole organism. But trying to figure out what a certain process is good for in inanimate nature is an entirely different story.... The atom symbolized by *Ag*, for silver, and the atom symbolized by *Cl*, for chlorine, will immediately combine into a compound symbolized by *AgCl* which is white and turns black under the influence of light. You of course recognize in this process the beginning of photography.... Why is it good for them to be together? We do not know and we may never know. But that does not stop chemists from being absolutely certain that *Ag* and *Cl* are always ready, existentially ready, to make *AgCl*, which in turn cannot help changing color from white to black, when exposed to light. The real reason, then, why chemists do not want to talk about finality in chemistry may well be simply because they do not know what most chemical processes are good for. At the same time, however, it is quite clear that we could not do chemistry, or any other science for that matter, without the notion of existential readiness in things.

The principle of gravity is an excellent example of how firmly we believe in existential readiness in physical nature at all levels. We know that whether on earth or the moon or any other celestial body, unsupported objects must fall to the ground. We construct houses and send probes into space on the basis of this existential readiness of matter, even though we really do not understand its purpose. What is the good of this universal attraction? Without it, some have said the universe could not hold together. That does not sound particularly arbitrary, but I for one would not consider it to be a rigorous explanation of the principle of gravity. Would anyone believe that *Ag* and *Cl* make *AgCl* so that we may take snapshots? Thus while I remain convinced that wherever there is movement or process there is finality by metaphysical necessity, I also believe that in our common efforts to understand inanimate nature, we can do better with existential readiness. Because even the most stubborn of mechanists cannot help recognizing this readiness whenever [*sic*: wherever] they turn in nature, calling it existential readiness rather than finality may open new and fruitful exchanges among different schools of thought in both the philosophy of science and the philosophy of nature.

What is also interesting to recall in the present context is the fact that until sometime in the seventeenth century, when mechanistic interpretation of nature began to prevail, the presence of this existential readiness in things of nature was spontaneously referred to as their "virtues"....

When Kant speaks of the starry skies above and the moral law within, he wants to bring out not what they have in common but what sets them apart. By contrast, in Shakespeare no less than in Aristotle, there is continuity between the laws of nature and the laws of morality, and the "virtue" of a physical thing is so called because of perceived resemblance to moral virtue. They are both seen as instances of existential readiness, which makes for trust, confidence, dependability, reliability, and indeed predictability.

The all-important difference between "natural virtues" found in things and moral virtues is, of course, that the latter proceed not from nature directly but from voluntariness and free choice. The chemical interaction of elements is determined by their nature. But it is not simply human nature that makes a man virtuous; it is his acquired and proved human excellence. A virtuous man acts the way he does, not because he cannot help it, but rather because he wants to act that way and, moreover, he knows exactly what he is doing. The predictability of his action will thus appear to deny his freedom only to those who automatically associate free choice with indeterminism....

What kind of readiness is present in habit? ... Habit embodies both qualitative and existential readiness. Clearly, habit is qualitatively specific, as we would not expect anyone to do out of habit the opposite of what he does out of habit. But neither would we call it a habit if it was not done regularly when the proper occasion arose. On this account, then, habit is far more like virtue than like science or art, which, as we said, includes only qualitative and not existential readiness. Yet the virtue habit resembles most is not moral virtue—it is the natural virtue of Shakespeare's rocks and flowers....

We are all habituated to hit the brake when the traffic light turns red. We do not have to think about it, we do it out of habit. Yet there is a sound moral reason why we have become so habituated. Behind the wheels of our cars, we want to be not only good drivers but also responsible citizens, and this habit is an almost fail-proof instrument of our deliberate, rational decision to make the right use of our automobiles. Moreover, we do not really mind if the existential readiness of our driving habits comes to approximate that found in chemicals, stones, and herbs. In fact the more it does so the better, for this makes us both good drivers and good citizens at reduced cost, so to speak.

Thus the importance of instrumental habits in matters of morality can never, in my opinion, be overestimated. But what is equally interesting to note is that a similar situation prevails also in science. I am of course not referring to the subjective habits of mind that make up Hume's notion of science. By science I mean here objective demonstrative knowledge as defined by Aristotle and aspired to by most practicing scientists. . . . Even geniuses run their daily programs by habit, more or less as they drive their cars, in a confident and relaxed manner but always alert to anything out of the ordinary. And when they spot something that does not fit the established patterns, they will then be ready for an intelligent struggle against the ingrained habits of thought. Thus . . . the whole history of science speaks against Hume, because virtually every advance in science has meant breaking some existing mental habit. But that does not make habits unimportant in science. To get anywhere in science, we must do much of it out of habit. Virtues thrive on instrumental habits.

In fact, without confirmed habits, I do not see how anybody's virtue could be trusted. Take, for instance, the case of a man who after years of dissipation undergoes a moral conversion. You know him well, and you have every reason to believe that he is sincere, that his change of mind and heart is genuine. But you still will not let him drive the school bus the next day. While he may indeed never take another drink for the rest of his life, in the beginning you cannot be completely sure. What you want to do is to give the man time to build up the habit of moderation, and he cannot do that simply by abstaining from drinking alcoholic beverages for twenty-four hours. His moral conversion has turned him in the right direction, but he still has to acquire the habit of stopping after the first glass or two, which is to drinking what braking at the change of the traffic light to red is to driving. In other words, existential readiness of the virtue of temperance requires the habit of moderation as its instrument. Without firm moral resolve, an alcoholic cannot stop being an alcoholic. But whatever in his metabolism, nervous system, or psychological make-up drove him to drink is still there the day after his big decision to quit. Thus in order to know that he has finally conquered these forces behind his addiction, known to defy even the strongest wills, what he also needs is a steady practice of moderation over a decent period of time.

Now there is an age-old rumor that virtues for Aristotle are nothing but good habits.... But this is not Aristotle's position. For if there is anything certain in his philosophy, it is the principle that human excellence demands a rational, and that means not only free and voluntary but also an objective, way of acting, which certainly is not the way of habit. Recall David Hume's principle: The necessity of habit is subjective, not objective necessity. Yet for Aristotle nothing is more objectively related to the good of man than moral virtue. He would have fully approved of the way St. Augustine put it more than 700 years later: "Virtue is a good quality of the mind, by which we live righteously, and of which no one can make a bad use" (*De Libero Arbitrio*, II.19).[2]

But how can virtue confirm an objective and necessary relation at the same time as it expresses what is most voluntary and free in a person? ... Here I merely want to draw your attention to the consequences of such common human failings as intemperance, lack of courage, imprudence, and the temptation to take advantage of other people. The unfortunate person suffering from such a lack of virtues can hardly be considered acting either freely or objectively; on the contrary, he is plainly seen as harming himself and others precisely because he cannot—subjectively—help himself. But what would happen if this man acquired temperance, courage, prudence, and justice? He would be able to do not [only] what seems right for him subjectively but what is right objectively. In possession of virtues, then, one freely abstains from doing wrong because it is wrong, and one freely does right because it is the thing to do.

To sum up the entire preceding discussion, let us repeat that virtue is neither science nor a habit. It is not a science, because its readiness is existential as well as qualitative; and it is not a habit, because it is an objective not a subjective quality. Aristotle puts it this way: Virtue is the state of character which makes a man good (as man) and which makes him do his own work (as man) well. Indeed, he goes on to say, virtue—like nature—is more exact and better than any art. We shall understand all this still better when we now turn to consider virtue precisely as a disposition....

To position means to put, and to dispose means to put things in a certain order. Its primary sense is to arrange things in place, probably because of the way our mind is connected to our senses. But "to dispose" also means, in all cases, to arrange the parts of a given whole with a view to an effect pertaining to the whole. For instance, after a visit with some new friends, you may remark—without malice—that while the Smiths have really nice furniture, their living room is not particularly attractive. That sometimes happens. Every single piece of furniture is quite nice, but the living room still looks dreadful, because of the way it is arranged....

What we have here is a notion of great scope and profundity, which has the added advantage of meaning exactly the same thing in both daily and philosophical usage. In its primary sense, etymologically and psychologically speaking, and I would say also logically speaking, we use it to refer to the arrangement of wholes that have parts external to each another. But we also speak, normally and spontaneously, of the disposition of a person. "I don't like to see Mr. So-and-so at our meetings," you say, "because I know that he is not well disposed toward our organization." This usage is most revealing, because what we mean here to designate by "being disposed" is also an order of a whole, which has parts. The whole in question is Mr. So-and-so's soul, or if you are ashamed to use the word "soul," his psyche. Of course, the parts of a man's psyche—or personality—are not external to each other spatially. But there is no doubt that what we call a man's disposition is the effect of several parts arranged in a particular order....

How shall we characterize the whole represented by the disposition of a person?... I would like to designate it as "dynamic." Perhaps we could also call it a functional whole with functional parts, but dynamic is better: the "psychological totality" which represents a person's moral character is a dynamic whole with dynamic parts....

A dynamic whole, I suggest, is one whose parts represent a multiplicity of virtualities, potentialities, and real possibilities.... Take, for instance, the personality of a youngster about twelve years old or a little older.... To make the case as clear as possible, let us assume that this youngster is truly exceptional: keen intelligence, good health and looks, excellent memory, artistic talent, practical sense, social adaptability—this youngster has it all.... At this age, all these many potentialities, virtualities, and possibilities have not yet been set in any particular order: his character is still unformed. So we try to imagine, we speculate, what this youngster will be like fifteen years from now, when his personality will have achieved some sort of disposition. Of course, we hope this will be felicitous, that it will be good. But we also know that... this promising youngster may conceivably end with a rotten disposition. The bright young mind may grow in the ways of truth, but it may also fall into most vicious error. In fact, the boy as he grows older may even become stupid, as sometimes happens to gifted people who abuse their mind, and who then become not just the worst idiots but dangerous, because of their mental prowess. There is, likewise, no guarantee that while growing stronger this youngster's will will always adhere to the good, and that none of his passions and emotions will get out of hand and come to dominate his psyche. All these things are clearly possible, and in realizing this we also realize that what this youngster's many fine qualities and talents are most in need of is precisely a proper disposition....

Finally, a word about art. While most people would agree that taste in art is an acquired disposition, there will probably never be an end to the disputes whether this disposition is subjective or objective. Of course, we all know that some people can look at an awful painting and declare it beautiful, just as others can drink cheap wine and say that it tastes good. Moreover, we are constantly reminded by eager freshmen that what is beautiful for the Chinese is not beautiful for us and vice versa. But I do not know about that. A lot of people, including myself, just love those Chinese paintings, landscapes, animals, portraits. Besides, I do not think that there exists a reputable art critic, no matter how relativistic in outlook, who does not recognize the reality of bad taste. All this speaks against total aesthetic relativism. And yet, the question of the nature of aesthetic judgment is not so easily settled.

To tell the truth, this is one question on which my old teacher and friend Jacques Maritain and I remain divided. Is artistic taste always a matter of opinion, or can it be raised to the level of habitus? In the latest edition of his great book *Art and Scholasticism*, Maritain has added a footnote, which I know is addressed to me, reiterating his view that while art itself is definitely a full-bodied habitus, aesthetic taste is merely subjective habitual disposition. But I remain convinced that, if there is objectivity in the creation of beauty, it must be possible for its appreciation also to become objective.

Still, in the present context what is important is not so much whether a disposition is objective or subjective; what is important is to see that it is needed. Whenever the parts consist of multiple possibilities, the order of the whole depends on disposition. And if we recognize opinion, aesthetic taste, and even science as such wholes, we should have no trouble understanding that a person's moral character is also the unique arrangement of all his moral traits. And when this arrangement makes him totally reliable and dependable in human affairs, we call both the man and his disposition virtuous.

This, as we noted in the beginning, has always been the common understanding of the meaning of virtue: dependability in matters pertaining to the good of man as man. But, as we have also seen, there is more than one theory as to how this dependability, desirable for the sake of individual happiness as well as of social peace and progress, can be achieved. While Aristotle saw it as a compound product of nature, habit, and reason, achieved literally by good disposition of personal inclinations and qualities, modern writers have looked for simpler and easier methods. But I am afraid that there is no cheap or automatic way of solving the problem of how we should live. . . .

[The] flaw in the romantic substitute for virtue is exposed far better by modern psychology than by Aristotle. Among the lasting achievements of modern psychoanalysis perhaps none is more significant than its having shown that an individual's strongest and most idiosyncratic tendencies are sometimes caused by childhood accidents. An authoritarian father, an authoritarian mother, or two quarreling parents, can easily and often do warp their children's sound native inclinations into all sorts of harmful neurotic behaviors. These are the sad facts of life.

But even in the absence of such accidents, the many virtualities, potentialities, and real possibilities that make up the yet-unformed personality of a youngster can hardly be expected to arrange themselves in the best of all possible orders by themselves....

Why is it, then, that Emerson's call to give "perfect faith to our involuntary perception" rather than to trust "the voluntary acts of our minds," continues to appeal to so many people? The answer is simple. Compared to "native goodness," the cost of achieving a truly virtuous disposition is incomparably higher.

The sort of mean cost-accounting seems to me to be also the unconscious motive behind at least the more extravagant claims for the potential results of modern psychology. Even though such claims are not voiced directly, one gets the impression that some of the practitioners actually believe that, if and when their techniques are perfected, there will be very few problems with people left over. But as we have seen, even though the soundness of inclinations, passions, and emotions is very important when it comes to being or not being dependable, the absence of pathological aberrations is no guarantee of morality. Being of sound mind and having normal appetites still leaves wide open the question of what to do with them. Whether one is or is not dependable hinges not so much on the goodness in nature as on the goodness in the use of natures, including especially one's own qualities and abilities. The disposition required to decide correctly about right and wrong in human action lies thus beyond the reach of psychology....

Finally, in evaluating again the effectiveness of "social engineering" in assuring human dependability, we may as well call briefly on Plato, who has not been read and re-read for nothing these twenty-four-hundred years.... He not only recognized the social order as a unique problem of the one and the many, but he also saw clearly that its solution requires not one but two distinct arrangements. Thus in contrast to, say, Marx or Fourier, among others, Plato holds firmly that in order to establish a properly working political system, there has to be disposition not only among the many but also within each of them. The personal whole needs to be set in order no less than the social whole.... Before we can match them, moral character and the form of the regime both need to be worked on. "Social engineering" looks for an easier way out. But I am convinced that as long as we keep reading Plato, we shall not fall into complete barbarism. . . .

The only way to face realistically the human problem is to acknowledge the need for a deliberate disposition of the dynamic parts of our psyche that would make us existentially ready to do the right thing at the right time. In other words, from what has already been said, we know that virtue must be both a qualitative and existential disposition. The only problem is that not all qualitative existential dispositions are virtues, and so we have to distinguish and clarify some more.

Take, for instance, the case of a businessman who always pays his bills and fulfills every single provision of his contracts in the most scrupulous fashion. He always does the right thing at the right time, and he should be praised for it. But even though he is thus rightly disposed and quite dependable, he may still not possess the virtue of justice. He may be practicing honesty as "the best policy," which would make him a good businessman but not a good man without any qualifications. His readiness to deal fairly with everyone is socially very constructive, and if all businessmen did the same, the economic life of the nation would be greatly improved. Thus honesty as the best policy is strongly to be recommended in all social transactions. But if it is pursued exclusively for the sake of business, it does not constitute moral virtue, because virtues are supposed to make us not only dependable citizens but also good people. As St. Augustine put it, virtue is the good quality of the soul by which we live rightly—*qua recte vivemus*—not in pursuit of our various occupations but as human beings. . . .

At this point, however, we run into a serious gap in Aristotle's ethical theory. He defines virtue as a disposition relative to choice, and we understand that he includes in it what we have called existential readiness. But we also now realize that such a disposition relative to what makes a man good as man presupposes a system of moral axioms. A choice lying in a mean that makes the difference between a good man and a bad man clearly requires a general understanding of what makes men good or bad. Does Aristotle cover this by saying that the choice of the mean is determined by a "rational principle"? Perhaps, but the whole issue is rather ambiguous. . . . Does he have a theory of how we know the basic premises of the moral order? Aristotle is not very clear on this matter. . . . How do we know what makes man good as man, and consequently what is right and what is wrong for man to do?

In our time, this is called the problem of values, and it is a question of what is valuable for man, what makes for a happy human life. Still, we must be very cautious here, because more often than not consideration of "values" today takes place within the framework of an idealistic, mechanistic philosophy whose vision of the world excludes finality. In this vision, things, including man, have no ends and have, therefore, to be assigned "values" from outside. Without a nature of his own that would determine what is good and bad for him, man has no other choice but to let his imagination create his own "values." No wonder so many people today suffer from existentialist despair of one kind or another. In a world devoid of finality, all values must of necessity be both subjective and artificial; and when these "values" collapse, despair is all that is left. By contrast, in a world of natures, value resides in the nature of things. Thus if man has a nature, he also has a destiny, and we can relate what is right and wrong for him to do to his nature and to his end objectively.

Now, it goes without saying that, even though in his philosophy Aristotle (and the same goes for Plato) did not work out fully a theory of knowledge of the right and wrong, this knowledge in his philosophy is plainly related to reality and to the finalities of things. To know what to do, one must consider the nature of things. For instance, man being what man is, suicide is wrong. Similarly, society being what it is by reason of what man is, it is clearly better not to lie than to lie. But even if we grant that there is such a thing as human nature, the understanding of which brings out the difference between right and wrong, we still have another extremely important question to consider. How do we come to know moral axioms? What is the mode of our apprehension of moral principles? Are they known rationally or by inclination? The ancient Greeks were not very explicit on this issue.

How do you know that it is better not to cut the throat of a child than to cut it? How do you know that it is wrong to steal, rape, burn? Do you grasp it rationally, or do you know because you "feel" it? Or do you do both? On this subject I would recommend a few pages from a book by my old teacher and friend Jacques Maritain, entitled *Man and the State*. I cannot say that I like every part of that book, but its few pages on natural law are absolutely excellent. Natural law, Maritain explains, is known first of all by inclination. That does not mean, of course, that it cannot be known rationally, or that rational knowledge of its principles is not desirable. It is simply that primordially, primitively, and primarily, natural law, whose core is constituted by the premises of the moral order, is known by inclination. I think that is indeed the case. We know these things first by a sort of instinct. For instance, why refrain from lying? How do you know that lying is wrong? You feel it. Is that irrational? Not at all. Irrational means extraneous and opposed to reason, which certainly does not apply to telling the truth. Thus what is known by inclination is not irrational, even though it may not yet be rational knowledge in the strict and full sense.

Now what goes for moral axioms, principles, and laws, goes with even greater force for the particular decisions, the unique choices that have to be made with regard to those principles in given situations. When a choice is to be made, the determination of the right and the wrong is carried over into the world of contingency where formal rationality, formal logic, is not much help. By what, then, is this determination effected? It can be effected only by the virtue of prudence....

Whenever the contingent is relevant to a decision, logical connection with ethical principles is either loose or purely and simply impossible. In all such cases, which covers practically every moral choice we have to make, the decision must be determined by the subjective psychological disposition of the actor. But within its own system of causality, that prudential judgment, supported by all the virtues, is fully capable of absolute objectivity.

Suppose I decide that my family needs a vacation, that it would be good for all of us to break up the routine, to experience a change in environment, and also to have a chance to be together not just at mealtime but for all sorts of fun and games as well as serious talk. Now they all like my idea, but it is mainly up to me to make the actual arrangements. We are agreed as to where we shall go, but I have to decide how to get there. Shall we go by plane, take the train, or drive? There is something to be said for—as well as against—each of these ways, but let us say that I decide that going by car would be most economical and also most convenient. So I take the car to the service station to be checked out, and the man in charge tells me that while everything is fine, I might want to keep an eye on my front tires. He is honest enough, and he does not say that he would be glad to sell me a couple of tires at a discount; he is simply informing me that the tread on my front tires is wearing down and that I should think of replacing them in the not too distant future. So I have a relatively small practical problem here—whether to spend our limited money supply on tires before the vacation, or wait until later. Yet this small problem clearly has potentially grave consequences. What if one of these tires blew out either while we are going to the mountains or coming back? Should I trust the expert who has told me that the tires are O. K. for now, especially since the family cannot afford to spend money unnecessarily? This is the kind of stuff practical decisions are made of. Marked by contingency and thus impossible to connect with any theoretical principle, they are left for the subject responsible for making them to decide by inclination. Can I do that objectively? Well, if I love my family, my tendency, my object, will be to do what is best for them. And if at the same time I have trained myself not to be unduly afraid of life's accidents and not to be extravagant in any way but to give all claims pertaining to the common good of the family their due, I do not see how my decision in this case, or any other similar situation, could be objectively wrong. It is I who must determine what is to be done; but if I possess the virtue of prudence, I will subjectively make my decision be the right one.

The object in this case is, what should be done in the best interest of the family? That is what I am after, and I would not be deliberating if I was not after that object. But how can I reach it? Because the case involves multiple contingencies, there is no way in which the object could be reached by logical analysis. To reach it, therefore, one must rely on properly disposed subjectivity, a psychological reality constituted by what Brentano calls *Gemütsbewegungen*, that is, "affective motions" in the broadest sense. And if this system of feeling and aversion is properly disposed by what we call the virtues, the object will be mine, because here indeed "in der Subjektivität liegt die Wahrheit." Kierkegaard implies that truth and objectivity "reside" in subjectivity. I prefer to say that they are "attained" through it. But the meaning of either expression is rather clear: the object of the inclination that determines our actions depends on our subjective disposition and nothing else....

Now while it is true that Aristotle might be a bit short of specific standards by which to judge moral right and wrong, he nevertheless makes it quite clear that these standards must be related to the good of man as man, to the good life as befits a human being who has developed to the fullest his human potential. Understanding human nature, we can train ourselves in virtues according to objective standards. And whoever succeeds in acquiring virtues will be easily recognized, as we suggested at the start of our discussion, by his or her unshakable dependability in human affairs....

According to Aristotle, moral virtues are connected with each other first of all in prudence. We have seen how the prudential judgment is determined. Because it applies to situations characterized by contingency, this judgment cannot be logically derived from any general principles of morality. Instead, it is determined by inclination. But clearly, in order to be right, this inclination cannot be virtuous only in some respects and not in others; it must be virtuous in all essential respects. Take, for example, the principle that in the case of extreme necessity private ownership is suspended. In such cases, "things become common," as Aristotle puts it. Yes, but how does one determine that that extreme emergency exists? By inclination, of course, for logic does not apply in such cases. Suppose you and your child are starving, and you wonder whether you have the right to take some food that belongs to your neighbor. This is essentially a problem of justice, but in order to make the correct decision you clearly also need both temperance and fortitude. You do not want to take what is not yours just because you are hungry; but if you delay taking action out of cowardice, your baby might die. Thus in order to make a prudential judgment in such a situation, you need not only a keen sense of justice; you need also temperance and courage. To save your life and the life of your child, you have a moral right to appropriate what belongs to your neighbor. But to make that determination, your prudence needs all the other virtues. And that is the whole story: all moral virtues are knotted together in prudence. In any moral situation, we need prudence in order to find the mean, that is, the right answer. But prudence cannot determine this mean by logical derivation from general principles. To know what is the right thing to do in this unique existential situation, the prudent man relies on inclination which, in order to be reliable, must be sound not just in some but in all respects. . . .

Any virtue, in order to be itself, needs the modalities procured by the other virtues. Each virtue needs every other virtue for the sake, we may say, of its own perfection. Thus in order to be temperate, a man must certainly use the modality supplied by justice, as well as the modality supplied by fortitude. A man wants, and needs, to be temperate with justice and courage, and vice-versa. Can one be truly courageous without moderation? How do we tell the difference between courage and recklessness? Being without fear does not of itself define courage. But not being reckless clearly involves a modality procured in temperance. . . .

If one virtue is badly lacking, other virtues do not have a chance. Suppose a decent person with a strong sense of justice becomes addicted to drugs. He or she will not long remain just. From what you hear about the cost of drug addiction, you know that to supply their "need" the unfortunate young man will sooner or later turn to stealing and robbing and the unfortunate young woman to other unethical means. . . . A coward can never really be honest. As long as everything is more or less normal, a businessman may pay his taxes and live up to his contracts regularly. But what happens if you put him in an unusual situation under high pressure? Without courage, he will lie, cheat, and do other things contrary to justice. He may even hate being dishonest, but his lack of courage leaves him no other choice. . . .

Lest these remarks make it appear that when all is said and done the Aristotelian teaching is not so much different from the Stoic doctrine of unqualified unity of virtue, let me point out that, while the theory of interdependence of virtues requires the presence of all virtues, it does not require that all virtues be possessed in the same degree. . . . For instance, a man may be possessed of justice in an excellent condition without possessing the virtue of temperance in the same condition. . . . What about a man who likes a couple of drinks before a meal, a glass or two of wine with his meals, and regularly takes also an after-dinner drink? I would not say he is a paragon of temperance. But that does not mean that this man cannot be just in the most excellent degree. . . .

Because ours is a life of contingency, there are no guarantees in interpersonal relations. But annoying as the qualified honesty and courage of an average person may be, they are far better than having nothing at all. In fact, even though people cannot be relied upon under absolutely all circumstances, life in society is made possible because most people possess a certain inclination toward justice, as well as some fortitude and temperance. For the dogmatic Stoic, this is quite a problem. But not for the Aristotelian. Virtue is acquired by habit, and a man need not be perfect in all respects in order to become or even be a good man. An inclination is where virtue must begin, and no one need despair because, say, his courage lags behind his temperance. Just being aware of it is a sign of a desire to do something about it, though no one should expect total conversion overnight. For, no less than in any other human endeavor, in our quest for moral virtues the law of progress is one of gradual perfection.

Notes

1. [Editor's Note: I selected texts from a specified range; the contributor then approved my choice.]

2. [Editor's Note: Vukan Kuic footnoted this, also referencing Thomas's *Summa Theologiae* I-II, q. 55, a. 4.]

CHAPTER 13

Freedom of Intellect

The theme of these pages is one of the most ancient and characteristic themes of political philosophy. It is also the theme of perhaps the most celebrated image in the history of philosophy: the image of the cave from the seventh book of Plato's *Republic*. That story concerns the ineliminable tension between the rational and political elements in human nature. It is common for both readers and teachers to focus on the escape from the cave, but it must not be forgotten that the man who has seen the truth returns to the cave, which is more than once called a "home" or "dwelling." The human community is one dominated by opinion, and the quest for truth emerges out of and against this environment. For Plato's Socrates, truth is related to another important good: freedom. These two themes come together in the selections from Simon that follow. Freedom is only possible when anchored in truth, but the quest for truth is complicated by the common world of opinion, the political-cultural world, and the influence of truth on public affairs requires constant vigilance: it must be fought for and pursued with clarity and determination. This means that freedom itself is work. Freedom must be achieved and reachieved.

This view of the connection between freedom and truth and the necessity of achieving freedom again and again distinguishes Simon's liberalism (liberalism, of course, is derived from the word for "free" and freedom is undoubtedly a good for Simon) from modern political liberalism. The first selection below was originally published in Simon's *The Community of the Free* (1947), and was written against the backdrop of prewar European liberalism, which tended to abstract from considerations of truth and see freedom simply as the absence of authority. Simon saw this facile kind of liberalism as culpable in the suppression of freedom in Europe and the necessary, albeit terrible, struggle to regain it that followed.

The first selection emphasizes the unity of truth and the unfortunate tendency of those who love truth in purely scientific matters to eschew its pursuit in practical, especially political, life. It was precisely the indifference of highly intelligent people that made possible the triumph of monstrous untruths in the years preceding World War II. Here again, Simon endorses Plato's definition of the true philosopher in the *Republic* as one who loves all knowledge and never just a part. This is a call for the unity of life in the love of truth that has effects well beyond the contemplative life, but that is grounded in a contemplative attitude.

Here, of course, we face the objection that the truth is divisive, that there is too little agreement on important questions to unify society. Such concerns underlie the contemporary debate on the nature of "public reason," a notion made central in the later work of John Rawls and still the subject of extensive debate and discussion. It is astonishing to see in the second selection below, from Simon's *A General Theory of Authority*, that Simon anticipated these objections and this great issue before his death in 1961, long before Rawls's first essays on the subject.

Simon notes the common distinction between "positive" and "transcendent" systems of truth, the positive referring to the natural sciences and matters of social convention, and the transcendent referring to more abstract matters beyond experimental verification. The dichotomy itself is misleading, since at the very base of the sciences are assumptions that could only be fully argued for in the transcendent manner. This epistemological distinction is a commonplace in the contemporary world, but it is not itself the essence of liberalism with respect to the place of truth in public life. That essence is found by Simon in a distinctive thesis about the "sociology of truth."

Society always imposes some positive truths on citizens, but to what degree can it or should it take a stand on transcendent matters, about which there is much less agreement among citizens? The modern liberal thesis is an answer to this question. Simon defines liberalism as the view that society's commitment in transcendent matters should be minimized in the service of freedom of conscience and the free competition of ideas. In so doing, he accurately anticipates Rawls's view that political society's abstention from transcendent truths (at least with respect to the most important constitutional matters) is a decisive principle of political liberalism and that a liberal society practices such abstention regardless of its contingent circumstances as a matter of principle. Simon, on the other hand, suggests that such abstention may reflect a reasonable prudential determination in a particularly divided society.

Simon does not propose any straightforward rules to guide such a determination, but, in his characteristic way, reframes the question, bringing new clarity via categories both grounded in Thomistic-Aristotelian philosophy and more subtle and sophisticated than the often sweeping and mechanical rules of contemporary liberal theory. What, asks Simon, makes propositions relatively more or less publicly accessible? He distinguishes between truths that are by nature incommunicable, that is, irreducibly personal and individual, for example, how a certain sense experience revives in one a childhood experience, and truths that are communicable. Truths that are *de jure* communicable can be less communicable *de facto* because of particular social conditions. This is especially the case with respect to metaphysical propositions and some foundational aspects of ethics, but it is important to note that there is nothing about those subject matters in themselves that renders them incommunicable; this derives rather from their interaction with contingent social-historical conditions. A particular society that takes a stand on such de facto less communicable matters takes a risk, one justified or not less by reference to any simple principle but relative to the contingencies of its history and character.

Simon may agree in practice with many liberal judgments about just how far a particular society might go in taking a stand on important truths, but his approach is at once more flexible and more solidly based on a defensible principle. The flexibility comes from Simon's recognition that just how much truth can be represented by a society is conditioned by its particular circumstances; the more defensible principle is the relationship of freedom to truth, itself grounded in his understanding of human nature. The texts of our second selection, therefore, are perhaps even more relevant now than when they were originally published.

V. Bradley Lewis

The Community of the Free
("Freedom in Daily Life," 13–21)

The Love of Truth Is Indivisible

The love of truth is the most natural thing in the world.¹ Why, then, is it that, as a matter of fact, truth is so little loved? Let us not be satisfied with accusing the perversity of human nature. In the commerce of souls with truth, there are possibly certain elements of illusion, to expose which would suffice to deprive falsehood of some effective instruments.

To recall that there are diverse kinds of truth, that the truth of a necessary proposition and that of an historical proposition, the truth of a theoretical proposition and that of a practical proposition, are different in nature, is but to repeat a commonplace. But in the order of moral and concrete psychology we have still much to learn concerning the consequences of this commonplace.

The diversity of truths conceals the unity of truth. Here is a psychological accident which occurs very frequently and is too little known. The natural tendency which carries our minds towards truth finds satisfaction in a certain realm of knowledge; satisfied, it stops there, and he who would give his life for a truth of a certain kind is found, in some other realm, to be indifferent to truth and falsehood. The absurdity of such a practice often remains concealed from the scrutiny of our consciences. For the absurdity to appear, the instinct for truth must show signs of being unappeased. Now it has found peace, it has illusorily satisfied its hunger, by acting in a limited field.

So it comes about that a positive scientist—a physicist, a chemist, a biologist—displays an admirable honesty in criticizing his own discoveries and theories, and a complete indifference in regards to the truth of metaphysics and religion. Nothing could be more edifying than his search for truth in the scientific field in which he is interested. If he suspects the presence of some factor which could make their meaning uncertain, he does not hesitate to regard experiments which have cost him years of work as null and void. His generalizations are exactly measured by the frequency of incontestable facts. He refuses himself the pleasure of indulging in brilliant but risky theories. He publishes little, because there are few results of which he is perfectly certain. Always ready to recognize his errors and the infinitesimal extent of his knowledge, he willingly bears the mockery of less scrupulous colleagues. What does he care for fame? His consciousness of scientific probity suffices him. That too-happy consciousness allows him to pass a thoroughly agreeable life without concerning himself about truth and falsehood in fields removed from his specialty. Has God spoken? Does God exist? Our conscientious researcher turns away from such questions with a loftiness that expresses his sense of an incontestable right. Outside the field of his choice, truth has no further rights to the assent of this intellect. His intellect has all rights.

From the point of view defined by the object of his study, what is supremely important here is the monstrous but frequent association of a splendid intransigence in respect to religious, metaphysical, and moral truths, with a degrading indifference in respect to what we shall call historico-practical truth. (By this I mean the entire aggregation of historical facts, whether recent or remote, which are of such a nature as to affect our attitudes as party men, our interests, our habitual tastes, and the esteem in which we hold the past. For example: Are the Protocols of the Elders of Zion authentic? Did Hitler save Germany and Austria from communism? Did the German air force bomb Guernica?) Here, as in the case of the scientist just described, the natural desire for truth is illusorily satisfied, then falls asleep, although truth demands that it remain awake. A sacrilegious paradox: the desire for truth is illusorily satisfied with the most sublime of foods, and the mind refuses to perceive that the truth which has nourished it imposes upon it a sacred duty to seek truth in all things, without setting any limits to the rights of truth.

Anyone who has understood in what a basic and absolute sense the possession of liberty is dependent upon submission to truth will recognize that the quality of a free man demands a love of truth which is not conditional and limited, but total and indivisible. In respect to things moral, social, and political, problems of truth can be reduced to two systems which we have just mentioned: the system of religious, metaphysical, and moral truths, and the system of historico-practical truths. There must, then, in the daily life of a free man be moments wrested from business, from pleasures, from passions, from work, in which the mind withdraws into itself and strengthens its adherence to these same two systems of truths. The need to consecrate a certain time each day to meditation upon eternal truths is well known to all those who have had the benefit of an elevated moral discipline and of a spiritual education. But—especially if they have the dangerous responsibility of teaching others—let them not neglect to consecrate as well a time of generous attention to forming true judgments upon historical facts whose interpretation determines their attitudes in the development of temporal history. Love of truth remains authentic only so long as it remains undivided.

Freedom and Autonomy

However well we know that freedom is a divine name, we find it hard to prevent ourselves from treating it as a suspect person. Common experience, as well as history, has a great deal to say on the subject of its extravagances. In the eyes of a reasonable, thoughtful, prudent man any operation which promotes freedom is a risky one, and must be accompanied by guarantees against license, rebellion, and the misuse of freedom. These common-sense views are not false: they are unhappily incomplete. Unless we go beyond them in our dealing with freedom, we shall more than likely adopt an empirical and inconsistent course of conduct.

According to the felicitous terminology employed by Maritain in a well-known study (*Freedom in the Modern World* [New York: Charles Scribner's Sons, 1936]),[2] mere free will, mere freedom of choice, has the character only of an initial freedom. It is freedom in its primitive, in its native state. Now, according to the law of progressiveness, which is the law of our whole nature, there is a great distance between the native state and the truly natural state, between the primitive condition in which a perfection exists only in a mixed and precarious form, and the terminal condition of a perfection that is stable and pure. Terminal freedom is not merely freedom of choice, but also freedom of autonomy. Here [in its initial, native, state] freedom of choice contains the possibility of making bad choices. Freedom of autonomy, in the measure in which it is actually realized, excludes that dreadful possibility. Freedom of autonomy is constituted by the presence of law within liberty. It is won by a process of interiorization of the law. At this point, in order to avoid misunderstanding, let us point out that the term *law*, here and in the following pages, refers either to natural laws, which are not man-made, or to those man-made laws which are just. We take it for granted that an unjust law, having no connection with the principle of law, is not a law at all. Let it not be objected that it is sometimes morally good, indeed obligatory, to obey an unjust law. When we feel obliged to obey an unjust law, it is generally because by disobeying it we should cause disorder and set an example which would be exploited against genuine laws by a spirit of disobedience; thus, we comply with a "law" which has no binding power in order not to disobey the obviously genuine and binding law that disobedience to laws should not be encouraged.

The wrong use of freedom occupies so large a place in our meditations that we have difficulty in preserving ourselves from the feeling that free will necessarily implies the possibility of doing wrong. Thus, a will whose adherence to the good should be infallible would have abdicated its freedom; and what, by an abuse of language, is called terminal freedom would be reduced to the necessity of willing the good—a privileged necessity, but in the long run one as foreign to freedom as, for example, the fidelity of vegetable life in following its cycles.

Such a concept contains a basic error fraught with consequences. Adherence to the good does not eliminate freedom of choice: within the limits of the good, numerous possibilities are still offered to our faculty of choosing. Far from eliminating freedom of choice, adherence to the good renders it perfect, *precisely as freedom of choice*. This is the point which it is important to understand. The object of the act of choosing is a means. Now, a bad means leads us away from our supreme end; in the final analysis, it is not a means because it does not lead to the end. There is only the appearance of a means and of an object of choice. To remove the possibility of a bad choice is simply to liberate free will from a deceitful appearance and to restore to it its genuine object—the veritable means, the means which leads to the end. Terminal freedom includes a freedom of choice which has attained to the purity of its idea.

An agent is said to be autonomous, in an absolute sense, when it is identical with its law. This kind of autonomy belongs only to God. An agent is said to be autonomous, in a relative yet entirely proper sense, when its law, without being identical to its being, dwells in it and governs it from within, so that the spontaneous inclinations of the agent coincide with the exigencies of the law. For creatures not endowed with reason, autonomy has the character of a datum: it suffices that they are what they are for their tendencies to conform with their law. For reasonable creatures, autonomy has the character of a vocation and a conquest. In the native state, man's will is an indeterminate complex of tendencies in which the order of nature will be established only by the action of reason. So long as this imposition of order remains unaccomplished, the law remains in some measure exterior to the will. The distance which separates it from the will is manifested by conflicts and defeats. The faculty of choosing is divided between the veritable means and the illusory means, which latter often carries off the victory. The interiorization of the law is effected by an oscillating movement between two lines of progress, one of which consists in an ever better understanding of what it is needful to know in order to act rightly, the other in an ever-deepening, spontaneous, and voluntary adherence to the necessary ends of our activity.

Thus, once the aspirations of free nature are precisely understood, freedom ceases to present the appearance of a fantastical and ambitious personage, always ready, if not duly confined and repressed, to destroy order and arrest life; useful in critical periods, when there are obstacles to be overcome, but little inclined to creative activity, and consequently not suitable for use in periods of construction or reconstruction. Freedom, correctly understood, is the most ordered thing in the world. It causes order to descend into the depths of the human will. This is the thing for which despotism will not forgive it. Collusions between despotism and anarchy, of which contemporary history furnishes so many examples, are a phenomenon easily comprehended. Despotism needs anarchy, in order that it may have a reason for existing: it cannot reign except over subjects refractory to autonomy, who call it to their aid, or at least tolerate it, because an external law is after all better than a total absence of law. The sure means of starving despotism out of existence is to realize, at all levels of personal and social life, the fusion of law and freedom—an operation which has nothing of the character of a compromise, since it brings both freedom and law to a state of perfection.

A General Theory of Authority
("The Search for Truth," 100–115)

THE FREEDOM OF THE INTELLECT

The expression "freedom of the intellect," which admits of multiple meanings, sometimes designates nothing else than the defeat of such forces of error and ignorance as passions and prejudices, blind traditions and unreasonable fashions, the imperialism of schools and the arbitrary dogmatism of their programs, the prestige of national groups, the imposture of false witnesses, insincerity in all its descriptions and, above all, the tough selfishness of the intellectual ego by reason of which systems, instead of bringing truth into the mind, act as screens between the mind and the truth. If the question is to achieve all this and nothing more, whoever loves truth cherishes with the same heart the freedom of the intellect, and no one is interested in intellectual freedom unless he loves truth. So understood, intellectual freedom has the character of a cause, most precious and always in danger. It transcends the programs of all schools of thought and parties. It has no particular connection with the philosophical and historical entity known under the name of liberalism. In spite of its many adversaries, it remains a universally human cause and cannot constitute the disruptive purpose of any system or movement.

Turning to the notion of intellectual freedom such as it is conceived in liberalism, let us try to determine what is distinctively liberal about it. The answer would be relatively simple if it were possible to say that of all interpretations of intellectual freedom, only one belongs properly to liberalism. But this is not the case. In the historical reality of the liberal movements, the freedom of the intellect is the subject of several interpretations, all of which deserve, on diverse grounds and in diverse degrees, to be considered typical expressions of liberal thought. Our exposition of these interpretations will begin with the most radical, which is also the least frequently expressed, and end with the most constant, which is also the least radical.

The structure of the mind can be described in terms of a polar opposition. Judgments possessed of immediate or demonstrative obviousness make up the *pole of rational determination*, and judgments relative to particular goods make up the *pole of practical indifference*. It is easy to imagine what reductions to unity the philosophers will be tempted to effect. Everything would be incomparably simpler and our vision of human life would be rid of much mystery—though perhaps at the cost of much absurdity—if it were possible to suppress one of the two centers of attraction and to place all judgments in the area defined by the remaining center. Since necessity is really and logically anterior to freedom, reduction to the system of rational determination was to be attempted first. Rationalistic determinism had been in existence for many centuries when the opposite attempt was favored by unprecedented developments, pertaining mostly to the moral and political order. Beginning with Charles Renouvier (1815–1903) the dialogue of the philosophers comprises a character whose role is to extend systematically the domain of voluntary assent. This character is cautious and often noncommittal; most of the time he operates silently. It is generally hard to know what significance he attributes to his own pronouncements. Yet it is clear that at the logical limit of his undertakings there no longer is such a thing as necessitating obviousness: even the first principles have become objects of free belief. The pole of rational determination and its field of attraction have disappeared.

It cannot be said that this most radical interpretation of intellectual freedom belongs to the essence of liberalism. To be sure, a true liberal may confess that the principle of noncontradiction does not in any way depend upon the dispositions of our freedom. Only a few extremists openly hold the theory of a free adherence to the first principles. Yet the influence of this theory has not been negligible. The paradoxes of the extremists often convey the thoughts which are present and active, perhaps subconsciously, in the minds of the moderates. Though professed by few persons, the theory of a free domination over obviousness itself has been haunting the liberal movement after the fashion of a ghost, hidden most of the time and skilled at concealing his identity, but always ready to lead liberal conscience into subtle temptations.

(The trend described here, which originated in moral and social attitudes, often combined its energy with that of a trend altogether relative to epistemological issues. Ever since the time of the Greek geometricians the axioms of mathematics had been held to constitute the clearest and most unmistakable examples of rational necessity. Over a period of many centuries, mathematical education was, by general assent, in charge of developing and maintaining, in the minds of men, a sense for those necessities that are not of factual but of essential and intelligible character. Now, in the last generations, a thorough reconsideration of mathematical premises has taken place. It has been brought forth that propositions which play the role of premises in one system may be conclusions in another system: the term axiom, which used to convey the inflexible necessity and absolute primacy of the self-evident propositions, has come to be taken as a mere synonym of postulate. It is hardly possible to exaggerate the importance of this reinterpretation of mathematics in modern culture. Indeed, the grounds on which a system of postulates is *chosen* often remains obscure. It is reasonable to suppose that the emphasis on the postulational character of mathematical premises is still due, at least in part, to a reaction against old misconceptions concerning the relation between mathematical necessity and the necessity proper to things of the real world. From the point of view of the history of culture, what is decisive is that the idea of *choice* among principles, of a human initiative in matters of first premises, of a human *control* over primary determinations, is active precisely in the area which, for so many centuries, has been reputed to supply the ideal pattern of determination by objective evidence. [James R. Newman in *Introduction* to W. K. Clifford, *The Common Sense of the Exact Sciences*, p. xlii.] Clear statements of the case are extremely rare: but it is easy to detect, in the common discussion of the most important subjects, the underlying theory that, since the first premises of mathematics from being axioms have become postulates, there can be no domain of thought where principles escape the condition of mere assumptions selected by the human mind with some degree of arbitrariness.)[3]

Another interpretation of intellectual freedom connects liberalism with agnosticism. Indeed, the first great synthesis of agnostic thought was built, under the name of positive philosophy, by an adversary of most liberal ideas. Paradoxically, many liberal thinkers, whether missing or ignoring the deep intention of Auguste Comte (1798–1857), held that the men of their own spirit were greatly indebted to the founder of positivism. What interested them in Auguste Comte was not the high priest of a distinctly ridiculous religion, narrowly dogmatic and big with the threat of clerical power; neither was it the political heir to Joseph de Maistre and de Bonald, eager to end revolutionary criticism and to establish a definite state of affairs; nor was it the legislator of scientific thought, who sets limits to the audacity of laboratory men as well as to that of theorists, and who blamed with the same heart hypotheses of structure and microscopic investigations. It was the serene assurance, pervading like a harmony, with which Auguste Comte had proclaimed the end of the absolute. To this disquieting theocratist, liberalism was grateful for having emancipated man from the transcendent dogmas of theology and metaphysics. The mind had simultaneously won its freedom and found the ways of its progress.

Agnostic liberalism does not deny that objects can determine, in unique and necessary fashion, the assent of the human mind. But it holds that this property belongs only to observable relations, and to the logical principles which govern the construction of the sciences. Thus, the universe of knowledge is divided into two systems: that of experience organized by logic—let it be called *the positive system*—and that of the propositions which do not admit of experimental verification—let it be called *the transcendent system*. Within the positive system, it is granted, and sometimes affirmed with fanatic dogmatism, that the mind enjoys no choice. But any assent to transcendent propositions is treated with diffidence, as if it were expressive of intellectual debasement. In the willingness to be ruled by the absolute, many positivists saw the ultimate cause of every servitude. All this looks wonderfully clear as long as no one remarks that the actual life of the intellect, within the positive system itself, implies assent to some transcendent propositions, and that the separation proclaimed with such complete assurance by the agnostic negation has never been actually observed in any work of thought.[4]

Great difficulties are felt as soon as there is a question of going beyond cheap generalities and of defining with any accuracy the content of the two systems. The transcendent system comprises all the propositions relative to the divine mysteries and the mysterious history of the relations between God and man. It comprises propositions relative to metaphysical objects, such as the first cause of the world and its last end. Consistency would require that it comprise also the great epistemological problems, e.g., the relation of universal ideas to reality and the significance of scientific theories—but then science would prove impossible. It should also comprise the supreme principles of morality, viz., views relative to human destiny, to the meaning of human life to genuine happiness, to the origin of obligation, etc.—but then would ethics still be possible?

The positive system comprises experimental sciences such as physics, chemistry, and biology; mathematics and a minimum of logic; the so-called observational sciences—geography, ethnology, anthropology, sociology—; such techniques as industrial mechanics, medicine, psychiatry; positive law, practical ethics, i.e., the rules of behavior recommended both by the moralists in repute and the people commonly held honest. With a not too exacting mind, with no taste for intellectual adventures, no interest in greatness and no sense for God, a man may remain all his life within the positive system and feel perfectly satisfied.

The association of liberalism with agnostic attitudes is common. However, it would be arbitrary to say that it belongs to the essence of liberalism. In fact, many deists and some ardent believers are among the most typical representatives of liberal psychology. Like the idea of free adherence to first principles, the agnostic attitude is for liberalism no more than a disquieting connection. However, between these two interpretations of intellectual freedom, there is a difference of great historical significance: because it is less radical and less paradoxical, the second does not need to wear a mask. Of the two familiar personages that haunt the liberal conscience, one generally works secretly and the other openly. Both play important roles, but neither can be identified with the liberal concept of intellectual freedom.

The essence of liberalism, as far as intellectual freedom is concerned, must be defined in relation to the sociology of truth. The contrast between the positive and the transcendent systems is provocative in spite of its obscurities: let it be kept in mind. Everyone holds, without taking the trouble of thinking of it explicitly, that society has the right and the duty to take stands on many issues belonging to the positive system. No social life is possible without rules of positive law promulgated by society and guaranteed by sanctions that no one can escape. No society would be possible without a code of practical ethics concerning human life, marriage and family, contracts, property and honor. No society is possible, in modern times at least, without the embodiment in positive law of many scientific and technical conclusions—as the control of food and drugs, and in the prevention of infectious diseases or accidents. All this is clear, and disagreements concern only particular cases. It may be argued, for instance, that such and such an inheritance law proceeds from an unsound notion of property, but no one would argue that society has no right to have ideas about property. The efficacy of a vaccination and the desirability of making it mandatory may be questioned; but no one questions the right of society to have ideas in matters of public health. On the contrary, society is commonly denied the right to have ideas in transcendent matters. It is commonly denied the right to take stands on metaphysical issues and on issues pertaining to the ultimate vindication of legal and ethical rules. The transcendent system is held to be the domain of private conscience and of spiritual power, if there is such a thing. Let society inflict punishment in case of theft or murder; but the principles which vindicate ultimately the prohibition of theft and murder are the concern of my conscience and yours—and of our church, if we please to recognize any. Whether these principles are firm or illusory, whether they effectively guarantee or badly jeopardize the code of practical morality without which no social life is possible, is none of society's business. According to your inclination and your lights, you will adopt, as final vindication of the prohibition of crimes and felonies, the commands of a revealed religion or the precepts of an irreligious rationalism, the inspirations of sentiment or the calculations of self-interest, the desire to be happy in your own way, the absoluteness of duty or the absoluteness of the supreme good, the requirements of an aesthetic harmony or those of a biological equilibrium: you may also, if you are a pure empiricist, refrain from inquiring into the principles of your actions. All these questions pertain to individual conscience. Society has nothing to say about them, it practices agnosticism without professing it: to profess it would already imply a stand on a transcendent issue.

By identifying this "sociological agnosticism," we think that we have reached what is constant, necessary and distinguishing in the liberal claim for freedom of thought. Whoever holds that society must refrain from any act relative to transcendent truths, and the search for such truth must be neither directed nor helped in any way by society, is a liberal. And whoever holds that society normally should be concerned with transcendent truths, or some of them, has rejected the liberal notion of intellectual freedom; at least he has decided to keep its dynamism under control.[5]

A man who professes agnosticism cannot help objecting to society's taking stands on questions which according to his philosophy cannot be answered. What is remarkable is that many minds by no means inclined toward agnostic attitudes, nay, provided with firm convictions in religion, in ethics, and even in metaphysics, hold that society should never say or do anything on behalf of their most cherished beliefs. Further, it often happens that the same person interprets sociological agnosticism not as a prudential disposition made necessary by the particularities of a spiritually divided society, but as a philosophy which would still hold under circumstances of spiritual unity.[6]

The arguments of sociological agnosticism can be summed up as follows: in order not to inflict any violence upon minds and consciences—the worst kind of violence, indeed—a society should never assert any proposition that is not commonly accepted by its members. The application of this rule causes no particular difficulty in the case of societies which are joined voluntarily and which anyone can leave at will. If you hold that the dogmas professed by spiritualistic groups are a challenge to common sense, keep away from these groups. But everyone involuntarily becomes a member of the state, and from the state no one can secede. The problem of the indispensable harmony between the beliefs of society and those of its members cannot be solved, in the case of the state, by the spontaneous operation of intellectual affinities. The only way to solve it is to reduce the intellectual content of public life to a minimum of propositions so chosen that no normal person can disagree. At this point the distinction between the transcendent and the positive systems plays a significant part, independently of any agnostic proposition. In fact, positive truths, or at least those of them which directly concern the welfare of temporal society, are commonly accepted by normal persons. Thus, such a general rule as the communicability of infectious germs is hardly questioned by anybody. Only a few rebels object to the basic rules of positive law. And most precepts of daily ethics are acknowledged almost unanimously.

The social destiny of transcendent problems is altogether different. Even if one holds that they admit of definite solutions, it must be granted that in many cases they fail to win the assent of minds. When specialists in these questions meet, they can hardly talk to each other for lack of agreement on definitions and principles. One affirms that God exists and that he can prove His existence; another says that we shall never know whether or not there exists a God; another holds that such questions cannot be decided except by revelation; another, that the question of the existence of God has merely a pragmatic sense; and still another that it has no sense at all. How could the great number of men be expected to reach unanimity where experts are so far from being unanimous?[7] And yet it is necessary to keep unsegregated, in the society to which everyone belongs by right of birth and from which no one can secede, these theists and these atheists, these believers in theoretical truth and these pragmatists, these utilitarians, these Kantians, these hedonists, these evolutionists, these traditionalists, all these intellectual species which can stand some sort of unity when there is a question of positive issues, but prove refractory to any discipline when transcendent issues are in question. To give any of these species a privilege is to do violence to all the others. For lack of a common assent, the only possible policy is one of abstention.

In order to clarify the meaning of this argumentation it is necessary to consider the general problem of the communication of truth. Some truths are incommunicable by nature; thus, I shall never succeed in making you know exactly what I mean when I say that the smell of a damp underwood revives in me, in confused and moving fashion, such and such experiences of my childhood. Such incommunicable truths are very important, but whatever their nature and their worth, it is plain that they cannot be included in the collective beliefs of a society.[8]

The obscurity of the problem results from a discrepancy between *de jure* and *de facto* possibilities within the system of communicable truth. Every demonstrable proposition is, *de jure*, communicable without limits. But it often happens that the understanding of a fully demonstrated proposition, or even that of an immediately obvious one,[9] requires conditions which are not commonly satisfied in any society. *De jure*, some propositions of metaphysics and ethics are no less communicable than any theorems of geometry or law or biology. But whereas the conditions required for the understanding of mathematics and biology seem to be well assured by our schools and other learned organizations, the conditions necessary to understand the most fundamental theories of metaphysics have never been commonly satisfied in any society. At philosophical conventions deaf men make speeches for other deaf men, and blind men play pantomimes for other blind men, and this will never prove anything against the intrinsic communicability of philosophic truth. Such facts prove nothing else than the reality of contingency and its ability to bring about the broadest discrepancies between the life of the mind such as it would be, if nothing interfered with the necessity of objective laws, and the real life of our minds, where factors of disturbance are powerful.

As positive science becomes more aware of its social destiny, it evidences greater determination to cut down the discrepancy between *de jure* and *de facto* communicability—as far, at least, as the experts are concerned. Enrico Fermi used to say that the physicist needs to express himself in "sharp statements," and is inclined to keep away from areas where such a mode of expression is impossible. A sharp statement is one which, though possibly inaccessible to unprepared minds, can be communicated by one expert to another in such a way that the latter soon is ready to determine whether he agrees or not, or at least soon knows what he should do in order to ascertain his own stand on the subject. In the selection of its topics, in the determination of its standpoints, positive science often resorts to costly exclusions that philosophers are tempted to deem arbitrary. For instance, the method which ignores, as far as possible, the qualitative aspect of things and substitutes a system of measurable data for the more complex world of our experience, is motivated, to a large extent, by the privilege of propositions that anyone can easily verify provided he submits to a code of clearly defined and relatively simple operational rules. The philosopher has no right and no inclination to practice such exclusions and must resign himself never to win unanimity, no matter how rigorous his demonstrations, except within small groups of kindred minds. As far as communicability is concerned, the difference between positive science and philosophy, and more generally between positive and transcendent truth, should be expressed in terms of tendencies. Positive science systematically seeks *de facto* communicability among persons concerned. But the exclusions necessarily entailed by such a systematic search are strictly forbidden philosophers. The law of philosophic thinking is altogether concerned with the objective significance of issues and cannot tolerate a tendency to make sacrifices for the sake of factual communicability.

When temporal society takes a stand on a positive proposition, it is—except for possible accidents and abuses—an easily communicable one. Little risk is involved. Opposition, if there is any, will soon be defeated by the felicitous consequences of the principle newly introduced into social life. But when society takes a stand on a truth whose communication involves great difficulties, it accepts all the hardships and all the risks of a struggle which is likely never to end.

At this point, attention should be called to the historical association of liberal doctrines with the ways of knowledge which become predominant in modern times. Positive science, by bringing about constantly repeated evidence of the conquering power of truth, has filled minds with patterns highly favorable to liberal expectations. The telescope of Galileo sufficed to destroy stubborn errors concerning celestial bodies. A few experiments conducted with rigor transformed into scientific propositions, soon accepted by all, the hypotheses of Pasteur concerning the role of micro-organisms in diseases. The history of the sciences, at least since the Renaissance, fully vindicates an optimistic vision of the conflict between truth and error in the positive system. It is very tempting to extend this vision to all orders of human knowledge without asking whether the factors which, in the positive science and technique, determine the success of truth, work also, and with the same regularity, in transcendent matters. Justice Holmes summed up the liberal tradition when he declared that "The best test of truth is the power of the thought to get itself accepted in the competition of the market." The preceding remarks on *de facto* communicability raise the question of whether this celebrated statement is of general significance, or holds only in a distinguished domain, viz., in the domain where the success of truth is favored by the firm communicability of proof.

Notes

1. [Editor's Note: I selected texts from a specified range; the contributor then approved my choice.]

2. [Editor's Note: The reference in parentheses was a footnote in Simon's text.]

3. [Editor's Note: Simon's editor placed Simon's material in this parenthesis as a footnote in his original text. The text was being readied for publication at Simon's death. Its editor evidently found a reference in it to Newman's work, and so he placed the reference within this footnote.]

4. Emile Meyerson has convincingly established that the "products of scientific thought," in other words, the things that the scientific mind actually has brought about in its effort to create a scientific interpretation of the universe, do not agree on any point with the program set by early positivism. His famous investigations (*Identity and Reality*, *On Explanation in the Sciences*, etc.) are limited to the domains of mathematical and physical sciences. Similar investigations in the moral and social fields would easily show that here also the "products of scientific thought" express thorough disregard for the restrictions that positivism holds to be indispensable conditions of scientific research.

5. It is hardly necessary to remark that in the concrete history of ideologies adherence to the liberal principle admits of many degrees. Some great liberal traditions, viz., those which still prevail in Anglo-Saxon countries, do not forbid the agents of the temporal power to take stands on some metaphysical and religious issues. Atheistic propaganda and the most destructive ethical theories are freely expressed in Great Britain and in the United States; but British and American liberals, with the possible exception of a few fanatics, do not object to the Prime Minister's and the President's recommending, in public speeches and by public acts, prayer and the reading of the Holy Scripture. In most Latin countries on the contrary, the liberal tradition hardly allows that God be mentioned in a public speech. If a statesman in these countries happened to recommend the reading of the Gospel, even believers would feel that he is minding someone else's business.

6. The following discussion will be principally concerned with those transcendent truths which do not claim any supernatural character, and the word society will stand for civil society. But what holds for civil society often admits of application to other societies and the disposition which forbids civil society to have ideas in transcendent matters may also determine opposition to organized religion, to all forms of community worship and generally recommend individualistic methods whenever transcendent subjects are involved.

7. We intend to leave entirely out of the discussion the question of a possible guilt involved in the failure to find the truth about some transcendent issues. The reader will notice that leaving a question out is not the same as holding it unsettled in all respects.

8. We are speaking here of propositions relative to real situations. As recalled in the first chapter, a proposition concerning what ought to be done by a community may, in spite of contingency, demand the assent of all. The ground of common assent, which is not supplied by rational communicability, may be supplied by affective communion.

9. I refer to the difficulties involved in the formulation of the first principles. Every sane man grasps the principle of causality and applies it many times a day. But phrasing this principle is an immensely difficult task, which will never be accomplished in such conditions of finality as to exclude further improvements through new discussion.

CHAPTER 14

Society and the Formation of Free Persons

One of the great paradoxes of life in democratic society is that civil authority cannot—at least, not without considerable qualification—be entrusted with the formation of the very moral and spiritual values on which that society depends and which that authority is supposed to serve. Perhaps, in the ideal order of utopian political philosophy, authority might be thought synonymous with the power entrusted to it for purposes of governance. But history tells a different story, and the writings of Simon selected below are mindful of the need for something other than the invariably bureaucratic methods of the secular state in the formation of the free persons needed for the citizenry of a free society.

A sophisticated notion of freedom is needed here. Much as one might cherish being able to do and say what one likes, without fear or constraint, so long as one does no harm to one's neighbor thereby, it is not enough for a free society of free persons. The libertarian notion of freedom that is conceived in terms of negative liberty and the right to be left alone is ultimately only an adolescent's dream, and one that presumes a level of prosperity that in turn depends on the good and peaceful order of a community to which this libertarian solitude makes no contribution. Culturally, this would be to live off one's principle rather than the interest.

In addition to those aspects of freedom that need to be defined negatively (the absence of physical restraint, intellectual constraint, psychological pressure, and so on), there is also need to articulate its positive constituents, including self-mastery, self-determination, and self-donation. For Simon, genuine freedom is not merely the freedom of spontaneity in following one's animal desires, but a mastery of all one's inclinations. In his discussion, for instance, of the ways in which the free love movement has tried to co-opt the political idea of freedom for the purposes of hedonism, he distinguishes carefully between the legitimate human desire for freedom (including the freedom for political participation in civil society) and the degree of an individual's or a people's readiness for the good use of the freedom that they are moved to demand. At one point, for instance, he writes: "Whoever thinks that, in the relation of man and woman, free union alone can keep him free, and holds that marriage would enslave him, has left out of the picture the most interesting possibility: a mastery over desire such that, for the sake of a law, for the sake of the good, for the sake of God, a man must be free to choose, if he pleases, and without a struggle against overwhelming difficulties, the dignity and the exclusive dedication of indissoluble marriage."

This view of marriage, of course, and of its contribution to the well-being of the individual spouses, of the family, and of a free society is much contested in contemporary debates. Proponents of the traditional view of marriage often seem inarticulate, if not simply question-begging, in their efforts to provide a rational vindication for their beliefs. It may well be that the objections to the traditional view are simply disingenuous and that anyone who has been brought up in a virtuous way simply ought to see the truth about the traditional idea of marriage without need for any elaborate argument. But even topics on which the reasoning behind a traditional view of things might seem less difficult, such as the right to private property or the absolute prohibition on the taking of innocent life, are subject to widespread contention.

The common beliefs needed about such basic elements of life in a free society far surpass the resources of a libertarian approach or the noncommittal live-and-let-live policies of social Darwinism. If virtually everyone agreed about the sanctity of human life, the need for respecting property, the binding nature of contracts, and the fundamental structures of family life, the duties of state authorities could presumably be fulfilled without any special attention on their part for the formation of character in their citizens. But the sharpness of disagreements regarding what is criminal and what is praiseworthy belies that prospect. As Simon observes, what some call suicide, others praise as heroic sacrifice. What some call exploitation, others take to be the normal operation of the market. What some call violations of human rights, others see as the consequences of the workings of evolution.

But if the state cannot be entrusted with the duty of moral formation and yet the matter cannot be left purely to individual taste, what is one to do? For Simon, a minimal view of authority is not enough. Those political theorists who conceive the main functions of a state to be the restraint of criminals and the enforcement of contracts have not yet accounted for how we are to take the sort of decisions that are needed for common action, so that we will be able to marshal the energies of a community for projects that individuals or small groups could never accomplish on their own. But the powers with which authorities are entrusted for the sake of various kinds of progress also need to be limited. Power intoxicates, and the historical record of the vast powers accorded to modern states gives little reason to expect that the very features that make such large organizations work—whether the slow but relentless efficiencies of bureaucracy or the sophisticated shaping of popular opinion through the new media technology—will enhance the wisdom needed in society to protect the order of truth about transcendent values. By contrast, Simon offers positive arguments for the legitimacy of public authority while at the same time making a profound case for an ethics by which to govern authority and secure limitations on the powers granted to authority.

For Simon, it would be a false dichotomy to restrict one's options to a choice between the libertarian ideal of maximal personal liberty and the communitarian concession of personal liberty only to the extent necessary to prevent generating so much individual resentment as to impede collective realization of the common good. His thinking constantly takes us back to the need for the virtue of prudence and for the moral formation of citizens, as the way to create the ordered liberty that a free society requires. The most important means for communicating a sense of human excellence and for cultivating personal commitment to the acquisition of the crucial individual and social virtues is through love and friendship. At the social level, one sees this in the benefit and the joy that comes from the privilege of working under a truly able leader, a person of good will who wants to do the things that the common good demands, who actually knows what those things are, and who does them. As the following readings show, the development and protection of the specific arrangements that will ensure the proper formation of free and mature people and a free society depend on intermediary institutions, such as the traditional family, and on a sound philosophy of the person and society.

Joseph W. Koterski, SJ

Freedom and Community
("Autonomy and Authority," 93–101 and 109–13)

In countless daily instances society is what saves the human mind from doubt and desperation.[1] We expect of society a constant declaration of the rational. We are so convinced that what is rational must also be recognized and proclaimed by society that when social sanction is lacking, rationality is doubted. Thus, against the view that metaphysical propositions admit of demonstration, it is everlastingly objected that if such were the case some sort of consensus concerning these propositions would take place; from the absence of consensus the absence of demonstrativeness is inferred.

Notice the difference, in this connection, between metaphysics and other difficult disciplines. It has been said that only a dozen men were able to follow the most advanced theories of Einstein; it used to be said that only three men in the world could follow the last theorems of Henri Poincaré. However, society never left minds without guidance in the domains explored by Poincaré and Einstein. Society backed them, certified that they were reliable witnesses. How can society certify the testimony of witnesses who can communicate with only a few other individuals? In such a difficult discipline as physics, there is a concatenation of testimonies which finally reaches the common man and fills him with confidence. The vanguard scientist communicates his most advanced theories to extremely few, but those few communicate with a larger group of experts, and the latter with still larger groups and so on down to the common people. . . .

How then are we to explain this difference between social possibilities in physics and metaphysics? The obvious answer is that in physics experts are agreed, to a large extent, at all levels of expertness, whereas in metaphysics the experts themselves are divided. But this is still a shortsighted approach. . . . In metaphysics as well as in other domains, the qualities that we refer to when we say that a man is able, that he has a great worth, that his knowledge is broad and profound are recognized by society with sufficient regularity. The thing that society cannot do, in metaphysics and related domains, is to decide whether the doctrine proposed with ability, profundity and amplitude, expresses truth or error. It is precisely in relation to truth and error that the metaphysical expert is not regularly distinguished by society from the scientific expert. Society recognizes only the kind of expertness to which we refer when we speak of ability, profundity, amplitude, etc. It seems to have no criterion as to expertness regarding truth and consequently concludes that the experts are divided....

The process of moral improvement, by which the possibility of wrong choices is ruled out—though never in absolute and unqualified fashion—changes freedom of choice into itself, not into something else. The process consists of an interiorization of the law. One is not interested in freedom as autonomy unless he respects the law so deeply as to want it to get hold of his innermost self. In truth, there are two interpretations of autonomy, one characterized by emphasis on self which inevitably gives way to the spirit of arbitrariness. Another is characterized by such dedication to law that I do not want to be ruled by anything else than the law. I so hate arbitrariness, especially if I have anything to do with it, that I want my own self to be the abode of law and my own inclination strictly to coincide with the directions of the law. I can then speak of autonomy without sophistry. I have not erected my will into law, but the law has become the soul and form of my will. The interiorization of the law is then an operation involving much sacrifice. The rebel is unwilling to consent to such sacrifice because the law is something he does not care to have within himself. He finds it bad enough that the law hovers over him as a threat.

So long as the tendencies of a person are at variance with the law that he is bound to obey, the law remains, in varying degree, external to him. The development of virtues is the gradual constitution of steady tendencies in strict coincidence with the law. Insofar as a man is genuinely virtuous, acts at variance with the law stir in him horror and aversion.... Yet in pain and struggle and exposure the just man can be said, in the proper sense, to be free from subjection to the law; insofar as love for what the law prescribes actually predominates in him, insofar as the rebellious law is actually kept under control, the just man no longer is placed under the law; rather he is one with the law by reason of victorious inclinations made of love for what the law demands and aversion to what it forbids. . . .

The autonomy of the things of nature does not entail absolute regularity of operation; yet operation according to law, in the sense of nature, is hampered by contingency alone: a minor factor of disorder in comparison with the initial condition of man, which is open to disorder not only by reason of contingency, but also by reason of ability to make wrong choices. Hence the feeling of contrast between the reliability of nature and the unreliability of man. . . .

The interpretation of nature as a system of autonomy attained the highest degree of firmness and consistency in the philosophy of Aristotle. The hylomorphic theory means that in a universe of perishability and within the stream of universal becoming, things have a way of being what they are and of acting according to what they are. In the metaphysically more complete vision of St. Thomas a nature is "a certain idea, viz., of the divine art, placed in things and by which things are moved towards their ends". . . .

After having considered the meaning of autonomy in the individual person, and in physical nature, let us consider it in society. . . .

It is normal for every society to rule itself; precisely why is this the case?—the more autonomous the rule, the closer it is to the matter to be ruled, the more effective it is. Here, as well as in the individual person, the perfection of autonomy is identical with perfect orderliness. Observance of the law is perfect when the law is so totally interiorized that there is no longer subjection to it. In what sense can it be said that there is no subjection in the case of a law which is that of our own group? There remains subjection of each to the law of the group, but insofar as the group is theirs, in other words, insofar as we as persons are members of their group, the law is our law and subjection has disappeared. The individual as such has the character of a part and the part is irreducibly subjected to the law of the whole; but because the person as such has a character of a whole, one may conceive, at the limit, a coincidence between the law of the person and the law of the group. . . .

Developments in diverse personalistic movements between the two world wars include Maritain's personalism in *Three Reformers* and subsequent studies, Mounier and his team, the New Order, Berdyaev, von Hildebrand, and before him Scheler, the Californian journal *The Personalist*, etc. These movements are, to a large extent, independent of each other, and it would be altogether unreasonable to treat "personalism" as one doctrine. However, these several personalistic movements, which are apt to clash with each other on very important issues, have some aversions in common. For one thing, the personalistic movements are all opposed to the totalitarian state.... Secondly, they all evidence some sort of aversion to the old individualism....

With regard to the right to lead a life of contemplation, I have used the expression "to secede into contemplation," but the propriety of the expression "to secede" raises an interesting problem. In spite of appearances, the contemplative may be so related to society as not to be seceding from it.... In fact, in what ways can it be said that a contemplative is useful to society? (1) By his example. But if his example is useful, the life of which he sets an example is understood to be worth imitating. (2) The contemplative is useful by his teaching. But here there is the serious difficulty: the teaching of the contemplative may be considered in relation to contemplation itself and we are again confronted by the problem of the worth of contemplation considered in itself....

Vindication in terms of utility is not the only kind of vindication. Indeed, it would make no sense if it were not understood to hold in relation to a vindication in terms of intrinsic excellence. In all orders, things excellent lie beyond utility, as for example, health beyond the means used to preserve it or restore it. To ask about health the kind of questions that we ask about medicines and diets would make no sense. Likewise, contemplation does not have to be justified in relation to some further goal to which it would be a way: it is itself the best life whose excellence ultimately justifies the other ways of life. The contemplative is related to society as the fruit to the tree.

Is the contemplative then outside society? The contemplative belongs to society by the action he takes in the order of final causality. Just as the mover by efficient causality is, in a very proper sense, present in what it moves, so there is a presence of the thing desired in whatever desires it. This supplies a new approach to the question: for it asks in what sense is the contemplative *good* for society? Again, his essential goodness does not consist in a relation of utility. The decisive insight may be this—to be useful is only one way of being "good for": the end is "good for" whatever strives toward it and is present in whatever strives toward it. Even if the contemplative, as soon as he has attained his state of accomplishment, should disappear into the wilderness and never be heard of again, he would remain present in society by the order that he causes in it in the capacity of final cause and intended fruit. . . .

It is rarely said that it is the beneficial presence of the contemplative in society which will do most to explain a society dedicated to culture and to the perfection of minds. But the fact could be substantiated. It would then be possible to show how the community procures the freedom of contemplation and how the freedom of the contemplative procures the order of the community.

Let us finally emphasize that in all acts of common life, the most profound is communion in immanent actions. True, immanent acts of knowing the same truth, if exercised by solitary individuals with no awareness that the truth they know is also known by others, would be a collection of strictly individual acts, not a communion. But what was said in the foregoing of the solitary character of contemplative life does not entail individualistic isolation. . . . In contemplative hermits the community exercises its loftiest and most intense act of communion. Such acts do not need to be exercised directly by all members of a community; their loftiness and intensity are perhaps inversely proportioned to the number of those who achieve genuine contemplation.

A General Theory of Authority
("The Search for Truth," 126–31;
"The Communication of Excellence," 148–56)

Let us now bring together these two sets of considerations, those relative to the fact that temporal society cannot shirk concern with the thoughts of men, even on the deepest levels, and still discharge its more obvious duties—say, protecting innocent life, giving property a guarantee against evil doers and assuring some kind of dignity in marriage—and those relative to the *immanence* of what is most essential in common life, in other words, to the fact that the principal part of our common good is contained within our souls. As soon as these two sets of very simple considerations are taken together, the interest of society in transcendent issues—or some of them—becomes obvious. Who would believe that the temporal society, the society whose duty is to protect, with a power of unconditional coercion, life, property, honor, and dignity, should restrict its field of communion to what we have called the positive system: propositions of empiriological science and technique, the minimum of logic indispensable to organize experience, and rules of action carefully kept apart from the principles which might give them a meaning and a soul? The suggested restrictions amount to depriving the temporal community of what is deepest, most essential, and most vital in its common action. Against these restrictions we do protest whenever such an occasion as a public ceremony gives us a chance to commune in any of the "transcendent" propositions, relative to the rights of men, relative to the purposes of civil society, and relative to God, which make up the soul of our temporal common good. Promoting the order of truth in social life of the transcendent intellect requires the operation of wisdom; it may be the most significant, as well as the loftiest, of all the duties entrusted to the wisdom of societies.

But the suggestion that the temporal society, the civil society, the state, could be, in any way and under any circumstances, trusted with the maintenance and the promotion of transcendent propositions seems to involve a lack of respect for what is most precious in truth. As we think of what temporal society would do if it undertook to serve truth in transcendent matters, our mind is promptly filled with repulsive pictures. We imagine a system of censorship run by men that power intoxicates. Brains are hammered by dead truths and by deadly errors, propaganda pervades scholarly work, rewritten syllabi leave out the really embarrassing questions, social pressure substitutes for certainty and probability, the call of the hero is silenced by decree, academic life, at all levels, is defiled by informing and related practices. Where the loftier kind of truth is supposed to be served, fraud and deceit prevail.

These pictures are not entirely the work of rebellious imagination. They originate in history and the difficulties that they bring forth are perennial.... How will the possibilities of wisdom be determined? Assuming that these possibilities are real and that the wisdom of society can effectively promote the order of truth in the transcendent life of our intellects, how will the ways and means of such an immensely difficult enterprise be determined? Plainly, it is up to prudence, to practical wisdom in the full sense of this expression, it is up to a judgment fully coincident with the complexity and mutability of the circumstances to answer this question.... No one will question that in society some things go on according to patterns that are more vital, and other things according to patterns that are more bureaucratic. This common remark may supply direction in a prudential search for the ways and means that a particular society should use as it endeavors to promote the order of truth. Briefly, the loftier the function, the more strongly it demands to be exercised according to the ways of life, and the less it admits of bureaucratic management. As already said—though in tentative language—promoting the order of truth in the social life of the transcendent intellect is the highest function of the civil community. It is not a function which admits of bureaucratic methods. It calls for the actualization of what is most vital in society. From this consideration it may follow that problems of truth often call for a sharp distinction between the state and the civil, or temporal, society—a distinction which we have not been using so far. When a function is directly exercised by the state, according to the ways which are those of any governing apparatus, it is inevitably exposed to what is damaging in bureaucracy. We can reasonably conclude that in most cases the loftier problems of truth, which we have described in making up the transcendent system, should not directly concern the state apparatus. Again, the state cannot leave these problems out of its consideration. In most cases, however, it will discharge its duty best by concerning itself indirectly with such things as the maintenance and promotion of transcendent truth. Bureaucracy should better deal with problems that are not so lofty and do not pertain so directly to the deep life of our souls. . . .

Like authority and hierarchy, obedience has a bad name. The words of W. K. Clifford, "There is one thing in the world more wicked than the desire to command and that is the will to obey," express an opinion which, without being common, has never lacked supporters especially among intellectuals. But it is also a widespread belief that obedience, which is obviously indispensable in the life of communities and in the upbringing of the youth, may work wonders in the progress of persons who are already mature and good. Is it paradoxical to say that the best approach to this problem is supplied by the theory of freedom? The paradox exists for those who identify freedom with primitiveness and fancy, not for those who have understood that it consists in an active and dominating indifference, in a mastery over a plurality of possible ways of action. According to the latter theory, not all obstacles to freedom are external. Some—and, in a way, the worst—lie within myself. Regardless of what happens in external nature and in the actions of my fellow men, I see that various forces existent in me restrict my freedom. Of these the most sublime are not the least dreadful. Considering the lower first and then the more lofty, let us mention the power of habit, sensuous desires, lust for wealth, attachment to beloved things and persons, and, in my relation to truth, excessive concern with the contributions of my own self. . . . The use of the word slave in such a context shows how commonly freedom is interpreted as mastery, or dominating indifference, so long as we have not been indoctrinated by the ideology of spontaneity and primitiveness. . . . Whoever thinks that, in the relation of man and woman, free union alone can keep him free, and holds that marriage would enslave him, has left out of the picture the most interesting possibility: a mastery over desire such that, for the sake of a law, for the sake of the good, for the sake of God, a man may be free to choose, if he pleases, and without a struggle against overwhelming difficulties, the dignity and the exclusive dedication of indissoluble marriage. These expressions, "free love," "free union," are dishonestly loaded with a philosophy which interprets freedom as spontaneity, and preferably as the spontaneity of animal desires.... An old habit, or a native disposition, are obstacles to our freedom if, when we see that it would be *good* to act at variance with this habit or disposition, we must confess that the power of those internal forces is all but insuperable....

A thing which is not God cannot *be* except by being deprived of indefinitely many forms and perfections. To this situation, knowledge, according to St. Thomas' words, is a remedy, inasmuch as every knowing subject is able to have, over and above its own form, the form of other things. This remedy is, so to say, complete in the case of intellectual knowledge, for intelligent beings can have the forms of all things and *be* all things spiritually, intentionally, transsubjectively, objectively. In the order of judgment as distinct from that of mere apprehension, objectivity is one with truth, and a shortcoming in the knowledge of truth is a failure to achieve the objective and infinite existence by reason of which man is said to be an image of God.... The most desirable of all freedoms is the freedom to be all things, as becomes a faithful image of God. No condition is dearer to the spirit than freedom from the matter-like impulses which so often force upon us the narrow capacities of subjective existence....

Obedience may well be the closest approximation to a general method for dealing with the weight of subjectivity in the uppermost part of our self. There are many forms of obedience, and their distinguishing characteristics are relevant to the discussion of the present issue. One type of obedience corresponds to paternal authority, another to the essential functions that authority exercises in community life. The necessity of obedience may result from a membership that has not been freely chosen and it may result from the free decision to be a member of a particular community. Finally, obedience may be chosen on account of some excellence of its own....

Even though obedience is due to God alone in the domain of interior acts, there is one kind of judgment which is covered by the obedience that man owes to man. True, this judgment is not a purely internal act, since it is the form of external action; yet its being covered by a duty of obedience implies a decisive surrender on the part of the self. All that is exacted by pirates is money or merchandise, but whenever an act is done out of obedience, I will that any judgment and volition of mine should yield, if necessary, to the judgment and volition of those in charge of the common good. The decisive step has been taken. Inasmuch as the practical judgments, which are the forms of my exterior actions, also are acts of my mind and will, the rebellious moods of my subjectivity are curbed, and this happens voluntarily and freely. Whatever excellence is communicated in the exercise of authority uses ways of distinguished significance, for the ways of obedience are kept in order by a constant process of emancipation from the powers which threaten most profoundly my freedom to do what I please for the sake of the law, for the sake of the good, for the sake of God.

Philosophy of Democratic Government
("The Training of Free Men," 296–307)

We may not trust romantic descriptions in which the wretchedness of the assembly-line worker is pathetically contrasted with the bliss of the medieval artisan. But one hard act stands: highly divided labor does little for the intellectual culture of the laborer. By general assent, many functions of big industry require only a very short apprenticeship, and years of experience add little to the skill acquired in a few weeks. In order to estimate the significance of this fact, consider that the core of all intellectual culture is constituted by intellectual qualities which, on account of their object, imply essential steadiness, necessity, certainty, indefectibility.... Intellectual qualities devoid of certainty and necessity are of great human and social worth when their growth centers upon habitus and supplements them with an element of flexibility and charm. But if habitus are wanting, the mind can hardly rise above the level of amateurish adornment. The most serious effect of extremely divided and monotonous work is that it deprives men of their chance to acquire intellectual habitus during their working hours.... No technical habitus can be acquired without steady participation in the planning of action upon nature, and every planning is concerned with wholes. In Aristotle's philosophy of labor it seems that the only functions endowed with the privilege of generating intellectual culture are the so-called "architectonic" ones; the manual laborer, exemplified by the mason, is described as a mere agent of execution, whose virtue consists mainly in carrying out the orders that he is given. The stain attaching to manual labor, as a result of its being commonly done by slaves, seems to have blinded Aristotle to the large amount of technical thinking and planning required of all skilled workers. The connection established by him between architectonic thinking and the art habitus holds; Aristotle's error consists in his failure to see that every skilled worker performs intellectual operations similar to those which make up the dignity of the architect. In so far as he exercises domination over a plurality of parts and arranges this plurality for the sake of an end, the artisan does, on various levels, what the architect does on a high level, and, like the architect, he normally acquires an intellectual habitus. But, in so far as the object with which a worker is concerned has the character of a part, there is less opportunity to exercise domination, to arrange, distribute, subordinate, and co-ordinate—in short, to exercise technical thinking....

As a result of extreme division of labor, an unprecedented separation has taken place between planning and execution. Architectonic functions have been taken over by a large minority possessed of increasingly distinguished knowledge and ability. But simultaneously a great number of industrial workers were assigned to tasks which, on account of their being concerned with parts rather than with wholes, are altogether devoid of architectonic character. Many industrial workers exercise no self-government in the labor process; government is concerned with wholes.

Lack of autonomy in such an important phase of human life as daily work is by itself a grave privation. Considering, further, that there is inevitably a certain amount of interdependence between intellectual functions, it is reasonable to fear that a man deprived of a chance to govern himself in the process of labor will have a hard time learning to govern himself in moral and social life....

In contrast with industry, agriculture does not admit of extremely divided labor.[2] The biological rhythm of nature and the alternation of the seasons make it generally impossible for a man to repeat the same operation throughout the year, as often happens in industry....

These characteristics of wholeness and integration are due in part to the nature of the living processes with which the agricultural worker is concerned, but they are principally due to the nature of the unit within which these processes take place. Inasmuch as production processes are aimed at satisfying all the needs of the farm, the integrating center of work lies in man. *The essence of humanism is the use of a reference to man as principle of integration.* When labor processes are calculated to satisfy the needs of the human unit within which and by which they are planned and executed, the laborer is given a guarantee of human finality. In order that human labor may be properly related to man, two things are necessary: (a) that the product of labor be designed to satisfy some real human need and (b) that proportions measuring various products be determined by proportions existing among human needs. . . .

Thus farm work normally has, both in reference to technique itself and in reference to man, a character of wholeness and integration that industrial work cannot, in most cases, be expected to possess. All other things being equal, the farm worker finds in the conditions of his work an opportunity for training in self-government, both in the technical order and in the human order, which industrial conditions do not furnish. If the industrial laborer is to possess, with regard to self-government, a chance equal to that of the farm worker, it will be through the operation of factors capable of compensating for serious deficiencies. . . .

The wide and enduring influence exercised in our century by a variety of personalistic doctrines and movements is plainly due to the common experience of threats made to personality by the circumstances of modern life. Of those threats, the most apparent and perhaps the most central originate in technological organization. The type of organization promoted by technology makes for large and sometimes huge units in which the uniqueness of the individual person is, in many cases, unlikely to be remarked, remembered, pondered over, and sympathetically understood. . . . There is something depressing about the feeling that one is lost in a multitude. . . . Such a feeling discourages or perverts the natural urge toward autonomy. The orderly pursuit of self-government requires that I should be aware of the true law of myself, that I should perceive, beyond the confusing whims of pleasure and passion, the real meaning of my uniqueness. I am unlikely to achieve sound understanding of those things if I know they are inevitably ignored by society. . . .

Inasmuch as personal freedom implies freedom from interference by authority in the pursuit of personal good, the farm community is not the framework in which the greater amount of personal freedom can be achieved. All other things being equal, the industrial setup would give personal freedom a better chance. In many cases the migration of the youth from the farms to the big cities has been a movement away from paternal rule, toward conditions of more complete personal independence. Attention must be called, however, to the particular version of paternalistic government that party bureaucracy or a state bureaucracy, when given a free hand, usually inflicts upon industrial masses. This variety of paternalism is characterized by impersonality, rationality, efficiency, and the finality of decisions. . . .

Over and above resistance to unfair management, labor organizations have accomplished the double feat of helping to establish discipline among masses of men and of giving such discipline the higher meaning of autonomy. What this great product of the technological society—the labor union—has done for autonomy is of such exceptional value that any reform which would jeopardize the operation of labor unions or alter their essential constitution is bound to arouse the suspicion of the democratic mind. . . .

With regard to autonomy, the small unit of public life is distinguished by the following features: (a) The uniqueness of the individual person has a better chance of being recognized. In this connection the remarks made above concerning the farm hold for the small community of farmers, and those made concerning the big industrial plants holds for the big city. (b) The small rural community is about the only place, in modern public life, where some sort of rotation in power is practicable. The management of such a community requires no high degree of expertness; it may, consequently, be intrusted [sic: entrusted] to any prudent person. True, violence is done to the nature of public life whenever government is in the hands of an expert rather than in those of a prudent man. In public life government by experts is government by outsiders. But in technological societies the expert often becomes so important that it is hard to keep him in purely instrumental functions. Rule by experts is a frequent accident in modern states and in big cities as well. Against such accident the small rural community asserts the autonomy of public life by intrusting [sic: entrusting] leadership to persons that have no other distinction than their being good and experienced citizens.

A state directly governed by the people is hardly conceivable under modern circumstances, and, anyway, many disadvantages attach to government without distinct governing personnel. Yet direct democracy remains the archetype of all democratic organizations, and, if it were to perish from the earth, representative democracy might soon be transformed into some sort of oligarchic or aristocratic polity. Large cities are not different from states with regard to the need for distinct governing personnel; but in the town and village elected councilors and officers are in such relation to the whole of the people that local government amounts to a close approximation of direct democracy. The modern democratic state draws much of its spirit from the small rural unit of public administration. Democracy on the level of the state depends to a large extent on the intensity of democratic life in the rural community. A democratic polity is hardly possible in a nation in which the countryside is subjected to oligarchic rule, whether by landlords of the old-fashioned type or by companies.

Notes

1. [Editor's Note: I selected texts from an indicated range, and this was then approved by the contributor.]

2. [Editor's note: Simon earlier had limited his discussion of agriculture to the "family-size farm," as opposed to "industrial agriculture." At the time Simon wrote, the former was more prevalent than it is seventy years later.]

PART IV

Community

CHAPTER 15

Political Society

Yves R. Simon explains what a "common good" is understood to be. A common good is not "opposed" to a private good; one cannot really have one good without the other. Strictly speaking, no real good is opposed to another good unless it is out of proper order, in which case the problem is with the mislocation of the good, not with the good itself, which remains good even in disorder. A "common" good, moreover, makes private goods flourish as goods and as private.

Following the notion that wholes cannot be wholes unless parts be parts, Simon, following a remark of Aristotle about the danger of the ideal city in the *Republic* (1261a15–20), explains why a common good is not an absorption of parts into an undifferentiated whole. Rather, it is a protection of parts in order that there may be a real whole. The function of authority relative to the common good is to allow and promote the parts, in their very organization, to be what they are, as themselves necessary for the good of the whole by being what they are.

The authority responsible for carrying out the particular compromises or laws that may indeed affect private goods does not intend to discourage or destroy private or lesser social institutions, with their own authority structures to keep them what they are. Rather, what it intends is to provide an opportunity of parts to be parts precisely by finding a place for them alongside other goods that are also parts of the whole complexus of goods that is made possible by an authoritative common good.

The common good is the end or purpose of a state understood in Aristotle's sense that man is "by nature a political being." This famous phrase means that in order to be what he is intended to be, man will need many other institutions and activities, including the family, whereby what he is can be actively manifested and fostered through his own participation. Since no one, by himself, can accomplish all the varied things possible to human beings, the polity or the state is a natural, but humanly organized, institution whose purpose is to permit and encourage the wide variety of good things that are possible to human beings through their own prudence and skill and intelligence.

This same civil institution by default will also be responsible for limiting or preventing, as part of this same common good, evil acts directed against the parts, individuals, or groups within the whole. This latter function, however, is called "substitutional" by Simon. That is, it is now necessary that a coercive function within the polity exists, because of the actual human condition in its fallen state. But the directive functions of the polity would be present even if there were no wickedness manifested in human experience. These latter or coercive functions are occasioned only by improper or evil uses of the will in free choice.

Simon is careful to insist that the metaphysical being of the polity is not itself another "being" to be found separately from the parts that constitute the polity in the first place. The polity is not a "substance," but a "relation," an intelligible order of things as they are related to one another. Nor is the common good some plan that exists apart from the actual members of the polity, to be superimposed on it by some outside movement or force or politician. The common good does not have totalitarian overtones.

In a brief, brilliant sentence, Simon writes, "The principal part of our common good is contained within our souls" (*A General Theory of Authority*, 126). What does this phrase mean? We are rational beings whose proper acts are through our knowing and willing what is true and good. The diversity and variety of things are, as such, good things. How is it possible that what is not directly my good is also my good, while at the same time being the good of the social order? This is the problem that the common good sets out to answer. As Simon writes in *Work, Society, and Culture*, "An order is in principle a part of an integrated society defined by a function relative to an aspect of the common good." What is contained in our souls is the understanding that our part, our private good, is also a good allowed to be what it is because all good is worthy of being manifested and fostered.

The true is what we should know because we see the evidence for it. The good is something we should choose because we see that it is worthy of choice. Simon argues that the promotion of the good and the true on the part of the state or society is now substitutional. But he suggests that if the example of someone can inspire me to the good or the instruction of a teacher can guide me to what is true, then it is a worthy thing to embrace the help, even though we only understand the true, for instance, when we see the evidence for it. As he put it in *A General Theory of Authority*, "promoting the order of truth in the social life of the transcendent intellect is the highest function of the civil community" (129).

The ultimate common good of the universe is God, for it is by him that all goods *are*. It is an essential element in the common good that those beings that can know *what is*, in their own activity actually *do* know. Knowledge, Simon says, is that by which we know *all* that is. This is the power by which all things not ourselves become ours without ceasing to be themselves. This is why the "principal part of the common good is within our souls," for in no place else is what is common seen to be precisely common, save by a particular being in his own soul.

James V. Schall, SJ

Freedom of Choice
("The Will," 25–26 and 31–34)

The comprehensive good is not determinately finite; yet it cannot be identified with the infinite good.[1] A good determinately infinite cannot exist in combination with any evil, or with any limitation of goodness. The comprehensive good does *admit of* coincidence with the infinite good; it should be said the climax of its intelligibility is attained in such a coincidence. Likewise, the concept of being exercises the fullness of its energy when it comes to signify being without privation or limitation—the unreceived and unrestricted act of to be. But just as the common concept of being admits of limited realizations and excludes no limitation—it excludes only contradiction, which would annihilate it—so the comprehensive good excludes no conceivable limitation of goodness: it admits of all the limitations that it transcends and excludes only the fiction of an evil subsisting by itself. The comprehensive good is embodied in the most particular objects of desire, e.g., in the short-lived sweetness of vengeance obtained at the cost of hideous felony. But any particular thing in which it is embodied fails, by an infinite distance, to coincide with it. In short, the infinity of the comprehensive good is that of a form which admits of existence in particular bearers, but whose power cannot be exhausted by any bearer distinct from itself. . . .

In animals, luxury and disorder do not have the character of devouring frenzy, save perhaps in a small number of cases. In man, on the contrary, biological desires, as soon as they are not controlled by the virtuous reason, expand indefinitely, become frantic, miss their object and destroy their subject. If such facts of furious destruction are relatively rare, it is because the conditions upon which they depend are seldom realized. Few men succeed in destroying completely the structure of rational rules built in their souls by religion and society. Let it be said that insofar as the rules of the virtuous reason are lacking, frenzy gets hold of desires. This does not happen only as an exception but constantly. Every rebel bears witness to the destructive infinity of emancipated desires.

Let us make clear the paradox contained in these familiar facts. The rules of action resulting from biological structure and animal instinct should, if all things were equal, suffice to assure the government of man in his animal life. A purely sensible desire would be a matter proportionate to the forms of instinct; but the matter that instinct vainly endeavors to control is a desire animated, agitated, tormented, expanded and sometimes devastated by the quest for infinity which is characteristic of the spirit....

All our perceptions are human and pervaded with intellectuality....

Let us call exasperation the process in which emotions and passions, through their indefinite amplitude, disclose the infinite nature of the will and of the energy capable of all the good. Under the name of Dionysian emotions Nietzsche describes a sublime form of exasperation. A delirium shaken by the shivers of sacred awe is brought about by the inebriation of the senses. How could this be, if there were not, within inebriation, an appetite capable of finding its joy in the metaphysical attributes of being? Universal harmony, superabundance, common and unanimous life, liberty, peace, the original unity rejoined at the cost of an immense negation of the distinctions of forms, mystery and joy invading the entire soul: all these metaphysical marvels come forward at the call of spring, under the influence of fermented drinks, of dance and strident sounds, through emotions expressive of a love greater than the world and capable of the absolute.

The Tradition of Natural Law
("The Definition of Law," 89–96)

Let us remove the pernicious and all too frequent illusion that the tendency of men to form communities proceeds exclusively from need, poverty, lacks, and wants of every description. Some forms of sociability do proceed from our not having, all by ourselves, the things that we must have in order to survive and to live well. But other forms of sociability, perhaps less conspicuous but not less profound, proceed from our accomplishments, our fulfillments, our plenitude, from the abundance and superabundance of successful life. There is such a thing as disinterested sociability. And since divine love alone can be absolutely disinterested in all respects, there is such a thing as a need to give, a need to be generous, a need to act disinterestedly. This need is so deeply rooted in our rational nature that when it is frustrated it soon breeds a singular power of destruction.

These fundamentals concerning human sociability ought to be borne in mind in order that the common good be safely distinguished from its counterfeits and from the substitutes which make it possible, at least seemingly, to do without it in individualistic philosophies. "The greatest good of the greatest number," in the language of the utilitarians, is such a substitute excluding the common good by the premises of the system. No doubt a substitute is better than nothing, and men have laid down their lives for a common good which was inadequately represented in their minds by "the greatest good of the greatest number." To bring forth the qualitative difference between the common and the private good, let us remark that a good is common if, and only if, it is of such a nature as to call for common pursuit and common enjoyment. It is not an addition, or a multiplication, but an objective relation of the thing desirable to the powers of desire and attainment which distinguishes the common from the private good. Public safety is an aspect of the common good, for it certainly is a thing which by nature has to be pursued by common effort and, if obtained, is enjoyed in common. The same holds for the training of characters by the irresistible power of state coercion, and the same holds for the treasures of knowledge available in our schools and libraries.... Above all it holds for the constant action, silent most of the time, by which society maintains in each of us some clarity of moral conscience, some willingness to prefer the right to the wrong, and some comforting energy against the forces of desperation. When the structures of society break down, as they sometimes do in periods of critical changes, in revolutions and in wars, ordinary people soon yield to hideous crime. Then it becomes appallingly clear that whatever moral conscience can be expected to exist in large numbers of men, whatever decency, whatever resistance to perversion or to desperation can be expected of them, are goods of such a nature as to be pursued in common and procured by the distinct causality which belongs to a multitude unified, differentiated, and stabilized in its differentiated unity. It may be difficult to say in what respects a man is, and in what respects he is not, a part of the community. What is not open to doubt is that insofar as the individual has the character of a part, the principle of the primacy of the whole signifies not only that the common good is greater, but also that the private good may have to be sacrificed to the greater good of the community....

The illusion of the community of men represented as a work of art is powerful; to destroy it several approaches may be needed....

It should be recalled that no art solves any problem of human use. One may possess an art excellently and remain idle. And it is always possible to make a humanly good or a humanly wrong use of whatever art one masters, whether excellently or in a rudimentary condition. Moreover, the master of an art may use his mastery against the very purposes of his art if he pleases to do so.... If politics were an art, a virtue would still be needed to decide what use should be made of it, but this prudence is politics itself....

The myth which identifies the common good with the perfection of a work of art and thus represents it as something nonhuman is constantly strengthened by the assumption that society, or at least the temporal, as distinct from the spiritual society, is conceived only with external actions, such as digging, orderly conduct in the street, marching, charging and retreating according to orders, paying taxes, fulfilling contracts, etc. Political society, in this view, would have nothing to do with what goes on in the heart of men. To ascertain the worth of this current opinion, we must consider the kind of reality that social and political life is made of.

As social sciences tried to profit by the experimental method which was so successful in the knowledge of nature, the notion of *social fact* acquired a central importance. What facts are social in a proper sense? To what types are the main social facts reducible? The most obvious example of social fact is constituted by the cooperation of men engaged in a transitive action of such nature as to require the unified effort of a multitude. The digging of a canal, the clearing of a jungle, the building of a railroad, the reclamation of swamp land, all are clear examples of social facts, and the good condition of such facts, the successful cooperation of men in the performance of collective transitive actions is an aspect of the common good. But when men are aware of their unity in knowing and loving or hating, we speak with entire propriety of their communing in acts of cognition and love or hatred. Here are immanent actions which, because of the awareness of unity, assume a social character.[2] Clearly, these communions are the most genuine and the most profound of all social facts, and the good condition of these communions, the good condition of whatever pertains to acting together in these immanent actions, is the deepest and the most precious part of the common good. We may imagine isolated prisoners watching the same play at the same time, each on a particular screen, without any awareness of what goes on in the other cells, without even knowing whether other cells are occupied. There is nothing social about the unity in enjoyment of the play by these isolated spectators. Suppose now that the doors of the prison are opened. The men are free, with no restriction of their craving for community life. (Every community is in some way or other what Aristotle says of the state, a community of the free.) Should they happen to watch a performance together, we would recognize the familiar picture of communion in interest, in terror or pity, in expectation and suspense, in admiration and enthusiasm which also makes up the social significance of Greek tragedies, football games, and bullfights as well. With their experience in confinement and freedom, in isolation and community, these fellows would be exceptionally qualified witnesses about the true nature of the common good. By listening to the words springing from the abundance of their hearts we would come to realize quite clearly that the most important part of community life takes place in the heart of man.

Practical Knowledge
("Practical Knowledge of Social Science," 123)

If we notice that a trend has prevailed over a large part of society and for a long time, shall we infer, from its sheer prevalence in these dimensions of social existence, that some excellence belongs to this trend, although the connection may still not be clearly intelligible? In the last fifty years the divorce rate has increased considerably, especially in societies characterized by readiness to welcome technical progress and to give up the traditional ways of life. Should it be said that the trend, by the very fact of its persistence, takes over a value in terms of rightness and progress? If this were the case, the divorce rate, other things being equal, should not decline, and the eccentrics who remain faithful to the principle of strict monogamy should be blamed for refusing to cooperate in the progress of mores. Whenever such inferences are drawn, it is easy to recognize the operation of the postulated principle that the law of mankind is one of inescapable progress. This law is supposed to be so strict as to tolerate no deviation of any considerable size or duration; as soon as a process assumes the character of a trend, one may be sure that the benevolent genius of history is at work. Clearly, such a transmutation of facts into values proceeds from a mythological theory of the fact. It is not a solution to the problem of the relation between fact and value.

A General Theory of Authority
(Selections: 29–30, 36–39, and 122–26)

In this world of change, individuals come and go. The law of generation and corruption covers the whole universe of nature. This law is transcended in a very proper sense by the incorruptibility of the species and the immortality of human association. The masterpiece of the natural world cannot be found in the transient individual. Nor can it be found in the species, which is not imperishable except in the state of universality; but in this state it is no longer unqualifiedly real. Human communities are the highest attainments of nature, for they are virtually unlimited with regard to diversity of perfection, and virtually immortal. Beyond the satisfaction of individual needs the association of men serves a good unique in plenitude and duration, the common good of the human community. . . .

We still need to inquire into the basic forms of association. These are the mere partnership and the community. Let us consider familiar examples. A merchant succeeds in convincing an owner of capital that money invested in his business would bring nice dividends. By the terms of their contract, any profits will be divided according to a definite ratio. Then the merchant goes to the market, and the money-lender sits back and awaits the event. Their "common interest" was celebrated in expectant toasts, but they are not engaged in any common action designed to promote any "common interest." The merchant works by himself or with his employees; he does not work with the money-lender, who remains a silent partner. Where there is no common action, there is no common good. These two men do not make up a community. What they call their "common interest" is in fact a sum of private interests that happen to be interdependent.

In contradistinction to mere partners, the members of a community—family, factory, football team, army, state, church . . .—are engaged in a common action whose object is qualitatively different from a sum of interdependent goods. . . .

It is not by accident that nobody can demonstrate what the rule of justice consists in under historically conditioned, absolutely concrete, individual, and possibly unprecedented and unrenewable circumstances. Here the rule of justice is not uttered by an essence and cannot be grasped by the demonstrative power of the intellect. It is uttered by the love which is the soul of the just and it can be learned only by listening to the teaching of love. Take for instance the problem of ownership of extreme necessity. Our sense of justice acknowledges that a starving person, without money and without liberal friends, has a right to save his life with food that he cannot pay for. No doubt, such a proposition can be demonstrated, and St. Thomas successfully designated the middle term of the demonstration when he remarked that in case of necessity all things become common. But argumentation will never establish a logical connection between the theory of property and the answer that *I* am looking for when, already weakened by hunger, I wonder whether my case is actually one of extreme necessity. A man in need will know for sure whether his necessity is extreme or not if and only if he is so just as to feel how far the right of his neighbor and his own right go, so temperate as not to mistake an accidental urge for a real need, and so strong as to fear neither the sufferings of hunger nor the resentment of his illiberal neighbors.

Thus, whereas a question relative to an ethical essence can be answered both by way of cognition and by way of inclination, the way of inclination alone can procure an answer when a question of human conduct involves contingency. This holds for the rules of common action as well as for those of individual conduct. Political prudence is no less dependent upon the obscure forces of the appetite than prudence in the government of individual life....

Every certain judgment concerning what we have to do under concrete circumstances is dictated by an affective motion and owes its certain truth to its agreement with dependable inclination. But when the pursuit is that of a common good, the part played by affective and secret determination is no longer an obstacle to unity of judgment among men. Wills properly inclined toward the same common good cannot but react in the same way to the same proposition, if what this proposition expresses is definitely what the common good demands....

Granted that the wisdom of society should work toward conditions favorable to the order in truth in transcendent matters, the next question is whether *temporal* society has anything to do with such problems of truth and error....

The political ideal of liberalism was a state whose only functions were to restrain criminals and to make sure that contracts were lived up to. But at this point let us ask what common beliefs these purposes imply on the part of the citizens as well as on the part of the governing personnel. All would be easy if it were possible to assume that, with the negligible exception of the very few, the inhabitants of civilized nations agree on such subjects as the preservation of human life, the respect for property, the observance of contracts, the fundamental principles of family life, etc. If that much agreement could be taken for granted, it would seem natural to hold that the duties of the state can be fulfilled without any concern for what is going on in the souls of men. But experience shows that even in small and closely knit groups disagreement can be sharp with regard to crime and good action. Here is a party of old friends who belong to the same section of society and whose background is much the same. Yet some call sheer murder what others consider altogether beneficial surgery; some call suicide what others praise as heroic sacrifice; some call exploitation and robbery what others understand to be the fully normal operation of the market and some call violations of human rights what others interpret as the consequences of facts obviously designed by providence. Civil society cannot afford indifference to opinion on such subjects as murder, suicide, honesty in economic life, and justice and brotherhood in the relations between groups distinguished by color or language. A well-organized police force does not suffice, under all circumstances, to protect innocent life.... Indeed, if society wants to protect innocent life effectively, it must be concerned not only with external behavior, but also with the thoughts of men on various levels, the deepest ones not being excluded....

By reflecting, no matter how briefly, on the nature of the acts which constitute the life of communities, we shall find ourselves in a better position to understand the interests of society, be it purely temporal, in the deep thoughts and feelings of men. Let us mention first the collective actions designed to bring about changes in external nature. A team of men pulling a boat from the bank of a river supplies a perfect example of a community in act. Of these men, none could cause the boat to move—a thing that the united team does easily. Next to these transitive actions that are collective by necessity come certain kinds of communication among men. Indeed, communications may be entirely interindividual and may not involve the power of the social whole. Those that are social are distinguished from the merely interindividual ones by their being designed to cause communions among the men who communicate. A speech by a public person and the raising of the flag every morning in the schoolyards of the nation are clear examples of communion-causing communications. Thus, we are led to understand the principal act of social life is immanent in the souls of men. It is a communion in some belief, love, or aversion. . . . The common good is actually attained when a collective action upon external nature has brought about, in fact, the change for which it was designed. Again, there is actual attainment of the common good when a communication has succeeded in causing a communion. But, most of all, the common good exists in act when we know and feel that we are one in adhering to a certain truth and in dedicating our lives to what we hold to be right and good.

Philosophy of Democratic Government
("General Theory of Government," 62–67)

It has been established that authority, considered in its essential functions, is as natural as the association of men for a common good. Thus civil government is as natural as civil society if, and only if, a common good is the object of civil association. The only way to escape the conclusion that civil government is produced "by our want"—in other words by the nature of things—would be to show that civil society has no common good for its object. The question boils down to this: Is it possible to conceive civil society after the fashion of a mere partnership, involving no common existence, no common life, no common love, and no common action?[3] . . . .

Let us assume, for the sake of greater precision, that what is in question is not civil society as such but its being a society relative to a common good, and let us further define civil society as the society within which all the tendencies of man, so far as temporal life is concerned, can normally find satisfaction. In order to determine the nature of the good that such a society proposes to procure, viz., whether it is a common good or a sum of particular goods, let us disengage, from typical examples, the distinguishing features of a society relative to a common good. Then we shall see whether these are recognizable in civil society as defined above.

As typical examples of societies relative to a common good let the football team, the team of workers, and the army be singled out. Let the contrasting example of the handicraftsman and moneylender association be borne in mind. And, in order to simplify our vocabulary, let us call "community" the society which is relative to a common good; "mere partnership," the society which is not.

1. That the football team, the team of workers, and the army are communities is evidenced, first of all and most strikingly, by the fact that some transitive actions are traceable not to any particular individual but to the team or to the participation of all. Such operations do not

necessarily involve the actual participation of all; an act exercised by some remains the act of the whole if those who are actually engaged in action act as the organ of the whole. This is plainly what happens in the case of an attacking army: the attack is traceable to the army as to the cause of which it is the action; yet members of the army, possibly many, are waiting, watching, resting, healing their wounds, not attacking. In mere partnership each action is traceable to some partner, e.g., all the work is traceable to the handicraftsman and the financing to the money-lender, none is traceable to the partnership itself.

2. The transitive actions of a community are prepared and intrinsically conditioned by immanent actions of knowledge and desire in which members commune. The members of a football team or of an orchestra always know very well why they are gathered together and always desire very ardently the attainment of the common objective. Members of a working group do not always understand very clearly what they are doing together and do not always desire ardently the effect of their common action. Members of an army are often unaware of the cause for which they are fighting. Such failures constitute a telling counterproof, for, in so far as there is lack of knowledge or love with regard to the object of common action, the community is poorly integrated, incompletely constituted, and its efficiency is uncertain. Let it be noticed, further, that communion in immanent actions does not consist in the sheer fact that several know the same object and wish it to be brought about. Prisoners toiling in isolation would contribute to the production of a certain effect, would all know what this effect is, and would all desire its coming into existence without there being any communion between them. Communion implies, in addition to immanent acts relative to the same object, my knowing that the others know and desire the same object and want it to be effected by the action of our community. Communions in immanent actions make up the most profound part of social reality; theirs is a world of peace where ennui is impossible and where death itself can be sweet—there alone the individual is freed from solitude and anxiety. Mere partnership, on the other hand, does not do anything to put an end to the solitude of the partners. They may be better off as a result of their contract, but their contract will not relieve their lonesomeness. There is not, between

them, any communion in an immanent action. It may be that in our time mere partnership plays too great a role in the life of men at work; according to certain criticisms, this would be a major cause of the anxiety prevalent in our societies.

3. Communications, as such, are merely interindividual processes. They obviously play an essential part in mere partnership. But in communities they assume a new character, inasmuch as they are calculated to produce communions and to entertain them. In the teams and in the army as well there is a constant exchange of signs, not all of which are words, whose purpose it is to cause in souls certain cognitions and certain emotions and awareness that the objects of these cognitions and emotions of mine are also the objects for the cognitions and emotions of my companions, superiors, and subordinates. Presiding over these communion-causing communications is one of the major tasks of a leader and a very precise test of his ability. A good leader sends the appropriate messages—words, gestures, examples, silences—at the proper time, this may be the easiest part of his job. It is more difficult to obtain a steady flow of appropriate messages from his subordinates, and the most difficult and finest accomplishment would be to assure the regular operation of communion-causing communication among equals, at all levels of the hierarchy.

To sum up: collective causality, communion in immanent actions, and communion-causing communications are the criteria of the community as distinct from the mere partnership.

But who can fail to recognize these criteria in anything that deserves in any degree the name of civil society? Directing attention to a few obvious facts should suffice to bring our inquiry to a firm conclusion. Under the first heading, i.e., effects traceable to the civil multitude as to its proper cause, let us mention the following: security against enemies, both foreign and domestic; building commitments with foreign societies; over-all status of expansion, both within existing boundaries and toward new boundaries; over-all status of ownership, of education, of temporal life in relation to the spiritual. Under the second heading (communion), refer to any aspect of the feelings known as patriotism, loyalty, or allegiance to one's country, especially as expressed in ceremonies whose purpose it is to give the individual comfort and the community more abundant life, by bringing civil communions to a high pitch of intensity, e.g., military parades, inaugurations, national funerals, the daily raising of the flag in the schoolyards of the United States. Third heading: these ceremonies themselves are perfect examples of communion-causing communications proper to the civil society and of such a nature as to demonstrate its being a community. To show how easily countless other examples could be found, let us merely mention the teaching of civics at school and such risky procedures as government-inspired propaganda.

Notes

1. [Editor's Note: I selected the texts from indications of the earlier editors; the contributor approved them.]

2. The distinction between transitive and immanent action is explained by Aristotle in *Meta.* 9.8, 1050a 30, translated by. W. D. Ross: "Where, then, the result is something apart from the exercise, the actuality is in the thing that is being made, e.g., the act of building is in the thing that is being built and that of weaving in the thing that is being woven, and similarly in all other cases, and in general the movement in the thing that is being moved; but where there is no product apart from the actuality, the actuality is present in the agents, e.g. the act of seeing is in the seeing subject and that of theorizing in the theorizing subject and the life is in the soul (and therefore well-being also, for it is a certain kind of life)."

3. That not every society is a community is hinted at by Aristotle in relation to animal societies (*History of Animals* 1.1 488a7–10): "Sociable animals are those which all together accomplish a work that is one and common to all: this is not always the case with animals living in herds. Such sociable animals are man, the bee, the wasp, the ant, the crane."

CHAPTER 16

The Definition of Law

We draw here on the "Definition of Law" chapter in Yves R. Simon, *The Tradition of Natural Law*.[1] Simon works, in defining law, from the first question of Thomas Aquinas's *Treatise on Law* (*Summa Theologiae* [*ST*] I-II, q. 90, a. 4).

It will be remembered that the four articles of question 90 of the *Treatise on Law* are the following:

1. Whether law is something pertaining to reason?
2. Whether law is always directed to the common good?
3. Whether the reason of any man is competent to make laws?
4. Whether promulgation is essential to law?

We can see in "Definition of Law" how much, and what kind, of a Thomist Simon was. We can also see how important Thomas's account, buttressed by Aristotle's insights, still is an account that develops this definition of law: "Law is an ordinance of reason for the common good, promulgated by him who has the care of the community" (*ST* I-II, q. 90, a. 1 ad 4).

There is relatively little here about Thomas's third article of question 90 (on who is authorized to issue laws), and there is virtually nothing about Thomas's fourth article (on the promulgation requirement).

Perhaps this is because the overall interest of this Simon book, on natural law and its applications, makes questions about who exercises authority and about how laws are promulgated less pressing. Such questions may be regarded as concerned with technical matters substantially dependent on "history" and circumstances.

On the other hand, there *is* in "Definition of Law" an extended discussion of the common good, of which a sample is provided below. We all have, of course, *some* notion both of what the common good calls for and what it looks like, however dependent the common good (or its extent and development) may often be on contingencies.

There is also an extended discussion of the role of reason in the shaping of law—and that discussion is here in our selection at greater length, particularly the effort to correct those who make much of *will*, instead of *reason*, in accounting for law. (A will-oriented approach can be seen in *Erie Railroad Company v. Tompkins*, 304 U.S. 64 [1938].) The Simon position can be said to be anticipated by Aquinas's dramatic observation in his *On Truth* (q. 23, a. 6):

> Because justice is a kind of "rightness" as Anselm teaches (*On Truth*, 12) or "equality," as the Philosopher teaches (*Nicomachean Ethics* 5.1), justice in its essential nature will depend primarily upon whatever has that measure by which the equality and rightness of justice are established among things. Now the will cannot be characterized as the first rule but rather as ruled, inasmuch as it is directed by reason and intellect. This is not only true for us but for God as well, although the will in us is really distinct from the intellect. This is why the will and its rightness are not the same thing. But in God the will is really identified with the intellect, so that the rightness of his will is really the same as the will itself. So the primary thing upon which the essential nature of all justice depends is the wisdom of the divine intellect, which establishes things perfectly, in proportion to one another and to their cause. The essential nature of created justice consists in this proportion. In asserting that justice depends only on the will, one is declaring that the divine will does not act according to the order of wisdom, a blasphemous assertion.

Simon's use of mathematics in the selections here provided is particularly instructive as to how reasoning itself is to be assessed. Simon is aware of the limits of rationality in the everyday conduct of human affairs. One is left to wonder what the rank of philosophy should be among the proper aspirations of the human being, particularly in comparison both with communal endeavors and with personal salvation. Is philosophy that reliable grasp of things that any community of rational beings somehow naturally yearns for?

Of particular interest is the orderly, even methodical, character of the typical Simon analysis, so much so as to make him appear almost naïve (if not even "Aristotelian") in his simplicity and earnestness. He starts with what is closest and most familiar to us, the laws of civil society. One may even be led to wonder whether the diversity of man-made laws itself suggests the law of nature—that law or set of standards by which we can assess what is offered and done, and why it is done, by human beings acting as officers of government.

It should be noticed, if only in passing, that there are here and there in the Simon discussion on the definition of law intriguing materials that draw upon the French tradition, including materials using Descartes, Pascal, Rousseau, and the French Revolution. The influence of that tradition upon Simon would be worth developing elsewhere, along with his remarkable adaptation to the American regime. Perhaps it is the French tradition that helps account for the emergence and importance of a sometimes anarchic individualism in the Western world. Much is said in "Definition of Law" about the relation of individualism to the common good, including the indications that reasonable provision for individuals should be assumed in any sound and enduring understanding of the common good.

A salutary warning is provided by Simon against much reliance by a people upon "executive agents." He advocates, instead, greater reliance upon "legislative prudence," an advocacy that may be even more timely today than it was when first ventured six decades ago by our old teacher.

George Anastaplo

The Tradition of Natural Law
("The Definition of Law," 69–87, 97–98, and 107–9)

[W]e now turn to the study of the concept of law.[2] Order requires that we consider first the kind of law which is, and which in all events will remain, the closest and most familiar to us. The study of law begins with the consideration of what this word signifies when we speak of the laws of the civil society, when we say, for instance, "This is the law of the land." This order is determined by reasons of diverse character. For one thing, it is clear that the law of society comes before the law of nature in a psychological and pedagogical sense. . . .

We find at the beginning of Thomas Aquinas' *Treatise on Laws* (*Summa Theologiae*, I-II, q. 90, a.1) this nominal and dialectical definition of law: law is a rule and a measure of human action. Establishing the real and scientific definition will consist in determining what conditions a thing should satisfy in order that it be a rule and a measure of human action. The search for the real definition of law is subdivided into four questions, the first of which is whether law is a work of the reason. (The others are: (2) concerning the end of law; (3) its cause; (4) the promulgation of law.)[3] The meaning of this question is made perfectly clear by referring (according to good historical and dialectical method) to the fact of legal voluntarism. What is not in dispute is that the legislator—whether king, representative assembly, or the people as a whole—wants a certain rule to be observed in certain circumstances. That every law involves an act of will is taken for granted. What is being asked is whether the role of the will in the constitution of the law is primary or subordinate. . . . [T]he history of voluntarism testifies that this problem is not an irrelevant subtlety. Thus the first question in our progression from the nominal and dialectical to the real definition of law is whether, in order to have the character of a rule and a measure of human action, the thing called law should be primarily a work of the reason or a work of the will.

Of the terms involved in this question (rule, measure, human action, reason, will), none has the quality of intelligible ultimacy.

Mathematicians—our teachers in rigorous thinking—are today more than ever particular about making their initial and indefinable concepts, as well as their initial and indemonstrable premises, entirely explicit. In philosophy, also, complete rigor requires that every concept be analyzed into its components up to the level of the indefinables. One reason why philosophy rarely exists in a perfectly rigorous and scientific condition is that the complete analysis of a philosophical term is an operation involving such strain that few people can stand it. A philosopher who cares to have any readers must generally stop short of the indefinables, just when he has reached a level where the reader experiences a feeling of sufficient clarity. If intellectual training is sound, this feeling is dependable, and if it is unsound, not much can be done anyway. Therefore, we shall confidently depend on the common understanding of such terms as "rule" and "measure." The latter term is somewhat unusual in the context of human affairs, but simple reference to its ordinary quantitative use suffices to make it clear, as well as graphic and effective, as a supplement to the term rule. If a thing is a rule and a measure of human action, what kind of thing is it supposed to be? Among the conditions that it ought to satisfy, shall we include its being primarily a work of the reason or its being primarily a work of the will? . . .

The proposition that "a thing which is a rule and a measure of human action is primarily the work of the reason" is axiomatic, and so we are again confronted by the particular difficulties that the handling of axioms involves in our time. Two factors should be considered. First, ever since the early ages of Greek culture men have looked up to mathematics for patterns of rigorous thought and held that if any propositions enjoy the power of absolute premises these should be the mathematical axioms. But in our time mathematicians commonly hold that no difference should be made between axioms and postulates. The so-called axiomatic proposition still plays the part of first premise but it is within a definite system that it plays such a part; in another system it would be a conclusion. Accordingly, the proposition *used as* first premise never has the character of an absolute premise. A day may come when the meaning of axioms in mathematics will be understood to involve unique particularities following upon the fundamental characteristics of mathematical abstraction. Then we may realize that looking up to mathematics for ideal patterns of axiomatic propositions was a precarious operation, jeopardized by illusions concerning the relation of mathematics to reality....

Secondly, the adventures of the theory of axioms in modern times are traceable in part to the confusion of logical issues with psychological issues. The sharp distinction to be made between logical immediacy, i.e., independence of any middle term and antecedent demonstration, and the psychological situation designated when we say that we are ready to do something immediately, vanishes in any theory which fails to express the difference between psychology and logic. The psychological interpretation of logical properties has been a common accident, especially since the seventeenth century. (One of the reasons for the success of what is called "symbolic logic" is that in this movement we find again, at long last, a sense for something which, no matter what its nature may be, is certainly not reducible to psychological processes)....

At this point it is relevant to ask whether some human societies may conceivably be governed by rules of instinct and animal intelligence rather than by rules of reason. What is it that makes the difference between so-called animal intelligence and intelligence (or understanding, or reason) properly so called? The distinguishing characteristics of reason, as compared with animal intelligence, are most certainly attained by reflecting upon the profundity and the necessity that rational consideration involves in an indefinite multiplicity of ways. The pattern is supplied by abstract thinking, logical and mathematical. If Plato believed that the science of mathematics is such a distinguished teacher of mankind, it is, above all, because it develops in the mind a familiarity with rational necessity. Such absolute necessity is absent from any combination of images, no matter how subtle; it is also absent from the complex which associates anticipated pleasure or pain with a sensation or an image; and it is also absent from the sheer feeling that the thing attained in a particular experience or image is useful or harmful. This feeling is precisely what Aristotle calls the sagacity, the prudence, the wisdom found in animals—man not excluded—and which we designate as instinct and animal intelligence (*Hist. Anim.* 8.1.588a20). If we want to decide whether primitive societies, or some of them, establish their rules of action by animal intelligence rather than by rational consideration, let us bear in mind the character of necessity which distinguishes the rational.... Thomas Aquinas expressed the belief that the circumstances of climate may be such as to prevent the development of the reason in men. If such underprivileged men made up a society, their rules of common behavior would be infrarational. These hypotheses are not disproved by any philosophical principle but the modern study of primitive societies does not seem to bear them out. The report accepted by Aquinas apparently was one of those amazing travellers' stories that our ancestors were so eager to believe....

Let us now ask in what capacity law is a work of reason and, more precisely, whether it is a work of reason in the capacity of conclusion or in that of premise. Sound method requires that we should consider first that which is ultimate in the system of practical reason, i.e., the fully determinate judgments which apply to action immediately. These judgments are as practical as the acts whose forms they are; accordingly, they involve reference to all the contingencies of particular situations. The individual case with which practical judgment ultimately has to deal may always be in some significant respect unique, unprecedented, and unrenewable. Thus, the last conclusion of the practical discourse is marked in essential fashion by features of strict singularity and of contingency. These features contradict in several ways the already established characteristics of law. In fact, a practical judgment fully adjusted to the circumstances is not so much the work of the reason as that of an inclination. It cannot be connected logically with any first principle. It ought indeed to be connected with principles but, owing to the contingency of its matter, the soundness of an inclination is the only thing that can effect this connection. No necessity of discourse deals with data that are not contained in any rational necessity. At the level of practical ultimacy, "love takes over the function of object" and the determination of truth is the work of affective connaturality. It is entirely reasonable that the last word about action be uttered by the inclination of the wise men, but there is less rationality in a judgment determined by sound inclination than in one determined by rational obviousness. Thus, considering this trait of law, viz., its being a work of the reason, let it be said that the conclusion of the practical discourse implies, in the most essential fashion, a trait opposed to the rational character of law. But more fundamentally, the last practical judgment, i.e., the one which is congruent to action as form is congruent to matter, is separated from law both by its singularity and by its contingency. A law is a rule and there is nothing more essential to it than the intelligible features implied in the concept of rule. These include universality and necessity. . . .

Between the concept of authority and that of law there exist enlightening relations. It is, indeed, perfectly appropriate to speak of the authority of the legislator, and it would be arbitrary to identify authority and executive power. However, authority and law evidence opposite intelligible tendencies inasmuch as the more a proposition is expressive of necessity, the more it participates—other things being equal—in the character of law, whereas there is nothing in the concept of authority that expresses aversion to contingency. When authority serves to insure the united action of a community under circumstances which render unanimity precarious, authority is exercising an essential function. But after we have discounted all factors of a negative character, such as ignorance, shortsightedness, and selfishness, it is the contingency of our ways, the possibility of attaining our goal one way or the other, which renders unanimity precarious and causes authority to be the indispensable condition of steady unity in common action. Authority is perfectly at home in the management of contingency and in the uttering of practical conclusions. Law is more at home in the realm of necessity. If any law is so grounded in a necessary state of affairs as to be unqualifiedly immutable, this is a law in the most excellent sense of the term. The expression "authoritarian government" may be considered redundant inasmuch as every government implies authority. Yet it is not by meaningless chance that this expression has come into existence, for in contrast to those governments which systematically proceed by law, as far as law can go, the governments which want their initiative to be, as far as possible, free from direction and restriction by law can be called authoritarian with some propriety.

Accordingly, the principle of government by law is held in check by the inevitable and fully normal contingency of the situations that government has to deal with. The significance of this principle is clear, for law admits of powerful and lasting guarantees against arbitrariness. Beyond the last settlement of law, man is but precariously protected against the arbitrariness of his decisions. A wise polity entrusts as little as possible to the good judgment of executive agents, but what it has to entrust to these agents, under penalty of destroying much human substance by doing violence to the works of history, may still be considerable. Government by law is a principle that must be asserted with special firmness and frequently recalled, precisely because it is inevitably restricted by opposite requirements. The principle of government by law is subject to such precarious conditions that, if it were not constantly reasserted, it soon would be destroyed by the opposite and complementary principle, viz., that of adequacy to contingent, changing, and unique circumstances....

The consideration that a law is a work of reason in the capacity of premise raises the following problem in regard to the constitution of every legislative system. "Premise" admits of being understood relatively, in government as well as in theoretical science. A proposition acting as a premise in relation to further propositions is not necessarily axiomatic. It may be derived from antecedent propositions. That every legislative system contains many propositions derived from antecedent premises is obvious. The relevant question concerns the nature of this derivation. Are these derived legal formulas determined by logical connections with axioms, or are some of them the work of prudential determination? The answer is plain: indefinitely many legal formulas are the work of a legislative prudence and their determination has been worked out by the sensible, the dependable inclinations of experienced and well-intentioned persons....

Not every rule of human action is a law. We may speak with entire propriety of the rules that we wish to observe in our own lives or in the government of our families. Occasionally, we may call these rules laws, but there is something metaphorical about such a way of speaking. We do not even use the word law to designate a regulation—an ordinance—issued by city or county authorities. But we speak of state and of federal laws. In actual signification, then, "law" stands for a rule relative to the common good, and more precisely, to the common good of a community distinguished by amplitude and completeness.[4] The rules of such communities are spontaneously treated as being rules and measures of human action in an excellent sense. To ask whether this understanding of law is warranted is the same as to ask whether the common good has primacy over the private good. Indeed, there are rules in reference to all sorts of private affairs, but it is also taken for granted that the rule of the civil community, called law, is something superior which should inspire dedication, reverence, and awe. If it is ever lawful to act at variance with the law, it is by reason of some accident, such as ungenuineness on the part of the law or extraordinary circumstances. Some would like to believe that law can never be ungenuine, and that no circumstance can ever suspend its efficacy. Between these and their opponents, the discussion is about the range of accident; they are agreed that the law as such is final. But this implies that the common good of the civil society is, in some way, final and supreme. Is law, then, essentially relative to the common good? The answer will consist in determining whether the common good (best exemplified by the good of the most complete society) enjoys primacy over the particular good (best exemplified by the good of the individual)....

Individualism, i.e., the philosophy according to which the common good is merely a useful one, in other words, is a mere means to the good of individuals, often derives energy from the misinterpretation of what is, in fact, an essential and most significant feature of the genuine common good precisely considered as residing in men. A thing which has the appearance of a common good, inasmuch as it cannot be realized without common desire and common action, is not a genuine common good and may amount to sheer destruction if it is kept apart from the persons who make up the community. Because society does not exist except in individuals (connected by definite relations), the good of society demands, by nature and not by accident, a constant distribution to individuals....

Not every rule and measure of human action is called law; the term is reserved for the rules issued by the state, which is a community distinguished by duration and completeness. To what purpose are such rules established? The spontaneous answer designates the end of the laws of the state as "the good of the society," "general interest," "the common good." But the almost universal agreement on this issue faces the difficulties attending all formulation of fundamental truths, and it dissolves in misinterpretations of the common good which these difficulties occasion. We have discussed two overlapping views, as stubborn as they are erroneous. The first is the myth of a common good external to man and conceived after the pattern of a work of art. The tendency, here, is to restrict social facts to material accomplishments and, consequently, to absolve politics of moral responsibilities. The second is the position defended by various schools of individualism, that the common good is merely a useful one, that is, "the greatest good of the greatest number." Its principal difficulties involve confusion regarding orders of means and ends and, in some cases, the familiar problem of the universals. In contrast with these views, we have tried to show that the common good indeed enjoys primacy over the private good of the individual, when both are of the same order, but that at the same time the common good is internal to man and by its very nature requires continuous distribution among the members of society. As such it is the end of the laws of the state. . . .

In this discussion . . . no exhaustive treatment of all relevant topics can be expected. We shall deal with the remaining components of the definition of law briefly. Recall that the first was its rational character, the second its relation to the common good. The third concerns its cause. The principle involved is that of proportion between purpose and cause. If the purpose of law is common, the cause also must be common. Thus, law is a rule of reason, relative to the common good which, on account of its relation to the common good, proceeds from the community. The relevant difficulties concern the variety of ways in which a rule may proceed from a community, as well as the variety of communities. The two obvious cases are the civil community and the family. Clearly, rules for the welfare of the family emanate from the family; but babies, while certainly included, do not make rules. Not so long ago the exposition of the case would have been simple, as it was taken for granted that the family community had one head, neither appointed nor elected but designated by nature, who made the rules. Perhaps this is still true, at least in some cases. Of course, it is assumed that everything is normal; if the man is incapacitated and the wife is a wise woman, she will take over. Also, there is no reason why an indefinite number of decisions should not be made by the wife or even by the growing children. But there are more decisive, final issues concerning the family where the power of decision is invested in a head who is designated not by election, not by appointment, not by heredity, but by nature. Now to whom does it pertain to issue rules in the civil community? To a person designated by nature? To a person designated by God? To persons designated by heredity? To persons designated by election? To the whole multitude? These are familiar questions. In their modern form, they were first formulated at the time of the Renaissance in the conflicts between church and state. If the king is the representative of the political society, why should not the pope also be the representative of the church? Do the laws of the spiritual society emanate from the spiritual society the way the laws of the civil society emanate from the civil society? Those who wanted to curb the power of the pope and assert the authority of the church as community over its head reasoned by analogy from the principles of the civil society. Is not the civil society, at least in a crisis, superior to its head whom, if he is unworthy, it may depose? So begun, the dispute continued through centuries gaining only in confusion. Let us merely recall that the use of the expressions "divine right" and "sovereignty of the people" is unwarranted unless the several and incompatible meanings of each of them are defined with the utmost care. For our purposes, the third component of the definition of law has been gathered: the making of law belongs either to the community as a whole or to someone who is in charge of the community. The fourth and last component will not be elaborated in this context: law has to be promulgated, it has to be conveyed to the knowledge of those who are subject to the law. The full definition then reads: "Law is an ordinance of reason for the common good, promulgated by him who has the care of the community" (*Summa Theologiae*, I-II, q. 90, a. 4, translated by Anton C. Pegis).

Notes

1. [Editor's Note: Simon, *The Tradition of Natural: A Philosopher's Reflections*, ed. Vukan Kuic (New York: Fordham University Press, 1965, 1967; rev. ed., 1993).]

2. [Editor's Note: Prior to his death, the contributor had given his preliminary approval to the selected texts.]

3. [Editor's Note: The sentence in parenthesis was a footnote in the original text.]

4. It is hardly necessary to say that the idea of completeness, in the present context, is affected by relativity. To define the state by the character of completeness is not to imply that any human society can ever be complete absolutely speaking; the most complete human society remains incomplete in many respects.

CHAPTER 17

The Common Good and Authority

Central, perhaps, among the important teachings of Yves R. Simon for political philosophy, in fact for all human relations, is his lucid expansion and modern application of the principles of Thomas Aquinas's understanding of authority. To come to know this teaching is to gain resources for the critical assessment of one of the most famous statements made by theorists of modern democratic government, namely, James Madison's observation in Federalist 51: "But what is government itself, but the greatest of all reflections on human nature? If men were angels, no government would be necessary."

In each of three major treatments of authority, Simon discussed its essential function: initially in his 1940 Aquinas Lecture at Marquette University (published in that year as *Nature and Functions of Authority*), next in his Walgreen Lectures of 1948 at the University of Chicago (published in 1951 as *Philosophy of Democratic Government*), and finally again approximately a decade later in *A General Theory of Authority* (published posthumously in 1962 and based largely on his "Common Good and Common Action" published in 1960 in *The Review of Politics*). The selections that follow are drawn from the latter two books, which contain his more substantial and developed thinking on the topic. Although the Aquinas Lecture approaches the topic, as does his 1948 treatment, in the context of the tension between liberty and authority, stresses the role of prudence in striking a balance between them, distinguishes coercion and authority, and offers provisional definitions of authority and its substitutional (e.g., paternal) and essential functions, there is in this early and abbreviated treatment no second essential function explicitly raised.

In his subsequent considerations of authority, Simon will give extensive and probing attention to what he terms "a most essential function" of authority. The most essential function is a willing of the material or specific common good as opposed to a mere formal willing of it expected of every good person. One might, perhaps, see the seeds of this later development of Simon's thought in his observation in *Nature and Functions of Authority* that "authority is the everlastingly good principle of the social unity in the pursuit of the common good" (30). It suggests that communal authority is entrusted, in the nature of things, with more than simply securing "unity of action of a united multitude" (17), which is his understanding of the first essential function, a function that becomes more rather than less necessary as a community develops toward excellence and a plenitude of means to the common good becomes ever more the case. It also appears that Jacques Maritain's critique of the Aquinas Lecture (noted by Simon, *Philosophy of Democratic Government*, 25) made him aware of a "serious error" in neglecting the possible affective basis for unanimity and unity of action, leaving him to rely on rational communication as sole basis of such unity. The most essential function that Simon introduces in *Philosophy of Democratic Government* brings forward to a central role the needed will and hence affective disposition required of authority, one that Simon is convinced cannot reasonably and responsibly be expected of non-authority-holding members of a community. Such members or citizens are rather to follow nature's lead and intend their various particular goods even as they formally intend the common good. Examples in *Philosophy of Democratic Government*, such as the strongly dedicated Latin teacher who sees all curricular decisions from his particular perspective (45ff.) and the wife of a murderer whose attachment to her husband leads her to oppose the common good's call for her husband's execution (41, see selection below), are portrayed by Simon so as nearly to invite resistance to authority in the name of particular goods. One is led to wonder why, when the common good is pointed out and understood, those but formally willing it would not be expected to embrace it with material intent. Simon seems to hold that such an expectation is unrealistic and dangerous.

Later in *A General Theory of Authority*, Simon—though he makes explicit that he is concerned for genuine individual autonomy (79, see selection below) and fears the "disappearance or impairment of the particular capacity" (58ff.) in the expectation that citizens materially embrace the common good—appears to be continuing to think through how to fit the most essential function of authority into his overall moral and political theory. Gone in this last work of his on authority are the unsettling examples of strong attachment to the particular good that marked his *Philosophy of Democratic Government*. Present is a section (the substantial third to last paragraph given here) where Simon cautions against a formalism that would seem to allow one not to care about the matter of her actions. Here, he utilizes a potential function of authority called "the communication of excellence," notably present in relationships of love and friendship, as an appropriate way a community's leaders would move towards closing the usual gap between the willing of the formal common good by all good people and embracing the material common good by virtuous holders of authority.

Just as Simon strives in this way for the unity of formal and material intention, so one might see in his distinction between an essential and most essential function of authority two sides or aspects of a single truly essential function of authority. Simon suggests as much the very first time he moves toward the concept of a "most essential" function in *Philosophy of Democratic Government* (36, see selection below): "The problem of united action is relative to means. Now it is perfectly evident that all operations concerning means are conditioned and sustained by more basic operations, i.e., the volition and intention of the end." Just as a formal intention of the common good ultimately detached from the material common good is short of the mark of excellence appropriate to human communities, so too is an authority that brings about unified action to anything but the common good.

Finally, Simon's *A General Theory of Authority*, just as its title suggests, moves away from the political problematic in which the

Aquinas and Walgreen Lectures are rooted. It moves to explore the authority of witness in intellectual matters of all sorts, and it comes even to illumine briefly the role of substitutional authority in the Christian church. Out of this exploration comes the concept of "communication of excellence" that, as seen above, functions for Simon as mediator between his insistence on the good of particular attachments and the superiority of the common good in political communities.

Walter J. Nicgorski

Philosophy of Democratic Government
(Selections: 7–9, 19–21, 26–42, 47–48, 70–71, and 139–41)

The issue of authority, just as much as the related issue of freedom, is one plagued by the kind of confusion that intractable emotions cause and entertain. A common mistake is to identify authority with coercion, which is but the most conspicuous of its *instruments*. It is important, also, not to postulate a necessary connection between the essence of authority and any of the particular forms in which this essence is embodied; yet many hold it axiomatic that authority means absolutism and exploitation. Finally, few, if any, bother about distinguishing, within authority itself, a diversity of *functions*; yet this diversity is so fundamental that, if it is not expressed, we hardly know what we are talking about when we speak of authority. Clouded by such confusions, an unfruitful dialogue goes on between those who feel inclined toward authority and those who, on principle, put an emphasis on liberty. Platitudes about the difficult task of maintaining the proper balance between the two are nearly all that can be expected.

Our present purpose is to describe the diverse functions of authority and to show that authority, according to the diversity of its functions, calls for diverse interpretations in terms of foundation, duration, relation to progress, and relation to freedom. Instruments and forms will be discussed in later parts of this book....

First, in this function, authority aims at the *proper* good of the governed. A child needs direction because he is not able to take care of *himself*, i.e., to direct himself toward his own preservation and perfection. Thus, apart from all consideration of social good or common good, authority is needed for the survival and development of the immature person.

Secondly, authority here is made necessary by a deficiency. Parents take care of the child, inasmuch and in so far as the child is *unable* to take care of himself. The father substitutes his mature judgment and will for the judgment and will of the child, which are still immature. The paternal function of authority is not essential but *substitutional*....

Authority as engaged in this substitutional and pedagogical function we call "paternal," following the good usage that extends to the whole genus the name of the most familiar species. Besides the father-to-son relationship, there are many situations in which authority of the paternal type is exercised....

We now must consider whether authority has essential functions. That it has no essential function at all is a proposition current among liberal writers.

Let us bear in mind the picture of a society made exclusively of clever and virtuous persons. If such a picture was necessarily utopian, it might still satisfy the conditions of a mental experiment. In fact, it is not unreal; e.g., a man and his wife make up a society; both of them may be virtuous and enlightened. There exist societies whose members are all perfectly good; but these societies are very small. We want to know whether such societies need authority. If they do, authority is not devoid of essential function.

Even in the smallest and most closely united community, unity of action cannot be taken for granted; it has to be caused, and, if it is to be steady, it has to be assured by a steady cause. Here a man and his wife—both are good and clever, but one thinks that the summer vacation should be spent on the seashore, and the other would rather spend it in the hills. If they remain divided, one goes to the seashore, the other to the hills, and common life ceases temporarily. It would come to an end if a similar divergence concerned an issue of lasting significance.

Now unity of action depends upon unity of judgment, and unity of judgment can be procured either by way of unanimity or by way of authority; no third possibility is conceivable. Either we all think that we should act in a certain way, or it is understood among us that, no matter how diverse our preferences, we shall all assent to one judgment and follow the line of action that it prescribes. Whether this judgment is uttered by a leading person or by the majority or by a majority within a leading minority makes, at this point, little difference. But to submit myself to a judgment which does not, or at least may not, express my own view of what should be done is to obey authority. Thus authority is needed to assure unity of action if, and only if, unanimity is uncertain. The question is whether unanimity can be established in better than casual fashion among the perfectly clever and well-intentioned members of a society which is, by hypothesis, free from deficiencies. . . .

Thus, in the field of scientific thought, unanimity is guaranteed, *de jure*, by a process of rational communication whose possibility results necessarily from the nature of scientific objects. Faultless scientific minds, no matter how many, would be unanimous with regard to scientific truth. The problem with which we are now concerned is whether what holds for scientific propositions holds also for those practical propositions which rule the action of a multitude: Do they possess the power of commanding unanimous assent, at least when conditions are entirely normal?

The theory of practical certainty and of practical truth, worked out by Aristotelianism, is a first step toward an answer. The very exacting definition of science in the *Posterior Analytics* seems to make hopeless the case of certainty in practical matters. If the certainty of science demands that the scientific object should possess the kind and degree of necessity that is found in universal essences alone, it seems that practical knowledge admits of no certainty, for human practice takes place in the universe of the things that can be otherwise than they are. Events constantly give the lie to our prudence. After careful deliberation we conclude that this course of action is the right one, yet what it brings about is a catastrophe. . . .

Consider a group of persons confronted with a duty of united action for the common good. We assume that they are all virtuous; by their virtues they are properly related to the common good as end. We assume also that they are all enlightened and that no ignorance or illusion interferes with their ability to determine the proper means. Unanimity cannot be brought about by demonstration, for the proposition that such and such a course of action ought to be followed is not demonstrable. Attempts at its rational establishment, no matter how sound and helpful, will fall short of necessitating the assent of the minds. Let an example be that of a nation threatened in its freedom and existence by an ambitious competitor. A time comes when survival demands war-readiness, and a time comes when fighting alone can preserve the common good. Yet it is never possible to demonstrate that whoever loves the common good must support a policy of war and that whoever opposes such a policy is wrong. Who knows? Decisive factors often are extremely unobvious. A policy of abstention may not bring about the calamities whose unfolding is considered evident by some. And war is a risky enterprise. The dialogue goes on, though the situation imperatively demands that all should contribute full measure of devotion, with all their minds and hearts, to a uniquely determined policy. The question is whether such disagreement can take place among citizens that are both good and enlightened.

One thing is plain: if unanimity can be achieved in non-fortuitous fashion, it is not by way of necessitating argumentation and rational communication. But the analysis of practical judgment, which rules out rational communication as a steady cause of unanimity in these matters, shows also that a steady cause of unanimity is found in the inclination of the appetite, whenever the means to the common good is uniquely determined. If there is only one means to the common good, only one proposition—viz., the proposition expressive of this means [is] the only one that admits of practical truth. It is the only one that conforms to the requirements of a properly disposed appetite, and a properly disposed appetite cannot make any other proposition win assent. The community of the end and the unique determination of the means bring about a situation distinguished by happy simplicity. . . .

Considering, thus, the function that authority plays as an indispensable principle of united action when there are several means to the common good, let the question be asked whether this function is essential or substitutional. Since the need for authority here is properly caused by the plurality of the means, the real question is whether this plurality of means is itself caused by a deficiency or by the good nature of things; in the latter case alone will the function under consideration prove to be an essential one. . . .

In short, wealth, health, and strength are factors that cause independence from particular courses of action, dominating indifference, mastery over several means, freedom. Destitution, ill health, uncertainty, weakness, are factors that cause dependence upon determinate means. Plenitude causes choice, poverty leaves no choice. Deficiency, such as lack of knowledge, may render the genuine means undistinguishable from the illusory one and thus make a plurality of means appear where there is really no more than one. But fulness [*sic*: fullness], actuality, determination, achievement, accomplishment, power and greatness, knowledge and stability, produce or increase liberty in societies and individuals as well. A society enjoying a supremely high degree of enlightenment would, all other things being equal, enjoy much more choice than ignorant societies and have to choose among many more possibilities. It would not need authority to choose between two courses of action one of which is bound to lead to disaster, since, by hypothesis, knowledge would rule out illusory means. But it would need authority, *more than ever*, to procure united action, for, thanks to better lights, the plurality of the genuine means would have increased considerably. The function of authority with which we are concerned, i.e., that of procuring united action when the means to the common good are several, does not disappear but grows, as deficiencies are made up; it originates not in the defects of men and societies but in the nature of society. It is an essential function. . . .

The problem of united action is relative to means. Now it is perfectly evident that all operations concerning means are conditioned and sustained by more basic operations, i.e., the volition and intention of the end. Associates may unify their action by way of authority or have to content themselves with the risky procedures of unanimity; clearly, there would be no action to be unified if these men had not antecedently determined that a certain object should have for all of them the character of an end to be pursued through common action. Thus, beyond the problem of united action, we have to inquire into a more profound issue, i.e., that of the very intention of the common good. We know that authority is necessary, under definite conditions, for the proper working of the means; the next question is whether the proper intention of the common good requires the operation of authority. . . .

That virtuous people, as a proper effect of their very virtue, love the common good and subordinate their choices to its requirements is an entirely unquestionable proposition. Thus, *in a certain way at least*, the volition and intention of the common good are guaranteed by virtue itself, independently of all authority. Of this way we do not know, as yet, anything, except that it is essential and basic; for it is not by accident or in any superficial fashion that the just love the common good and surrender for it their private interests. The problem, accordingly, is to determine whether the virtue of the private person regards the whole of the common good or merely some fundamental aspect of it. If, and only if, the latter is true, authority may have an essential part to play in the volition and intention of the common good. We are wondering, in other words, whether the *way* in which virtue guarantees adherence to the common good is an all-embracing one; should the guarantee supplied by virtue fail to cover some essential aspect of the common good, then direction by authority might be needed, in order that the adherence of society to all essential aspects of its good might be steadily assured....

The wife of the murderer, as she fights for the life of the man whom the common good wants to put to death, does precisely what the common good wants her to do. It is in a merely material fashion that she disagrees with the requirements of the common good: by doing what the common good wants her to do, she formally desires the common good. The common good formally understood is the concern of every genuine virtue, but it is the proper concern of the public person to procure the common good materially understood, which the private person may virtuously oppose....

Under the assumption that the society with which we are concerned is aiming at a common good, it is stated:

1. That virtue implies love for the common good, willingness to sacrifice one's own advantage to its requirements. 2. That the common good may be intended formally without being intended materially. 3. That the virtue of the private person guarantees the intention of the common good formally considered, not the intention of the common good materially considered. 4. That society would be harmed if everyone intended the common good not only formally but also materially; that, in a material sense, particular persons and groups ought to intend particular goods. 5. That the intention of the common good, materially considered, is the business of a public reason and a public will. 6. That the intention of the common good by the public reason and will necessarily develop into a *direction* of society, by the public reason and will, toward the common good considered not only formally but also materially; which is the same as to say that the intention of the common good, materially considered, demands the operation of authority....

Finally, let us again call attention to the illusion that the good will of each, if it were complete and enlightened, would suffice to guarantee the intention of the common good. This illusion is stubborn because it is hard to master the operation of the principles which, at the bottom of the question, seem to conflict but actually condition and supplement each other. The common good demands that particular persons should do full justice to the goodness of the particular good; but, if such is the case, an over-all direction toward the common good is necessary. Thus the most essential function of authority springs, in the last analysis, from the *autonomic* goodness of the particular good. The autonomy of the homestead and that of the function matter highly for the common good, but, without over-all government, these autonomies would mean the disintegration of society. Thus autonomy renders authority necessary and authority renders autonomy possible—this is what we find at the core of the most essential function of government....

At the conclusion of an inquiry into democratic freedom it is fitting to ponder over the common opinion which sets in opposition authority and democracy and, more generally, authority and freedom. According to this opinion, which is so firmly established in many minds that the need to formulate it clearly is almost never felt, authority and liberty, though both necessary, oppose each other in such fashion that the growth of one of them implies the decline of the other. Since both are held necessary, they must be supplementary in some way, but they are more opposite than supplementary. Circumstances may demand the strengthening of authority; so much the better, then, if authority grows stronger, but let us know where we are going and realize that liberty is being curtailed; and, if the progress of society implies the growth of liberty, let it be understood that a progressive society is a society in which authority is declining. In the same commonly held assemblage of thoughts, democracy is a device for the elimination of authority. It is liberty itself embodied in institutions proper to its genius. These views are not understood to imply that a community can do without authority; but if authority is held indestructible, then, in the same measure, democracy is held not to be entirely realizable. It is worth noticing that such views prevail among conservatives as well as among supporters of democratic progress....

Between authority and liberty there is both opposition and supplementariness. Which one of the two aspects ultimately predominates? The answer is obvious, since opposition prevails in the substitutional domain of authority, supplementariness in its essential domain.

A General Theory of Authority
(Selections: 40, 48–49, 55–57, 79, 84, 93, 134, 143–45, and 161)

But after having recognized the marvels that unity, or quasi-unanimity can work, let it be remarked that *unanimity is a precarious principle of united action whenever the common good can be attained in more than one way.* All that has been said in the foregoing about the power of unanimity simply makes no sense except when the way to the common good is uniquely determined. If the common good can be attained in more than one way, neither enlightenment nor virtue, but only chance, can bring about unanimity....

The power in charge of unifying common action through rules binding for all is what everyone calls authority. It may be a distinct person designated by nature, as in the couple and in the family. It may be a distinct person designated by God, as in the cases of Saul and Peter. It may be a distinct person designated by the people, as in the case of David. It may be a distinct person designated by birth and accepted by the people. It may be a distinct group of persons designated by heredity or by election or by lot. And it may be no distinct person or group of persons, but the community itself proceeding by majority vote. The problem of the need for authority and the problem of the need for a distinct governing personnel have often been confused: at this point, it is already clear that they are distinct and that the argumentation which establishes the need for authority, even in a society made of ideally enlightened and well-intentioned persons, leaves open the question of whether some communities may be provided with all the authority they need without there being among them any distinct group of governing persons....

Again, this virtuous citizen is dedicated to the common good at all times, whether or not the assembly is in session, and, unmistakably, the difference that we are trying to express concerns, not the common good and its opposite, but two relations to the common good. The private person, inasmuch as he is morally excellent, wills and intends the common good, and subordinates his private wishes to it. He may not know what action the common good demands, but he adheres to the common good formally understood, to the form of the common good, whatever may be the matter in which this form resides; as far as content or matter is concerned, it is his business to will and intend private goods. But the public person is defined by the duty of willing and intending the common good considered both in its form and in its matter. And because the service of the common good normally involves an arrangement of private things, and sometimes requires the sacrifice of private interests, the subject of the public capacity exercises authority over the private person, whose business it is to look after particular matters. . . .

The most essential function of authority is the issuance and carrying out of rules expressing the requirements of the common good considered materially. . . .

It is the excellence of autonomy which vindicates the particularity of the subject and whatever forms of authority are needed for the preservation of this particularity. Here, familiar contrasts are transcended, authority and autonomy no longer conflict with each other and no longer restrict each other. They cause and guarantee one another. But a rebel cannot perceive the great unity, the great peace which obtains at this very deep level of social reality. Autonomy implies the interiority of the law, a condition which, for human agents at least, is not native, but has to be achieved through arduous progress. . . .

In the study of the theoretical functions of authority let us never lose sight of this fundamental contrast: when an issue is one of action, not of truth, the person in authority has the character of a leader; but when the issue is one of truth, not of action, the person in authority has the character of a witness. . . .

The simple consideration that the role of authority in theoretical matters is entirely substitutional makes it easy to understand both how docility to reliable witnesses proceeds from the love of truth, and how the love of truth stirs an indefatigable eagerness for a cognition in which authority no longer plays any part. . . .

Indeed, excellence is communicated in relations of the father-to-son type. But under the present title what we propose to consider is a process independent of all deficiency. Once more we shall bear in mind a community free from ignorance and ill-will. In such a community there still is a problem of excellence to be communicated. Freedom from deficiency by no means implies equality in perfection. Moreover, if the members of a community were equal, it would still be desirable that those who are more proficient in one quality should help those whose proficiency has been of another kind to acquire this quality. . . .

In the second chapter of this book, we raised the question of whether enlightened virtue suffices to procure the volition of the common good. We saw that it does not, as far as *matter* is concerned. The man of good will, who adheres steadily to the *form* of the common good, should not be asked to take one more step and, all by himself, to *will what the common good demands. This he could not do without impairing all the perfections connected with the preservation of the particular capacity.* Yet no one would hold that the relation of a person to the common good—this relation which intrinsically pertains to personal virtue—is complete and free from deficiency as soon as the right form is willed. Formalism is not any more tenable here than it would be in regard to the more personal aspects of moral life. In all cases adherence to the right form implies a tendency toward the right matter, but the *determination* of this tendency is effected in widely different ways according as the good to be brought into existence is particular or common. Once more, the life of an honest man is filled with problems of agreement between matter and form: being honest he wants to do what is right; and determining what is right, determining the thing in which rightness actually resides under the circumstances—under circumstances which always may be new and unprecedented in some relevant respect—is the job of an intellectual and moral virtue whose name is prudence. True, a man of good will may well err as to the *thing which is* right; by reason of contingency and unpredictability, he inevitably makes such errors once in a while. Such occasional failures are compatible with moral perfection; but practical wisdom and virtue comprise, by essential necessity, a *steady tendency* toward the exact determination of the thing in which rightness resides. From the moment a man comes to consider that he should not bother too much about determining the matter or content of good actions since certainty in such determination is beyond his power—we know that he is light-minded and careless. His formalism destroys everything, his adherence to the form of the good not excluded. Because he does not care enough for the matter, he has come to miss the form.

As long as the intended achievement is personal, all takes place within the person. Only one capacity is involved. But two capacities are at work in the bringing about of the common good; individual good will procures the right form, authority determines the right matter. And thus *it is only by the operations of authority that the person enjoys the benefit of an orderly relation to the common good understood both with regard to form and with regard to matter.* No wonder that men of good will appreciate the privilege of working under a truly able leader. Thanks to his direction, the antimony is overcome; the man of good will who wants to do the thing that the common good demands, actually knows what that thing is and does it. But the truly able leader, inasmuch as he is directly concerned, both in a formal and in a material way, with the good which is "greater and more divine than the private good," is supposed to be a man of higher excellence. Here, over and above whatever is done by example, love, and friendship, the communication of excellence follows a way proper to authority, for the greater excellence of the able leader consists in his adequate relation to the common good, and it is precisely this relation which is communicated in the act of taking his orders. . . .

For the understanding of authority in matters of truth, much could be done by Christians if they realized better the relation of their faith to the promised vision. Christian faith merely substitutes, provisionally, for clear knowledge: statements of the Holy Scripture on this subject are unmistakable, "We see now through a mirror in an obscure manner, but then face to face." "Now faith is the substance of things to be hoped for, the evidence of things that are not seen." The center of Christian life is not found in faith and authority: it exists in a world of clear intuition. But between this true center of Christian life and our present condition there stand death and much natural dread.

CHAPTER 18

Work and Society

In his lectures gathered under the title *Work, Society, and Culture*, Yves R. Simon conducted a philosophical analysis that divides into equal theoretical and practical parts. In the former (lectures 1–3), he examines work from two related points of view: "psychological-metaphysical" and "socio-ethical." In the latter (lectures 4–6), he shows how these standpoints throw light on several aspects of the labor movement, wealth, and culture. Throughout, he relies on simple examples to help his students view each question from various angles until a persuasive answer emerges. Logically, the practical part is prior, because it suggests why Simon finds it desirable or necessary to offer a theoretical definition of work.

Twenty years passed between Simon's monograph *Trois Leçons sur le Travail* and "Work and the Workman," the University of Chicago course from which the present lectures are taken. Midway between the two, Simon contributed "The Concept of Work" to a Chicago symposium published in *The Works of the Mind*.[1]

His reflections on the significance of work and working in the larger contexts of human and social life belong to a comprehensive set of interests in theoretical and practical philosophy that developed over time in the course of examining knowledge and experience, freedom and community. For his student Vukan Kuic, editor of the lectures for posthumous publication, they contain a "complete prescription, difficult to fill but realistic, on how it may be possible to save the modern man from himself."

The authorities Simon cites in the lectures run from Aristotle to several modern figures in the humanities and social sciences, but in the main what underpins the argument is his own and others' experiences. Linking the two sources is a common awareness of dangers and difficulties confronting work and workers as a result of modern ideological forces arrayed against the classical tradition. Simon's work seems fundamentally inspired by the need to provide a philosophical critique of *laissez-faire* economic theories, which treat human labor as just another commodity to be bought and sold in the market.

In the fifth lecture, "Work and Wealth," Simon cites the Charter of the International Labor Organization as evidence that already by 1919 "the principle that human labor was *not* an item of merchandise ... had been accepted all over the world by most diverse sectors of opinion." Moreover, the Great Depression (1929–39) definitively showed the failure of *laissez-faire*: "abundance itself was a cause of poverty" because "wealth can never be distributed adequately by means of exchange alone." Compensation according to services rendered and distribution according to need—both admirable ideals, in his view—become impossible if human labor is treated as a commodity. And the unmasking of this error will lead to a moral review of all commodities: "From now on, they too must be evaluated by humane and social standards; ... the market place will increasingly be judged by rules pertaining to human labor."[2]

Among social units, Simon singles out the family for special attention in lecture 3, "Man at Work." He observes that in modern times there has been "an enormous separation between work and family life," which contradicts Aristotle's insistence that "what is daily an essential in the life of work be performed within the family unit." The natural sociability of work done in common lays a basis in the elementary human association for stability in community life by strengthening the bonds of love and friendship in the most natural way. Simon hopes and even predicts that the shortening of the work day will allow more time for working at home in the presence of the family. When he wrote, more than a generation ago, one could still assume that almost all workers would find a wife and children awaiting them at home.

Which brings us to Simon's third major consideration: the broader sphere of culture. In the final lecture, "Work and Culture," he enlarges upon the implications for culture of a worker's "right conduct... in his relations with members of social groups to which he belongs," especially "the right... uses of human freedom." Applying socio-ethical analysis, he emphasizes "the social utility of work" as an "essential" component of his theoretical definition. "To qualify as work, an activity must not only be honest [i.e., valuable in itself] but also socially productive." Even speculative activities must "render a service to society" if they are to be true works of the mind, because "the end [of work] is not in wealth but always in man."

Unlike artistic and contemplative activity, which has "a terminal character" and is therefore "better than useful," work occurs under the constraints of being, of the existing state of things, and is "always something serious." In contrast to Josef Pieper's famous dictum that leisure is the basis of culture, Simon insists that according to the psychological-metaphysical analysis of work, "the real basis of culture... is to be found rather in activities in the performance of which a workmanlike disposition is indispensable." A good it surely is, but the activities leisure permits transcend culture, because they benefit mainly the individual artist and contemplative. Conditions that facilitate work are what provide the real foundation for social development: "Holding out an ideal of culture based on freedom from work inevitably leads to a disorderly exaltation of the flowery element of culture, and this makes for subjectivism, arbitrariness, and an attitude of frivolous aversion to nature and its laws."

Therefore, in undertaking "the reformation of our concept of culture,... the immediate task before us appears to be the development of a theory of culture centered not on leisure but on work" broadly understood to include "moral, social, and intellectual, as well as technical and manual work." As a kind of "lover" concerned exclusively with the thing to be produced, something external to himself, "the good worker" has "much in common" with "the lover of truth." "Struggling" toward the good of one's fellows is "simultaneously struggling... toward an order of wisdom." Hence "social action in the community at large must be combined with the psychology of the lover if it is to be genuine. . . . How could work be social if it is not coupled with love for one's fellow man?" So "there is such a thing as love . . . in struggle," Simon had said when dealing with the worker "as a psychological type" in the first lecture. It is through love that work and rest enter a unity that is at once metaphysical (in origin) and cultural (in end).

The following selections from Simon's text present his general theoretical analysis of work and society (his second lecture) from which the above implications and applications are drawn.[3]

John A. Gueguen, Jr.

Work, Society, and Culture
("Work and Society," 33–59)

We have considered work primarily as an activity of an individual.[4] Let us now see in more detail how much the concept of work depends on man's essentially social nature. There are human activities besides hobbies, exercises, and make-work, already mentioned, which, though they fully satisfy the metaphysical definition of work, simply are not work in actual social contexts. For instance, the activity of a burglar digging a hole in a wall is not work. In saying that burglars do not like to be disturbed when they are at work, the word "work" is used with obvious irony. Burglars do not work. In fact, we think that they are doing something that is the exact opposite of work. Or consider the situation of two brothers, one of whom has decided to get rich by any means, foul or fair, while the other, though not indifferent to financial success, is determined to stick to hard work. This hard work, of course, does not have to be manual labor to qualify socially as work. But getting rich by any means might well involve activities which we would not consider to be work. In a word, what both these examples reveal is that, in order to qualify socially as work, an activity must also be honest. But beyond honesty, there is still another social qualification of work which is somewhat more difficult to explain.

Service to Society

I should like to begin by saying that an honest activity, accepted by society, may still not be work of any description if it is unproductive. Specifically, I maintain that operations called speculation are not work, even though they may be both legal and morally acceptable. To avoid misunderstanding, let me repeat: an activity does not have to be immoral in order to be undesirable. The decisive factor here is that we would not want the kind of operations we are talking about to become too frequent. For example, I know of an actual case in which a man had bought a tract of desert land for $4.00 per acre and thirty years later sold it for $1,700.00 per lot, with at least two lots per acre. Such deals have not been uncommon in the Southwest United States. Again, there is nothing vicious about it, and one cannot really blame the man for being smart enough to guess thirty years ago that this desert land, good for nothing and selling for a song, might some day sell for much more. If he bought ten acres, the worst that could ever happen to him would be to lose forty dollars. So he invested his money, and today that land is a wealthy suburb of Phoenix or Albuquerque. Everybody is happy. But is it desirable that these things should occur regularly? Should they be encouraged? I do not think so, because such activities are basically unproductive. True, the man has done nothing, literally—no wrong and no work. But precisely because no work was involved in this operation, a few thousand dollars simply leaked out of society.

The condemnation of commerce in Aristotle and reservations about commerce (*negotium*) in medieval theology refer specifically to operations consisting of a purchase at a lower price followed by a sale at a higher price, without any utility being produced in the meantime. Now, commerce is predicated also on the operation of buying oranges and grapefruit in Florida and selling them in Chicago, but this includes the considerable service of bringing vitamins in the winter to people who are almost snowbound in that dreadful climate. Here is a distinct production of service, and if the compensation of the merchant is about equal to that service, this is not commerce in the sense of Aristotle. Is it work? What does it mean to go to the orchards of Florida or Israel to purchase these crops and to see that they are delivered where needed? The answer is that it is an obvious service, and insofar as the compensation does not exceed the value of that service such an activity is socially productive. The man performing this service is thus not a merchant in the sense of Aristotle, medieval theology, or canon law. He is a producer of "space utility," as the economists call it, and there is no reason why he should be purely and simply excluded from the society of workers. The mark of a true speculator is that he produces absolutely nothing. In our example, he first by purchase effects a legal transfer of property, and then by sale at the market price thirty years later effects another legal transfer of property. The land of which that property consists was desert, and it has remained desert. One cannot even say that the man conserved the land, for he did absolutely nothing to it; he simply waited for the city to expand in the right direction....

First, let us consider the speculator in the exercise of individual acts of buying and selling. Provided that the rules of the game are observed—i.e., provided that the market has not been sophisticated in any way—all the transactions appear to be absolutely honest. For all we know, the money this man pays for anything he buys is what the thing is worth when he buys it, and the money he receives for anything he sells is what the thing is worth when he sells it. Secondly, however, we must consider the speculator also in his general relation to society. We imagine him close to retirement after a life characterized by skill as well as honesty. He has never indulged in practices designed to influence the market, but he has been so skillful and so lucky in his innumerable transactions that on balance he has gained much more than he lost. Thus his fortune has been acquired by a long series of operations, each of which was absolutely fair and honest. But assuming that he had been a pure speculator—that is, a pure merchant and not a producer of any utility—it is plain that, when his career is considered as a whole, there has been between this honest man and society no real exchange. All the wealth went one way.

In this abstract example, we can see how, through a succession of actions each of which is entirely lawful, wealth can leak out of society. But what happens most clearly in the case of the pure speculator happens to a lesser extent also in the case of the mixed type whose income is part compensation for his services as a producer of some utility and part speculative gain. The important point is that in all speculation, as defined, wealth leaks out of society through operations each of which is perfectly legal and even morally acceptable. Moreover, the market system makes for a permanent possibility of such a leak, and if speculation and activities tending to speculation multiply, burglars, robbers, and swindlers will not be needed to cause social bankruptcy—the regular and perfectly honest operations of the system will suffice.

Let us dare spell it out: the man who does nothing but speculate—that is, who does nothing but buy and sell—does not work because he does not render a service to society. To qualify as work, an activity must not only be honest but also socially productive. To avoid misunderstanding, as well as the charge of dogmatism, let us again grant that "commerce," in current usage, may well be a necessary component in the system of division of labor in society. But let us also notice that even in this usage—that is, understood not as pure speculation but as a productive activity—everyone recognizes that there can be too much of it and that then it is not good for society. Thus while commerce, even vigorous commerce, may be conducive to social development and betterment, the moment commerce turns into "commercialism" the social benefits derived from it tend to diminish rapidly. Notice that even in our "business culture" such terms as "speculator," "operator," and "wheeler-dealer" are not particularly complimentary, and how much more contumelious they become as antonyms of "honest worker" or "hard worker." Because the speculator tries so hard to "make money," we sometimes fail to see him as completely unproductive—that is, a non-worker. But common sense does not give up so easily, and the frequent complaints about the people who make all the money while others do all the work point directly to the truth of the matter: only socially productive activities qualify to be called work.

THE ETHICS OF THE WORKER

The economists' staunch denial that there can ever be such a thing as pure speculation is derived, interestingly enough, from a source that has also inspired various socialist proposals for the reorganization of society intended to eliminate all possibility of speculation. For instance, on May 17, 1846, Pierre-Joseph Proudhon (1809–1865) answered a letter from a young German doctor of philosophy named Karl Marx, who was asking him to enter into some kind of political association. Marx at that time was 28, Proudhon nearly ten years older and incomparably more important in the socialist movement. In Marx's letter there were some things that did not please Proudhon, in particular a veiled allusion to violent revolution. The hint was not very clear, but Proudhon thought it unmistakable, and he wrote back that though he had once believed in revolution—and though he still respected the idea of it—he no longer agreed that it was the best method of social transformation. The best way to solve the problems and difficulties of the capitalist system, Proudhon explained, was to work out a system of economic relationships which would prevent wealth from leaking out of society. In its simplest form, this idea may be said to represent the beginning and the end of Proudhonian socialism.[5]

The common source of these opposing positions in regard to speculation is what we shall call here the ethic or the ethics of the worker, according to our emphasis on ideas or sentiments. There can be no doubt that these notions and feelings represent one of the most interesting cultural trends in modern times. Their origin can be traced to the rising middle class which carried out the commercial and industrial revolutions between the sixteenth and the nineteenth centuries, at which time these ideas and sentiments were eventually taken over in somewhat modified form by various labor movements. The belief that work is the highest value, the fullest and perhaps the only meaningful form of human activity appears to have been expressed most forcefully in the bourgeois literature of the transitional period. "Work alone is noble," Thomas Carlyle wrote in *Past and Present*, while James Russell Lowell "blessed . . . the horny hands of toil," and Henry Wadsworth Longfellow celebrated *The Village Blacksmith* in these rhymes: "His brow is wet with honest sweat, He earns whate'er he can, And looks the whole world in the face, For he owes not any man."[6] Against this background, it is indeed no wonder that when it consciously came into being the modern working class proclaimed through its own spokesmen that it should be the ruling class.[7]

For our purposes here, the general idea and the sentiment behind this glorification of work may be reduced to the proposition that whoever lives in society owes society a debt which has to be repaid by the continual exercise of socially useful activities. While not unfamiliar, this notion of social debt remains rather vague, and if philosophers are good for anything, it should be for analyzing and clarifying concepts which, no matter how vague, convey something of great significance. That one owes a debt to society may be clearer to a person born into a well-to-do family than to a person born into a destitute family. But in either case it is fairly clear that one cannot be alive and active, healthy, trained, educated, and protected, at least most of the time, without incurring some sort of obligation to society, the proper repayment for which might well be in activities that are socially useful. In the ethic of the worker, this proposition has the rank of the first principle. What are its consequences?

Again, the case of the pure speculator is relatively simple (we leave people who engage in socially harmful actions out of the picture altogether). Like everybody else, such an individual in his lifetime has collected all kinds of services from society. He has been protected by the police, he has used public roads, and he has learned geometry because somebody cared to preserve the works of Euclid and Archimedes. Yet, he has never repaid his debt. According to the ethics of modern times, such an individual is absolutely despicable, and that is why liberal economists deny the existence of pure speculation in their economic theories, while socialist reformers are bent on eliminating all possibility of speculation in social practice.

But what about some other types who may not be paying their debts because they are not engaged in socially productive activities? I have in mind in particular persons answering the description of the contemplative sketched above. This contemplative, it will be recalled, is the only social character whom we have already disqualified from the general category of workers by our initial, metaphysical definition of work. The contemplative cannot be a worker in any sense, because contemplation is the exact opposite of worklike activities. But if he is not working, he cannot be paying any debts. Even if what he does may be something better than work, as he contemplates he does not have society on his mind. Contemplation is an activity of the scientific intellect at the term of successful research, and what the contemplative considers are conclusions which, without being exhaustive, are genuine conclusions because they are true. We may also call him a theorist, which is closer to Aristotle's θεωρός, derived from θεωρειν, which here means to look at the truth. According to Aristotle, this is the happy man living the best life. But does he have any excuse for living in modern times?

It must be emphasized that the contemplative has received immensely from society. If he is achieving a peak of human excellence, it is because he has been granted rather exceptional privileges. And yet his proper activity is not of itself socially productive. It is, of course, granted that the contemplative does some good in society. For instance, when he happens to speak he speaks so much better than others; he needs to say only a few words in order to be socially very useful. Then there is also the value of the example of rest and of dedication embodied in his life. But all this is factual, not essential. We are asking: Is there a theoretical vindication of the life of the contemplative in the ethic of the worker?

It appears that though there have always remained islands of contemplative life, which might even have spread in the last fifteen years or so, the contemplative as a type has been relatively rare in our busy society. Yet if we consider China, India, and Persia together with the medieval Christian, Jewish, and Moslem world, the practice of contemplation or meditation reveals itself as something rather voluminous in the history of mankind. In all these societies we find men who, like the happy man of Aristotle, are more or less completely withdrawn from society. They may live a solitary eremitical life; but since surviving in solitude is rather difficult, hermits generally tend to congregate. What is really interesting is that (*Ethics* 10.7, *Politics* 7.3) at these other times and places the contemplatives were not only tolerated but were respected and often maintained by the society that they renounced.

It may be considered somewhat of a paradox that, in the bourgeois industrialist liberal society with all its emphasis on individualism and private rights, there is such an undercurrent of contemptuous resentment of contemplatives, whether philosophic or mystical. Generally they are considered idlers, and the only way in which they could perhaps redeem themselves is by some sort of service to society. But if they just contemplate, there is absolutely no justification for their existence. Our puzzlement becomes even greater when we compare the case of the contemplative with that of the financial speculator. The latter like the former is performing no useful service, he is not paying any debts to society, and he is certainly not a worker. But if a man who plays at the stock market is not necessarily considered a dishonest man, why should the contemplative be held up to opprobrium for not paying his debt to society?

It is on this particular issue that we must recognize that the ethic of the worker has serious limitations, and that before it is accepted as a satisfactory system something has to be done in it on the subject of contemplatives. The contemplatives are not workers in either the social or the metaphysical sense of the term. They are not, as contemplatives, useful to society. And yet, these useless people may embody the peak of human excellence. For modern society, this is a very keen problem. In most historic societies, the contemplatives were not much of a problem, because if a man could live there without working, and if his happiness was meditation, he could withdraw into a den to be fed by birds without people being upset about it. But in our society, in which everyone is expected to pay his debt to society in socially useful activities, the contemplative is more often than not considered a parasite. Yet how can a man who is "looking at the truth" be despised? How did we ever get involved in this paradox?

I should like to suggest that the main source of this limitation and weakness in the ethic of the worker is to be found in its tendency to identify useful activity with the exploitation of physical nature for human purposes. And since this tendency is also the key to the understanding of many other aspects pertaining to industrial societies, it is of some importance that we consider its concrete social and historical origins, as well as its influence on the social movements in the last six or seven generations.

Useful Activity and Modern Social Thought

To understand modern times, it is essential to understand the Saint-Simonists. Saint-Simon, born in 1760, was a man of great but undisciplined intelligence, an adventurer without regular training in any field of knowledge. "He is wrong inasmuch as he mistakes himself for a scientist, for a scholar," the celebrated mathematician and statesman Hippolyte Carnot (1801–1888) said. "He is not one; but I have never known another man with such daring visions." When he was seventeen years old, Saint-Simon fought for American independence under Lafayette. He then went on through a life of incredible adventures, starting many things, finishing nothing. It has been said that his written work improved considerably whenever he had a secretary of genius, and among his secretaries there were two who qualified, each in his own way. The first was the romantic historian Augustin Thierry (1795–1856), undependable as an historian but important in the history of historiography and in the romantic revival of interest in the Middle Ages. The other, nineteen years old when Saint-Simon hired him, was Auguste Comte (1789–1857), the founder of Positivism. . . .

The main point to which I wish to call attention is typical of Saint-Simonism, especially in its early period. Put simply, it is the idea that up to now men have been mostly interested in lording it over other men. Too much human effort has been spent in establishing dominion of man over man, with subsequent exploitation of man by man. Again, it is important to realize that this idea comes in the wake of twenty-five years of furious military activity which had demonstrated the potential of modern organization. In fact, the genius behind Saint-Simonism and behind socialism in general is that of Napoleon. It was Napoleon who demonstrated that it was possible to collect an army of half-a-million men who spoke different languages—many of whom were former enemies—and to move it from one end of the continent to another. And what was Napoleon's secret? Organization. By the sheer power of organization, he was able to take this great mass of mankind all the way to Moscow (that he did not bring them back is another issue). The Saint-Simonists were impressed by such feats at the same time as they deplored them as inhuman waste. Thus the central idea of Saint-Simonism, particularly in its early phase, is the contrast between (a) military activities whose purpose is the domination of man over man and hence of exploitation of man by man, and (b) the activity of man upon physical nature for the benefit of mankind.

> It is impossible to repeat too often that man cannot exercise any useful action except his action over things. The action of man over man is always in itself harmful to the human species through the double destruction of energies that it involves. It becomes useful only inasmuch as it is secondary and only helps to exercise a greater action over nature.[8]

This "double destruction" obviously means that, while the man who is acted upon is being destroyed, the one who seeks power over other men also wastes his energy. Accordingly, the Saint-Simonists believed that, with the advantages of the alternative of exploiting nature made clear, the exploitation of man by man was bound to disappear. Of course, if a canal is to be dug, there will have to be leaders, and there will therefore also be men who must take orders; but the purpose of it all would not be to set some men over other men. It would be jointly to serve mankind by exploiting physical nature.[9]

It is in this Saint-Simonist view that we find the strictest identification of socially useful action with what we have distinguished in the preceding chapter as manual and technical work, and it is of special importance to note that this idea also was taken over more or less intact by Marxism. On this subject, the Marxists are the followers of Saint-Simon, even though they may lack the roughness and the simplicity of the originators.

In the history of ideas, I have found a law which says that the early phases of great movements are characterized by a lack of inhibitions. That is why I am so interested in these early phases. The Pre-Socratics, for instance, are fascinating because they are completely free from inhibitions that decent academic people experience every time they have something to say. Having said it, academicians immediately back up a little in order to show that they are not quite so naïve and that they are able to achieve a balanced view. The Pre-Socratics have not reached that stage. For instance, Parmenides holds that Being exists and that non-being does not exist, so that Being is for him one big sphere. Whatever is not that sphere simply does not exist but belongs to a world of appearances. We may not know exactly what he meant, but the least that can be said is that his expressions are blunt and uninhibited. When Thales says that everything is made of water, he presents us with another example of a thinker who has the courage of his opinion. And finally, in Cratylus we find a completely consistent philosopher: He refused to talk at all, because by the time one utters a sentence the flux of becoming has passed on, and so whatever one says can never correspond to the real state of affairs.[10]

Now if we consider the Marxists of the late nineteenth century, we see that they have become in some respects more sophisticated on the subject of socially useful activities. But the early socialists are not afraid of being unpolished and of proclaiming bluntly that men act in two ways and only two. One way leads to the exploitation of man by man and is nothing but waste. Therefore, it is the other, consisting in collective effort aimed at the transformation of physical nature for the service of mankind, that is alone useful.

We must also note that though early Saint-Simonism was rather anarchistic, this did not last long, because all organizers have a passion for authority, especially the engineers. The early nineteenth century had had some experience with machines which ran fairly smoothly, and while they were certainly not as good as machines are today, they were already then much more reliable than men. In this respect, there has been an enormous change even, say, in the last thirty years. To start a car used to be quite a problem. Today our cars still break down more often than we would wish; but the number of miles they go without repair is really very impressive. On a higher level of technological precision, there are many parts of our installations that never get out of order. But men get out of order all the time; it is always the human factor which restricts our expectations. Those Saint-Simonist engineers were very conscious of this problem and reacted to it with a super-Platonic system of centralization of planning and of thought-control. Within a few years, they became a most dogmatic and authoritarian sect. We understand very well how this happened; with their passion for organization and huge teamwork it was inescapable. In our time, and not only in totalitarian states, the patterns of indefectible regularity which constitute the norms of the industrial system have created a new passion for authority for the control of men, who appear to be the only things around that get out of control and out of order.

These aspirations of Saint-Simonism are echoed forth in the famous words of Engels about the new society [in which] we would be able "to replace the government of persons by administration of things."[11] Together with the previously quoted statement of Saint-Simon about the nature and scope of useful human activity, this expectation expresses the hopes of both early Saint-Simonism and genuine Marxism. Whether the rulers of the Soviet Union would still today contend that all they want to do is to administer things rather than to govern people is a moot question. In twentieth century Bolshevism, this distinction has been somewhat blurred by the struggles we know so well. *The State and Revolution* (1916), where this idea is still accepted, is said to have been written by Lenin in order to reassure the leaders of labor unions, among whom the philosophy of anarcho-syndicalism was still prevalent. But in subsequent developments the withering away of the state was relegated to the inexplorable part of the future, and the distinction between the government of persons and the administration of things has been all but forgotten. It now belongs to the history of socialism in the nineteenth century, the century that ended with the First World War and the Russian Revolution.[12]

So much for the European developments. But let us also take it with a grain of salt when we hear it said that the American labor movement is not ideological in character. Even though it certainly is not as doctrinaire as those of Spain or France or Germany, the American labor movement too has had its visions of the society of the future. Samuel Gompers, for instance, was a very astute and practical leader of men and a conservative in many respects. Nevertheless, he too cherished the belief that, when labor came to be sufficiently organized, all really important social problems would be taken care of, so that political government would naturally pass into non-existence.[13] We often read in the documents of the Labor Movement that work or labor (the first if we speak of the activity, the second if we speak of the men who exercise this activity) ought to be supreme in society. At the bottom of this view is the old Saint-Simonist idea that men may struggle either to lord it over other men, to exploit them and be served by them, or to control physical nature for the benefit of all mankind. As the former involves a "double destruction," only the latter activity is of any real use to society. All human effort, therefore, should be directed to administration of things.

Again, the broad intention of socialism is to return to society, either by violent action or by some particular economic scheme, the wealth that leaks out of it under the capitalist system; the moral vision which accompanies these social plans is the ethic of the workers, whose pride it is that through daily activity upon physical nature they pay society back for services rendered. Let us not hesitate to declare openly that recognizing this debt to society represents the glory of the ethical disposition of socialism. But let us at the same time not forget that in this view anything pertaining to political government is judged as being an inferior kind of activity. This too is a characteristic of the ethic of the worker, and its origin must be traced to the view that "socially useful activity"—which is in itself not a bad definition of work—is restricted to action upon physical nature.

This restricted view of socially useful activities is what is really behind the suspicion of politics so prevalent in modern ideologies, liberal as well as socialist. It is also what is behind the resentment of the contemplatives. Now, interestingly enough, the problem of the debt which every individual owes to society is found also in Aristotle, who does not restrict socially useful activity to action upon physical nature. As is well known, the first place among social activities in Aristotle's philosophy is reserved for politics, and for him it is the statesman or the citizen rather than the worker who is considered to be paying his social debt in full. Nevertheless, the decisive standard in both cases is social utility, as Aristotle judges the citizen according to his contribution to the common good. And yet, for Aristotle, the very best life is that of the man who withdraws from society into solitude to contemplate and to keep seeking after truth. Does this mean that Aristotle is inconsistent? Does it mean that, by denying any exceptions for the contemplatives, the modern view on social obligations is more consistent than Aristotle's? I do not think so, for a rather simple reason. Contemplative life can easily be justified in Aristotle's philosophy, because he has an idea of the good that is not merely useful but is better than useful, because it is desirable for itself, because it is an end in itself. Such a notion of the good is absent in much of modern philosophical thought, and that is ultimately why in this thought there is no ground on which to justify the autonomy of science, of philosophy, or even of political activity. Thus when all is said and done, what we have identified above as a major shortcoming of the ethic of the worker, namely, the resentment of the contemplatives, cannot really be overcome without first recognizing the goodness of things that have nothing to do with social utility.

The Sociological Conception of the Working Man

We may conclude these remarks on work as a social activity by distinguishing briefly between what I call the socio-ethical and the sociological conceptions of the worker. As mentioned above, some years ago I had proposed a definition of the working man that included only people professionally busy with some action exercised upon physical nature. According to this definition, professional activities ultimately concerned with pure science or with social order were not considered work strictly speaking. This narrow view was sharply criticized by a number of writers,[14] and further reflection on the problem of the definition of work has led me to conclude that at least some of that criticism was the result of my failure to distinguish clearly between two points of view which are indeed profoundly distinct from one another; namely, the *socio-ethical* and the *sociological*. Here, we must make sure of that distinction.

Ethics being the science which deals with the order to be assured by reason in the voluntary actions of man, let us say that a consideration is relevant to the ethical point of view when it is dominated by the purpose of discovering the right order to be established in the uses of human freedom. Accordingly, considerations relevant to the socio-ethical point of view are those which are dominated by the purpose of establishing the right conduct for the individual in his relations with members of social groups to which he belongs. From this point of view, work may be defined simply as an activity implying a service rendered to society, which confers on the person performing this service the right to receive an equitable compensation for it. For instance, we all recognize that statesmen and clergymen, policemen and psychiatrists, perform services useful both to society at large and to individuals, and most of us believe that these people are entitled to a decent remuneration for their services. And yet, in the current and spontaneous use of words, there is a strong repugnance toward designating such persons as judges, soldiers, members of representative assemblies, or clergymen, teachers of philosophy, physicians, and the like, as workers, working men, members of the working or laboring class. We say that a priest is *working* when he is not resting. We say that like anyone else who works, he deserves a just salary. But it would sound strange and even ridiculous to say that he belongs, as a priest, to the social category called "workers." Thus what actually happens here is that, in the first instance ("the priest is working"), we adopt spontaneously a psychological and metaphysical point of view; in the second instance ("he deserves a just salary"), a socio-ethical point of view; and in the third instance ("he is not a workman"), a sociological point of view.

The nature of sociological science may still be disputed, but the least that can be said without embracing any particular school is that sociology properly so-called is the science which refers to *social causality*—that is, to the causal power of social beings—as the proper principle of its explanations. In other words, the proper effect to be explained by sociology being the social fact *qua* social, and the proper cause to which the sociological explanation makes appeal being the social group as such, a consideration is relevant to the sociological point of view inasmuch as it is formally concerned with some proper effect issued by the causal power of such social beings. Einstein is reputed to have said that when he wanted to elucidate some notion he asked himself in the first place: What does this notion mean to me *as a mathematician*? When we consider the notion of work formally *as sociologists*, the aspect which is predominant for us is the ability of labor-activity to determine a special kind of grouping among men. Such terms as "working classes," "labor groups," and "working section of the society" do not express fictions arbitrarily invented by theorists. They express the factual grouping of men in specific communities, and the sociological definition of the worker is determined by the factual boundaries of such a community. And here we see that, as a matter of fact, social theorists in the most different conditions of time, environment, theoretical principles, and practical aims oppose almost constantly the category of workman not only to the category of idlers, and to the smaller category of wise men, but also to such categories as soldiers, statesmen, judges, and clergymen.

Many classical economists and some contemporary socialists have strongly indicated that they consider statesmen, soldiers, and clergymen to be good for nothing.[15] By contrast, Plato recognizes these people as the most useful to the city. But no more than these other theorists does he bear in mind that they might ever be counted among the workmen. Thus when Veblen describes the working class as "this great body of people" which in its everyday life is "at work to turn things to human use" [*Essays in Our Changing Order*, p. 84], and when in opposition to this working class he defines as a leisure class those occupied throughout all history with "government, warfare, religious observances and sports" [*The Theory of the Leisure Class* (New York: Modern Library, 1934), p. 2], he expresses a conception which is most generally accepted among social theorists.

The specifically sociological concept of "the worker," then, is relatively a narrow one. Letting it appear decisive for an overall definition of work was a serious flaw in my early position, and it is no wonder that it caused resentment among so many who did not feel that they should be excluded from the category of workers. I have since learned a great deal about moral and social work, about the theoretical features of manual work as compared to art, and about the psychology of the worker. From the sociological standpoint, however, I cannot say that my views have changed. I wish to repeat that being excluded from the sociological category of workers cannot be an insult to anyone, unless it is postulated that the working man alone is respectable, that he alone has the right to food rations. Unfortunately, many social movements since about the end of the eighteenth century have more or less explicitly embraced precisely such a postulation. It is voiced uninhibitedly by the Saint-Simonists and echoed in a hundred ways by both conservative and liberal as well as socialist champions of industrial life. The pressure which these ideologies exert against an objective inquiry into the place of work in human life and society is very great, and no clarification in these matters is possible without firmest resistance to all ideological influences.

In this resistance, we may take courage from the fact that sociological theory, as distinguished from ideologies, follows a line already traced by our theoretical inquiry into the nature of work. We have seen that, from a metaphysical point of view, manual work is the fullest realization of the idea of work, and sociological investigations confirm that social consciousness designates the manual worker as the archetype of the working man. Correspondingly, the sociological term "working class" designates primarily the class of manual workers, and while it may also refer to people who direct manual work, such as various types of foremen and master craftsmen, it definitely excludes all those who are not concerned with action exercised upon physical nature. Moreover, in a sociological classification of social groups, people engaged in what we have called the works of the mind—technical, social, and purely intellectual work—are placed at distances from the working class corresponding faithfully to the place of their activity on our diagram of the polar opposition between work and contemplation. Thus while these people may be considered workers in several senses, including the socio-ethical, they definitely are not workers in the sociological sense. From the sociological standpoint, the only group considered collectively as workmen is the group whose members are habitually engaged in action upon physical nature.

Notes

1. [Contributor's Note: Yves R. Simon, *Trois Leçons sur le Travail* (Paris: Chez Pierre Téqui, 1938); Simon, "The Concept of Work," in *The Works of the Mind*, ed. Robert B. Heywood (Chicago: University of Chicago Press, 1947), 3–17. The three lessons are on "The Definition of Work," "Work and Wealth," and "The Worker's Culture." His Chicago seminar (1958) was one of twenty-six that he directed while a member of the Committee on Social Thought between 1948 and 1959.]

2. [Contributor's Note: Simon, *Trois Leçons sur le Travail*, 132, 138–40. John Paul II made that element of Christian social teaching emphatic in his 1981 encyclical *Laborem exercens* (*On Human Work*) (Boston: St. Paul Editions, 1981): "From the point of view of man's good ... work is probably *the essential key* to the whole social question" (sec. 3). For the pope, the greatest economic challenge of our day is to prevent "the objective dimension of work" (roughly equivalent to Simon's psychological-metaphysical standpoint) from overwhelming "the subjective dimension" (which Simon calls socio-ethical), thereby depriving workers of their personal dignity and corresponding inalienable rights (secs. 5 and 6).]

3. [Contributor's Note: This introduction abstracts from my graduate seminars on Simon at Illinois State University (1993, 1996), a paper presented to the American Maritain Association's 1988 conference, and the corresponding contribution, John Gueguen, "Parallels on Work, Theory, and Practice in Yves R. Simon and John Paul II," in *Freedom in the Modern World*, ed. Michael D. Torre (Notre Dame, IN: American Maritain Association, 1989), 153–61. I wish to acknowledge Anthony O. Simon and others who encouraged my studies of Simon, with whom I worked briefly while pursuing graduate study at the University of Chicago in 1961.]

4. [Editor's Note: Rather exceptionally for this work (yet see Schindler's selection of texts from the same source in chapter 20), a number of the longer footnotes have here been retained; see also Green's selections (chapter 11) from *The Definition of Moral Virtue*, and V. Bradley Lewis's selection (chapter 13) from *A General Theory of Authority*.

All of the subsequent notes are from Vukac Kuic, the editor of Simon's posthumous book. It would seem that sometimes Kuic included references that he had found amidst Simon's papers and sometimes he included references to works that appeared after Simon's death. He did not distinguish between these groups for us, although obviously he and not Simon is at least responsible for the second works, as in notes 5 and 12.]

5. See *Selected Writings of Pierre-Joseph Proudhon*, edited by Stewart Edwards, translated by Elizabeth Fraser (Garden City, NY: Doubleday, 1969), pp. 150–54. The relevant passage concludes as follows: [Proudhon states,] "In other words, through Political Economy we must turn the theory of Property against Property in such a way as to create what you German socialists call *community* and which for the moment I will only go so far as calling *liberty* or *equality*. Now I think I know the way in which this problem may be very quickly solved. Therefore I would rather burn Property little by little than give it renewed strength by making a Saint Bartholomew's Day of property owners. My next work, which at present is in the middle of being printed, will explain this to you further (*System of Economic Contradictions or the Philosophy of Poverty*)." See also J. Hampden Jackson, *Marx, Proudhon and European Socialism* (New York: Collier, 1962). For a number of Simon's writings on Proudhon, see the Select Bibliography.

6. The full stanza from Lowell's *A Glance Behind the Curtain* reads: "No man is born into the world whose work / Is not born with him; there is always work, / And tools to work withal, for those who will / And blessed are the horny hands of toil." In the same spirit, Angela Morgan wrote in the 1920s in *Work: A Song of Triumph*: "Work! / Thank God for the swing of it, / For the clamoring, hammering ring of it, / Passion of labor daily hurled / On the mighty anvils of the world."

7. Cf. Hannah Arendt, *The Human Condition* (Chicago: University of Chicago Press, 1958), p. 101: "The sudden rise of labor from the lowest, most despised position to the highest rank, as the most esteemed of all human activities, began when Locke discovered that labor is the source of all property. It followed its course when Adam Smith asserted that labor was the source of all wealth and found its climax in Marx's 'system of labor,' where labor became the source of all productivity and the expression of the very humanity of man."

8. From the *Organizateur*, Nov. 1819–Feb. 1820. *Oeuvres de Saint-Simon et d'Enfantin* (Paris: Dentu, 1865–1878), Vol. 20, p. 192.

9. *Doctrine de Saint-Simon. Exposition. Première Année* (1929), edited by C. Bouglé and Elie Halèvy (Paris, Rivière, 1924), p. 144: "The basis of societies in antiquity was slavery. War was for these people the only way of becoming

supplied with slaves, and consequently with the things capable of satisfying the material needs of life; in these people the strongest were the wealthiest; their industry consisted merely in knowing how to plunder." P. 162: "Material activity is presented in the past by the twofold action of war and industry, in the future by industry alone, since the exploitation of man by man will be replaced by the harmonious action of men over nature." P. 225: "The exploitation of man by man, this is the state of human relations in the past; the exploitation of nature by man associated with man, such is the picture that the future presents."

10. Aristotle, *Meta.* 10l0a13. See also G. S. Kirk and J. E. Raven, *The Pre-Socratic Philosophers* (Cambridge: Cambridge University Press, 1957), pp. 74ff. on Thales, pp. 263ff. on Parmenides, and pp. 182, 198 on Cratylus.

11. *Socialism: Utopian and Scientific*, in *Marx and Engels*, p. 106. [Editor's Note: This refers to *Marx & Engels: Basic Writings on Politics and Philosophy*, ed. Lewis S. Feuer (New York: Doubleday, 1959).]

12. In 1959, Nikita Khrushchev gave the following interpretation of this famous dogma: "Marxism-Leninism teaches us that under communism the state will wither away and that the functions of public administration will no longer have a political character, and will pass under the people's direct administration. But we should not take an oversimplified view of the process. We should not imagine that the withering away of the state will resemble the falling leaves in autumn, when the trees are left bare. The withering away of the state, if we approach the question dialectically, implies the development of the socialist state into communist public self-administration. For under communism, too, there will remain certain public functions similar to those that are performed by the state, but their nature, and the methods by which they be exercised, will differ from those obtaining in the present stage" (*Control Figures for the Economic Development of the U.S.S.R. for 1959–1965* [Moscow, 1959], p. 123). This was Khrushchev's report to the Twenty-first Party Congress. By the time of the next Congress, this dialectical process had produced the expression "the state of the whole people." "The draft Programme of the Party raises, and resolves, a new important question of communist theory and practice—the development of the dictatorship of the working class into a state of the whole people, the character and the tasks of this state, and its future under communism. *The state of the whole people is a new stage in the development of the socialist state, an all-important milestone on the road from socialist statehood to communist public self-government*" ("On the Programme of the C. P. S. U.," in *The Road to Communism* [Moscow, 1962], p. 148; italics in the original).

13. For instance, in an editorial in the *American Federationist*, August, 1923, p. 624, Gompers wrote: "I have said and I should like to repeat here that

political government has definite limitations in the ordering of affairs, and it can go beyond these limitations only at the peril of the people and their social and economic organization. Political government, for example, is simply not competent to conduct industry, to work out the salvation of industry, or to teach industry which paths to walk. There is a great gulf between politics and industry. Industry must work out its own salvation, build up its own great governing forces, apply democratic principles to its own structure and meet the needs of humanity out of its own intelligence." See also his *Seventy Years of Life and Labor*, 2 vols. (New York: Dutton, 1925). A convenient secondary source is Louis S. Reed, *The Labor Philosophy of Samuel Gompers* (New York: Columbia University Press, 1930). On page 127, Reed quotes Gompers as saying: "I still believe with Jefferson that that government is best which governs least."

14. See José Todoli, O.P., *Filosofia del Trabajo* (Madrid: Instituto social Leon XIII, 1954), pp. 11–15, 20–25.

15. It was Adam Smith who wrote: "The whole, or almost the whole public revenue, is in most countries employed in maintaining unproductive hands" (*The Wealth of Nations* [New York: Modem Library, 1937], p. 325).

CHAPTER 19

Economic Justice

Yves R. Simon rejected the postulate of economics as a value-free science. Economics is inevitably linked to the good of the community of persons. Moreover, he rejected contemporary ideologies, because his rich, ontologically, and morally rooted thinking could not countenance their false assumptions. Concerning classical liberal economics, Simon argued that it fundamentally glossed over the distinction between individual goods and the common good, while overemphasizing and even glorifying the role of the individual and his elementary, spontaneous drives in the economic organization of society. He was deeply concerned about the moral need for adequate distribution and thought it highly unlikely that the market would ever produce an adequate distribution of needed goods. He therefore defended the principles of distribution according to needs and what he called "free distribution," and *argued for their institutionalization*, though preferably not via the state. This latter proviso, however, would never for Simon simply be an argument in favor of cutting welfare, for *the moral imperative is that society take responsibility for these alternative systems of distribution*, and not simply leave the results to chance or to the arbitrary decisions of individuals. Moreover, Simon acknowledged that the state had a role to play in ensuring that no particular dimension of the common good ever be allowed to dominate the others. Hence, the state must ensure that the pursuit of economic goods not compromise other political, social, and cultural goods. On the other hand, Simon shared the liberal concern for the aggrandizing tendencies of the state, and saw in private property and the Catholic principle of subsidiarity necessary safeguards. No utopian, Simon believed that property should be forgiven much for all that it accomplishes for liberty (Proudhon). Among his gravest concerns is that state intervention stifles precisely the imagination, creativity, and initiative needed to discover and institutionalize alternative mechanisms of distribution.

Simon questions the uncritical equation of just prices and just wages with the results of the free market. Concerning the justice of prices, the problem is that modern, market-oriented production tends to replace production for use by production for exchange. As a result, profit becomes separate from service, with two unsavory but increasingly frequent results: (1) inequality between the value of a good and its monetary remuneration, and (2) services that are in fact illusory yet rewarded monetarily. Simon is here aware that the professional economist will cry foul, because the principle of ethical neutrality has here been violated. Simon finds the charge arbitrary, especially since the economist's position stands on a claim everyone knows is false, namely, that there is no distinction between a desire and a need.

Given that there is a distinction between genuine service of work and the mere indiscriminate satisfaction of desires, it follows that, in the modern industrial economy, there is a considerable amount of unequal exchange. In addition to illusory services, there are also "one-way exchanges": commercial exchanges in which all of the value goes in one direction. This occurs in commercial activity when profit is made from price changes that correspond to no useful production. The best example of a one-way exchange would be profits made on speculation. Although Simon does not think that to profit from price changes alone is intrinsically immoral, he does think that society should find ways to curtail this process, by which wealth "leaks out of society." Given the explosion of speculative economic activities today, from the stock market (partially speculative) to currency markets, commodities' markets, and futures' markets, this *desideratum* is particularly timely.

The just wage is another area of concern to Simon. Despite legal guarantees of equality, Simon insists that exploitation of the worker exists whenever the compensation is lower than the value of the service rendered. He laments that, in many cases, workers continue to accept low wages out of necessity. Again, Simon links economics with a broad conception of the common good. At issue here is not simply mathematical calculations as to the monetary value of what is produced, but the fact that the one involved in production is a human person with objective needs whose fulfillment is the end wages should intend. Labor cannot be reduced to a commodity subject only to the law of supply and demand.

Simon's concerns about inequality in economics prompt him to make two judgments concerning democratic capitalism. First, he says that it has remained, to a degree unrealized by many, an affair of the privileged. Second, he believes that the goal of ending the alienation that results from unequal exchange needs to be a special focus of democracy today.

Simon's treatment of economics is so rich because he acknowledges always the organic connection between the economic good and the broader goods of human society. One of his biggest concerns about modern work is that the individualism at the root of contemporary market economies undermines the social nature of work and all that the latter entails. What is lost is precisely the experience of work as a common good, an experience of that communion-in-desire that creates real human solidarity. When the profit motive looms large, the sense of loneliness and alienation grows, together with a sense of boredom and lack of purpose in work. Simon suggests that this is one of the roots of the anxiety and depression so prevalent in our society. Given the available evidence on the proliferation of these conditions today, Simon again appears particularly insightful and timely.

Simon's economic thought is rich and not ideological, a wonderful corrective to both the Right and the Left. Its implications have been insufficiently explored in secondary literature.

Thomas R. Rourke

Philosophy of Democratic Government
("Equality versus Exploitation," 232–53)

There is alienation in the case of the slave as just defined; slaves are unpaid labor, which means that they are not recompensed for their work but are merely given maintenance. There is also alienation in the case of the ill-paid wage-earner. By saying that he is ill-paid, we imply that his wage is not equal to his work; thus part of his work is dedicated, in involuntary fashion, to the welfare of a private person, his employer. There is alienation in the case of the small truck-farmer when market prices are so low that he cannot make a decent living out of the sale of his vegetables. There is alienation in the case of victims of usury, including tenants who pay too high a rent. There is alienation in the case of consumers who pay excessive prices for any commodities or services. These people are not slaves, inasmuch as the alienation of their labors is not established by a legal relation of authority. We thus come to understand that the exploitation of man by man can be managed in either of two ways: (1) through an authority relationship sanctioned by law or (2) through unequal exchange. No legal formula compels the wage-earner to remain under the authority of the employer; the small truck-farmer is not under the authority of his customers, the debtor is not under the authority of the creditor, and the tenant of a house is not under the authority of the owner. But, like slaves, these people undergo alienation when they have to be content with processes of exchange in which they give more than they receive, which means that part of their contribution is, involuntarily, given for nothing to another person. It would be arbitrary to describe as slavery the situation brought about by unequal exchange, but it often can be described as a sort of servitude.

According to such a witness as Tocqueville, the history of freedom is, to a frightful extent, the history of a conflict between freedom and equality. Be that as it may, there is one case at least in which freedom and equality, far from conflicting, agree, coincide, and become indistinguishable from each other. It is the comprehensive case of freedom as opposed to servitude, of freedom from alienation, of freedom from exploitation. The work done yesterday by a slave may be done today by a free laborer; suppose, for the sake of clarity, that the latter receives a recompense fully equal to his service. Transition from the state of the slave to the state of the normally paid laborer signifies, undividedly, achievement of freedom and achievement of equality. If inadequate wage maintains inequality, the legal abolition of slavery and serfdom, for having failed to end exploitation, would be described as having failed also to end servitude.

In rough outline, the social history of modern times is dominated by two great revolutions. The first began in the late eighteenth century; its main parts are over, although it is still going on, and still has to go on, in some countries, for a long time. The second had hardly begun before the first World War; we know that it is going on; we know that it is still very far from termination; whether it is still in its initial stage or is already beyond it we do not know. Giving these revolutions names is an embarrassing duty. If the first is called the "democratic" revolution, a few questions are begged with regard to the second; and if the second is called "socialistic," more questions are begged. Let these terms be used, if indispensably needed, in purely conventional and provisional fashion. What relation there is between these two revolutions is by no means obvious. Some historians perceive mostly resemblances and continuities, others contrasts. Some would say that they are merely two phases of one and the same revolutionary process. They certainly have in common a feature of central importance: in either case there is a question of putting an end to a system of exploitation or alienation.

The democratic revolution asserted with great vigor the proposition that political government is dominion over free men; it endeavored to destroy the myths and practices which had, to some extent, corrupted civil government into a master-to-servant relationship. It also opposed with success processes of alienation connected with the division of society into castes and orders, with slavery and serfdom. But it did little about processes of alienation that had no special connection with political structures, with the aristocratic constitution of society, or with institutional servitude. It even seems that in countless instances it released forces of exploitation that the old regimes used to keep under control.

As a result of the democratic revolution, which abolished slavery, serfdom, and feudalism, unequal exchange became the main factor of alienation. It was often noticed that liberalism brought down to a minimum gratuitousness in human relations. Such a thing as the free distribution of wealth, which played a considerable part in more primitive economic systems, was excluded from normal relations, except within the limits of a narrowing family circle. Beyond these limits the communication of wealth had to be effected by way of exchange alone. With economic transactions reaching unprecedented magnitude, alienation through unequal exchange assumed overwhelming importance at the time when alienation through legal bondage was formally abolished and factually declining.

It is axiomatic that exchange is just if, and only if, the exchanged values are equal; then, and only then, the partners treat each other as equal; then, and only then, both are free from alienation and exploitation. Here justice is equality and freedom, and all is ready for the growth of friendship. On these principles there can be no disagreement among honest persons. But the question is pervaded by anxiety as soon as the problem of *recognition* is envisaged. What values are equal? What is the criterion of equality of value? Here are a farmer and a shoemaker; exchanging wheat against shoes is for them the most natural thing in the world. But what weight of wheat equals in value a pair of shoes? We certainly can define an *insignificant* amount of wheat and know for sure that it is inferior in value to a pair of shoes; and we can define a huge amount of wheat, such that nobody would doubt that it is worth more than one pair of shoes. Between the insignificant and the huge the distance is hopelessly wide.

We have already called attention to the difficulties of the problem of recognition in ethics. These difficulties cover the whole domain of moral life; we like to think that there are safe regions in which the right and the wrong are recognized without any special inquiry; this is an illusion, possible under ordinary circumstances, violently shaken in wars and revolutions as the identities of things and persons become uncertain. To know crime from virtue in time of war, I need to know whether this war is just; assuming that it is, I still do not know crime from duty so long as I do not know whether these shadows are enemies, friends, or nonbelligerents. Common behavior in wars and revolutions shows that when the problem of recognition becomes exceedingly difficult, most persons give up all interest in the answer and soon come to ignore and to deny the problem itself. Let us be allowed to express this hypothesis: the adventures of human conscience, with regard to equality of values, are partly to be understood as an effect of fatigue and discouragement. In the wars of our time resignation to indiscriminate destruction of life often resulted from the difficulty of determining who is a belligerent. For lack of a better criterion, fliers would treat as belligerent, at the cost of many innocent lives, anything that moves within a distance of twenty miles behind the enemy lines; such a rule of action shows that hope of finding a working criterion has been given up. We are suggesting that with regard to equality of values most men use or are ready to use, without circumstances being upset by any war or revolution, almost any conventional criterion, no matter how crudely inadequate, out of a sense of hopeless difficulty and out of a biological realization that life cannot wait and that exchanges must go on.

In an economy using money as an instrument and measure, the problem of the equality of values becomes the problem of the just price. Among the methods employed in the determination of prices, that of the market enjoys an obvious privilege. It is assumed that the best possible way to obtain a fair estimation of the value of a service or a commodity is to leave it up to those whom it directly concerns, i.e., prospective purchasers and sellers. They meet in a public place and a deliberation goes on, with clashes and compromises, mutual pressure, mutual control, and control by the public. It is not claimed that this method enjoys any kind of indefectibility. It would be granted that in each particular case it probably falls short of the rule of justice; but it is held, not unreasonably, that casual influences work one day in one direction, another day in another direction, so that in the long run the rule of justice is approximated as closely as it can be by any human method. Under exceptional circumstances prices are fixed by government decree; this, too, is not a procedure free from risks, and it may be held that in many respects, especially with regard to the protection of liberty against government arbitrariness, the risks of the market system are lesser than those of price-fixing by government decision.

What does honesty mean to a businessman operating under the market system? Let us suppose that he is a person of uncompromising righteousness. In order to know what he has to do, to what sacrifices he has to consent, and what returns he can expect, he merely has to know about the situation of the unsophisticated market. The most common temptation of dishonesty regards operations calculated to sophisticate the market. One may, for instance, spread false news or overemphasize the significance of an actual fact in order to have prices go up or down at will. There is also sophistication of the market when a group of businessmen sell at abnormally low prices in order to get rid of a competitor. So long as the market price genuinely expresses the conclusions of a deliberation between prospective purchasers and prospective sellers, buying and selling at the market price is buying and selling at the just price, as far as it can be determined under the circumstances.

Since prices change, the system implies the possibility of making profits without performing any operation except purchase at a low price and sale at a higher price. This defines "commerce." But a tedious experience of idle discussions makes it necessary for us to elaborate on this definition. Economic subjects lend themselves so nicely to rhetoric and dogmatism that people who would not fail to grasp the meaning of an abstraction, say, in chemistry, can talk indefinitely to demonstrate that they have not understood the meaning of an ideal type in economics. When a physician says that some conditions demand a diet free from sodium chloride, he does not imply that the thing contained in the saltshaker is ideally pure sodium chloride; he does not even imply that it is in the power of any chemist to isolate one gram of NaCl without any admixture of any other chemical; all that he implies is that there is a relation between the ingestion of a chemical essence symbolized by NaCl and the evolution of a disease, so that, in so far as the patient ingests NaCl, whether in a pure form or in mixture, he can expect to undergo such and such symptoms. Now, when the century-old definition of commerce just recalled is voiced in certain circles, it is tempestuously objected that a merchant patterned after this definition is a mythical character impossible to find in the world of experience (a fiction of philosophers and theologians, just as NaCl is a fiction of chemists). It is argued that between the purchase and the sale the merchant produces space utility (e.g., if he moves grapefruit from Florida to Quebec) or time utility (e.g., if, just by keeping merchandise in his basement, he transforms new wine into old, or butter in July, when cows have plenty of milk, into butter in January, when milk flows less abundantly). If it were not for the literary habits of thought commonly exercised on such topics, it would be clear to everybody that *in so far* as a man creates space utility by moving a commodity from a place where it is plentiful to a place where it is scarce or time utility by keeping a commodity from a time when it is plentiful to a time when it is scarce, there is no question of describing him as a merchant; he is a producer of utility, just as is a woodcutter or a miner. The relevant question is this: Over and above compensations obtained for such services as wood cutting or coal mining or space utility-producing or time utility-producing, is there such a thing as a profit corresponding to no production at all, but merely to an advantageous difference between price at the time of the purchase and price at the time of the sale? If such a thing exists, commerce exists and is definable, and the description of its laws is relevant both in a theoretical sense and in a practical sense, whether or not there exist individuals specialized in commerce and determined not to produce any utility under any circumstances. The thing contained in the saltshaker is certainly not pure sodium chloride, and the thing contained in our atmosphere is certainly not pure oxygen. To deny the reality of commerce, as defined above, for the reason that most or all businessmen produce some utility is as good logic as to deny the reality of oxygen for the reason that in our atmosphere the molecules of nitrogen are the overwhelming majority.

For the sake of clarity, we are going to consider the abstraction of the pure merchant, just as a chemist considers the abstraction called NaCl without having to decide whether or not it is possible to realize this abstraction in a state of absolute purity. What does profit mean in relation to the law of commutative justice, which is one of strict equality between the exchanged values? This is the problem.

It is necessary to subject the commercial practice to a twofold examination. Let us consider the merchant, first, in the exercise of an individual act of buying or selling. Provided that the rules of the game are observed, viz., provided that the market has not been sophisticated in any way, the purchase is just and the sale is just. So far as we can know, the money that he gave up when he bought was equal in value to the commodity that he acquired, and the money that he received when he sold was equal to the commodity that he sold. There is in the school of Aristotle a great deal of diffidence toward commerce even when it is not accompanied by any sophistication of the market, for the mover of commercial activity is the desire to make money, and this desire contains a threat, inasmuch as its immediate object does not impose on it any measure. If I desire such real wealth as food or shelter, the very nature of the thing desired involves a principle of measure: one house in town and one in the country are about as much as I can enjoy, and the amount of proteins and carbohydrates that I can use per unit of time is contained within very narrow limits. On the other hand, it takes no particularly perverse disposition to experience unmeasured desire for money. Precisely because money is means in the second power, means in view of means and instrument in view of instruments, it presents the desire with no specification and no measure. From this it follows that profit-making is always a disquieting and risky proposition. However, Aquinas and other great theologians explain that honesty can be preserved in commerce if specification and measure are supplied by the ends to which desire for money is subordinated. Taking advantage of a difference in price on the unsophisticated market is an action which does not possess its justification within itself; it is not good of itself; but it is not, either, bad of itself, and it may receive from the appropriate end the justification that it does not possess in itself. Taking advantage of a difference in price in order to support one's family or to relieve the needy is a perfectly justified action. Its justification does not spring from its own nature; it springs from the end to which it is related. Such justification by the end is possible because there is nothing intrinsically evil about a purchase and a sale at the market price.

A distinct and supplementary approach is effected when we consider not individual acts of purchasing and selling but the general relation of the merchant to society. Let us suppose that a businessman reaches the end of a life characterized by skill and honesty. He never indulged in practices designed to sophisticate the market, but he was so skillful and so lucky as to gain much more than he lost. He has acquired a large amount of property through a series of operations each of which was absolutely fair. But, assuming that he has been a pure merchant, by no means a producer, it is plain that, if his career is considered as a whole and related to society, there has been between this honest man and society no real exchange. *All the wealth went one way. Through a succession of actions each of which was entirely lawful, wealth leaked out of society.* Exchange has been more apparent than real. Notice, further, that what happens most clearly in the case of the pure merchant, happens no less really in the case of the mixed character whose income is made partly of compensation for his services as a producer and partly of profit. The significant fact is that, in a system which identifies the just price with the unsophisticated market price, wealth leaks out of society through operations each of which is perfectly legal and lawful. The significant fact is that the market system makes for the permanent possibility of a leak without there being dishonesty on the side of any partner. The significant fact is that, if the operation of the genuine market is accepted as the safest way to approach the determination of the just price, burglars, robbers, brigands, and swindlers are unnecessary to cause wealth to leak out of society: the regular and perfectly honest operation of the system suffices.

To sum up: nobody questions that exchange is just if, and only if, the exchanged values are equal. The whole problem is to measure values in such a way as to know what values equal what values. The answer that the just price is identical with the market price, provided that the market is unsophisticated, may not be the last word on the subject, for the market system admits of one-way transactions and illusory exchanges. The least that can be said is that greater accuracy in the determination of the just price is highly desirable, if it can be achieved at all.

Since there is no reason why constructs should be less lawful and less useful in philosophy than anywhere else, let us indulge in the construct of a businessman of such unusually exacting conscience that he wants to sell merchandise for what it is, instead of following the common rule of taking as much money as possible from the customer within the limits of the unsophisticated market. His first concern is to determine his cost of production. Suppose that this virtuous man is an innkeeper and that the commodity whose cost of production he would like to know is the use of a particular room for one night. Let us try to understand what operations and what difficulties are involved in determining the cost of production of such a commodity. Some entries are very clear, some are essentially obscure. It is easy to know what figures should be entered for rent, fire insurance, taxes, interest, etc. The figure to be entered for wages is less certain, but, except in time of inflation, the margin within which it is contained is rather narrow. But I have also to enter my own salary, and here, according to the familiar paradox of prudence, there is no chance to know the truth except through the influence of virtue. The customary view is that I can look for the highest possible remuneration so long as it does not involve any violence to my associates or any sophistication of the market. To say the least, such a view cannot be expected to deliver the most accurate answer to the problem of the just price. The way to the answer is a deliberation in terms of human needs conducted in a disposition of entire generosity. Covetousness and pride would make me feel that no income is too big a reward for me; but temperance and humility cut the figure down. Fear would incline me to overdo the amount to be set apart for purposes of security—in fact, it is the craving for security more than lust for pleasure that causes the evil of boundless desire. Thus fortitude is needed in order that desire for security should not cause me to trespass the boundaries of the just price. The ultimate rule is an estimation of human needs, and this estimation cannot be effected without the unique light that proceeds from virtue. It goes without saying that it is only for the purpose of simplicity that we are imagining a solitary research by an individual conscience; such deliberations have to be conducted, so far as possible, by the wisdom of society. Yet ultimately there is always some amount of indetermination to be actualized by the operation of individual prudence, and it is not possible to disregard entirely, no matter how much we would like to do without it, the trivial consideration that there cannot be justice in society without a minimum of good will in the individuals who make up society.

Let human needs be divided, according to tradition, into those which are biologically determined (*necessarium vitae*) and those which are sociologically determined (*necessarium status*). With regard to the former, science and technology have brought about significant conditions of extraordinary novelty. For one thing, the appreciation of these needs has become subject to fast change; for another, the change always takes place in the same direction, inasmuch as the more recent view is more exacting than the less recent. Our children are reputed to need, in order to survive and to keep well, a huge amount of costly things which fifty years ago were considered luxuries or were totally unheard of. From the point of view of the present inquiry the most relevant fact is that the increasingly high estimation of biological needs entails equalitarian consequences. The case can be simply described as follows: Assuming that society is determined to assure the satisfaction of biological needs, let us compare a period in which biological needs are measured by 2 units with a period in which they are measured by 20 units. Since biological needs are, roughly, the same for all, higher estimation causes a greater amount of wealth to be distributed equally. As the estimation of the biological minimum goes up, technology makes it possible to procure this increasing minimum for all. So long as low production ruled out the distribution of the biological minimum to all, the estimation of this minimum was likely to be much below the truth; it is heartbreaking to declare, as necessary to life, commodities that one knows to be far beyond the range of most of one's fellow-citizens. Abundant production, whether it be a fact or merely a technical possibility, pushes up the estimation of the biological minimum by making the expert free to heed all the suggestions of experience.

With regard to the needs resulting from a social state of affairs, let us first remark that they are sometimes as imperative as items included in the biological minimum. For many men it is easier to do without their full ration of calories than to do without a white shirt. Thus no notion of luxury or futility should be systematically connected with the concept of merely sociological necessity.

Here is a telling fact: whereas the estimation of biological needs has steadily gone up in recent times and, by going up, has brought about equalitarian consequences of great significance, awareness of needs connected with social rank has declined in significant respects; and this also entailed equalitarian consequences. These two movements with one effect favor each other; that is, as more units of wealth are assigned to biological needs, fewer are left for needs of merely sociological character, and, as fewer units of wealth are assigned to "conspicuous consumption," more are left for the salvation of human life. What we mean is not that the total ratio of wealth allocated to sociologically determined needs has declined; in democratic mores the common people have social obligations which, taken as a whole, are extremely costly (decent apparel, good-looking homes, clean lawns, etc.); the significant change concerns the needs connected with high rank in society. The rationalism of democracy produces here its most certain and least harmful effects. So long as expenses declared necessary on account of rank are moderate (e.g., white collars for office workers), they admit of rational justification; but, in order to believe that one's social status imperatively demands a huge sacrifice of wealth—at the cost, possibly, of human lives—one's view of social hierarchy must be colored by mythological belief. The aristocracy-aping bourgeoisie of the nineteenth century gravely took over the nonrational postulates which made it possible to enjoy murderous expenses of conspicuous consumption with a feeling of mere submission to the eternal laws of the social order. It is worth remarking that little was accomplished, in this connection, by the democratic revolution, or by its first phase. A good sign that a new revolutionary phase is irresistibly going on is that it has become impossible for men possessed with a normal conscience to understand how pleasure can be found in meals as costly as those which were such an important part of social life for the upperclass gentlemen of the Victorian era.

This is how a philosophy of human needs—which implies, of course, a whole philosophy of human destiny—has a central part to play in the computation of costs of production. The social conscience of the nineteenth century revolted against the treatment of human labor as an item of merchandise. But if human labor ought not to be treated as an item of merchandise, no item of merchandise ought to be treated as a mere item of merchandise, for there is always, at the core of the cost of production, the recompense of human labor and the answer to human needs. Incorrect estimation of human needs, one way or the other, entails error concerning the cost of production, inequality in exchange, rupture of balance, alienation.

But suppose that the cost of production of a service or commodity has been exactly computed. The construct of the virtuous businessman can be of further help, for a question of no negligible importance remains to be examined. Is the just price equal to the cost of production?

There is a strong appearance that it is. Once more, justice in exchange is nothing else than the equality of the exchanged values. Does not equality demand that the sum surrendered by the purchaser be no greater than the total cost of the commodity purchased?

If producers sold their products at a price equal to the cost of production, they would set a fine example of disinterestedness, but society would not be well served, for there would be no provision for two social needs of the most essential character, viz., *capitalization* and *free distribution*. The meaning of capitalization is clear, but in oral discussion of these ideas I have had many opportunities to notice that the expression "free distribution" fills minds with horrifying pictures related to that of the wealthy man showering bills, from a window, upon a cheering crowd. Free distribution is, indeed, fittingly defined in opposition to exchange. Wealth is made available to the consumer in either of two ways, according as the surrender of equal value is or is not the condition under which wealth is made available. In the first case there is exchange; in the second case wealth is distributed freely. Upset souls are generally pacified not by this definition or any definition but by examples leading to the realization that in the daily life of our societies a huge amount of wealth is distributed freely, that the survival of our societies without extensive processes of free distribution is absolutely inconceivable, and that an economic system in which wealth is made available by way of exchange alone has never existed (although societies tended toward it in the golden age of liberalism). Let it be recalled, further, that abundance causes exchange to be more insufficient than ever as means of distribution. As a matter of fact, we are constantly using a hundred ways of maintaining scarcity, for we know well that, under the circumstances, abundance or some forms of it would entail poverty.

Thus the hypothesis of the price equal to the cost of production leaves unanswered the question of capitalization and that of free distribution. It takes little imagination to find a solution to both these problems and to the problem of determining the cost of production as well: in an extensive system of state ownership, public powers fix prices and have a monopoly on capital and on free distribution. It is the government which distributes relief, education, family allowances, bonuses of all descriptions, and free room and board in its army and in its concentration camps. Nothing can prevent state bureaucracy from determining the just price of each item of merchandise as equal to the cost of production, plus a certain ratio for capitalization and another ratio for distribution. Wealth no longer leaks out of society through unequal exchange; any amount of money paid over and above the cost of production is assigned to functions of capitalization and distribution directly and exclusively relative to the public welfare. Alienation has come to an end. By keeping effectively all wealth within society, such a system properly deserves the name of "socialism." It is important to recall the ideas which were commonly held on the subject of the state at the time when socialist doctrines were constructed. The background of socialism in the nineteenth century is constituted by economic and political liberalism, a system in which the state apparatus is made necessary only by deficiencies that are likely to be gradually remedied. Roughly, the basic duty of the state is to see that contracts are lived up to and to protect honest people against mischievous men. Further, there is hope that, as a result of a better understanding of the laws of society, there will be, in the not too remote future, fewer disorders to correct and less need for the coercive power of the state. In its daring expressions, bourgeois liberalism is very close to anarchism.

In uncertain relation to bourgeois liberalism, which is mostly centered about economic life, a more popular trend of thought, rooted in the French Revolution, cherishes the notion that the dangers of tyranny inherent in the ancient structure of the state can be safely excluded by democracy. Elimination of government may come later; within the explorable portion of the future, what matters is that government should be in the hands of the people and work for the people. Here are the two patterns which exercised decisive influence upon the treatment of the state in nineteenth-century socialism: let the first be described as the theory of the withering away of the state, the latter as the theory of the democratic transformation of the state.

The experiences of our century, inasmuch as they evidenced the connection between state socialism and totalitarianism, have made us receptive to the criticism of Proudhon, already cited in the second chapter of this book. Not a believer in the democratic transformation of the state, Proudhon shows that the proper way to contain the imperialistic dynamism of the state is to have it faced by a force possessed with equally uncompromising imperialistic ambition. This force is property. It alone can preserve society from exhaustion by the development of the state into totalitarian machinery. The last thought of Proudhon on the subject would be nicely expressed by the consideration that much should be forgiven to property on account of what it does for liberty. To put into the same hands the power of unconditional coercion which belongs to the state and the power of ultimate decision concerning earthly goods, which constitutes the right of property, is an arrangement fateful to freedom.

The problem of alienation through unequal exchange admits of undemocratic solutions, in which mercantile exploitation is replaced by incomparably worse forms of servitude. Democratic complacency, in our time, identifies itself with the opinion that dictatorships and totalitarian practices can be avoided without the issue of alienation through unequal exchange being treated in any thorough fashion. Confusedly, many like to think that this is the kind of issue which ceases to be burning as soon as living standards are adequately raised. In several countries social politics is a dialogue between an antidemocratic party which proudly asserts a solution of its own and a democratic party which cherishes, without daring to voice it too loudly, the hope that the question will be dodged indefinitely. *Yet alienation through unequal exchange is the thing that democracy, in the second phase of its revolutionary development, has to deal with, just as alienation through institutional bondage was the thing that democracy had to deal with in its first revolutionary phase.*

Are there elements of a solution in actual democratic practice? Before attempting an answer to this question it is necessary to sum up the data of the problem.

We have understood that the market system is but a primitive method of approximating the just price. Even if controlled, in spite of verisimilitude, by unflinching honesty, the market system implies a continual allowance for profits. (By "profit" we mean any appropriation of wealth made possible by the market situation or by a relation between market situations over and above the recompense equal to the commodity sold or the service rendered.) Without trying to define a better method, we tried to show what better things a better method would do. It would treat the just price as a total made of (1) the cost of production and (2) a surplus for purposes of capitalization and free distribution. The part constituted by the cost of production corresponds to the interindividual aspect of exchange. The surplus is social by essence; its meaning is best expressed by contrast with the methods of state ownership: in a state-socialistic organization it is up to the central administration to save money for capital goods and to effect investments; it is up to the central administration to save money for free distribution and to effect the distribution. Private ownership embodies the principle of autonomy; it relieves the state of tasks that can be fulfilled by individuals, families, and associations, but it also assumes that private persons and private groups will actually perform duties which have to be performed anyway. For instance, subsidizing education on a broad scale is a thing which has to be done in any modern society. One way to get that thing done is for the state to collect through taxation all the money needed for the schools, plus a suitable percentage for the maintenance of the bureaucratic machinery and a few other forms of waste, and to distribute help to schools according to rules and whims which are those of the men in power. There is more autonomous life and there is less waste if money goes directly from private persons and groups to the schools. But when distribution is not effected by public powers, private persons and groups are intrusted [*sic*: entrusted] with a social responsibility and cannot arbitrarily allocate to private pursuits the money needed for the schools.

With regard to the cost of production, the all-important item is human labor. Iniquity creeps in here. Should the conclusion arrived at by the market-place deliberation be my only rule, I would often undervalue my neighbor's labor to the point of making him destitute and overrate my own labor beyond all reasonable limit. (Such things happened commonly at the time when societies allowed themselves to be governed according to the dogmas of economic "science.") As an effect of the moral work carried out in the last three generations, it is now a common opinion that human labor is not an item of merchandise and that recompense for my neighbor's labor cannot be allowed to fall below the minimum needed for a decent life. This worthy step in the enlightenment of the common conscience still has to be supplemented by the realization that, on the other hand, the recompense for my own labor cannot be allowed to go up with no limit. There is somewhere an upper limit beyond which income no longer is a compensation for service but assumes the character of a one-way traffic of wealth. Just as we have come to outlaw destitution, which was still considered an inescapable phase of the economic cycle three generations ago, so a day will come when the conscience of the just will realize that the recompense of human labor, though admitting of inequalities, is comprised between a lower limit, which cannot be very low—for it takes a terrific amount of money to prevent children from dying and to bring them up decently—and an upper limit, which cannot be very high—for no aspect of the common good demands that any person should enjoy an income many times greater than his avowable needs.

Let us use as the background the picture of industrial societies during the golden age of laissez faire economy; against this picture it is easy to distinguish, in the democratic practice of modern societies, institutions and trends designed to promote equality in exchanges, to prevent wealth from leaking out of society, to procure greater accuracy in the estimation of human needs, and to assure the social use of everyone's surplus. The following examples should not be mistaken for the outline of a system; they are meant merely to suggest hopeful research.

1. The first place belongs to the labor union. Prior to the organization of working people, the labor contract was bound to be heavily unequal in the vast majority of cases. It would take a miracle of wisdom and disinterestedness for an equal contract to take place between two parties, one of which—the employer—can wait and cannot be replaced, whereas the other—the isolated laborer—can be replaced and cannot wait. But organized labor can wait and cannot be replaced. Its position is roughly equal to that of management. As an effect of this equality of position, genuine, i.e., equal, contracts can be negotiated between management and labor without any superhuman virtue being presupposed on either side. With due allowance for countless failures and abusive actions, what labor unions have done for a fair estimation of human needs is to be admired among the greatest accomplishments of mankind's social genius.

2. Co-operatives tend to establish strict equality between cost of production and sale price by returning profits to their members.

It should be remarked that the co-operative movement, in its more recent phases, has often lacked the conquering energy which marked its early progress. Most communities are very far from having exhausted the possibilities of co-operation with regard to equality in exchanges. This failure may be due, in part, to habits of passivity generated by the state management of social problems.

3. Concerning free distribution, the great problem is to make it independent of the arbitrariness of individual whims without delivering it up to the arbitrariness of public powers and their bureaucracy. This twofold freedom is actually achieved, in a considerable measure, by numerous organizations which collect and distribute huge sums for relief, scientific research, art, education, and religion. True, the successful operation of autonomy, here and elsewhere, demands industry, labor, obstinacy, imagination, creativeness. An inquiry into the varieties of institutionally organized free distribution throughout the history of economic life might render great service by stimulating the imagination of planners. The worst thing about state management is that it makes people unimaginative; now, when people lack imagination, all that is left is state management.

4. It is hardly necessary to recall that in countless instances freedom from exploitation was served by diverse measures of state intervention. Such measures were eagerly promoted by those democracies which are historically inclined toward state socialism. In other democratic countries they were envisaged with extreme reluctance, then adopted and maintained under the pressure of obvious necessity (minimum salary, social security, subsidies to agriculture, etc.). It happens, not infrequently, that state intervention ought to be accepted in spite of its involving a curtailment of autonomy. But there are cases in which the intervention of the state serves to strengthen autonomic institutions and to increase social guarantees against all threats of imperialism, including those which may come from the democratic state. An example would be supplied by laws designed to protect the farmer's ownership of the land. If such laws are applied successfully, the resulting situation contains a new line of defense against the appetites of financial oligarchies and against those of public powers as well.

CHAPTER 20

Community, Truth, and Culture

In *The Idea of a University*, John Henry Newman argued that the goal of a liberal education was to acquire a "connected view or grasp of things" by virtue of a comprehensive curriculum. The fruits of such a holistic education are immediately evident in the writings of Yves R. Simon. Simon examined a great diversity of subjects, ranging from ethics to political theory to the philosophy of science, in such works as *Practical Knowledge*, *The Philosophy of Democratic Government*, and *The Great Dialogue of Nature and Space*. Yet, although Simon's corpus is remarkably wide-ranging, it does not sacrifice depth for breadth; it is marked by a deep engagement with and careful analysis of the subject at hand.

The subjects treated in the selections in this chapter receive this kind of attention. The reader will find in these pages a mind that is truly philosophic, animated by a single impulse: the love of truth. He will also find a writer who combines the poetic wonder of a Hopkins, the analytic rigor of an Aquinas, and the spare eloquence of a Bernanos. All of these are evident in Simon's examination of the great themes of community, truth, and culture.

It is no accident that Simon takes up these themes. His concern with these matters reflects a basic philosophical orientation that sees community, truth, and culture as intimately related. Simon works in the

Aristotelian-Thomistic tradition, which views human beings as intrinsically social, truth-seeking, and culture-building. Yet, though Simon is a self-conscious heir to this tradition, he recognizes both its strengths and its weaknesses, building on the former, attempting to remedy the latter. He also brings the formidable resources of the tradition to bear upon new topics that uniquely confront the modern mind. For his willingness to engage present problems from a Thomistic perspective, Ralph McInerny praises Simon as a worthy follower of St. Thomas. Not simply a faithful expositor of Thomas's texts, Simon is, in McInerny's words, "all the more a Thomist in that, having assimilated that tradition, he carries it forward into uncharted territory."[1]

Simon's discussion of intellectual freedom in *A General Theory of Authority* (see chapter 13 in this volume) is especially relevant to contemporary cultural questions. His careful defense of the role of authority in intellectual progress, for instance, will add nuance to current discussions about such things as "academic freedom" and the proper role of the teacher, and his argument for the communicability of moral truth and the necessity of public support of such truth will enrich the debates over "public reason" and state neutrality.

The themes of community, truth, and culture are addressed in our selection from *Work, Society, and Culture*. Simon here undertakes a subtle examination of the nature of work and its connection to social life and the development of culture. We see a truly philosophic mind at work, as Simon looks at a problem from many sides, attempting to understand it using the best resources from his own and other intellectual traditions, and also from a variety of disciplines. In the course of Simon's examination, the reader is treated to a careful explication and refinement of Aristotle's account of the intellectual virtues, which paves the way for Simon's ingenious distinction between the structural foundations of culture and the achievements built upon them.

Though composed more than sixty years ago, Simon's analysis of culture bears relevance to our situation today. Having changed from an industrial to a service and information economy, most Americans find themselves having ever less contact with the world of manual labor, becoming ever-more distant from the class of workers who earn their living with their hands. This historically novel situation yields at least two effects. First, there is for most people more time for leisure, which raises the question of how we ought to spend our time. Second, there is a vast discrepancy between the ways of life of the wealthy and the working poor, which raises the question of how the two should relate to one another. Simon's examination of the nature of work and its connection to culture sheds light upon these difficult questions. He argues compellingly that the fruits of culture found in the fine arts and the contemplative life rest ultimately upon a foundation of work and that manual labor in particular encourages certain disciplines that are essential to the right use of free time. In so doing, Simon bridges the gap conventionally placed between work and leisure, provides an important insight into the danger of an affluent, leisured society, and lays the groundwork for a genuinely humanistic culture based upon collaboration among persons from a wide range of social sectors, from manual workers to philosophers, from technicians to artists.

The following selections promise to enrich the reader's understanding of the important themes of community, truth, and culture. Simon's writing requires patient attention on account of its profundity, but it is well worth it, for, as one commentator observed, "You will find that you will understand any problem better if you can read something that Yves Simon has written on it. 'He touched nothing that he did not adorn.'"

Jeanne Heffernan Schindler

Work, Society, and Culture
("Work and Culture," 154–67 and 182–88)

Culture and Civilization

Next, let us approach our subject analytically.[2] We have no ready-made definition, but there are common notions about what culture means, which we can use to begin to work toward a definition. Again, I do not promise that we shall be able to put one together, but it may be enough if we get started on the right track.

"Culture," *cultura* in Latin, was already used in its present derived meaning in ancient times. Originally, it referred to the cultivating of the soil. There is a difference between a field where things grow wild, and where by luck we may find a few plants useful to man, and a field cultivated with the purpose of obtaining a harvest over and above what nature would produce if left to itself. When we transfer this idea to the case of man, we understand very well that what we mean by culture is not something produced by nature but something superadded to the effects of nature by the agency of the human will and reason. The expressions "physical culture" and "physical education" are quite significant here. When we observe how far primitive people are from being able-bodied, we understand that in order to obtain the proper development of muscles alone and a proper balance of muscles and other components of the human body, it is necessary for the body to be educated and cultivated; such results are not obtained by just letting nature take its course. Clearly, then, the general notion of culture refers to rationally controlled processes. But the word is used in a wide range of senses, from the extremely vague and all-embracing to those which are rather narrow and perhaps arbitrarily restricted. Let us consider a few accepted meanings.

The broadest meaning of culture is to be found in anthropology and ethnology. Ethnologists and anthropologists speak of the culture of the Tasmanians just as they speak of the culture of the Mayas, the

Chinese, or the British. They mean by culture anything and everything added by human initiative to the biological results of human existence. Thus the use of extremely crude pottery would be a culture phenomenon just as definitely as are the tragedies of Shakespeare. This meaning is firmly established in ethnology today, and there is no use trying to change it. But we should be aware that when we speak of the culture of the Chinese, the word does not have exactly the same meaning as when we speak of the culture of the Tasmanians. For instance, when we ask "How much culture did Marco Polo find in China?" we do not mean the same thing as when we ask "How much culture was there in Tasmania when the island was first discovered?" In the latter case, we definitely use a much broader meaning.

Among the diverse meanings of the word "culture," especially in regard to the contrast in amplitude and restriction, I call attention to possible opposition between the notions of culture and civilization. This idea was conceived toward the end of the nineteenth century by the Germans and was later adopted by the Russians.[3] "Culture" in this conception has a favorable meaning, "civilization" a pejorative one. Culture is all that expresses life, genuineness, and spontaneity, while civilization includes much that is artificial, mechanical, and contrived. This is a particularly grave distinction, because we cannot change the etymology of "civilization." In many cases the origin of a word may be lost, but that is not the case of "civilization." The root of this word is civic, citizen. Taken seriously, then, such contrast between culture and civilization would imply that what pertains to man as a citizen is something artificial or mechanical, rather than genuine and spontaneous. For instance, legal relationships would thus be relegated to civilization, to the domain of the contrived, at a far remove from what is alive and personal to man, and culture in its relation to law would change from something that develops from within men to something that is imposed on them from the outside.

That these matters are awfully confused is precisely the point: we must be aware of the power of confused ideas. Jacques Maritain, in noting this contrast between "culture" and "civilization" in a number of German and Russian writers, warns the reader that he will not make any such distinction. The interesting question, however, is whether this contrast pertains only to these particular philosophies of life and society or whether it could be significant independently of their specific postulates. In those passages in which Maritain declares that he himself will make no distinction between "culture" and "civilization," he obviously implies that the contrast is not relevant except from a rather specific philosophic position. But I see a problem here.

On the one hand, it is obvious that the notion of civilization comprises the whole system of legal and political relations in any given society. If the word has any meaning, it certainly includes, among other things, the whole range of relations embodied in constitutions, laws, and legal and political practice. But can it be said, on the other hand, without being somewhat arbitrary, that legal and political relations belong specifically to culture? I do not think so, unless "culture" is understood in the all-embracing meaning of the ethnologists (which is another problem). We all agree that culture is more or less connected with civilization and therefore with the legal and political system of a particular society.[4] But take the example of the French. So far as culture is concerned, they consider themselves first in the world (they of course exaggerate a little). Yet, so far as their constitutional and political practices are concerned, I do not think that they even pretend to distinction: Here is a striking discrepancy which I consider significative as well as significant. There is apparently something we call "culture" that can be possessed eminently by a society while the civic relations of that society are by no means remarkable. Since the latter are determinant of civilization, we may have here a hint of opposition. This, I think, holds independently of the more or less dubious views of the contrast between what is spontaneous and what is artificial in human and social life, allied by some to be embodied respectively in culture and in civilization.

The Hard Core of Culture

This discussion of the meanings of the word "culture" has been indispensable in preparation for an analysis of the thing itself. Again, we are not taking "culture" in the broad sense of the anthropologists and ethnologists. Moreover, we have in mind primarily intellectual culture rather than moral culture. There are people of excellent morality who have no sense for poetry or painting or sciences, and who may even lack good manners. We describe such people as uncultured, although we respect them for their moral excellence. On the other hand, there exist also supercultured people who have sunk to the bottom of moral debasement. They are sometimes called sophisticated, but, needless to say, even if we here mean by "culture" primarily what pertains to intellectual excellence rather than to moral qualities, that does not mean that we are overly impressed by this kind of person.

To start this discussion of intellectual culture, it seems best to begin with what is structural in it. I use "structural" here in a metaphorical sense derived from the way in which we speak of a building, because I conceive of this structural component of culture to be like a frame that supports it. For instance, in Aristotle's theory of culture this structural frame is found in two works: in book six of the *Ethics* and in the *Posterior Analytics*. Now, *Analytica Posterior* is a great and difficult treatise on logic, which from the beginning to the end seems concerned with nothing but the logic of demonstration, and this has led some to hold that for Aristotle intellectual culture is something exclusively theoretical and highly abstract. In this view we have one of those stubborn errors known as half-truths; but, to get the whole truth, we have merely to turn to book six of the *Ethics*, where Aristotle treats of the intellectual virtues. In my view, these intellectual virtues constitute an integral part of Aristotle's theory of culture and may indeed be considered its foundation.

"Intellectual virtues" is an expression which has been injected into the veins of American academic life by Robert M. Hutchins. At the beginning of his presidency at the University of Chicago in 1929, he somewhat shocked the academic world by asking, point-blank, what the purpose of higher education was. Was it to turn out superbiological organisms, wonderfully adjusted to life in society, or was it to develop intellectual virtues? While this controversy still swirls around us, Mr. Hutchins has staunchly persevered in his view that the latter is the only legitimate purpose of higher education. But what are these intellectual virtues?

According to Aristotle, the intellectual virtues are understanding, science, wisdom, art, and prudence, and before we go on, let us make sure that we know what each of them means.

The first intellectual virtue, νοῦς, is translated by W. D. Ross as "intuitive reason." I prefer "understanding," not only because it is closer to tradition, but because "reason" is essentially discursive—as in *Hamlet* [Act I, scene ii], "a beast that lacks the discourse of reason." To speak of intuitive reason, therefore, is somewhat contradictory; if reason is taken properly, it is not intuitive, and intuition is not discursive. At the same time, the faculty by which we perceive the truth of immediate propositions is what we call understanding. These definitions, or more exactly definitional propositions, do not need a middle term to manifest their truth. They simply state that this is the definition of this subject. If we know what we are talking about (for instance, if we know what "whole" and "part" mean), such propositions are understood without demonstration; they are antecedent to any possibility of demonstration (viz., "a whole is greater than any one of its parts"). We clearly cannot demonstrate that a subject has a certain property, if we do not know what that subject is. And to express our knowledge of what a subject is, we need definitional propositions worked out by the faculty called "understanding." My final reason for preferring this word to "intuitive reason" is in order to keep, as in Greek, the same word for intellectual power itself and for this most fundamental faculty by which those propositions are understood, which having no middle term are above mediation and demonstration. Aristotle's word, νουσ, also means "mind" in Greek.

Is this ability to understand immediate propositions just a part of intellectual culture or an indispensable foundation of it? The answer is that it is the foundation, for, while it may not be in act prior to experience, understanding is certainly in act prior to the cultivation of the intellect. An extremely uncultured person may possess understanding, sometimes even to a considerable degree. In fact, we find some rather refined people who say, "If two plus two equals five on the moon, I have no objection," and we find uncultured people who object. Aristotelian philosophy is here on the side of the latter, because they have retained their understanding of immediate propositions: two plus two does not equal five—all other things being equal. The reservation is necessary because of the strange things going on in mathematics in our time. Today it could be easily demonstrated that a square can be a circle, and vice versa, by simply shifting from one system of postulates when speaking of circles to another system of postulates when speaking of squares. But these mathematical procedures do not contradict the understanding of basic propositions.

We shall call the second intellectual virtue, επιστήμη, "science" rather than "knowledge," because the latter term may refer both to the intellectual and to the sensory. Science, in this Aristotelian sense, is the intellectual quality by virtue of which the mind is at ease in the field of demonstrable conclusions. The third intellectual virtue, wisdom, σοφία, is a particular case of science. We shall not treat it as a separate virtue, though as a science it has a character of supremacy and is also called by Aristotle metaphysics, first philosophy, and theological science or science of things divine—that is, those beyond the world of motion. This science which is concerned with the first causes and the first principles enjoys a unique privilege insofar as organization is concerned, for one of its functions is to set the whole universe of knowledge in order. Setting things in order is what we expect of a wise person; a wise person is not necessarily one who knows a lot but rather one who puts everything in its proper place. The science which enables him to do so is called wisdom.

The fourth intellectual virtue, art or τέχνη is, as we have already learned, the intellectual quality which renders a man at ease in the domain of things to be made, while the fifth and last intellectual virtue, prudence, renders him at ease in the domain of actions to be done. For the latter there are difficult problems pertaining to either my personal conduct or to my behavior as a member of a group, or to what I must do as a leader of a group. To solve these problems one needs a distinct intellectual quality which Aristotle calls φρόνησις. This is translated by W. D. Ross as "practical wisdom." But even though the meaning is correct I still prefer to call it "prudence" because Aristotle's term has for centuries been translated by the Latin *prudentia*.

These five virtues represent, in my view, the core of the intellectual culture in Aristotle. But are they really virtues, properly speaking? Robert M. Hutchins called them intellectual virtues, and this usage is supported by a long line of precedents beginning with Aristotle himself, who calls these things αρεται which indeed means virtues. Yet if we consider carefully the definition of virtue in book two of the *Ethics*, we realize that it does not apply to all these qualities, because virtue strictly speaking includes rightness of use. For instance, it is not easy to see how a person could make a wrong use of the virtues of justice or temperance by employing them against their purpose. In fact, that is absurd and contradictory, because to have the virtue of temperance is to possess a quality which guarantees the right use of the virtue itself. The same, however, cannot be said, without qualification, of art or of science, and so we have a problem here.

There is in the *Ethics* a passage which annually drove at least one student in the Committee on Social Thought to my office, and the first time this happened I was seriously embarrassed. The passage is translated by W. D. Ross as follows: "But further, while there is such thing as an excellence in art, there is no such thing as excellence in practical wisdom." What could that mean? I suspect Ross did not try to find out, otherwise he would have produced a better translation. He is a great translator, among the very best, which simply indicates the difficulty of these matters. What he translates by "excellence" is αρετη so that if we translate literally we have, "There is virtue in art, and there is no virtue in prudence." But still, what does that mean? Something frightfully simple: It means that having mastered an art, one still needs virtue in order to make proper use of his art; whereas if one has the virtue of prudence, or practical wisdom, he already possesses the principle of good use and needs nothing else to apply it rightly in action.

So we arrive at the strange conclusion that of the above five qualities only one is a virtue in the full sense, and that is the one which is not purely intellectual. In other words, there is really no such thing as an "intellectual virtue." But if we want to blame anyone for this curious usage, we must not blame Robert M. Hutchins. It is really Aristotle's own fault. He was a thinker who, when he needed extreme precision of language, provided it; but on the next page when extreme precision was no longer required, he no longer cared. A virtue properly so-called is moral virtue—that is, a state of character or a stable quality which, by definition, procures its own good use. Understanding, science, wisdom, and art are not of that nature, because they are indifferent to the use to which they may be put. With his immortal naïveté Aristotle remarks that the grammarian is the man best qualified to make grammatical mistakes, if he wants to tease. For us, a chemical engineer is the logical choice for sabotaging a chemical plant.

The conception of the structural in intellectual culture which I want to propose here is closely related to these so-called intellectual virtues of Aristotle. Excluding the understanding of first principles, which is natural rather than cultural, we have science, wisdom, prudence, and art left, and, as we have just noted, only one of these—i.e., prudence—is a virtue unqualifiedly. But whatever these things may be, I believe that it is possible to demonstrate convincingly that they constitute the structural part of culture. Structure of course does not mean the whole. If our dwellings were reduced to their frameworks we would be at a severe disadvantage, and we could hardly call them dwellings. Likewise, a notion of culture restricted to what is structural in it may not correspond to anything that would look like a satisfactory definition of culture. There is a lot more to culture than just structure, and we shall get to it soon enough. But if science, wisdom, art, and prudence which make up the structural component of culture are not "intellectual virtues," what are they?

In my opinion, a better name for these intellectual qualities is habitus, rather than virtues. But this name must be traced to a different root meaning than is commonly supposed. In most books, that word, *habitus* in Latin, is translated with etymological crudity as "habit." Yet when a truly precise meaning is needed, "habit" is worse than useless, because it means exactly the contrary of "habitus." This is why I have been struggling for thirty years for the acceptance of the word habitus in the vernacular. It makes no sense to call our five virtues intellectual habits. In the history of science, habits of thought have been mistaken all too frequently for objective necessity. For instance, in a civilization in which it has always been taken for granted that there is no alteration in celestial bodies, it will be considered axiomatic that celestial bodies are incorruptible. I do not know whether it started with the Babylonians or much earlier, but I know that this habit lasted until the seventeenth century and was broken only when Galileo with his telescope was able to show stars whose qualitative appearances changed. This is one example among a thousand, and the same is evident in the history of moral ideas. How often have rules of action been held axiomatic, when as a matter of fact they were merely customs that had never been subjected to rational analysis? How often indeed have such social customs been at variance with conclusions of rational analysis? We all know that such instances have been all too frequent in history, and they all point to the difference between the kind of necessity which proceeds from habits of thought and the kind of necessity which proceeds from objects of thought. The despairing skepticism of Hume consists precisely in saying "There is no objective necessity, all you can find in the mind is the subjective necessitation of habit."[5] Thus, to call *science* an intellectual habit is to miss what is essential in it, namely the search for and (in the best cases) the grasping of a necessity which is not the effect of repetitive activity of the mind but the expression of what constitutes a form of being. In widely different ways, there is also objective necessity in *art* and in *wisdom*, and that is why these things are, if not virtues in the full sense of the term, still something greatly different from mere habit. They are qualities which owe their character of certainty to being grounded in a necessity of an objective nature.

To get back to our etymological argument, let us note that there is among philosophers some controversy about the translation of Aristotle's ἕξις. This noun is related to the verb ἔχειν (which means "to have,") and came into Latin, perhaps through Cicero, as *habitus*, related to *habere*. Cicero was a great popularizer of Greek philosophy who, though not always profoundly understanding, did a lot of vocabulary work. His habitus is a good translation from the Greek original: it has something to do with "to have." But why is there no exact equivalent of this term in modern philosophical language? I believe that the notion expressed by that word was lost sight of in the seventeenth century at the time when philosophical vernaculars were taking shape. We would not expect to find a word like that in Descartes, who has no use for intellectual habitus, so to speak, because he has his four rules of method. Nor would we expect to find it in Hobbes, another mechanist though of a different stripe. Yet these two were the first great philosophers writing in the vernacular, with the result that habitus was never translated from the Latin. Somebody once told me that in an obscure seventeenth-century French writing, habitus is rendered by *ayance* which is related to *ayant*, the present participle of *avoir*. That is a lovely word, but I do not think that it could be revived. At any rate, it would not give us a solution in English, for I cannot think of a coinage related to "having" that would do the job. So what is left for us to do is to use the Latin term, *habitus*, with its original meaning, in English. ("Habitus" is in fact found in unabridged English dictionaries, though not in our sense but rather referring to the general disposition of an organism, the sense in which it is used in medicine.)

This apparent semantic digression on the etymology of habitus has been quite intentional. My point is that in the intellectual habitus—whether of the contemplative type as in science and wisdom, or of the productive type as in art, or of the active type as in prudence—there is a stable quality which is essentially relative to an objective necessity. By this I do not mean that, for instance, everything taught in a scientific department at a university is objectively necessary. What goes on there under the name of science is to a very large extent made up of factual information, educated opinion, and probability; yet this aggregate owes its existence to a nucleus of hard, objective necessity, to which it is connected by the scientific habitus. Likewise, though we speak of miracles of production and of relativity in moral judgments, we know that neither of these activities admits of complete arbitrariness. A core of objective necessity supports our achievements in arts and prudence as well as in science. That is what really matters for the understanding of habitus as the structural component of culture. But this insight is also decisive for the understanding of the relation between work and culture.

In the early part of our analysis of the concept of work, we set in contrast to what we called activities of legal fulfillment certain other activities which we said expressed free development. To go to a coffee shop for a cup of tea because one has just met an old friend with whom it is pleasant to chat is not the same as to rush in for a cup of tea because one has been exposed to bad weather and hopes that drinking something hot may prevent a cold. The latter action pertains to legal fulfillment, the former to free expansion. Now, intellectual habitus clearly represent activities of legal fulfillment. In them there is no fancy, no frills, no jokes; they, like work, pertain to what is serious in human life. Stable and certain, because they are built on objective necessity, they are capable of constituting the structural in culture, its hard core. But as life is not all work, we cannot have a theory of culture without postulating also a lot of activities of free development independent of objective necessity. Indeed, some think that such activities are precisely and exclusively what constitutes culture, what culture is. We want to examine this matter closely, and we want to pay special attention to the alleged opposition between this unnecessary, subjective, free aspect of culture and what we have just identified as its hard core.

THE PLENITUDE OF CULTURE

An important element in the contrast between the component of free expansion in culture and its hard core of legal fulfillment has been expressed by Jacques Maritain in a single sentence which I am eager to quote in the original because it is as nicely phrased as it is profound. Maritain writes: "*Les gens du monde, polis sur toutes les faces, n'aiment pas l'homme à habitus avec ses aspérités.*"[6] I read that thirty years ago and could never forget it. *Les gens du monde* are the "beautiful people," the society people who go to parties but also support and participate in what are called cultural activities. They are *polis sur toutes les faces*: very polished in their ways; but they *n'aiment pas l'homme à habitus*: they do not love the man possessed of habitus; *avec ses aspérités:* with, or rather because of, his roughness....

LEISURE, WORK, AND CULTURE

Finally, we come to the popular question of the relationship between leisure and culture, which is of course inseparable from the consideration of the place of work in human and social life. Let us recall the title of the book by Josef Pieper, *Leisure: The Basis of Culture.* What does it mean? If it means that in order to do things cultural we need time to do them, it is fairly clear. For instance, studying classical literature is a component of culture of which many people are deprived who have to work from dawn to dusk, when they are completely exhausted and could not care less about the classics. But to say that we need leisure to do things does not seem very significant; if we call leisure the time left after biologically necessary functions and duties have been fulfilled, then we need leisure for work every bit as much as for culture. So, obviously, leisure does not mean just free time, but rather specifically freedom from work, as in the phrase "a life of leisure." Our question, then, must be put as follows: Is culture necessarily centered on a life free from work (taking the latter in the broadest possible sense as any activity of legal fulfillment that is also socially productive)?

The fact is that we can find several periods in history in which culture consisted principally of frivolity decorating the idleness of a distinct social class. The period spanning the late seventeenth and the early eighteenth century is a good example. In that period, even scientists, philosophers, physicists, and mathematicians had to be socialites and had to speak the kind of language that members of high society used in their conversations. To be sure, these society people were interested in both arts and sciences. But they considered themselves too refined to master technical scientific terms, and they simply assumed that anything really worth knowing or saying could be expressed elegantly in their own language. The works of Leibniz (1646–1716), for instance, are fairly representative of this approach and style, and this becomes quite evident when we compare his writings with, say, Kant's. Kant (1724–1804) no longer wrote for society people but rather for professional philosophers and serious students of philosophy.

Another example of this frivolous culture is the celebrated *Logic* of Port-Royal. This was a Jansenist institution used as a retreat by a few distinguished gentlemen of leisure (the most important of whom was Pascal), where, about 1660, two members of this group—their names are not important—fancied to write a treatise on logic.[7] This treatise is still being read, and there are some who hold that it is a typical example of Aristotelian as opposed to modern mathematical symbolic logic.[8] To me, it is just an historical curiosity. Indulging in an eclecticism of the second and third power and offering an aggregate of scholastic aberrations mixed with some Cartesian components, the book is altogether a logic-monster. But—this must be admitted—it is written in beautiful language. As I see it, what happened was something like this. When they came across logical subjects that could be expressed only in technical terms, these *gens du monde, polis sur toutes les faces*, these would-be part-time logicians, seem to have concluded with really delightful naivety, "Thank goodness that these things are of no importance." Yet some of the concepts that they dismiss so cavalierly are of the very essence of logic, and without them it would never be possible to say what logic is all about. But to the members of the Port Royal group this did not matter, because they were not serious students of logic; they were gentlemen of leisure for whom culture was all decoration—all flowers. I sometimes wonder whether they would have cared had they realized that their culture was made of cut flowers that were soon to dry up.

In my view, the connection with a life of leisure which has often been held essential for the development of culture has to do mainly with what we have called above the flower-like component of culture. The structural component of culture, its hard core of intellectual habitus, does not seem to demand a life of social leisure, at least not necessarily. For instance, there is precious little leisure in the life of a philosopher who teaches fifteen hours a week at a university and must also teach in the summer school, because without that additional fee his salary would not be sufficient to maintain his family. The same can be said about a painter who is not yet famous enough to sell one canvas a year at some fantastic price, and who must therefore paint one picture after another to make ends meet. Even the scientist who is paid a handsome salary for doing nothing but disinterested, pure research in physics cannot be said to lead a life of leisure. True, none of these people belongs to the working class, but they are not members of a leisure class either. In the broad sense, they spend their lives working—that is, engaged in activities of legal fulfillment that are not only honest but also socially useful. But does that mean that they are incapable of contributing to the flower-like component of culture? Does it mean that because theirs is not a life of leisure they cannot break through, so to speak, into activities of free expansion corresponding to their habitus? I do not think so, as I have never believed that social leisure—that is, freedom from any kind of work—is an essential requirement of culture.

In our time there is much speculation about the possibility of a life of leisure for practically everybody, and the question of the relationship between leisure and culture assumes under these conditions a radically different aspect than it has had historically. In all the past experience of mankind, there was a division of functions between the many who worked hard to maintain society and the few who maintained culture and enjoyed a life of leisure. But as leisure comes to be enjoyed by the many, it becomes much easier to see that all that a life of leisure was ever able to support for any length of time were a few flower like ornaments of culture. With more people enjoying more social leisure than it had ever been thought possible, we can now see much more clearly that, instead of a life of leisure, the real basis of culture—its supporting structure and hard core—is to be found rather in activities in the performance of which a workmanlike disposition is indispensable.

The immediate task before us, therefore, appears to be the development of a theory of culture centered not on leisure but on work in the broadest sense, including moral, social, and intellectual, as well as technical and manual work. Indeed, we may find in the most humble kinds of work those patterns and rules which can exercise a sound influence upon every search for culture and intellectual perfection. Let us say that technical work, especially on the level of execution, has the privilege of arousing in man a sense of honesty and an interest in perfection. Manual work is an activity which admits of no cheating. In intellectual work, particularly in its loftier forms, it is all too easy to cheat. For instance, take a theory designed to answer a philosophical problem. The answer is wrong, but the theory evidences a great deal of erudition and intellectual ingenuity; it is received as a magnificent piece of scholarship, and this brings the philosopher all the satisfaction he cares for. A manual laborer cannot expect satisfaction of this kind. The slightest defect in a key makes it impossible to unlock the door, and nobody can be fooled. Moreover, manual work is a field in which perfection is certainly obtainable. In many domains of intellectual work we are strongly tempted no longer to look for perfection because we know that we shall have to stop short of it. The temptation is very great for an artist, a writer, or a philosopher to give up interest in perfection, for they all know that their achievements are unlikely to be perfect.

But is such a thing possible? Can we really hope to develop today a culture that is neither frivolous nor obsessed with exploitation of physical nature? On the one hand, praising work and its prototype, manual work, seems to lead to the prevalence of the demiurgical ideal in our societies, sometimes called materialism. On the other hand, holding out an ideal of culture as this term has been understood in the last few centuries seems an ill-inspired remedy. If we cherish the element of refinement, of flexibility, of charm, and let everything which is sound—life, nature, energy, work, certainty, necessity—die out, we are confronted by the nihilistic monster which plagues, today, the oldest civilizations of the West and threatens to deliver them up to barbarism. Once they are cut off from the principles which make up the deep life of the soul, the blossoming externals of culture can only bring about a vacuum in which some kind of devastating frenzy is likely to develop.

Thus we must conclude that holding out an ideal of culture based on freedom from work is not the answer. Erecting such a culture into an ideal inevitably leads to a disorderly exaltation of the flowery element of culture, and this makes for subjectivism, arbitrariness, and an attitude of frivolous aversion to nature and its laws. Therefore, we must insist that knowledge of truth, not possession of culture, be our regulating ideal. And let us not doubt that, if truth is sought according to its own laws and to its own spirit, culture also will be attained. Everything is in perfect order if the factors of refinement, flexibility, and charm spring from what is strong and determinate and of itself hard. For lack of a logically satisfactory definition of culture, we may use a metaphorical one and say that true culture is a "bush of habitus" in blossom.

Years ago, in conclusion to a brief paper on the concept of work in a symposium entitled *The Works of the Mind*, I suggested that it was up to the manual worker to keep alive among us a certain spirit of honesty and perfection which ought to be carried from level to level up to that supreme sphere of intellectual life where all work comes to an end and the image of eternal life appears. The good worker and the lover of truth, I wrote, have much in common, and the promotion of their understanding could do a great deal for the reformation of our concept of culture. Here, I wish to add a further suggestion. It is my feeling that our best immediate chances to begin to develop the culture with a contemplative ideal may lie in promoting collaboration between all kinds of technical work and the fine arts. Such a rapprochement has been enormously facilitated by the truly fantastic developments in modern technology, of which we should take utmost advantage. As a general rule, the more powerful the technique at his disposal, the greater the possibilities for creative choices open to any worker. I believe that once these creative possibilities are fully recognized, modern technology, traditionally held to be hostile to culture, could become an important contributing factor to the development of a truly humanistic culture.

Notes

1. [Editor's note: Schindler is here quoting from Ralph McInerny's preface—"Yves R. Simon as a Moral Philosopher"—to his translation of Simon, *A Critique of Moral Knowledge* (New York: Fordham University Press, 2002), vii.]

2. [Editor's Note: As with John Gueguen's use of *Work, Society, and Culture*, the footnotes have been retained. All remaining notes in this chapter are those of Kuic (referencing works often published after Simon's death).]

3. Jacques Maritain, *True Humanism* (New York: Charles Scribner's Sons, 1938) p. 88; [Maritain,] "Religion and Culture," in *The Social and Political Philosophy of Jacques Maritain*, edited by Joseph W. Evans and Leo R. Ward (New York: Charles Scribner's Sons, 1965), pp. 217–218.

4. Cf. Jacob Burkhardt, *Force and Freedom*, edited by James Hastings Nicholls (New York: Meridian, 1955). See also Raymond Williams, *Culture and Society* (New York: Columbia University Press, 1958).

5. David Hume, *A Treatise of Human Nature*, Book I, Section XIV, "Of the Idea of Necessary Connexion": "Upon the whole, necessity is something, that exists in the mind, not in objects; nor is it possible for us ever to form the most distant idea of it, considered as a quality in bodies" (*The Philosophy of David Hume*, edited by V.C. Chappell [New York: Modern Library, 1963], p. 112).

6. See Jacques Maritain, *Art and Scholasticism*, translated by Joseph W. Evans (New York: Charles Scribner's Sons, 1961), p. 12.

7. The most recent issue is Antoine Arnauld and Pierre Nicole, *La logique de Port-Royal*, edited by Bruno Baron von Freytag Loringhoff and Herbert E. Brekle (Stuttgart: Frommann, 1965). The latest English edition is *Art of Thinking: Port-Royal Logic*, translated by James and Patricia Dickoff (New York: Bobbs-Merrill, 1964).

8. See Ferdinand Gonseth, *Qu'est-ce que la logique?* (Paris: Hermann, 1937).

Epilogue
Problems in International Order

Practical wisdom and theoretical wisdom are not only two different disciplines. They tend to be pursued by two different kinds of people. The careful attention to multiple details and the weighing of various possibilities and permutations, with an eye towards making a decision, calls for the kind of person who is relatively tranquil amidst incomplete data and unavoidable uncertainties. Indeed, the ability to make practical decisions calls for a special form of courage undeterred by the possibility of error or failure. By contrast, theoretical wisdom typically proceeds by sharply limiting the number of variables in play and by directing attention on those realities with the aim of arriving at certain conclusions. And theoreticians, therefore, by nature like problems that admit of clear and demonstrable answers possessing the status of settled science. All of us are required in the course of life to take up both approaches, but rare is the person who can do so at a high intellectual level, especially on matters involving large-scale national and international questions whose resolution often only gives rise to further complexities and puzzles.

As our previous chapters in this volume have shown, Yves R. Simon was that very rare mind who functioned at the very highest level of theory and, unusually, also with great practical insight. The following selections confirm that not only did he see the public questions facing France in great detail, but he also had a firm grasp on the international scene and its meaning for human history. The two most urgent international questions in Simon's time, of course, were the challenge of communism at home and abroad, and the aggression of Nazism/fascism in several guises. In the first pages of *Philosophy of Democratic Government*, he asserts, as others have done, that the two ideologies are quite similar, though partisans of either are horrified at the comparison. He then goes on to show in depth and detail why that is the case, and why both are deficient from a democratic stance that is defensible in both theory and practice. Typically for Simon, he also explores questions of authority, a difficult enough problem in both democratic and totalitarian states. But it has become even more so, in his time and ours, at the level of international relations, on account of the lack of worldwide institutional structures that command respect and that would, therefore, possess the authority needed to oversee something resembling a just world order.

Simon had already discerned the main lines of the problem during the Italian Fascist invasion of Ethiopia in 1935, a seemingly insignificant colonial adventure, little remembered today. He correctly foresaw that the failure of the international community to defend Ethiopia, a member of the League of Nations, was the beginning of the end of that body and the aspirations it represented. Simon was under no illusions about the imperfections and weaknesses of such political instruments. He would probably make sharp criticisms of the United Nations and other international organizations today. But collective security is a good that all nations can agree to pursue. And those in France and elsewhere who thought that indulging the fascists and getting rid of the League of Nations would free their nations to pursue their own legitimate interests thereby became partly guilty of the series of subsequent events that led to the disaster of World War II.

One of Simon's strengths as a political observer is his ability to hold to principle, without fanaticism, while appraising various factors. His practice parallels his own theoretical efforts to explain the mysterious ways in which virtuous character and moral principles are needed to reach the point of "command" at which action may be undertaken with confidence. In the battle over Nazism/fascism, for instance, he is clear in his mind about the goal of liberty and political decency—and at the same time critical of various French Catholics and others who were willing, in Simon's view, to betray France to the Germans in order to settle old scores. Since the French Revolution, French Catholics had a justifiable suspicion about the ideals of the Republicans, who had slaughtered Catholics and, in the government of Émile Combes, suppressed religious institutions in the name of liberty, equality, and fraternity. That ancient division into the "two Frances" made many Catholics vulnerable to the fascist propaganda that sought to portray quite vicious authoritarians as virtuous restorers of a properly hierarchical society and a resistance to the atheistic depredations of international communism. In the 1930s, the anti-Catholic atrocities of the Spanish Republicans, who had links to the Soviet Union, only seemed to confirm that portrait.

Simon deplored the French and Spanish Republican outrages as much as any Catholic and was not in the least sympathetic to the communist cause anywhere, least of all in France. But he was also not deluded that fascism promised any good in the world. It took real courage to say this openly, because highly influential figures in France and Rome, such as Réginald Garrigou-Lagrange (one of Jacques Maritain's teachers and later Karol Wojtyła's dissertation director), were also strong supporters of right-wing forces. Action Française, the French monarchist movement, had drawn the allegiance of many, including the young Maritain, who later repented of this confusion between Thomist principles and authoritarian politics. Although it was condemned for its atheism in 1926, and Catholics who continued to be members after early 1927 were barred from the sacraments, the condemnation was lifted by Pius XII in 1939, partly in response to the slaughter the Republicans had carried out in the Spanish Civil War.

Simon understood that the French tragedy, which resulted in its submission to Nazi Germany, was the result of many internal factors. The only solution he believed to have been available—alliance with the Soviets against Nazi aggression, while resisting communist ascendancy within France—was not one that the French were able to carry out, owing to long-standing intellectual and historical circumstances.

Perhaps this colossal failure also shows the effective limits of practical wisdom, at times. It is not a "science" in the strong sense of the word, but even when deliberation and good judgment result in what appears a wise course to pursue, it is not always possible actually to take such a course. Simon allowed himself angry denunciations of the "fools" and "traitors" who prepared the downfall of France and the spread of Nazism by their inability to analyze the situation properly and their readiness to rationalize collaboration with Germany. The United Kingdom and the United States, by contrast, were able to ally themselves with the Soviets against the Nazis without much fuss, but they were not countries with France's history of a strong communist presence. That tragic situation meant that France in a way had earlier prepared its own downfall. But there is a lesson for practical wisdom here: human beings are not the masters of themselves and, therefore, not of human history. History can become a kind of cross on which even the best practical wisdom is crucified.

Towards the end of *The Road to Vichy*, Simon explicitly states a principle that had been implicit throughout that book and in much of his thinking elsewhere about practical wisdom in public affairs: the need of an energizing *myth* to unite various, otherwise ineffectual, aspirations. It may seem odd for a philosopher to be recommending myth as a form of wisdom or practicality—something in dispute at least since the Pre-Socratics. But it is one measure of the "practically practical wisdom" Simon spent much effort trying to identify to see that, in order to move groups of men, such entities as myth are necessary. A cool science will never do, either theoretically or practically; for the philosopher who is not going to withdraw from human affairs as beneath the notice of an Olympian rationality is going to have to reckon with the perennial role of myth in human communities. Indeed, with or without philosophers, myths—either good or bad—will move public opinion. Better, then, a myth of freedom that cannot entirely describe the future, since the future will depend on the uses made of freedom. The myth of freedom can nevertheless assert with passion that the things the tyrants cannot offer, "neither truth nor freedom nor justice" (*The Road to Vichy*, 203), are precisely the goals sought by all who pursue what is right in every country. The international cooperation of various peoples—the Free French, the Free Poles, even the Free Germans—was "already converging to form one great vision which will be the victorious myth of the future: *the sublime vision of the liberation of the world*" (202).

That myth still awaits fulfillment, to say nothing of adequate expression, and needs to be rescued from many false starts and misconceptions about its meaning. In the *March to Liberation*, Simon himself explains that many people misunderstand the proper meaning of myth, assuming it merely signifies a false story. So he decided to replace "myth" with the term "heroic faith" and—borrowing from Charles Péguy—suggests that a heroic faith draws on those mystiques "in which truth and justice predominate (23)." *And it is only such faith that can lead to true liberation.*

"Liberation," in the twenty-first century, means for many people, however, liberation from the very virtues and moral principles that are the only basis of a well-lived life of freedom. And even more than in some of the false moves of the League of Nations, the contemporary international order—that Simon like many other good thinkers believed should be precisely "inter-national," in the sense of helping individual nations with their human tasks—is now marked by a cohort of international elites who regard themselves not as servants but as the masters of nations, whose functions they seek to control or to absorb in a new and threatening ideology of radical individual autonomy. In the continuing confusion about the nature of practical wisdom and its uses in a now globalized world, Simon's work continues to offer a rich reflection on what international order may yet be and how a wise practicality may yet make it a reality.

Robert Royal

Philosophy of Democratic Government
("General Theory of Government," 1–6)

Communism and national socialism have come to resemble each other in so many respects that their historical diversity and their lasting opposition arouse wonder.[1] In spite of common features that are profound and increasingly obvious, they prove altogether repugnant to effecting any kind of merger. The task of fighting them would be greatly eased if followers, actual and potential, were led to believe that one system, i.e., the one which appeals to them, is substantially identical with the other, i.e., the one which they hate; but such identification never was very successful as a polemical instrument. Conservatives in the 1930s were given a fair chance to understand that Nazism was but brown bolshevism; yet many of them helped the Nazis. Today it seems that it should be easy for all concerned to recognize in communism the very features that they hated most in Nazism; but not all do.

The persistent conflict of these two systems is traceable in part to their opposite stands on the class struggle and to the operation of class allegiances. But in the minds of many followers the decisive influence is exercised by representations of the ultimate future. For with regard to the future and more particularly to the remote portions of the future, where the assertion of an ideal cannot be hampered by any experience or fact, the two totalitarian systems differ widely. In fascism or Nazism, the totalitarian state is exalted as the highest product of life and history. In spite of the evolutionistic language in which such things are spoken of, it plainly enjoys the character of a terminal accomplishment. Is it going to endure forever? At any rate, not a word is said about how it might come to an end and what might come after it. Communism, on the other hand, promises the withering away of the state.

At an early stage of its history, socialism was characterized as pessimistic with regard to accomplished facts and optimistic with regard to facts to be accomplished. Communism, in our time, remains optimistic about facts to be accomplished ultimately. Its gruesome view of the non-Communist society and the ruthlessness of its revolutionary means are associated with a picture as radiant as anything ever produced by the spirit of utopia. The rational organization of economic relations will bring to an end the division of society into classes, the exploitation of man by man, the war of man against man. But the state is born of this division, this exploitation, this war. The classless society will be a stateless society. The totalitarian increase of the powers of the state is a temporary measure necessary to bring about a social structure that will render the state unnecessary and establish forever the brotherhood of men.

In Marxian communism the philosophy of evil is characterized by a sort of monism which proves very handy when there is a question of stirring men to action; for, if all particular injustices ultimately merge into one absolute injustice, it should be possible to do away with injustice, once and for all, in a Napoleonic victory. Social visions, in the tradition of liberal democracy, lack such tragic and appealing simplicity; yet the basic theory that evil alone makes the state organization necessary appeared first in liberal democracy. Recall the celebrated propositions of Tom Paine: "Society is produced by our wants and government by our wickedness; the former promotes our happiness positively by uniting our affections, the latter negatively by restraining our vices ... the first is a patron, the last a punisher." Strikingly, a theory worked out by men whose great concern was to limit the powers of the state was not rejected, but rather transfigured, by the planners and by the founders of the first modern totalitarian state.

The theory that government is rendered necessary not by nature but by deficiencies—let it be called, from now on "The deficiency theory of government"—should not be confused with the theory of describing government as a necessary evil. A Fascist would never grant that the state is an evil; on the contrary, he proudly asserts that it is the highest value. Yet, if he undertakes to set forth the reasons why the state is thought to be such a noble thing, he is likely to indulge in a pessimistic description of human societies and to declare that overwhelming force is everlastingly needed to crush ever recurrent evil. In so far as the Fascist exaltation of the state is linked to such pessimism, the deficiency theory is not foreign to fascism itself. Contrary to a belief current in classical democracy, this theory does not constitute a guarantee against overgovernment. In fact, systematic determination to prevent the government from doing more than a very small amount of governing did not originate in the deficiency theory. It originated in the belief that the greatest good of the greatest number is most safely brought about by the operation of individual initiatives. Even the needed convergence of multiple endeavors was reputed to be best achieved without any human management; for it was assumed—explicitly or implicitly and always confusedly—that there exists, inside the spontaneous course of events, a highly dependable person who inconspicuously directs chance occurrences toward a definite goal. According to times and circumstances, this person was called "nature," "Providence," or "evolution."

The naturalistic optimism on which early liberalism thrived is a thing of the past. We are aware of the shortcomings of human management, but dire experience has made it impossible for us to intrust [*sic*: entrust] the destiny of men and the survival of nations to the hazards of universal competition. We have come to recognize the jungle character of the wilderness which our fathers mistook for a land of harmony. The case is so plain as to be reflected in the meaning of words. In the golden age of liberalism, the word "liberal" designated a supporter of the laissez faire system, and one was reputed to be a liberal in so far as he was known to oppose state intervention, the organization of the workers, etc. The most radical among liberals were hardly distinguishable from individualistic anarchists. Today, a systematic adversary of economic planning, price control, labor laws, etc., is what everybody calls a "reactionary" and nobody is considered a liberal unless he is willing to support heavy programs of state intervention. The liberals of our time confess that a huge amount of government has become a condition for the preservation and normal growth of all the goods that society stands for. In terms of the deficiency theory, this is a bewildering situation. If evil alone makes government necessary, a demand for increased government activity means either increased evil or better awareness of evil or both. True, we feel that some things have become worse, and we have developed an ability to see many shortcomings that used to pass almost unnoticed, but there are not a few circumstances in which the call for more government activity seems to result from unqualified progress. It then becomes supremely important that the boundaries of the domain conceded to the state should never be left uncertain. If it is granted that progress itself, in a certain way, demands the growth of the state, it is more necessary than ever that disorderly expansion of the state machinery—a frequent accident under all circumstances—be held in check by the power of clearly defined principles.

Nature and Functions of Authority
(Selections: 1–7, 12–18, and 28–30)

Radical anarchists excepted, no social thinker ever questioned the fact that social happiness is based upon a felicitous combination of authority and liberty . . . it is quite clear that authority, when it is not fairly balanced by liberty, is but tyranny, and that liberty, when it is not fairly balanced by authority, is but abusive license. . . . There would be hardly any exaggeration in the statement that the essential question, for every social group, is that of combining rightly the forces of authority and liberty. . . .

Political and social consciousness, in modern times, evidences an obscure belief that the progress of freedom is synonymous with social progress, that social progress is, at bottom, the progress of freedom. This identification of the progress of liberty with social progress is proclaimed by those who call themselves liberals or progressives; it is rarely denied by those who call themselves conservatives or even reactionaries. It is very striking to observe that conservatives, in most cases, content themselves with accusing progressives, liberals, even revolutionaries, of precipitating the pace of social progress by asking for an amount of liberty that society, in its factual state, cannot stand. Thus they admit, no less than liberals and progressives, the basic assumption that social progress is identical with the progress of liberty. Now this progress of liberty is ordinarily conceived as implying a decay of authority, so that these three terms, social progress, the progress of liberty, and the decay of authority, are currently identified. . . .

It seems that a provisional definition [of authority] . . . can be of help. . . . Let us propose the following one:

Authority is an active power, residing in a person and exercised through a command, that is through a practical judgment to be taken as a rule of conduct by the free-will of another person. . . .

Let us now inquire into the reasons why it may be good that a person be regulated in his conduct by a person rather than by his own reason. To be ruled by another may be expedient or even necessary on the ground of one's inability to rule one's self. This is the case with children, and this is also the case with the insane, the feeble-minded, or the criminal, who are legally considered, as well as children, to be minors. A minor is a person supposedly unable to govern *himself*, that is, to provide for the right order to be assured in his actions, even within the field of his personal aims. A minor is supposed to be incapable of knowing what is good for him—this is why another person has to guide him in the very pursuit of his proper good. The inability of the minor to govern himself, to pursue his proper aims by himself, is always based on some deficiency.

Thus . . . authority enjoys substitutional functions. The question is now whether authority has any essential function; whether the necessity of authority always results from some deficiency; whether authority, when necessary, is necessary solely on the ground of some defect in the one who is subjected to it. The idea that authority has no essential function but only substitutional ones, is in fact very widespread. It is current among anarchists and liberal theorists. Let us mention, as particularly representative, Proudhon and J. S. Mill. . . .

The assumption that authority has but substitutional functions has far-reaching consequences, for if authority is made necessary by deficiencies alone, it will be destined to disappear insofar as the deficiencies which make it necessary disappear. . . . Thus, the law of progress would take the form of an asymptotic curve at whose unattainable term there would be a complete elimination of authority.

The best means of ascertaining whether there is such a thing as an essential function of authority is to consider a community of adults, intelligent and of perfect good will, and to inquire into the requirements of the common life of that community. . . . This community, however small it may be, must be regulated in its common action by decisions which bind all members. How will these decisions be made? They can be made unanimously, but the unanimity is not guaranteed. There is no steady principle which could indefectibly assure this unanimity. Any member of the community can disagree with the others as to the best course to take in a common action. In case of persistent disagreement, either the unity of action of the community will be broken, or one judgment will prevail, which means that some person or some group of persons will be recognized as having authority. I say: *a person or a group of persons*, because the decision which is to prevail can be issued by a single individual or by a majority-vote of the whole community, or by a majority-vote of a selected group within the community as well: as far as the principle of authority is concerned, it makes no difference.

And thus we have pointed out the essential function of authority: to assure the unity of action of a united multitude. A multitude aiming at a common good which can be attained only through a common action, must be united in its action by some steady principle. This principle is precisely what we call authority. . . .

Contingency prevents us from knowing exhaustively the factors with which our decision is concerned and from predicting their future with any kind of certainty. In the complex matters of collective behavior, more than anywhere else, the theoretical considerations on which the prudential judgment is based cannot be demonstrated. Accordingly, it can never be shown evidently that this or that practical judgment, to be taken as a rule for our common action, is the best possible one. However conscientious deliberation may be, since it cannot afford to prove its conclusions, anybody can, at any time, object that a better course of action could be conceived, and the unity of action which is supposed to be required by the pursuit of the common good will be ceaselessly jeopardized unless all members of the community agree to follow one prudential decision and only one—which is to submit themselves to some authority.

Thus, beyond necessities and conveniences which result from the unreasonableness, ignorance and wickedness of men, the principle of authority answers a necessity which is no way accidental, which is not a consequence of any sin, evil or deficiency, a necessity which is but a metaphysical consequence of the nature of things. Considered in its principle, authority is neither a necessary evil nor the consequence of any evil, nor a lesser good, but an absolutely good thing founded upon the metaphysical goodness of nature. Considered in its essential function, as identical with the prudence of society in its collective action, authority is the everlastingly good principle of the social unity in the pursuit of the common good.

The Ethiopian Campaign and French Political Thought

(Selections: 74–78)

If we go over the various accepted meanings of the term *force* as it is currently used with respect to human relations, it seems that the decisive elements in its meaning can be summarized in the following formula: force is an active causality, having as its object a person or society, and whose proper effects are of a physical nature; the person or society who uses force pursues a physical effect, or an ensemble of physical effects, as the proper means to their ends. . . .

Among the multiple use of the term *law*, the first in the order of intelligibility seems to be the objective usage: law, which is before everything else just, is the action that renders to another what is due; law is before all else *the object of justice*. We use law, in a second place, for the *rule* of just action (the *formal* meaning of the term *law*); finally, we call law that faculty that someone possesses to whom something is owed to assert his due (*subjective* meaning). There exists an objective natural law whose rule is the natural law; there exists an objective positive law, whose rule is the human institution: that rule is sometimes a contract agreed upon between persons or communities, sometimes a law established by a community. If we understand the term *law* in the formal sense (in the sense of the rule or measure of justice) there are then three great species of law: natural law, positive contractual law, and positive legislative law. In a complete juridical system, the contractual relations are subordinated to positive laws, which are only true laws to the extent that they conform to natural laws. The inner regime of a state is in principle a complete juridical system. The regime of international relations, so long as there does not exist any international community capable of establishing laws and imposing their implementation, is an incomplete juridical system: it only admits as other rules of law the natural laws and contractual stipulations; *positive legislative law is wanting here.*

Within an organized community, furnished with a positive legislative law, force is nothing other than the instrument of the rule of law, nothing other than the instrument of the positive law in its function of effectively regulating juridical matter....

Let us now consider the formal juridical situation of sovereign nations still not committed to an international community. What are the character and role of force in such a situation?... We will ... try to put the question more precisely by asking if a national force is *forbidden* in the absence of positive international law to play the role of an instrument of a rule of law. Surely, the possibility of such a role for national force is not excluded; every time it is used to ensure the observation of a natural law or a contractual stipulation itself conforming to natural law, national force has played the role of an instrument of the rule of law; but nothing guarantees, unless it is the virtue of a specific government, that it will play this role rather than the opposite role; nothing guarantees that it will not be checked or crushed by a rival force. The first benefit of organized communities, capable of establishing laws and imposing respect for them by collective force, is to increase immensely the chance of success for a rule of law. Is it possible to extend this inestimable benefit to international relations, to the very limit of the border of states? This, in a few words and stripped of all parasitic ideology, is the problem of the League of Nations....

We mean by the term *violence* not, as is often the case, the unjust use of force, but every use of force that lacks the character of an instrument of positive law; a just war, a just strike, a just insurrection, are in this sense acts of violence; arresting a delinquent, stopping a riot, sanctions applied by the international community to a state unfaithful to the international law are acts not of violence but of legal force. Now, it must be observed that justified violence—without speaking about what is not just—has aspects that are lacking in legal force.... Justified violence aims in the first place at the application of the rule of law, and secondarily at the exaltation of the group that uses it....

However, that subjective end of just violence is only a secondary end; its primary end is the triumph of the rule of law, and if that primary end can be attained more surely, more constantly and at less cost by legal force, such force must be unconditionally preferred.

The Road to Vichy
(Selections: 13–15, 42–43, 50–51, 102–3,
111, 115, 136–37, 163–65, 196–97, 201–4)

The spirit of the French Revolution survived the defeat of Napoleon by more than a century. It blew upon the entire world during the First World War. It conquered, and then died out on November 11th [1918] without anyone being aware of what was happening. THE FRENCH REVOLUTION? 1789–1918....

The worship of liberty, justice and right was in many ways an idolatrous one: it was also a homage paid to the *unknown God,* for liberty and justice are names of the true God. The collapse of revolutionary beliefs gave practical atheism an unexpected opportunity. Soon Mussolini will speak of the rotten corpse of the goddess of liberty: many people will not make any distinction between the rotten corpse and the Divine Name. The Divine Name will be scoffed at more surely than the goddess whom our fathers adored....

At the end of the movement described by Péguy [i.e., post-WWI], there will be the *realistic little* cads of whom Bernanos speaks—readers of *Le Jour,* of *Candide,* of *Gringoire,* of *Je Suis Partout,* insulters of the oppressed and lovers of force. These scoundrels were truly atheists, even though they went to mass. Whoever mocks those divine names, liberty, justice, mercy cannot remain a worshipper of the true God....

Powerful among all the intelligentsia, the *Action Française* exercised at the time we are describing an almost complete dictatorship over Catholic intellectual circles. Whoever came out as a democrat in these circles was doomed to be the object of an ironical and scornful pity; he was looked down upon as a person behind the times, a survivor of another age. In order to appear up to date and to succeed in your career you had to denounce liberal errors with an air of self-satisfied superiority, scoff at liberty, equality and fraternity, joke about progress, look skeptical when human dignity and the rights of conscience were spoken of, affirm authoritatively that every plan for international order was a bloody dream, and sneer at the League of Nations. All of this went on in an atmosphere of impudent arrogance....

We [members of *Jeune République*] were not absolute pacifists, but we fell into another error, an error not of doctrine, but of historical and political judgment. In the first postwar years, we used to stress the fact that there were two Germanies: the militaristic Germany which sought revenge, and the democratic Germany (partly Catholic and partly Socialist) which wanted peace and could not help but want peace. Franco-German rapprochement and Franco-German collaboration seemed to us possible and extremely desirable because, as we used to say, democratic Germany was in power. If we had been logical and true to our initial position, we should have demanded a policy of uncompromising resistance immediately after the defeat of democratic Germany. We should have demanded the same policy of uncompromising resistance toward Italian Fascism. We did not have enough fortitude to do this....

It is inevitable, and to a certain extent perfectly normal, that the people most interested in national defense[2] are those who are the least interested in social progress; whereas the people who are most interested in social progress are those least interested in national defense. This division of labor is not simply the result of temperamental differences: it derives from a real conflict between the ends which are pursued. Social progress, whether real or illusory, is expensive; national defense is expensive also. It is natural that each category of expenditure should have its habitual supporters. Moreover, the institutions which foster social progress, whether real or illusory, are not always the most favorable to national defense and vice versa. All goes as well as possible when the balance is maintained between the forces of social progress and those of national defense. All is jeopardized if party-spirit prevails on either side; if the advocates of social progress refuse the most necessary sacrifices for national defense and if the advocates of national defense refuse any concession to the demands of social progress. But the worst happens when one of the two groups becomes unfaithful to its vocation and abandons its role. The role thus abandoned will not be taken up by anybody else, for the other group is absolutely incapable of assuming it in addition to its own, or of substituting it for its own. If the nationalist groups fail in their duty of providing for national defense, it is certain that nobody will provide for it.

Now this is what happened in France: owing to a complicated set of circumstances, and to a lot of maneuvering and connivance, the French nationalists were led to abandon their role as guardians of the city....

The adversaries of Mussolini were the men of the newly formed People's Front, and a great number of Catholics. The Right, the conservatives and reactionaries, the nationalist party, whose members I have described as the *guardians of the city*, stood up almost unanimously against the League of Nations, against international law, and against the treatises signed by France; they supported the Italian aggression with a feverish enthusiasm....

The fate of Europe was sealed in 1935–1936.... Owing to the sabotage of the League of Nations, a new era was about to begin in which law would no longer be made by assemblies of jurists, but by the force of arms, as in Ethiopia....

It is impossible to understand anything of what took place in France in the last few years and is taking place there today, unless it is realized that during the last prewar years a whole class of people grew up, for whom the supremely important thing was neither money, nor honor, nor pleasure, nor God, but hatred. The starvation rations, the lack of coal, the heel of the Nazi boot and the enslavement of the nation itself are things they can stand, since such little inconveniences are counter-balanced by a most delightful experience: the complete crushing of the enemy. For certain Frenchmen are today in a triumphant mood. They are those for whom the enemy was not so much Nazi Germany as the People's Front....

The Spanish [Civil War] was an altogether different case. What a godsend for the enemies of France was this thirty months slaughter in which one million three hundred thousand persons lost their lives! What a godsend for the enemies of France were the killings of priests, the desecrations of churches, which stirred up, in France as elsewhere, so much anger against the Spanish Reds.... The consequence was that not only liars or fools, as in the Ethiopian war, but also really virtuous men, favored the victory of the Fascist and Nazi armies. Innumerable Frenchmen—and not only rascals and idiots, as during the Ethiopian conflict—supported in their speeches and in their hearts the armies of Mussolini and Hitler....

Was it psychologically possible for these millions of Frenchmen, in a few months after the (official) conclusion of hostilities, to turn as one man on Hitler and his allies, and fight them with unwavering resolution? It was much to hope for. . . .

What was exhausted in the France of the last twenty years was the power of generating, maintaining and exalting the collective beliefs which assure simultaneously the strength, the efficiency and the discipline of collective action. In speaking of the psychology of the French during the great economic crisis I used the expression: *Twilight of the Myths*. This expression really holds for the whole period between the victory of 1918 and the defeat of yesterday. There is no reason to believe that the French became worse, absolutely speaking, during these last twenty years. In should even be said that in many respects they became better. But, against the inroads of destructive passions and ideologies, they lacked the protection of a *myth*. The disappearance of the spirit of the French Revolution dried up for a while, in the soul of the French people, the power that creates myths. *Yet societies which have the initiative of historical movement, the societies which truly make history, are those which are animated by powerful myths.* Because they no longer had a myth, the French had lost the initiative of their own history and the sense of their national destiny. . . .

Here is a phenomenon unprecedented in history: the living and active forces of freedom are uniting citizens of all countries. . . . These combatants from all over the world have a common consciousness; the visions of freedom which haunt their minds are converging to form one great vision which will be the victorious myth of the future: *the sublime vision of the liberation of the world.* . . .

I shall not try to describe the order which shall be brought about by the victory of the forces of Freedom. The only certain thing (and after all, is it not the all-essential thing?) is that the very nature of these forces will compel them to evolve a world where the principle of equal justice for all will prevail, a world where Jews will have the same rights to justice as Aryans, Negroes the same as Whites, the poor the same as the rich; a world where religion will neither be persecuted, nor corrupted, but free; a world where the word of truth will be free to resound. This is all we have to know and we need know no more than this in order to give our lives.

The March to Liberation
(Selections: 8–10, 15–18, 23, 33–34, 84–96)

When it is a question of exploring the future, even the best minds experience the temptation to construct utopias. A utopia is an edifice erected by a thinker in the clear region of rational speculation. It often happens that such a construction is incapable of realization. But many utopias can be realized, provided one is willing to pay the price. What then is the cost of realizing a utopia? By reason of its very character as an intellectual construction, a utopia has no chance of becoming a fact unless an absolute power, capable of holding in check the rebellious forces of social spontaneity, imposes and maintains it in spite of the most powerful opposition. A utopia produces absolutism because it cannot enter history save through the grace of an absolute power....

Whether utopia calls itself State socialism, collectivism, the New Order, Corporativism, National Revolution—the words matter very little. Nor does it matter whether utopia dresses itself up in modern, ultra-modern, or revolutionary clothes, whether it wears the trappings of traditionalism, conservatism, or reaction. What does matter is that utopia, by a perfectly intelligible development, gives birth to a monster which devours all liberties, personalities, and autonomies. What matters is that a utopia, in order to impose the triumph of its rational constructions on the living forces of history, must necessarily give birth to a monster which devours history....

It is worthy of note that the mystery of the future only appears insurmountable and depressing in certain periods of history and within certain defined social groups. The paralyzing uncertainty about the future, which produces such redoubtable effects of doubt and inertia, is itself an effect of doubt and inertia: it is observable only within groups which have lost their faith; it is a disposition unknown in societies animated by a *heroic faith*....

A heroic faith achieves what a utopia does not: it realizes the indissoluble and living unity of the future and the present. It transforms the present as a function of the future because it is the representation of a future which will not realize itself by itself alone, which will not be realized, like a utopia, by means of the intervention of an all-powerful force, but which will be realized only at the cost of effort and sacrifice every moment of the day. . . .

When a group of men decide to persist in a task which appears impossible, which all prudent men declare to be impossible, which the most brilliant demonstrations have proved to be impossible; when these obstinate people have been convinced that they have no answer to make to these demonstrations, that it would be better to stop the discussion, that they will always be beaten by the advocates of capitulation if they consent to argue with them; when they know that they have nothing else left but to say "No," and an insolent *no*, to the rationalizers of their defeat; when they understand that their will to accomplish their task can and ought to show itself more potent, more effective, more in accord with reality than all the ratiocinations of "realists"; when they have accepted the alternative of descending into a mysterious abyss rather than accept the clearly demonstrable advantages of perjury, it is then that the heroic faith is born. . . .

Repeated experiences have convinced me that one can do nothing to drive out of the mind of a reader the idea that a myth is a fable, an illusion, a mirage, and that to go to one's death under the impulsion of a myth is to give one's life for a cause which really is not worth the trouble. I have therefore substituted for the expression employed by Sorel that of *heroic faith*. . . . We propose, then, to call heroic faiths those *mystiques* in which truth and justice predominate, and to reserve the name of *myths* for those in which error and evil predominate. . . .

We have learnt again to appreciate the worth of liberty. Scoffers and cynics cannot hinder us. There are certain experiences which will not be effaced: concentration camps, hostages shot to death, curfew at nine o'clock, spies everywhere, informers to be feared in every nook and cranny, an iron law hanging over suspect groups, fatality attached to the blood-strain, friend interdicted from giving aid to friend, friendship itself proscribed and legal processes suspended, and that solitude of death where anguish and despair take possession of the strongest wills. Those who have had these experiences will never, without clenching their fists, meet those nihilist poisoners of our youth who represented the spirit of liberty as an "irresistible solvent," fatal to all societies! We have realized and we shall never forget: no more liberty, no more social community; consequently, no more joy in life and no more peace in death. Those who have learnt how to find again, in that life of sacrifice, which this war of liberation demands of them, the sentiment of social communion, the power of living joyfully and of dying serenely, have already reconquered liberty. They have altered the course of history and laid the foundations of the better future....

The true function of universal suffrage is to give the most numerous and needy classes a regular means of assuring the protection of their rights.... To say that universal suffrage establishes the dictatorship of numbers at the expense of intelligence and culture, of tradition and good manners, of which the privileged section of society is allegedly the depository, is arrant nonsense: the privileged section, which does not have numbers on its side, has a hundred other means of influence. It possesses money and luxury, science and technical facilities, the art of writing and the art of speaking, and that imponderable but enormous power which results from the existence of regular relations among its members. Except for the force of numbers, it has everything that can serve to make it known and respected.... The common people, the petty property holders, tenant farmers, farm workers, the lower middle class, unskilled workers, orphans without fortune, negroes—these have none of all this: they have nothing on their side but the power of numbers. Take from them this force of numbers so detested by the privileged of fortune and of culture, suppress universal suffrage, and the great mass of the little people have no longer any constitutional means of making themselves heard and respected. They are given over to the tender mercies of a minority of masters.

The fundamental postulate of traditional paternalism is precisely that the good will and intelligence of this minority, the enlightened conscience of the governing classes, constitute the best guarantees of justice for all. This postulate must be accepted or rejected. It will be accepted if one is willing to ignore this great fact, abundantly demonstrated by history and by psychology, that justice is empty and disappears very quickly when it is not guaranteed by force. The paternalistic utopia is the most unreal of all reactionary utopias. Withdraw from the great number of men the sole force which they are able to possess, the force of numbers, and only one alternative remains: either you admit that the ruling minority will render justice freely and voluntarily, without any constraint, and out of pure love of the right; or, if you refuse to entertain an illusion so silly, you renounce the principle of equal justice for all. . . . Every government which excludes universal suffrage—or reduces it to the role of a mere counter, as in the plebiscites of the totalitarian States—is or becomes a system of exploitation more or less tempered with philanthropy—that philanthropy which the people of France execrates as soon as it suspects it to be a substitute for justice. . . .

One of the striking characteristics of the new movement in favor of liberty is that it is not accompanied by that defiance of authority which haunted the old liberalism. . . .

As we have remarked insistently, the meaning of liberty has been reawakened in us by experiences which will not be effaced. Many minds which in other epochs would have yielded to the liberal or anarchistic revolt have acquired the sense of authority in the course of experiences which will not be effaced either. Never will we forget that a society in which authority breaks down is a society in which liberty is on its deathbed. We will never forget the nightmare of the last years of the Third Republic when the exhaustion of authority permitted the growth of all the forces of disorder, and in particular of the forces of exploitation, of despotism, and of tyranny which were soon to seize power and to destroy the liberties of the nation with the collaboration of the enemy. The alternative, we know, is absolute: either authority has all the power necessary for safeguarding and promoting all the advantages of social life, and above all that liberty which is at once the principle of social life and its chief glory, or, for want of a power necessary for safeguarding and promoting them, all the advantages of social life and above all liberty will be exterminated by the nihilism of tyranny. These great and simple truths have assumed ardent vitality in the consciousness and in the actions of innumerable Frenchmen. Such is the wretchedness and the grandeur of the human condition: it is through extremes of suffering that the eternal verities reveal themselves in all their force and incorporate themselves into the movement of history. . . .

The alternative, economic liberalism or totalitarianism, is an arbitrary decision which can have nothing else for its motive than the desire of conferring on totalitarianism the prestige of inevitability. It is this infamous prestige which must above all be destroyed. Nothing hinders us from believing, indeed everything positively impels us to think, that the modern economy, *with its unprecedented capacity for producing abundance*, can become, for the great number of men, the instrument of an unprecedented and true liberty....

The task of the Republic, in the matter of property, will be to travel the way of the dictators in reverse, not in order to return to the point at which society found itself before the totalitarian Revolution, that is to say at the end of the liberal era, but rather with the design of pushing the victory of real liberty incomparably farther than liberalism ever did. The Republic will restore to property its ability to guarantee individual and collective liberty against the encroaching and totalitarian tendencies which are the permanent temptation of every State.

The Community of the Free
("Pessimism and the Philosophy of Progress,"
88, 104–13, 118–21, 128–30, and 134–36)

The optimism of classical democracy found its clearest expression in a certain philosophy of progress. The decline of this philosophy coincided with the great crisis of democracy. The men of our generation have something to say about the history of the idea of progress during the time when democracy was no longer the order of the day. Immediately after the end of the First World War, our youthful minds were assailed by a host of influences hostile to any philosophy of progress. . . .

In regard to the problem of causality and finality, the philosophy of Aristotle and St. Thomas may be described as a doctrine of nature and necessity associated with a doctrine of contingency and chance. This philosophy rejects the concept of absolute contingency; it sets at the beginning of all becoming the determinations of being, the essences, which doubtless do not exist in a necessary manner, but which are necessarily *what* they are, and which in virtue of their identity with themselves necessarily tend to exercise certain activities and to reach certain ends. But within every natural essence there exists a principle of indeterminateness, matter. Contingency is thus introduced into the world of determinate essences. On the other hand, every natural agent, to attain its ends, has need of the positive co-operation of other agents: this positive co-operation is not guaranteed by any law. In fine, a natural agent can be prevented from attaining its perfection by the action of another agent: against such vexatious encounters nature supplies it with but an insufficient protection. . . .

If one indiscriminately accepts the thesis that the event of nature is actually produced in the majority of cases and that natural finalities are translated into facts by a frequency of successful results, one arrives at an image of the world in which evil appears only rarely. This image is contradicted by innumerable familiar experiences. . . . The victory of natural finalities appears to be a comparatively exceptional outcome, accomplished amongst a multitude of defeats. Sometimes the number of defeats is so great that the entire species disappears....

These brief indications suffice to show that the very real connection between finality and frequency in no wise justifies the opinion that in each of the species below the human kingdom good occurs more frequently than evil. (St. Thomas expressly states that the human species is the only one in which evil occurs more frequently than good. But this formulation appears in contexts which narrow its meaning: it is concerned only with the inner relation of an act to its end and does not imply necessarily any conjecture as to what occurs when the action of an agent demands the co-operation of other agents or is exposed to the contrary action of other agents)[3] ....

The true cosmic picture can suggest only pessimism—but a confident pessimism, since it reveals that, through all conflicts and sacrifices, nature still finds means to convey to our minds the mystery of divine wisdom and of impassive love....

The fatalism of progress, like all fatalisms, indubitably tends to produce an arrest of life. It is particularly in the order of common moral beliefs, and of the institutions which are related to those beliefs, that the fatalism of progress seems actually to have favored an attitude of passivity before evil. As an example, let us cite the evolution of the ideas, habits, and laws relative to marriage in the western world as a whole, from the end of the eighteenth century to our own time. This evolution, on the whole a great process of decadence, has been astonishingly general, profound, and tenacious. It is easy to understand what its promoters sought from this evolution. But it has been tolerated, accepted resignedly and unresistingly, by many who in no way approved of the growing lack of discipline in morals. This was because people saw in it an inevitable development, connected with other aspects of modern society, inseparable from what it had been agreed to call progress, and consequently mysteriously oriented towards a better state of things....

After having witnessed, with an extraordinary foisoning of evidence, to what lengths ignorance, naïveté, incompetence, stupidity, the cruel egotism and the felony of our betters can go, our contemporaries will be little disposed to become excited over the contrast—dear to all aristocracies—between the wisdom of the governing classes and the folly of the people. The groups whose function it is to preserve the ideas of authority and hierarchy will do well to resign themselves to this fact and to give up compromising those ideas by a selective optimism which is condemned by facts too serious, too numerous, and too obvious to be forgotten. The catastrophes of our epoch have taught us to extend our pessimism to all periods of history and to all sections of society....

The pessimism which we recommend is in no sense a metaphysical theory: it is a point of view upon moral reality and upon history, not a theory of being. In metaphysics, the fundamental truths are optimistic propositions; the pessimistic propositions express only subordinate truths, conditioned truths, circumscribed truths. Every being is good, existence is good, the Supreme Being is Supreme Goodness....

All that is essentially implied by moral pessimism is a profound feeling of the wretchedness of our condition; a perfectly sincere disposition to see evil wherever it shows itself, together with its frequency and extent; will and resolution to knock down the protective screens which our fear and our laziness manufacture to spare us the sight of evil; a thorough sense of the immense difficulties which the accomplishment of good presents. One could say that pessimism is nothing but *depth of moral intelligence*. In the life of study, what distinguishes really intelligent people from those who have only a brilliant appearance of intelligence is an ability to understand that the most trifling questions, once examined, will always turn out to be incomparably more difficult than one could have foreseen, to understand that any progress in the exploration of a question necessarily has the effect of making new difficulties apparent, difficulties greater than those already encountered. Only shallow minds believe that there are such things as easy questions in the sciences, in philosophy and history. Profound minds know that there are no easy questions....

It is the disillusioned optimist who has good reason for losing sight of the possibility of progress and the exigency for progress which are written in our nature: for him the practical solution is to let things go. But to the true pessimist this is an inadmissible solution: an exact knowledge of evil reveals the power of good and arouses in our souls an uncompromising will to act and to struggle for the better world whose realization our nature, from the depths of its wretchedness, demands....

We have learned to make a distinction between individual guilt and collective guilt. We have come to understand that a soldier taken prisoner by a just belligerent becomes—immediately, and by the very fact that he ceases to be engaged in an unjust collective action—a person enjoying the same presumption of innocence as any one of our fellow citizens. . . .

We have come to understand that, given certain technical improvements in combination with certain economic and social improvements, a workman who earns ten or twelve dollars a day can work with a zeal incomparably greater than that which was brought to their tasks by the destitute of old. Is not the outlawing of destitution by the consciences of just men an incontestable step forward, and a thousand times more important than the obvious examples of progress in techniques? . . .

Just men's consciences are sensitive to crimes which not long ago left them indifferent. The history of the reactions provoked throughout the world by the Italian campaign in Ethiopia is particularly significant in this regard. There were some who, without contesting the injustice of the Italian enterprise, asked us if it was really opportune, in connection with this expedition, to raise a question of conscience which had not been raised in connection with other colonial conquests apparently no less unjust. Thus, because the moral conscience of just men had often shown itself indifferent to the crimes of the past, it ought to have remained indifferent to the crimes of the present. The poor fellows who reasoned in this fashion ignored both the need of progress which is written in our nature and the fact of the progress recently accomplished by the moral conscience of just men in discerning certain concrete goods and certain concrete evils. . . .

Let us take an example drawn from contemporary history in the field of labor relations. In our time, what would be the reaction of an industrialist if someone should propose to him that he make children work twelve hours a day in unhealthy workshops? We assume that the industrialist in question is an ordinary man, neither more nor less enlightened than the people around him—one who insists that honesty is still the best policy, a decent man, incapable of heroism. The proposal will arouse him to sincere indignation: he will swear that he would rather turn beggar than become a torturer of children.

Let us now reflect upon the conditions under which children worked in the factories of only a century ago.... Did employers in those days have the souls of criminals? We have every reason to believe that many of them were very worthy men.... As for the lives, as for the souls, of the children whom their machines consumed at such a terrible rate—on that subject their consciences said nothing whatsoever; their consciences were reduced to silence by a system of protective images called "the inescapable laws of economic life," "painful necessities," "the natural order," "the necessary organization of society," and so forth....

In opposition to such an encouraging example, we could cite many facts which show that the moral conscience of the common man has retrograded badly in several departments, during the last few generations. The unprecedented scope of the crimes perpetrated by the tyrannies of our time absolutely excludes the optimistic theory which would exonerate the bulk of mankind by referring all the evil to bands of criminals. The bands of criminals who actually directed the movement could not have given it the scope we know that it attained, without the active complicity, at least the tacit consent, the indifference, of countless millions of men. Perfectly capable of sharing in the progress of the moral conscience, these millions of representatives of ordinary humanity demonstrated that the moral conscience of the common man lends itself to every kind of perversion when it no longer finds, in the daily framework of social relations, a discipline which ensures the protection and promotion of moral truths by conferring upon them the effectual reality of familiar impulses. Optimistic and individualistic liberalism has always postulated that moral truth spreads and maintains itself *easily*, by the very force of truth, without the necessity for intervention on the part of the conscious centers of society. This postulate has been refuted by the most striking fact in the history of morals in our time: confusion of conscience in the presence of colossal crimes, amongst ordinary people, decent people, worthy people.

Practical Knowledge
("Christian Humanism: A Way to World Order,"
137–44, 149–55)

We no longer believe that men trained in the sciences, techniques, and industrial crafts are thereby disinclined to lust for domination over their fellow men. In our worried inquiries into culture and education we listen with some eagerness to the suggestion that after all the so-called humane studies may have a unique way of tending to make men more human.... Let it be said that humanism can be understood both as an attitude and as a culture.... As an attitude it is characterized by respect for *all* men and confidence in the ability of mankind to accomplish good things in *this* world. It is not necessarily optimistic, but it is necessarily confident. And if a friend of man expects great things of his fellow men, but only in the other world, he cannot be described as a humanist....

The age of the Renaissance, which produced unprecedentedly important developments in humanistic culture, also produced the modern interpretation of nature. In relation to the problems of humanism, the most significant feature of the physical system founded by Galileo and Descartes is that it ignores finality. From now on man will be alone among the things of this world. He is a creature with tendencies, desires, purposes, and meaningful activities. Physical things will no longer be companions to him. The surrounding world is no longer a universe of natures: it is made of only one entity—call it extension or space—and this entity is not nature....

The exclusion of finalistic notions results from the nature of mathematical abstraction. Objects treated mathematically have lost the relation to existence that desirability implies. As Aristotle says, there is no goodness in mathematical entities. Mathematical sciences are good, but mathematical objects are not. You may fall in love with mathematics—many people do—but you cannot fall in love with the square root of minus one.

It is by no means obvious that the mathematical interpretation of nature, with its successes, rules out any other scientific approach to the physical world. If a philosophy of nature of the Aristotelian type, a philosophical physics, had maintained its position at the time of the Renaissance and had demonstrated its ability to achieve progress under the new circumstances, the cultural meaning of natural science might have been widely different from what it has come to be. In fact, the philosophy of nature has been displaced by modern physics. As a result of bewildering success in the mathematical interpretation of nature, the universe of culture was split.... As long as belief in natural law and in the metaphysical worth of man was strong, the vision of human affairs remained finalistic. But the threat of a violent reduction to unity appears as soon as the minds yield to the fascination of a social science which, in order to deal with mankind as successfully as physics does with nature, has to take on the scientific features and to dismiss "unscientific prejudices," the most flagrant of which is explanation by final causes. In contemporary atheism, the non-finalistic pattern is applied, regardless of the cost, to the totality of human affairs. Not only physical nature, but also mankind and its history have become a tale told by an idiot, signifying nothing. An all-embracing picture of absurdity expresses the last word of a mechanistic philosophy which has grown into a violent negation of all that humanism values. In some respects existentialism is an effort to achieve decency in a world whose meaninglessness extends to human actions....

Christian beliefs concerning original sin do not exclude the confident vision of man that humanism implies, but they contain a warning against the myths of naturalistic optimism. The Christian knows how easily the confidence of the humanist deteriorates into a rejection of the supernatural order. Correspondingly the humanist is permanently tempted to see in Christian mysteries a threat to his exalted notion of man. The solution lies in a humanistic theory that places at the center of its universe the union of divine and human natures in Christ. But we cannot expect a thing as precious as the *humanism of the Incarnation* (Maritain) to enjoy a peaceful existence and development, free from ruptures of equilibrium....

The condition of the human understanding is such that our knowledge of natural truth, with regard to subjects that concern our destiny in the most direct fashion, is badly deficient and precarious whenever the power of natural reason is not strengthened by the obscure certainties of faith. Natural reason can obtain many truths concerning God, but this rational ability is so subject to accident that the metaphysics of God seems bound to quick decadence as soon as faith is no longer there to direct the work of the reason.... The theory of the natural law is by definition something entirely natural and entirely rational. If our reason were in a perfect state of health, we should be able not only to perceive as absolutely obvious the axioms of the natural law but also able to establish with full clarity any particular proposition deductively connected with those axioms. But experience reveals a discrepancy between a *de jure* possibility and what is possible *de facto*. The circumstances of our time make it clear that the knowledge of the natural law is firmest and most lucid when it is associated with faith in God as cause of the supernatural order. Far from being tempted to use natural law as an argument against the divine government of mankind, we are aware that the theory of natural law, which is the foundation of all consistent humanism, finds its best guarantee within Christian faith....

It is easy to see by what features a humanistic education is able to counteract the disquieting tendencies brought about by the familiar acquaintance with scientific objects and technical creations. The humanistic approach to man is holistic. Think, for example, of the knowledge of man achieved through the study of the Greek tragedies, the plays of Shakespeare, the Spanish theater, and the French dramatists of the seventeenth century.... The spiritual link of totality and personality is always present. It is grasped intuitively. Even though the course of events be dominated by tragic inevitability, human freedom, whether defeated or not, stands at the center of the work....

Inasmuch as humanism is expected to remedy a situation brought about by science and technique, it is inevitable that the humanistic and technical cultures be set in opposition to one another.... The least that can be said of such an opposition is that it involves a waste of time, for there is not the slightest chance that mankind will give up its technological conquests.... An unhistorical humanism, a humanism with no understanding for what is going on in this world, is necessarily ungenuine, for humanism is not an abstract science of human nature: it is a sympathetic approach to what history has made of man....

The fruitful task is to establish, between the technical and humanistic cultures, a relation of instrument to principal cause, the kind of relation exemplified by the brush and the painter. . . .

Man is often dragged, by the sheer heaviness of his techniques, where he does not want to go. Can any general principle direct our effort to resolve, in every particular case, the conflict between the weight of our instruments and the law of instrumentality? The spirit of poverty supplies the answer. In the relation of the human to the technical, we keep our instruments under control insofar as we remain free from the attachment to things inferior to man. But it is not only in our relation to the physical world that we have to overcome the weight of things instrumental. Within all the system of our intellectual culture, what should be obedient often is heavy, and the freedom of the higher energies never can be taken for granted; again it is the spirit of poverty, the spirit of the freedom from attachment to things inferior, that preserves the order of human salvation and removes the danger of man's being crushed by the weight of his ideas, his systems, his experiences, his erudition, his constructs, his methods, and his postulations. The quest for freedom from whatever is heavy, within the mind as well as in man's dealing with nature and the works of his own art, thus leads us to consider the relation of humanism to what is above it. A program of humanistic studies should not exclude the masterpieces of mystical literature. Clearly, mysticism, which is totally concerned with eternal life, does not in any sense pertain to such an essentially human and historical thing as humanistic culture. But an inspiration derived from mystical life, and ultimately from the sovereign simplicity of mystical contemplation, is precisely what humanism needs in order to be vitally Christian and to ensure, in all domains and on all levels, the freedom of man from the weight of man's creations.

Notes

1. [Editor's Note: I selected the texts and this selection was subsequently approved by the contributor.]

2. [Editor's Note: Here and elsewhere, I have changed his spelling "defence" to the more usual "defense."]

3. [Editor's Note: The matter in parenthesis here was placed in a note in Simon's text.]

SELECT BIBLIOGRAPHY

Books of Yves R. Simon used in the Reader

These are given according to the date of their original publication. The work is given first according to the English publication used in this volume. Any previous edition of it, whether in English or French, is then given. To be clear: in his lifetime, Simon's books published in English consisted *only* of his Aquinas Lecture of 1940 (*Nature and Functions of Authority*), three brief works on contemporary political events (*The Road to Vichy* [1942], *The March to Liberation* [1942], *The Community of the Free* [1947]), and then his "magnum opus" of 1951, *Philosophy of Democratic Government*, and his later collaborative translation of John of St. Thomas's material logic (1955).

An Introduction to Metaphysics of Knowledge. Edited and translated by Vukan Kuic and Richard J. Thompson. New York: Fordham University Press, 1990.

Introduction à l'ontologie de connaître. Paris: Desclée de Brouwer, 1934. Reprint, Dubuque, IA: William C. Brown, 1965.

A Critique of Moral Knowledge. Translated and with an introduction by Ralph McInerny. New York: Fordham University Press, 2002.

Critique de la connaissance morale. Paris: Desclée de Brouwer, 1934.

The Ethiopian Campaign and French Political Thought. Edited by Anthony O. Simon. Translated by Robert Royal. Foreword by A. James McAdams. Notre Dame, IN: University of Notre Dame Press, 2009.

La campagne d'Éthiopie et la pensée politique française. Lille: Societé d'Impressions Littéraires, Industrielles, et Commerciales, 1936; 2nd ed., Paris: Desclée de Brouwer, 1937.

Nature and Functions of Authority [The 1940 Aquinas Lecture]. Milwaukee: Marquette University Press, 1940. Reprint, 1948.

The Road to Vichy, 1918–1938. Rev. English ed. Translated by James A. Corbett and Georges J. McMorrow. New introduction by John Hellman. Lanham, MD: University Press of America, 1988. Reprint, 1990. 1st English ed., New York: Sheed and Ward, 1942. (The English editions include a "Table of Events" not given in the French edition.)

La grande crise de la République Française: Observations sur la vie politique des français de 1918 à 1938. Montreal: Éditions de l'Arbre, 1941.

The March to Liberation. Translated by Victor M. Hamm. Milwaukee: Tower Press, 1942.

La marche à la délivrance. New York: Éditions de la Maison Française. 1942.

Foresight and Knowledge. Rev. English ed. Edited by Ralph Nelson and Anthony O. Simon. New York: Fordham University Press, 1995. (The English edition contains a bibliography and index not in the French edition.)

Prévoir et savoir: Études sur l'idée de nécessité dans la pensée scientifique et en philosophie. Montreal: Éditions de l'Arbre, 1944.

The Community of the Free. Rev. English ed. Translated by William R. Trask. Lanham, MD: University Press of America, 1984. (The revised English edition contains an index not in the original English edition.) 1st English ed., New York: Henry Holt and Company, 1947. (The English edition includes a final chapter 4 not included in the French original.)

Par delà de l'experience du désespoir. Montreal: Lucien Parizeau, 1945.

Philosophy of Democratic Government [The Charles R. Walgreen Foundation Lectures]. Rev. ed. Foreword by Jerome G. Kerwin. Notre Dame, IN: University of Notre Dame Press, 1993. (A detailed index and Simon's corrections to the text have been added.) 1st English ed., Chicago: University of Chicago Press, 1951. Reprint, 1977.

Philosophie du gouvernement démocratique. Translated by Clément Hubert. Preface by Florian Michel. Paris/Perpignan: Desclée de Brouwer/Artège, 2015. (The first edition has also been translated into Japanese, Portuguese, German, Korean, Italian, and Polish.)

Freedom of Choice. Rev. English ed. Edited, with preface, by Peter Wolff. Foreword by Mortimer J. Adler. New York: Fordham University Press, 1969. (Chapters 8, 9, and 10 of the original French Edition were not included.)

Traité du libre arbitre. Liège: Science et Lettres, 1951; second publication, Paris: Librairie Philosophique Jules Vrin, 1952. Rev. ed., Avant-propos by Patrick de Laubier. Preface by Pierre-Marie Emonet. Fribourg: Éditions Universitaire, 1989.

The Material Logic of John of St. Thomas: Basic Treatises. Edited and translated by Yves R. Simon, John J. Glanville, and G. Donald Hollenhurst. Preface by Jacques Maritain. Foreword by Yves R. Simon. Chicago: University of Chicago Press, 1955. Reprint, 1965.

A General Theory of Authority. Rev. ed. New Introduction by Vukan Kuic. Notre Dame, IN: University of Notre Dame Press, 1980, 1991 (paperback edition); 1st English ed., Introduction by A. Robert Caponigri. Notre Dame, IN: University of Notre Dame Press, 1962. Reprint, Westport, CT: Greenwood Press, 1973. (This is the first of nine new books, and English translations of six French books, to appear posthumously. Anthony O. Simon was instrumental in their publication. This well measures the debt we all owe to him.)

The Tradition of Natural Law: A Philosopher's Reflections. Rev. ed. Edited, with preface, by Vukan Kuic. Foreword by John H. Hallowell. New Introduction by Russell Hittinger. New York: Fordham University Press, 1992; 1st ed., New York: Fordham University Press, 1965, 1967.

Freedom and Community. Edited, with preface, by Charles P. O'Donnell. New York: Fordham University Press, 1968.

The Great Dialogue of Nature and Space. Edited, with preface, by Gerard J. Dalcourt. Albany, NY: Magi Press, 1970, 1973 (hardback edition).

Work, Society, and Culture. Edited, with preface, by Vukan Kuic. Appendix by Anthony O. Simon: "A Bibliography 1923–1970." New York: Fordham University Press, 1971, 1987 (paperback edition, without the bibliography). This work has recently been translated into Chinese (2008). This book is a substantial revision and expansion of material in (and thus a separate work from) a book originally published in French as *Trois leçons sur le travail.* Paris: Pierre Tequi, 1938.

Jacques Maritain: Homage in Words and Pictures. Coauthored with John Howard Griffin. Edited and with a foreword by Anthony O. Simon. Albany, NY: Magi Press, 1974.

The Definition of Moral Virtue. Edited, with preface, by Vukan Kuic. Bio-Bibliography by Marie-Vincent Leroy. New York: Fordham University Press, 1986. Reprint, 1989.

Enquête sur la vertu morale. Paris: Éditions Pierre Téqui, 2021.

Practical Knowledge. Edited, with a note, by Robert J. Mulvaney. New York: Fordham University Press, 1991.

Philosopher at Work. Edited, with a note, by Anthony O. Simon. Lanham, MD: Rowman and Littlefield, 1999. This work contains eight essays of Simon previously published:

"Maritain's Philosophy of the Sciences." In *The Maritain Volume of the Thomist*, 85–102. New York: Sheed and Ward, 1943; first published in *Thomist* 5 (1943): 85–102.

"The Concept of Work." In *The Works of the Mind*, edited by Robert B. Heywood; preface by John U. Nef, 3–17. Chicago: University of Chicago Press, 1947; rev., paperback ed., with a new preface by John U. Nef, 1966.

"The Rationality of the Christian Faith." *Thought: A Review of Culture and Idea* 31, no. 123 (1956–1957): 495–508.

"The Philosopher's Calling." *Proceedings of the American Catholic Philosophical Association* ("Role of the Christian Philosopher"), 32 (1958): 29–34 (the 1958 Cardinal Spellman-Aquinas Medalist Address).

"On Order in Analogical Sets." *New Scholasticism* 34, no. 1 (1960): 1–42.

"An Essay on Sensation." In *Philosophy of Knowledge*, edited by Roland Houde and Joseph Mullally, 55–95. Philadelphia: J. P. Lippincott, 1960.

"To Be and to Know." *Chicago Review* 14, no. 4 (1961): 83–100. This was the last of Simon's articles (indeed, the last of his works) that was published during his lifetime.

"Nature and the Process of Mathematical Abstraction," edited by Edward B. Simmons. *Thomist* 29, no. 2 (1965): 117–39.

Select Articles of Yves R. Simon Not Found in Works Used in the *Reader*

"Les idées artistiques et littéraires de Proudhon." *La Democratie*, n.s., 1, no. 6 (1924): 553–62.

"Le caractère religieux de premier socialism français." *Les Cahiers Catholiques*, "Part I: Saint-Simon et les Saint-Simoniens," no. 104 (10 Mars 1924): 2785–92; "Part II: Buchez et Proudhon," no. 106 (10 Avril 1924): 2870–74.

"Politique d'Alain." *La Vie Intellectuelle*, pt. 1, 1, no. 3 (1928): 417–30; pt. 2, 2, no. 4 (1929): 116–35. English, "The Politics of Alain" (translated by John M. Dunaway). *Interpretation* 13, no. 2 (1985): 215–31.

"Philosophia perennis." *La Vie Intellectuelle* 5, no. 1 (1929): 52–79.

"L'object de l'intelligence" (coauthor: Jacques de Monléon). *Revue de Philosophie* 36, no. 3 (1929): 314–35.

"La philosophie bergsonienne—Étude critique." *Revue de Philosophie*, n.s., 2, no. 3 (1931): 281–90.

"Positions aristotéliciennes concernant le problème de l'activité du sens." *Revue de Philosophie*, n.s., 4, no. 3 (1933): 229–58.

"Philosophie chrétienne—Notes compleméntaires." *Etudes Carmélitaines*, Tome XIX, Vol. 1 (Avril 1934): 107–19.

"Le problème de la transcendance et le défi de Proudhon." *Nova et Vetera*, IXème année, no. 3 (Juillet-Septembre 1934): 225–38. English, "The Problem of Transcendence and Proudhon's Challenge" (translated by Charles P. O'Donnell and Vukan Kuic). *Thought: A Review of Culture and Idea* 54, no. 2 (1979): 176–85.

"Philosophy of Science—Étude critique." *Revue de Philosophie*, n.s., 6, no. 1 (1935): 53–64.

"Note sure le féderalisme proudhonnien." *Esprit*, 5ème Année, no. 53 (1 Avril 1937): 53–65. English, "A Note on Proudhon's Federalism" (translated by Vukan Kuic), *Publius* 3, no. 1 (1973): 19–30. Also in *Federalism as Grand Design*, edited by Daniel J. Elazar, 223–34. Lanham, MD: University Press of America, 1989.

"Note sure la prévision scientifique." *Revue de Philosophie*, n.s., 7, no. 6 (1937): 508–13.

"La philosophie dans la foi: Extrait des mémoires d'un philosophe français." *La Nouvelle Revue*, Part 1: Vol. 1, no. 5 (Février 1942): 257–65; Part 2: Vol. 1, no. 6 (Mars 1942): 336–42. English, "Philosophy and the Faith: Extracts from the Memoires of a French Philosopher—Part 1 (translated and edited by Anthony O. Simon). *Notes et Documents*, n.s. XIIIème Année, no. 23 (Septembre-Décembre 1988): 76–82; Part 2 (translated by Vukan Kuic), *Notes et Documents*, Vème Année, no. 14 (Janvier-Mars 1979): 5–8. This last was in the Simon/Maritain issue edited by Anthony O. Simon.

"Thomism and Democracy." In *Science, Philosophy, and Religion*. Second Symposium, Vol. 2, edited by Louis Finkelstein and Lyman Bryson, 258–72. New York: Conference on Science, Philosophy, and Religion in Their Relations to the Democratic Way of Life, 1942.

"Beyond the Crisis of Liberalism." In *Essays in Thomism*, edited by Robert E. Brennan, 263–86. New York: Sheed and Ward, 1942.

"France and the United Nations." *Review of Politics* 5, no. 1 (1943): 26–37.

"Yves R. Simon." In *The Book of Catholic Authors*, edited by Walter Romig, 262–70. Detroit: Walter Romig Company, 1945. This is an autobiographical essay.

"Economic Organization in a Democracy." *Proceeding of the American Catholic Philosophical Association* ("The Philosophy of Democracy"), 20 (1945): 83–108.

"The Philosophical Study of Sensation" (coauthor: J. L. Péghaire). *Modern Schoolman* 23, no. 3 (1946): 111–19.

"Aristotelian Demonstration and Postulational Method" (coauthor: Karl Menger). *The Modern Schoolman* 25, no. 3 (1948): 183–92.

"On the Foreseeability of Free Acts." *New Scholasticism* 22, no. 4 (1948): 357–70.

"Three Lectures by Yves. R. Simon" ("Catholic Renascence: Background and Problems," "Catholic Renascence and Theology," and "Catholic Renascence and Temporal Problems"). *Renascence* 1, no. 1 (1948): 35–39 (as edited by *Renascence*'s editor, John Pick).

"Introduction." In *La civilization americaine*, edited and translated by Yves R. Simon, 7–20. Paris: Desclée de Brouwer, 1950.

"The Doctrinal Issue between the Church and Democracy." In *The Catholic Church in World Affairs*, edited by Waldemar Gurian and Matthew A. Fitzsimons, 87–114. Notre Dame, IN: University of Notre Dame Press, 1954. With a new introduction by Walter Nicgorski, in *Logos* 14, no. 1 (2011): 1–33.

"Common Good and Common Action." *Review of Politics* 22, no. 2 (1960): 202–44. This is the last of the articles in this section published during Simon's lifetime.

"La loi et la liberté." *Nova et Vetera*, XLIème Année, no. 1 (Janvier-Mars 1969): 42–53. English, "Law and Liberty" (translated by Peter Wolff). *Review of Politics* 52, no. 1 (1990): 107–18. This is the final chapter 10 in *Traité du libre arbitre* untranslated in *Freedom of Choice*.

"An Essay on the Classification of Action and the Understanding of Act." *Revue de l'Université d'Ottawa* 41, no. 4 (1971): 518–41. This essay was edited by John Deely, who also wrote the "Introductory Note" to it (518–19).

"A Comment on Censorship." *International Philosophical Quarterly* 17, no. 1 (1977): 33–42.

"Mes premiers souvenirs de Jacques Maritain." *New Scholasticism* 56, no. 2 (1982): 200–206. English, "My First Memories of Jacques Maritain" (translated and edited by Anthony O. Simon). *Notes et Documents*, n.s., nos. 2–3 (Avril-Septembre 1983): 106–10.

"Philosophy, The Humanities, and Education. *New Scholasticism* 62, no. 4 (1988): 467–71.

"Personality and Opinion" (edited by Raymond Dennehy and Anthony O. Simon). *Logos* 12, no. 1 (2009): 80–93.

Select Books and Articles on Yves R. Simon

Anastaplo, Georges. "Democracy and Philosophy: On Yves R. Simon and Mortimer J. Adler." In Torre, ed., *Freedom in the Modern World*, 79–85. See later entries for full bibliographical information on this book on Hancock's *Freedom, Virtue and the Common*, and on *Acquaintance with the Absolute*, edited by Anthony O. Simon.

Berns, Laurence. "Simon on Freedom: À propos of *Freedom of Choice*." *Revue de l'Université d'Ottawa* 42, no. 1 (1972): 35–45.

Borde, Hubert. "A l'école de la démocratie américaine: Jacques Maritain et Yves Simon." *Commentaire* 3, no. 163 (2018): 627–34.

Buckley, Joseph. "Logic and Mathematical Abstraction in the Philosophy of Yves R. Simon." *American Catholic Philosophical Quarterly* 49, no. 4 (1995): 573–83.

Burrell, David B. "A Note on Analogy." *New Scholasticism* 36, no. 2 (1962): 225–32.

Cahalan, John C. "Analogy and the Disrepute of Metaphysics." *Thomist* 34, no. 3 (1970): 387–422.

Caplin, Diane M. "The Good Citizen and the Demands of Democracy: An Application of the Political Philosophy of Yves. R. Simon." In Hancock and Simon, eds., *Freedom, Virtue, and the Common Good*, 293–306.

Chammings, Louis. "Yves Simon, philosophe des sciences et de la nature." *Cahiers Jacques Maritain*, no. 47 (December 2003): 23–39.

Cochrane, Clarke E. "Authority and Freedom: The Democratic Philosophy of Yves R. Simon." *Interpretation* 6, no. 2 (1977): 107–23.

———. "Authority and Community: The Contribution of Carl Friedrich, Yves R. Simon, and Michael Polanyi." *American Political Science Review* 71, no. 2 (1977): 546–58.

Cochrane, Clarke E., and Thomas R. Rourke, "The Common Good and Economic Justice: Reflections on the Thought of Yves R. Simon." *Review of Politics* 54, no. 2 (1992): 231–52.

———. "Beyond Ideology in Christian Economic Thought." In Hancock and Simon, eds., *Freedom, Virtue, and the Common Good*, 307–31.

Cuddeback, John A. "Yves R. Simon on Willing the Common Good." In *Maritain and America*, edited by Christopher M. Cullen, SJ, and Joseph Allan Clair, 65–81. Washington, DC: American Maritain Association, 2009.

De Haan, Daniel D. "Simon and Maritain on the Vocation of *Species in Medio*." In *Redeeming Philosophy: From Metaphysics to Aesthetics*, edited by John J. Conley, SJ, 54–82. Washington, DC: American Maritain Association, 2014.

de Laubier, Patrick. "Yves Simon et Leo Strauss: La loi naturelle comme enjeu de la philosophie politique." *Cahiers Jacques Maritain*, no. 47 (December 2003): 57–68.

Dennehy, Raymond L. "Yves R. Simon's Metaphysics of Action." In Anthony O. Simon, ed., *Acquaintance with the Absolute*, 19–56.

Doering, Bernard. "The Philosophy of Work and the Future of Civilization: Maritain, Weil, and Simon." In *From Twilight to Dawn*, edited by Peter A. Redpath, 49–71. Notre Dame, IN: American Maritain Association, 1988.

Fourcade, Michel. "Yves Simon entre S. Thomas et Proudhon." *Cahiers Jacques Maritain*, no. 47 (December 2003): 4–22.

Gallagher, Donald A. "Recollections of Three Thinkers, Adler, Simon, Maritain." In Torre, ed., *Freedom in the Modern World*, 13–30.

Green, Catherine. "Freedom and Determination: An Examination of Yves R. Simon's Ontology of Freedom." In Torre, ed., *Freedom in the Modern World*, 89–99.

Gueguen, John. "Parallels on Work, Theory, and Practice in Yves R. Simon and John Paul II." In Torre, ed., *Freedom in the Modern World*, 153–61.

Hancock, Curtis L., and Anthony O. Simon, eds. *Freedom, Virtue, and the Common Good*. Notre Dame, IN: American Maritain Association, 1995. This work contains six essays featuring Simon that are all detailed in this bibliography.

Hellman, John. "Introduction." In *The Road to Vichy, 1918–38*, rev. ed., translated by James A. Corbett and Georges J. McMorrow. Lanham, MD: University Press of America, 1988. Reprint, 1990. Retitled as "The Road to Vichy: Yves R. Simon's Lonely Fight against Fascism." *Crisis* 6, no. 5 (1988): 30–37; and *Notes et Documents*, n.s., nos. 24–25 (Janvier-Août 1989): 78–91.

———. "World War II and the Anti-Democratic Impulse in Catholicism." In *From Twilight to Dawn*, edited by Peter A. Redpath, 95–116. Notre Dame, IN: American Maritain Association, 1988.

———. "Maritain, Simon, and Vichy's Elite Schools." In Torre, ed., *Freedom in the Modern World*, 165–80.

———. "The Anti-Democratic Impulse in Catholicism: Jacques Maritain, Yves R. Simon, and Charles de Gaulle During World War II." *Journal of Church and State* 33, no. 3 (1991): 453–71.

Hittinger, John. "Approaches to Democratic Equality: Maritain, Simon, Kolnai." In Torre, ed., *Freedom in the Modern World*, 237–52.

———. "Jacques Maritain and Yves R. Simon's Use of Thomas Aquinas in Their Defense of Liberal Democracy." In *Thomas Aquinas and His Legacy*, edited by David Gallagher, 149–72. Washington, DC: Catholic University of America Press, 1994.

———. "The Achievement of Yves R. Simon." *Crisis* 14, no. 1 (1996): 36–40.

Hittinger, Russell. "Yves R. Simon on Law, Nature, and Practical Reason." In Anthony O. Simon, ed., *Acquaintance with the Absolute*, 101–27.

Hubert, Bernard. "Les années parisiennes d'Yves Simon et ses premiers pas avec Jacques Maritain (1920–1929)." *Cahiers Jacques Maritain* 79 (December 2019): 51–73.

Killoran, John. "A Moral Realist Perspective on Yves R. Simon's Interpretation of *Habitus*." In Hancock and Simon, eds., *Freedom, Virtue, and the Common Good*, 88–103.

Knasas, John F. X. "Yves R. Simon and the Neo-Thomist Tradition in Epistemology." In Anthony O. Simon, ed., *Acquaintance with the Absolute*, 83–100.

Koyzis, David T. "Yves R. Simon's Contribution to Structural Political Philosophy." In Torre, ed., *Freedom in the Modern World*, 131–39.

Kuic, Vukan. "The Contribution of Yves R. Simon to Political Science." *Political Science Reviewer* 4 (Fall 1974): 55–104.

———. "Jacques Maritain and Yves R. Simon on Truth, Liberty and the Role of the Philosopher in Society." *Notes et Documents*, Vème Année, no. 14 (Janvier-Mars 1979): 9–17.

———. "Yves R. Simon on Liberty and Authority." In Anthony O. Simon, ed., *Acquaintance with the Absolute*, 128–46.

———. *Yves R Simon: Real Democracy*. Lanham, MD: Rowman and Littlefield, 1999.

Lacombe, Olivier. "Yves R. Simon." *Revue de l'Université d'Ottawa* 42, no. 1 (1972): 5–7.

Leroy, Marie-Vincent. "Yves R. Simon, 1903–1961." *Revue Thomiste* 89, no. 4 (1979): 691–93.

———. "Yves R. Simon, 1903–1961: A Bio-Bibliography." *New Scholasticism* 54, no. 4 (1980): 512–18.

Long, Steven A. "Yves R. Simon's Approach to Natural Law." *Thomist* 59, no. 1 (1995): 125–35.

MacIntyre, Alasdair. "Review of *An Introduction to the Metaphysics of Knowledge* by Yves René Simon." *American Catholic Philosophical Quarterly* 65 (1991): 112–14.

Mahoney, Marianne. "Prudence as the Cornerstone of the Contemporary Thomistic Philosophy of Freedom." In Torre, ed., *Freedom in the Modern World*, 117–29.

Maritain, Jacques. "Yves R. Simon: Mon frère d'armes" (translated by Paule Simon). *Nova et Vetera*, 48ème Année, no. 1 (Janvier-Mars 1973): 43–45. English, "Yves R. Simon: Brother-in-Arms." *Notes et Documents*, Vème Année, no. 14 (Janvier-Mars 1979): 3–4.

McInerny, Ralph. "On Yves R. Simon as a Moral Philosopher." In Hancock and Simon, eds., *Freedom, Virtue, and the Common Good*, 76–87.

Michel, Florian. "Yves Simon à la bataille de Chicago (1948–1961)." *Cahiers Jacques Maritain*, no. 47 (December 2003): 40–56.

———. *Jacques Maritain, Yves Simon Correspondance*. Tome 1, *Les années françaises (1927–1940)*. Edited by Florian Michel, René Mougel, and Anthony O. Simon. Introduction by Philippe Chenaux. Tours: Éditions CLD, 2008.

———. *Jacques Maritain, Yves Simon Correspondance*. Tome 2, *Les années américaines (1941–1961)*. Edited by Florian Michel, René Mougel, and Anthony O. Simon. Introduction by Michel Fourcade. Paris: Éditions CLD, 2012.

———. *La Pensée Catholique en Amerique du Nord: Reseaux intellectuels et echanges culturel entre l'Europe, le Canada, et les Etats Unis (1920–1960)*. Paris: Desclée de Brouwer, 2010.

———. "L'américanisation d'un intellectual français: Le cas de Yves Simon (1903–1961)." *Transatlantica* (Online), 1 (2014). https://journals.openedition.org/transatlantica/6842.

Michelet, Edmond. "Mon ami Yves R. Simon." *Nova et Vetera*, XLIIIème Année, no. 3 (Juillet-Septembre 1968): 208–13. Translated into English by Paule Simon in *Listening Magazine* 5, nos. 2–3 (1970): 145–52.

Mougel, René. "Correspondances Simon-Maritain." *Cahiers Jacques Maritain* 47 (2003): Yves-René Simon (1903–1961): 70–129.

Mulvaney, Robert J. "Freedom and Practical Rationality in the Thought of Yves R. Simon." In Torre, ed., *Freedom in the Modern World*, 109–16.

———. "Practical Wisdom in the Thought of Yves R. Simon." In Anthony O. Simon, ed., *Acquaintance with the Absolute*, 147–81.

Murphy, J. Stanley, "Yves R. Simon and the Free World: A Canadian View." In *Revue de l'Université d'Ottawa* 42, no. 2 (1972): 245–51. This gives an historical survey of Simon's lectures and publications in Canada.

Nef, John U. "John U. Nef Recalls Yves R. Simon." *University of Chicago Magazine* 64, no. 5 (1972): 37–38.

Nelson, Ralph. "Freedom and Economic Organization in a Democracy." In Torre, ed., *Freedom in the Modern World*, 141–52.

———. "The Scope of Justice." In Hancock and Simon, eds., *Freedom, Virtue, and the Common Good*, 342–57.

———. "Yves R. Simon's Philosophy of Science." In Anthony O. Simon, ed., *Acquaintance with the Absolute*, 57–82.

Nicgorski, Walter. "Yves R. Simon: A Philosopher's Quest for Science and Prudence." In *Political Philosophy in the Twentieth Century: Authors and Arguments*, edited by Catherine Zuckert, 99–107. Cambridge: Cambridge University Press, 2011. First published in "Political Philosophy in the Twentieth Century: H. Arendt, L. Strauss, Yves R. Simon, I. Berlin." Special issue of *Review of Politics* 71, no. 1 (2009): 68–84.

Novak, Michael. *Free Persons and the Common Good*. Lanham, MD: Madison Books, 1989. This book contains a lengthy treatment of Simon, especially his concept of "the Common Good."

———. "A 'Catholic Whig' Replies." *Review of Politics* 58, no. 2 (1996): 259–64.

O'Donnell, Charles P. "Democracy in the Philosophy of Jacques Maritain and Yves R. Simon." *Notes et Documents* 5, no. 14 (1979): 18–27.

Pappin, Joseph, III. "Freedom and Solidarity in Sartre and Simon." *American Catholic Philosophical Quarterly* 70, no. 4 (1996): 569–84.

Plaza, Francisco. "Yves R. Simon's Metaphysics of Love: A Hidden Treasure." In *Love and Friendship: Maritain and the Tradition*, edited by Montague Brown, 145–54. Washington, DC: American Maritain Association, 2013.

Rourke, Thomas R. "Michael Novak and Yves Simon on the Common Good and Capitalism." In *Review of Politics* 58, no. 2 (1996): 226–58.

———. *A Conscience as Large as the World: Yves R. Simon versus the Catholic Neoconservatives*. Lanham, MD: Rowman and Littlefield, 1997.

———. "Yves R. Simon: 1903–1961." In *Enciclopedia della persona nel XX secolo*, edited by Antonio Pavan, 961–68. Napoli/Roma: Edizioni Scientifiche Italiane, 2008.

———. "Moral Problems in Economic Organization in the Works of Yves R. Simon: Unequal Exchange and the Principle of Integration." In *Redeeming Philosophy: From Metaphysics to Aesthetics*, edited by John J. Conley, SJ, 313–32. Washington, DC: American Maritain Association, 2014.

Simon, Anthony O. "Bibliographie de Yves René Simon, 1923–1968." *Revue Philosophique de Louvain* 67, no. 94 (1969): 285–305.

———. "Yves R. Simon: A Bibliography, 1923–1970." In *Work, Society, and Culture*, edited, with preface, by Vukan Kuic, 190–228. New York: Fordham University Press, 1971. This was included as an appendix to that work.

———. "Bibliographie de Yves René Simon: Complement, 1969–1974." *Revue Philosophique de Louvain* 73, no. 18 (1975): 362–67.

———. "Yves R. Simon: A Definitive Bibliography, 1923–1997." In Anthony O. Simon, ed., *Acquaintance with the Absolute*, 185–305.

———, ed. *Acquaintance with the Absolute: The Philosophy of Yves R. Simon*. Edited, with a Note, by Anthony O. Simon. Introduction by James V. Schall, SJ. New York: Fordham University Press, 1998. This work contains six essays and a bibliography on Simon that are all detailed in this bibliography.

Simon, Paule Yves. "The Papers of Yves R. Simon." *New Scholasticism* 32, no. 4 (1963): 501–7.

Simon, Pierre-Henri. "Yves R. Simon." *Revue de l'Université d'Ottawa* 42, no. 2 (1972): 227–31.

Smith, Gerard. "Eulogy for Yves R. Simon." *Renascence* 24, no. 3 (1972): 115–18.

Speaight, Robert. "A Frenchman Speaks." *Blackfriars* 23, no. 262 (1942): 15–17.

———. "Yves R. Simon: Friend and Ally." *Catholic World* 211, no. 1266 (1970): 268–69.

Stankiewicz, W. J. "Yves R. Simon's Transmission Theory of Consent." *In Defense of Sovereignty*, 34–37. New York: Oxford University Press, 1969.

———. "In Defense of Yves R. Simon." In *Approaches to Democracy: Philosophy of Government at the Close of the Twentieth Century*, 228–34. New York: St. Martin's Press, 1980.

Strauss, Leo. "Yves R. Simon, *Philosophy of Democratic Government*." In *What Is Political Philosophy?*, 306–11. New York: Free Press, 1959.

Torre, Michael D., ed., *Freedom in the Modern World: Jacques Maritain, Yves R. Simon, Mortimer J. Adler*. Notre Dame, IN: American Maritain Association, 1989. Reprinted, 1990. This work contains twelve essays featuring Simon that are all detailed in this bibliography.

———. "Yves Simon: The Merit and Limit of Federalism." *Notes et Documents*, n.s., 35 (Septembre-Décembre 1992): 53–63.

———. "Jacques Maritain and Yves R. Simon on Freedom of Choice." In *Human Nature, Contemplation, and the Political Order: Essays Inspired by Jacques Maritain's Scholasticism and Politics*, edited by Peter Karl Koritansky, 3–18. Washington DC: American Maritain Association, 2014.

———. "Yves R. Simon, Disciple of Maritain: The Idea of Fact and the Difference between Science and Philosophy." In *Facts Are Stubborn Things:*

Thomistic Perspectives in the Philosophies of Nature and Science, edited by Matthew K. Minerd, 19–30. Washington, DC: American Maritain Association, 2021.

Udoidem, Sylvanus Iniobong. "Metaphysical Foundations of Freedom in the Social and Political Thought of Yves R. Simon." In Torre, ed., *Freedom in the Modern World*, 101–7.

Vignaux, Paul. "Yves R. Simon: Par delà l'expérience du désespoir." *Revue Philosophique de Louvain* 70, no. 6 (1972): 237–39.

Von Simpson, Louise. *Happy Exile*. Darmstadt: Roetherdruck, 1981. This autobiography contains personal memoirs of Simon during his years at the universities of Notre Dame and Chicago.

Williams, Brooke. "Mystical Contemplation in the Thought of Yves R. Simon and Jacques Maritain." *Notes et Documents*, Vème Année, no. 14 (Janvier-Mars 1979): 28–35.

Woldring, H. E. S. "Dooyeweerd, Maritain, en Simon: Hun strijd om het behoud van de rechtsstaat." *Christen Democratische Verkenningen* (November 1994): 476–84. See Koyzis's PhD dissertation listed below for another comparison with Dooyeweerd.

Theses on Yves R. Simon

Cahalan, John C. "Necessary Truth and Philosophical Method: An Examination." PhD diss., University of Notre Dame, 1968.

Caplin, Diane M. "Authority, Freedom, and Community in the Political Philosophy of Yves R. Simon." Master's thesis, St. Louis University, 1990.

———. "Essentially Human: Democracy in the Thought of Yves R. Simon." PhD diss., Marquette University, 1993.

Chandler, Carolyn A. "The Concept of Political Authority in the Works of Emile Durkheim and Yves R. Simon." Master's thesis, Texas Tech University, 1983.

Connelly, Kathleen M. "The Political Activities of Five European Christian Democratic Scholars in Exile in the United States, 1938–1945 [Jacques Maritain, Yves R. Simon, Luigi Sturzo, Waldemar Gurian, and Ferdinand A. Hermans]." PhD diss., Boston College, 1995.

Gammon, Francis L. "A Study of the Theory of Authority of Yves R. Simon." Master's thesis, St. John's University, 1966.

Gehringer, Gerald. "The Concept of Political Liberty according to Mortimer J. Adler and Yves R. Simon." PhD diss., Pontificia Universitas Lateranensis, 1962.

Gichuci Theuri, John Baptist. "Democracy and Authority according to Yves R. Simon." Master's thesis, Roman Athenaeum of the Holy Cross, 1993.

Green, Catherine. "The Nature of Moral Actions: An Examination of Yves R. Simon's Metaphysics of Morals." Master's thesis, Catholic University of America, 1987.

———. "The Intentionality of Knowing and Willing in the Writings of Yves R. Simon." PhD diss., Catholic University of America, 1996.

Ikeme Ngozi, Anthony. "The Basic Principles of Democratic Freedom in the Political Philosophy of Yves R. Simon." PhD diss., Universidad de Navarra, 1993.

Koyzis, David T. "Towards a Christian Democratic Pluralism: A Comparative Study of Neo-Thomist and Neo-Calvinist Political Theory." PhD diss., University of Notre Dame, 1986. This is a comparative study between Yves R. Simon and the Dutch thinker Herman Dooyeweerd.

Lucal, John A. "Yves R. Simon's Theory of Authority." Master's thesis, Loyola University, Chicago, 1961.

Mariotti, Luisa. "Attività e verità nella filosofia di Yves R. Simon." PhD diss., Università Cattolica del Sacre Cuore, 1981.

O'Connell, Sean P. "A Treatment of Free Choice as Found in the Philosophical Writings of Yves R. Simon." Master's thesis, Catholic University of America, 1981.

Pollard, Christopher James. "The Concept of Virtue as *Habitus* in the Moral Philosophy of Yves R. Simon." Master's thesis, Catholic University of America, 1994.

Radzin, Patricia Pallasch. "The Development of the Relation between Authority and Freedom in the Political Philosophy of Yves R. Simon." PhD diss., Marquette University, 1995.

Rivera, José Antonio. "Political Authority and the Good in the Thought of Yves R. Simon and Luis Muñoz Marín." PhD diss., Catholic University of America, 1993.

Rourke, Thomas R. "Yves R. Simon and Contemporary Catholic Neo-Conservatism." PhD diss., Texas Tech University, 1994.

Turner, Phillip W. "Theological Anthropology and the State: A Study of the Political Ethics of Yves R. Simon and Helmut Thielicke." PhD diss., Princeton University, 1978.

Udoidem, Sylvanus Iniobong. "Authority and the Common Good in the Social and Political Philosophy of Yves R. Simon." PhD diss., Catholic University of America, 1985.

Vergara Villalobos, Miguel Ángel. "El cono del conocimiento práctico: Teoría de la accíon moral en la filosfía de Yves R. Simon." PhD diss., Universidad de Navarra, 2011.
Ward, Edward P. "Authority and Democracy: An Essay on the Political Thought of Yves R. Simon." Master's thesis, Catholic University of America, 1968.
Whipple, John Emory. "Some Contemporary Catholic Views on Democracy." Master's thesis, Duke University, 1969.

CONTRIBUTORS

George Anastaplo (November 7, 1925–February 14, 2014) studied with Leo Strauss and with Yves R. Simon in the Committee on Social Thought at the University of Chicago in the 1950s. In 1957, he joined the University of Chicago's Basic Program of Liberal Education for Adults faculty and continued to teach there for almost sixty years, through December 2013. He was the "heart and soul" of the program and was perfectly dubbed "the Socrates of Chicago." On principle, in the 1950s, he had insisted that the First Amendment of the U.S. Constitution protects the privacy of political affiliations; he thus refused to answer questions about membership in the Communist Party and was subsequently denied access to the Illinois bar. He appealed the ruling to the U.S. Supreme Court in *In re Anastaplo*. On a 5–4 vote, it upheld the lower court ruling, with Justice Hugo Black famously dissenting. He later became a professor at Loyola University Chicago School of Law. For one of his many essays, on Simon and Mortimer J. Adler, see the Select Bibliography.

Laurence Berns (March 15, 1928–March 7, 2011) was a close student of Leo Strauss at the University of Chicago, from which he graduated with a PhD in international relations. He taught at St. John's College in Annapolis from 1960 to 1999, and during his retirement he remained an active member of its college community as Richard Hammond Elliot Tutor Emeritus. An eminent teacher, his main interest at St. John's (and his main publications) focused on philosophy, political philosophy, and politics. Among his diverse publications, together with Georges Anastaplo, he coedited, cotranslated, and extensively annotated Plato's *Meno* (Focus Press, 2004).

David B. Burrell, CSC, Theodore Hesburgh Professor Emeritus in Philosophy and Theology at the University of Notre Dame, is currently serving the Holy Cross congregation at Notre Dame University in Dhaka, Bangladesh (david.b.burrell.2.nd@gmail.com). His service as rector of the Tantur Ecumenical Institute in Jerusalem (1980) spurred sustained inquiry into comparative theology: *Knowing the Unknowable God: Ibn-Sina, Maimonides, Aquinas* (1986); *Freedom and Creation in Three Traditions* (1993); *Original Peace* (with Elena Malits, 1998); *Friendship and Ways to Truth* (2000); and translations of Al-Ghazali: *Ninety-Nine Beautiful Names of God* (1993), and *Faith in Divine Unity and Trust in Divine Providence* (2001); followed by *Faith and Freedom* (2004) and *Learning to Trust in Freedom* (2010); a theological reflection on Job—*Deconstructing Theodicy* (2008); and, most recently, *Towards a Jewish-Christian-Muslim Theology* (2011).

John C. Cahalan, is a former philosophy professor and is now an independent scholar. He has been a Woodrow Wilson fellow, a National Defense Education Act fellow in symbolic logic, a visiting scholar at Harvard, and a member of the American Catholic Philosophical Association's Executive Committee. He has published numerous articles in American and European philosophical journals. His widely reviewed book, *Causal Realism*, uses Simon's insights on ordered analogical sets and Maritain's and Simon's insights on the problem of thing and object and ontological and empiriological concept formation to reply to empiricism: it refutes empiricism's critique of metaphysics, and it shows that metaphysics solves empiricism's own problems about empirical knowledge. It can be downloaded at no cost from the website he edits, Resources for Modern Aristotelian Philosophers, http://www.foraristotelians.info. He worked closely with Simon's son Anthony to make Simon's work available, and was assistant to the director of Notre Dame's Jacques Maritain Center at its inception.

John W. Carlson (September 17, 1943–December 12, 2012) earned his BA in philosophy from St. Mary's College (CA) in 1965 and his PhD in philosophy from the University of Notre Dame in 1970. He served successively as a member of the Philosophy faculty at St. Louis University, as associate dean and subsequently dean of Arts and Sciences at the University of Scranton, as dean and academic vice president of Le Moyne College, and as vice president for Academic Affairs at Creighton University. After stepping down from his role as vice president at Creighton, Carlson joined its Philosophy faculty full-time in 1995, teaching there for two decades. In addition to many scholarly articles, Carlson wrote and published several books to serve as resources for his courses, including *Understanding Our Being: An Introduction to Speculative Philosophy in the Perennial Tradition* (Catholic University of America Press, 2008), and *Words of Wisdom: A Philosophical Dictionary for the Perennial Tradition* (University of Notre Dame Press, 2012).

Raymond Dennehy (August 31, 1934–April 19, 2010) was a professor at the University of San Francisco, where he taught philosophy for forty-five years. He served in the U.S. Navy as a radar man, aboard the heavy cruiser USS *Rochester* (CA 124), principally in the South China Sea (1954–58). At the University of San Francisco, he majored in philosophy. He then did graduate work in philosophy at the University of California, Berkeley, and went on to acquire his PhD in philosophy from the University of Toronto. His graduate school teachers included Sir Karl Popper, C. B. MacPherson, and Anton Pegis. He was the author of *Jacques Maritain's Philosophy of Action*; *Soldier Boy: The War between Michael and Lucifer*; *Anti-Abortionist at Large*; and *Reason and Dignity*. In 2007, he received the Oleg Zinam Award for "Best Essay" in the *Journal of Interdisciplinary Studies*. In 2013, he received the Rupert and Timothy Smith Award for "Distinguished Contributions to Pro-Life Scholarship."

Jude P. Dougherty is dean emeritus and professor emeritus of the School of Philosophy, Catholic University of America. For more than forty years, he has been editor of the *Review of Metaphysics* and general editor of *Studies in Philosophy and the History of Philosophy*, published by Catholic University of America Press. His own publications continue unabated: for example, *The Nature of Scientific Explanation* (Catholic University of America Press, 2013); *Briefly Considered* (St. Augustine's Press, 2015); and the recently published *Interpretations: Using the Past to Understand the Present* (Catholic University of America Press, 2017).

Catherine Green practiced nursing, mostly in critical care areas, for more than twenty-five years, which led her to a consideration of the most basic questions of life. Subsequently, she studied philosophy at the Catholic University of America. Upon completion of her dissertation on the meanings of intention in the writings of Yves R. Simon, she was granted a faculty position at Rockhurst University in Kansas City, where she is currently emerita professor of philosophy. She has published essays in political philosophy, philosophy of knowledge, ethics, and philosophy of nursing. She continued to teach part-time at Rockhurst University and to write and lecture on issues of philosophy and nursing.

John A. Gueguen, Jr. (June 14, 1933–December 14, 2018) was professor emeritus of politics and government at Illinois State University (Normal). His webpage was in the faculty listing of the Department of Politics and Government at Illinois State: http://www.ilstu.edu/~jguegu. During the 1950s and 1960s, he was pleased to know and associate with Yves R. Simon and his son, Anthony, in South Bend, at Notre Dame, and at the University of Chicago (from which he received his PhD in 1970).

John P. Hittinger is professor of philosophy at the University of St. Thomas, Houston, and a member of the Center for Thomistic Studies. He holds degrees from the University of Notre Dame, the University of Dallas, and the Catholic University of America. He previously served on the Philosophy faculty at Benedictine College, the College of St. Francis, the U.S. Air Force Academy, Ave Maria University, and Sacred Heart Major Seminary of Detroit. He has published articles and presented papers on a variety of topics, including John Locke, Jacques Maritain, military ethics, liberal education, political philosophy, and the thought of John Paul II. He was the coeditor of *Liberalism at the Crossroads: An Introduction to Contemporary Liberal Theory and its Critics* (Rowman and Littlefield, 1994), of *Reassessing the Liberal State: Reading Maritain's Man and the State* (American Maritain Association, 2001), and editor of *The Vocation of the Catholic Philosopher: From Maritain to John Paul II* (American Maritain Association, 2010), and the author of a collection of essays entitled *Liberty, Wisdom and Grace: Thomism and Modern Democratic Theory* (Lexington Books, 2002). In 2008, Hittinger founded the Pope John Paul II Forum for the Church in the Modern World.

Joseph W. Koterski, SJ, has taught in the Philosophy Department of Fordham University (Bronx campus) since his priestly ordination in 1992. At Fordham, he serves as the editor in chief of the *International Philosophical Quarterly*, and as the editor of *Life and Learning*, the annual proceedings of the University Faculty for Life. From 2008 to 2014, he was the president of the Fellowship of Catholic Scholars. Among his recent publications is *Introduction to Medieval Philosophy*. He has produced three series of lectures for The Teaching Company: *Aristotle's Ethics*; *Natural Law and Human Nature*; and *Biblical Wisdom Literature*. In the courses that he teaches on the natural moral law, he regularly makes use of Yves R. Simon's *The Tradition of Natural Law*.

V. Bradley Lewis is associate professor in the School of Philosophy and a fellow in the Institute for Human Ecology at the Catholic University of America. He works in political and legal philosophy, especially the thought of Plato and Aristotle and the Thomistic tradition. He serves as associate editor of the *American Journal of Jurisprudence* and is currently working on a book on the idea of the common good.

Steven A. Long is an ordinary/full professor of theology in the Graduate Theology program at Ave Maria University, and an ordinary academician of the Pontifical Academy of St. Thomas Aquinas. He has authored three books: *The Teleological Grammar of the Moral Act*, whose second edition was published in

2015; *Natura Pura: On the Recovery of Nature in the Doctrine of Grace*; and *Analogia Entis: On the Analogy of Being, Metaphysics, and the Act of Faith*. And he has coedited *Reason and the Rule of Faith* with Dean Christopher Thompson of the St. Paul Seminary School of Divinity, and more recently (2016) coedited *Thomism & Predestination: Principles and Disputations*, with Roger Nutt and Thomas Joseph White, OP. He has recently served as guest editor for a special issue of the *National Catholic Bioethics Quarterly* devoted to a critique of the new natural law theory developed by Germain Grisez and further developed and applied by authors such as John Finnis and Robert George.

Ralph McInerny (February 24, 1929–January 29, 2010) was, during more than a half century at the University of Notre Dame and while serving as its Michael P. Grace Professor of Medieval Studies, and as the director of the Jacques Maritain Center there, a legend in his own time. He wrote more than fifty nonfiction books in philosophy, medieval studies, and theology, and also more than ninety novels, including the Father Dowling Murder Mystery series. He was beloved by his graduate students, forty-eight completing their dissertations under his careful direction, to which he always gave his immediate attention. He was truly a national (and, indeed, international) figure: president of the American Maritain Association, of the Fellowship of Catholic Scholars, and of the International Catholic University, fellow of the Pontifical Academy of St. Thomas Aquinas, Gifford lecturer, editor of *The New Scholasticism/American Catholic Philosophical Quarterly*, founder and editor of *Crisis*, EWTN TV host . . . the list goes on and on. For his translation of Simon's first work on moral philosophy and an essay on that philosophy, see the Select Bibliography.

Ralph Nelson (November 20, 1927–May 13, 2008) received his doctorate from the University of Notre Dame in 1961 under Joseph W. Evans, director of the Jacques Maritain Center. He went on to teach philosophy and political science for more than thirty years (1961–93) at the University of Windsor, Ontario. The main interest of his scholarly work was on democratic theory and practice. With Anthony O. Simon, he coedited *Foresight and Knowledge* (Fordham University Press, 1996), and wrote an essay on Simon's philosophy of science included in *Acquaintance with the Absolute: The Philosophy of Yves. R. Simon* (Fordham University Press, 1998). (For some other essays on Simon, see the Select Bibliography.) His articles include "Beyond the Sovereignty of Good," *Etudes Maritainiennes* 10 (1994): 124–41; "Moderating the Philosophy of Rights," in *Philosophical Theory and the Universal Declaration on Human Rights*, ed. William Sweet (University of Ottawa Press, 2003); and "Two Masters, Two Perspectives: Maritain and Gilson on the Philosophy of Nature," in *Wisdom's Apprentice: Thomistic Essays in Honor of Lawrence Dewan, O.P.*, ed. Peter A. Kwasniewski (Catholic University of America Press, 2007). He was a longtime and faithful contributor to the American Maritain Association.

Walter J. Nicgorski is an emeritus professor at the University of Notre Dame, whose faculty he joined in 1964, having taken his graduate degrees at the University of Chicago. He has been the editor of *The Review of Politics* (1994–2004) and has been chair of the Program of Liberal Studies, Notre Dame's sixty-six-year-old Great Books program. He has been a visiting scholar at Harvard University and at Cambridge University, and also a visiting tutor in the Graduate Institute of St. John's College (Santa Fe). He has published essays and books on Cicero, liberal and character education, American political foundations, Leo Strauss, Allan Bloom, and Yves R. Simon. He has presented Simon to contemporary Notre Dame undergraduates: "Passing the Torch: The Brownson Legacy and Yves Simon" (*The Brownson Journal*, 2007). He has written on Simon's sense of the vocation of philosopher: "Yves R. Simon: A Philosopher's Quest for Science and Prudence," in *Political Philosophy in the Twentieth Century* (Cambridge University Press, 2011). And he has introduced the republication of Simon's important essay, "The Doctrinal Issue between the Church and Democracy" (*Logos*, 2011). A longtime South Bend friend of the late "Tony" Simon, he has lectured widely in the United States, Mexico, and Europe.

Thomas R. Rourke, professor of politics at Clarion University of Pennsylvania, has published on Yves R. Simon throughout his career. His first book, *A Conscience as Large as the World* (Rowman and Littlefield, 1997), critiqued Catholic neoconservatism in the light of Simon. Three earlier articles, "The Common Good and Economic Justice: Reflections on the Thought of Yves R. Simon" (*Review of Politics*, 1992); "Beyond Ideology in Christian Economic Thought: Yves R. Simon and Recent Debates" (in *Freedom, Virtue, and the Common Good*, 1995); and "Michael Novak and Yves Simon on the Common Good and Capitalism" (*Review of Politics*, 1996), similarly critiqued economic theory, rooted in Simon's writings. He continued to publish on Simon for *The Review of Politics* ("Liberty and Authority," 2001), and, at the request of the Yves R. Simon Institute, he authored an entry on Simon's concept of personhood for the *Enciclopedia della Persona nel XX Secolo* (2009). More recently, he authored "Moral Problems in Economic Organization in the Work of Yves R. Simon: Unequal Exchange and Man as the Principle of Integration" (in *Redeeming Philosophy: From Metaphysics to Aesthetics*, 2014).

Robert Royal is the president and founder of the Faith & Reason Institute (Washington, DC) and editor in chief of *The Catholic Thing*. He is the author, editor, and translator of more than a dozen books, including editing *Jacques Maritain and the Jews* (American Maritain Association); *1492 and All That: Political Manipulations of History* (coeditor with George Weigel); *Building the Free Society: Democracy, Capitalism, and Catholic Social Teaching*; *The God That Did Not Fail*; *St. Thomas Aquinas: The Person and His Work* (translator); and, most recently, *A Deeper Vision: The Catholic Intellectual Tradition in the Twentieth Century*.

James V. Schall, SJ (January 20, 1928–April 17, 2019) was professor emeritus of Georgetown University. He contributed an article on Yves R. Simon, "Immanent in the Souls of Men," to *Acquaintance with the Absolute: The Philosophy of Yves Simon* (Fordham University Press, 1998). An indefatigable author, some of his numerous books include *At the Limits of Political Philosophy* (Catholic University of America Press, 1998); *On The Mind That Is Catholic* (Catholic University of America Press, 2011); *On the Unseriousness of Human Affairs* (Intercollegiate Studies Institute, 2012); *Reasonable Pleasures: The Strange Coherence of Catholicism* (Ignatius Press, 2013); and *Political Philosophy & Revelation* (Catholic University of American Press, 2013).

Jeanne Heffernan Schindler was formerly an associate professor in the Department of Humanities at Villanova University and is currently a research fellow at the John Paul II Institute for Studies on Marriage and Family in Washington, DC. She has long taken an interest in the work of Yves R. Simon, writing a dissertation on his theological anthropology and political vision: "Christianity and Modern Democracy: The Theological Anthropology and Political Vision of Reinhold Niebuhr and Yves R. Simon" (University of Notre Dame, 2000). She followed this work with articles and book chapters in which Simon's work played a critical role. See, for example, "Acknowledging Ambiguity and Difference in Politics: A Christian Realist Challenge to Thomists" (in *Reassessing the Liberal State: Reading Maritain's "Man and the State,"* 2001), and "Democracy and Tradition: A Catholic Alternative to American Pragmatism" (*Logos*, 2008). She has coedited (with her husband, D. C. Schindler) a collection of essays by the German philosopher Robert Spaemann: *A Robert Spaemann Reader* (Oxford University Press, 2015).

Anthony O. Simon (July 3, 1936–August 2, 2012) was director of the Yves R. Simon Institute and for many years the secretary of the American Maritain Association, whose vitality and work he was instrumental in furthering. He supported the creation of the Association's book series and served as its first general editor (1990–2004) for twelve of its volumes. He worked with former students of his father, and others, to ensure that his father's work received the recognition it deserves: nine new books, and the English translation of five others, were published in large measure from his efforts. He possessed a complete mastery of his father's oeuvre, as can be seen from his many bibliographies of it, especially in *Acquaintance with the Absolute*. He was also instrumental in seeing that many of his father's papers, and works pertaining to his father, were located in the Jacques Maritain Center at the University of Notre Dame, where they continue to await the exploration of future thinkers dedicated to revealing the philosophical wisdom and accomplishments of his father, whose work may serve as a model for future Thomist philosophers.

W. David Solomon began his legendary career at Notre Dame in 1968 and retired in May 2016. During his tenure, he served as the director of undergraduate studies in the Philosophy Department, founded and directed the Arts & Letters/Science Honors Program, and directed the Notre Dame London Program. An excellent academic administrator, his real passion was teaching and mentoring students. Each spring semester, more than 200 undergraduates took his signature ethics course, "Morality and Modernity," based on Alasdair MacIntyre's seminal book *After Virtue*. He also taught medical ethics to more than 250 undergraduate students each year, and also upper-division courses in contemporary ethics and special topics in ethics. At the graduate level, he taught the entry-level course "20th Century Ethical Theory" and directed more than forty doctoral dissertations. Solomon founded the Center for Ethics and Culture (CEC) in 1999 with the aim of bringing "the great treasures of the Catholic moral and intellectual tradition to bear upon the most pressing ethical questions of the day." He secured MacIntyre's return to Notre Dame to serve as the Center's inaugural permanent research fellow and established an interdisciplinary Board of Advisors from top-tier academic institutions to help guide the CEC's vision.

Michael D. Torre, associate professor of philosophy at the University of San Francisco, completed a four-year term as president of the American Maritain Association (AMA) in 2016. As its second general editor, he oversaw the publication of eight of its volumes between 2009 and 2013. The one he had edited (*Freedom in the Modern World: Jacques Maritain, Yves R. Simon, and Mortimer J. Adler*, 1989; second printing, 1990) assembled the first collection of essays published on Yves R. Simon. He has published two books dealing with man's responsibility for sin: *God's Permission of Sin* (Fribourg University

Press, 2009), and *Do Not Resist the Spirit's Call* (Catholic University of American Press, 2013). He has also published numerous articles in the AMA series of volumes and has written further articles on Yves R. Simon: "Yves R. Simon: The Merit and Limit of Federalism" (*Notes et Documents*, 1992), "Jacques Maritain and Yves R. Simon on Freedom of Choice" (in the AMA volume *Human Nature, Contemplation, and the Political Order*, 2014), and "Yves R. Simon, Disciple of Maritain: The Idea of Fact and the Difference between Science and Philosophy" (in the AMA volume *Facts Are Stubborn Things: Thomistic Perspectives in the Philosophies of Nature and Science*, 2021).

INDEX

absoluteness, 59–60, 104, 110, 155, 177, 191, 231, 258, 278, 286, 290, 291, 311, 381, 421, 430, 436
  contingency, 117, 438
  empirical/experimental, 33–34, 39, 117, 129–30
  good, 200, 217, 268
  necessity, 49, 92, 205, 230
  perfections, 101, 108–9
  power, 139, 433
  premise/proposition, 168, 208, 275, 329
  rejection of, 276
  sense, 215, 260, 271
  spontaneity, 73
absolutism, 341, 433. *See also* totalitarianism
abstraction, 11–12, 383–84
  analogical, 96–110
  Aristotelian, 14
  mathematical, 13, 94, 141, 329, 413
  metaphysical, 155
  and order, 103–6
  in practical thought, 49, 158
  and sensing, 122
accident, 68, 105, 106, 114, 124, 147, 161, 177, 267
action, 4, 10, 50, 119, 129, 132, 146, 152, 157–59, 161, 164, 176, 193, 198, 199–200n3, 203, 209, 212, 214, 216, 219–20n4, 224, 260, 271, 278, 292, 296, 298, 313, 331, 349–50, 355, 358, 373–74n9, 385–86, 394, 404–5, 408, 417, 421, 427, 436, 438–39
  collective, 319–20, 426, 432, 441
  common, 287, 294, 317, 318, 321–22, 332, 334, 345, 364–65, 425, 426
  definitions of, 60–67
  human (*see* human action)
  immanent, 55–78, 116, 122–23, 126, 293, 314, 322–23, 324n2
  upon physical nature, 299, 364, 367–69, 371–72
  and quality, 68–70
  reflex, 72, 240–41
  rules of, 167, 311, 330, 343, 382, 406
  transitive, 56–57, 64, 66–67, 70–72, 122, 127, 314, 320–22, 324n2
  united, 332, 338–39, 342–46, 348, 425–26
  voluntary, 180–81, 183, 189, 191, 219, 242, 249
Action Française, 417, 429
activity, 33–34, 37, 48, 55, 66–67, 69, 72, 102, 120, 122, 210–11, 215–16, 271, 309, 356, 360, 369–71, 373–74n9, 410, 412
  collective, 319–20, 426, 432, 441
  commercial, 377, 385
  contemplative, 354, 361
  government, 422–23
  immanent, 56–57, 62–64, 68, 70–71, 74, 120
  intellectual, 10, 407
  motionless, 70–71, 104–5, 119

activity (*cont.*)
  and objectivity, 59–60
  productive, 357, 359
  transitive, 56, 64–65, 116
  united, 338–39, 342–45, 348, 426
  useful, 363–68
  vital, 57, 60, 74
actuality, 35, 61, 71, 74, 101, 103, 104, 111, 159, 192, 216, 324n2, 345
  of the cause, 193–96, 198
Adler, Mortimer J., 5, 21nn14–15
aesthetics, 47, 237, 253–54, 278
affectivity, 318, 338
  communion, 164, 284n8
  connaturality, 154, 331
  knowledge, 153–54, 174
  motions, 259, 318
agents, 66, 72, 74
  "acts according as it is in act," 192, 197–98
  autonomous, 271
  cause (*see* cause)
  executive, 299, 322, 337
  free agent, 26, 43, 72
  power of, 225
agnosticism, 101, 275–79
agriculture, 300, 303n2, 395
alienation, 378–81, 389, 391–92
analogy, 5, 38, 56, 60–63, 67–68, 73, 108–9, 111–14, 138, 202, 208, 215, 216, 336
  abstraction, 97–103, 110
  attribution, 95–96, 100, 105
  metaphor, 95–96, 100
  proper proportionality, 95–97, 100–104, 106–7
  sets, 97–98, 101, 104, 106, 110, 197
anarchism, 271–72, 366–67, 391, 422, 424–45
angels, 73, 80, 85, 102, 337. *See also* spirit
animal intelligence, 211–13, 330
Aquinas. *See* Thomas Aquinas
Archimedes, 361
Arendt, Hannah, 373n7

Aristotle, 26, 62, 118, 131, 246, 249, 250, 254, 307, 325, 330, 405
  economic, political, and social philosophy, 299, 308, 314, 324n3, 353, 357, 368, 385
  ethics, 20n9, 112, 162, 167, 241–42, 256, 260
  finality, 174, 438, 443
  habitus, 251, 407
  and intellectual virtues, 397, 402, 403, 406
  logic, 29, 92, 101
  metaphysics, 13, 173, 324n2, 361–62
  philosophy of, xi, 5, 6, 23, 25, 31, 291, 368
  and Plato, 4, 6, 14, 27, 117, 134, 174, 257
  practical truth, 152, 169
  psychology, 75, 76, 113, 146
  senses, 119, 126
  virtue, 221–22, 234–35, 242, 252, 404
Aristotelianism, 6, 40, 126, 131, 343
artists, 10, 13, 125, 159, 182–83, 226, 253–54, 398, 412
asceticism, 26–27, 43, 50
assemblies, 100, 299, 338, 348
assent, 205–7, 344
  and judgment, 158, 166, 342
  common/general/unanimous/universal, 15, 284n8
  general, 275, 299
  of mind, 24, 33, 44, 86–87, 268, 276, 280, 343
  unanimous, 142, 343
  universal, 15
  voluntary, 274
atheism, 280, 283n5, 417, 429, 444
Augustine, 162, 186, 251, 256
Augustinians, 181
authority, 6, 11, 133, 142, 238, 285, 287, 296, 298, 301, 326, 333, 336, 337–40, 341, 379, 397, 416, 436, 440
  authoritarian, 254, 332, 366, 417
  and the common good, 337–51
  definition of, 424

essential function of, 34–35, 47, 297, 307, 321, 332, 339, 342, 344–45, 349, 351, 425–26
and freedom, 264, 347, 424
need for, 341–44, 348
substitutional ("paternal") function of, 297, 308, 341–42, 424
autonomy, 11, 33, 134–35, 290–91, 300–302, 339, 347, 349, 368, 393, 395, 419, 433
axioms, 45, 205–6, 242–43, 256–58, 275, 329–30, 333, 341, 381, 406, 445

Bacon, Francis, 141
Baudelaire, Charles, 13, 14
beauty, 146, 178–79, 212–13, 226, 237, 246, 253, 254, 409
becoming, 4, 57, 60, 71, 197, 291, 366, 438. *See also* change
being, 8, 24, 26, 34, 35, 38, 55, 59, 60, 61, 63, 64, 68, 86, 95, 97, 98, 101, 104, 105, 135, 144, 165, 190, 196, 198, 204, 271, 311, 356, 365, 407, 438
acted upon, 118–19, 122
concept of, 99, 100, 310
contingent/created, 56, 58, 66, 75
created, 63, 73
finite, 56, 61, 64, 75, 103, 110
genus, 35, 77–78, 88, 96, 100, 111
of God, 71, 74, 96, 101, 106, 109, 110
human beings (*see* humanity: being)
and knowing, 55, 57–58, 75–76, 83, 110, 113, 122
living, 36, 37, 41, 55, 57, 73
perfection of, 61, 108–9, 136, 186, 215
qua being, 36, 197
rational, 46, 73, 306, 327
of reason, 80, 81, 88, 90–94, 121, 143
sensible, 37, 61, 115
social, 245, 370–71
Supreme/First, 113, 114, 440
way of, 55, 57, 76, 103, 110, 112, 125, 291

beliefs, 46, 80, 116, 182, 205, 238, 274, 279–80, 296, 320, 331, 360, 367, 389, 422, 424, 429
Christian, 444
common, 286, 319, 432
moral, 439
in natural law, 444
See also opinions
Berdyaev, Nikolai, 292
Bergson, Henri, 10, 219n4
Berkeley, George, 16
Bernanos, Georges, 396, 429
biology, 25, 108, 134–35, 141, 210, 236, 277, 281, 300, 311, 388, 400
Bloy, Léon, 10
Bonaparte, Napoleon, 364, 429
Bréhier, Émile, 27, 48
Brentano, Franz, 94n3, 259
Buonarroti, Michelangelo, 13, 17
Burkhardt, Jacob, 414n4

Cajetan, Thomas, 7, 21n18, 78, 78n1
capitalization, 174, 317, 360, 367, 378, 390–91, 393
Carlson, John W., xii, xiii, xivn1, xivn4
Carlyle, Thomas, 360
Carnot, Hippolyte, 363
Cartesianism, 15, 31, 77, 116, 132, 410
categories, 99, 151, 265
of quality, 56, 67–68
of workers, 361, 369–71, 430
cause, 24, 31, 33, 36, 47, 50–51, 56, 63, 65, 68, 95, 103, 123, 147, 156, 158, 160, 163–64, 170, 176, 184, 196, 201–2, 206–8, 211, 215, 245, 271, 273, 320, 322, 326, 328, 335, 341–42, 344, 349, 357, 358, 386, 388, 390, 446
actuality of, 193–95, 197–98
determining, 137, 139
and effect, 102, 106, 197
efficient, 55, 59–60, 61, 66, 67, 72–73
final, 67, 100, 141, 152–53, 159, 204, 293, 444

cause (*cont.*)
  First Cause, 113, 277, 404, 445
  formal, 76, 100–101, 104, 152–53, 159, 190, 204, 212, 225
  of freedom, 46, 214, 217
  of indifference, 209, 216
  material, 100, 177–78, 183, 197–98
  proper, 102, 161, 323, 370
  ultimate, 73, 276
certainty, 15, 17, 30, 40, 63, 85, 121, 219n4, 295, 299, 344, 407, 426
  emotional, 65
  practical, 159, 163–64, 343, 350, 433
  of senses, 129
chance, 31, 44, 117, 144, 147, 212, 214, 348, 376, 422, 438
change, 34, 37, 40, 50, 56, 62, 64–65, 74, 90, 94, 118–20, 158, 197–98, 215
  activity and, 70
  definition of, 70
  occurring without, 55, 57
  source of, 60, 61
  subject of, 71
  world of, 196, 317
  See also becoming
choice, 160, 164, 169, 174–75, 193, 199–200n3, 242, 256–58, 261, 268, 275–76, 287, 290–91, 309, 344–45, 406, 414
Christianity, 27, 362, 446
  church, 340
  ethics, 50–51
  faith, 12, 48, 351, 445
  humanism, 443–44
  life, 351
  marriage, 251
  and non-Christianity, 51
  philosophy, 11–12, 26–27, 48–49
  social teaching, 372n2
  state of philosophy, 11, 48–49
Cicero, 407
citizens, 4, 250, 256, 265, 285, 287–88, 302, 319, 338–39, 344, 348, 368, 388, 400, 432, 441
civilization, 11, 82, 399–401, 406, 413
Clifford, W. K., 296

coercion, 11, 219n2, 294, 308, 313, 338, 341, 391–92
cognition, 35, 38, 45, 55, 57, 65, 67, 70, 74, 77, 79, 108, 110, 113, 122, 123, 149, 151, 159, 166–67, 201, 204, 210, 236, 314, 318, 323, 349
  and activity, 59–60
  powers, 132, 215
common good, 180, 259, 287–88, 298, 312–21, 325–26, 336, 368, 377–78, 394, 426
  and authority, 337–51
  formally intended, 338–39, 355, 346, 349
  individualism and, 327, 334–35
  materially intended, 338–40, 346
  means to, 343–45
  principal part of, 294, 308–9, 314
  vs. private good, 307, 333–35, 376
common sense, 25–26, 39, 44–46, 60, 64, 135, 149, 199, 201, 279, 359
common sensible, 115, 117, 128
communication, 10, 15, 17, 125, 142, 167, 280, 282, 294, 320, 323–24, 338–40, 343–44, 351, 381
communion, 164, 284n8, 293–94, 314, 320, 322–24, 378
communism, 268, 374n12, 416–18, 420–21
community, 11, 105, 161, 190, 283n6, 284n8, 285, 287, 294, 297, 313–15, 320, 323–24, 324n3, 325, 327, 332, 334, 336–37, 339, 342, 347–48, 352–53, 355, 370, 373, 396–98, 425–26, 435
  civil, 200, 295, 309, 333, 335
  international, 416, 427–28
  members of, 293, 317, 338, 350, 422
  and partnership, 321–23
  rural, 301–3
Comte, August, 117, 186, 276, 364
concepts, 26, 33–39, 80–81, 87, 88, 108, 125–45, 155, 163
  analogical, 100, 105, 106
  moral, 42–43
  objective, 124
  rudimentary, 25, 46, 237

Index 475

typology of, 45
universal, 100–101
univocal, 67, 105
connaturality, 151, 154, 186, 331
conscience, 31, 199–200n3, 228, 267, 279, 382, 386, 393–94, 441–42
   enlightened, 435
   freedom of, 265
   individual, 387
   liberal, 274, 277
   moral, 313, 341–42
   private, 278
   public, 11
   rights of, 429
   social, 389
conservative, 347, 367, 371, 420, 424, 431
contemplation, 10, 56, 62, 98, 120, 140–41, 181, 264, 292–93, 354, 361–63, 368, 398, 408, 413, 446
contingency, 4, 9, 11–12, 16, 56, 66, 83, 92, 115, 147, 262, 281, 284n8, 291, 318, 326, 331–33, 350, 426, 438
   non datur contingens in natura rerum (Spinoza), 92
contracts, 11, 112, 163, 167–68, 256, 261, 278, 287, 314, 319, 391, 394, 427
courage, 13, 14, 17, 68–69, 96, 160–61, 246, 251, 260–62, 365, 405, 415, 417, 430
Cratylus, 117, 365
culture, 16, 189, 239n2, 293, 352, 354, 396–97, 435, 444
   business, 359
   and civilization, 399–401
   frivolous, 410–13
   general, 31
   Greek, 140, 329
   hard core of, 401–9, 411
   humanistic, 398, 414, 443, 445–46
   intellectual, 299, 401–6, 446
   leisure and, 409, 412
   metaphorical definition of, 413
   modern, 275
   moral, 402
   "physical culture," 399
   plenitude of, 409
   Scholastic, 9
   scientific, 30
   structural part of, 402, 406, 408, 411–12
   work and, 408, 410, 412, 413

da Vinci, Leonardo, 13, 17
death, 29, 39, 157–58, 163, 179, 199, 212, 226, 322, 346, 351, 434–35
de Bonald, Louis, 276
Delacroix, Eugène, 13
democracy, 6, 133, 285, 302, 337, 347, 374–75n13, 378, 391, 421, 429, 438
   Germany, 430
   practice, 392, 394
   revolution, 380–81, 389, 392
   state, 303, 395, 416
dependability, 206, 222–23, 229, 234, 241, 244, 246, 249, 254, 256, 260, 318, 329, 333, 422
Descartes, René, 8, 77, 131, 133, 134, 141, 191, 239n3, 327, 407, 443
desire, 51, 67, 71–72, 120, 139, 173–74, 181, 185, 193, 201, 209, 217, 268, 296, 310–12, 322, 334, 346, 377, 437, 447
   determinate, 211–12, 218
   for happiness, 182, 186, 194, 207, 278
   infinity of, 186, 386–87
   movement of, 152–53
   for wealth, 385–86
determinism, 30–31, 128, 147, 160, 176, 193, 196, 198, 209, 219–20n4, 274
disorder, 31, 135, 176, 185, 192, 233, 270, 291, 307, 310, 354, 391, 413, 423
   and freedom, 176, 214
disposition, 56, 70, 88, 90, 129, 138, 161, 232, 236, 246, 252, 274, 279, 283n6, 297, 338, 367, 385, 397, 408, 433, 440
   defined, 68–69
   good, 160, 244, 254–56
   habitual, 69, 222, 254, 197
   objective, 254–55
   psychological, 90, 111, 258
   stable, 69, 222–23, 236
   subjective, 170, 253, 254–55, 260
   workmanlike, 354, 412

distinction, 32, 121, 129, 157, 182, 264, 302, 311, 367, 429
 between absolute and relative, 227
 between achievements and structural foundation of culture, 397
 between administration and government, 366–67
 between civilization and culture, 400–401
 between collective and individual guilt, 225
 between common and individual good, 376
 between common and proper sensible, 115
 between desire and need, 377
 between enunciation and judgment, 94n3
 between essential and most essential function of authority, 339
 between existential and qualitative readiness, 242
 between freedom of choice and terminal freedom, 5
 between idea and thing, 77
 between immanent and transitive action, 324n2
 between intransitive and transitive action, 56
 logical, 60
 between logical and psychological, 320
 between nature and use, 225
 between object and thing, 79–94
 between positive and transcendent system of truth, 265, 379
 real, 61, 70, 113
 between right and wrong use, 225
 between satisfaction and service, 377
 between society and state, 295
 between socio-ethical and sociology, 369
divorce, 50, 316
doubt, 34, 38, 41, 47, 84, 214, 216, 289, 433

Duhem, Pierre, 117
duty, 11, 16–17, 27, 102, 143, 156, 182, 268, 278, 287, 294, 296, 298, 343, 349, 381, 391, 430
Dwelshauvers, Georges, 210

economics, 367, 372n2, 381, 383, 491
 crisis, 431
 cycle, 394
 justice, 6, 376–95
 liberalism, 391, 437
 life, 256, 319, 391, 395, 442
 organization/planning, 375–76, 422
 relations, 360, 421
 "science," 393
 system, 381, 390
Eddington, A. S., 177
effects, 17, 67, 70, 96, 126, 142, 162, 184, 193, 195, 252, 299, 322–23, 382, 388–89, 394, 398–99, 427, 407, 433
 and cause, 66, 106, 197
 immanent and transitive, 56, 62, 72, 74
 multiplicity of, 7, 119, 202, 215
 proper, 102, 161, 206, 345, 370, 427
efficient cause. See under cause
Einstein, Albert, 239, 370
Emerson, Ralph Waldo, 255
emotions, 65, 124, 159–60, 199, 202, 203, 213, 218, 222, 227, 230–31, 234, 245, 253, 255, 259, 311, 323, 341
empiricism, 5, 14, 33, 39, 42, 46, 60, 108, 121, 125, 132, 135, 144, 238, 269, 278
empiriological science, 6, 36–37, 39, 115, 294
ends, 62, 68, 72, 91, 120, 140, 153, 154, 174, 196, 199, 199n3, 204, 206, 227, 229, 257, 291, 300, 308, 343, 345, 355, 368, 378, 385, 430, 438–39
 and means, 189, 199–200n3, 335, 427
 final/last, 27, 50, 73, 182–83, 187–92, 207, 271–72
 of a free agent, 26, 43

of law, 328, 334–35
particular, 73
primary, 428
proper, 233
of work, 354
See also goals
English, 111, 122, 123, 236
enlightenment, 128, 345, 393
entities, 77–78, 80, 92, 122, 443
Epicureanism, 7, 116, 176–78
epistemology, 12, 30, 79, 80, 82, 135, 141, 147, 163, 224, 264, 275, 277
equality, 37, 168, 324, 350, 373n5, 377–82, 388–90, 394–95, 417, 429
essence, 11, 33, 35, 46, 49, 51, 55–57, 61, 63–64, 67, 83, 89, 104, 120, 154, 161, 191, 194, 196, 264, 274, 277, 318, 343, 383, 393, 411, 438
   of authority, 341
   of freedom/free will, 176, 193
   of good, 194–95
   of humanism, 300
   of intellect, 108
   of justice, 76
   of liberalism, 264, 274, 277
   of logic, 411
   of multitude, 185
   of object, 84
   of subject, 176
   of wrong, 168
eternal, 9, 13, 27, 34, 120, 129, 269, 389, 436
ethicalness, 49, 133, 157, 200, 318, 367
   excellence, 161, 180
   neutrality, 145–47, 377
   philosophy, 131, 162
   point of view, 232
   principles and rules, 258, 278
   socio-ethical, 352, 354, 368–69, 371, 372n2
   thought, 240, 283n5
   unethicalness, 156, 261
ethics, 32, 49, 89, 187, 231, 240–41, 265, 277, 279, 280, 281, 287, 369, 381
   Christian, 50–51
   logic subordinated to (Pierce), 227
   natural, 27, 50

politics and, 6, 132, 174
practical, 277–78
rational, 50–51
theory of, 231, 234
of the worker, 359–63, 367–68
See also moral philosophy
Ethiopian war, 11, 416, 427, 431, 441
Euclid, 29, 236–37, 361
evil, 43, 164, 294, 308, 310, 387, 426, 434, 439–42
   choice, 200
   intrinsically, 385
   and joy, 184
   Marxist philosophy of, 421–22
   moral and physical, 102, 148
   mystery of, 135
   problem of, 143
   theory of, 121
   See also under good
exchange, 353, 377, 382, 384, 393–95
   just, 168, 381, 386, 390
   not real, 386
   unequal, 378–79, 381, 389, 391–92
existence, 46, 47, 55–57, 60–66, 72, 78, 83, 101, 104, 108, 111, 124, 125, 137, 146, 148, 162, 272, 310, 316, 321, 343, 361, 362, 400, 408, 440, 443, 444
   actual, 121–22
   come/brought into, 51, 197, 204, 322, 332, 350
   concrete, 9, 100
   of God, 174
   infinite, 109, 297
   logical, 105
   objective, 76, 77, 90, 91
   physical, 58, 74, 77
   real, 91, 93, 121
   second, 59, 90, 121
existential, 9, 74, 77, 110, 130, 147
   condition, 49, 51
   judgment, 35, 36, 38, 39
   order, 78, 98
   predetermination, 72–73
existential readiness, 8, 242, 246–51, 256, 261. See also qualitative readiness

existing, 33, 43, 83, 144, 165, 204, 272
  act of, 98, 111, 159, 161–62
experience, 29, 33, 35, 47, 64, 75,
    86–87, 102, 122, 178, 189, 191,
    211, 213, 225, 232, 276, 294, 299,
    315, 308, 319, 330, 352–53, 366,
    378, 388, 403, 412, 420, 422, 431,
    436, 438, 445–46
  aesthetic, 16
  childhood, 265, 280
  common, 24–26, 37–42, 184, 269, 301
  daily, 238
  data, 24, 34
  immediate, 129, 161
  moral, 16, 182
  mystical, 154
  ordinary, 115, 214
  philosophical, 25–26, 39–40
  scientific, 39–40, 42, 116, 142
  sense, 14, 24, 26, 115–17, 121, 125–29, 265
  world of our experience, 37, 45, 98, 108, 110, 281, 383
explanation, 24, 51–52, 106, 117, 125, 132, 135, 158, 162, 164, 166, 177, 179, 187, 238, 248, 370, 444
exploitation, 143, 287, 319, 363–65, 373–74n9, 377, 379–81, 392, 395, 412, 421, 436

fact, 11, 23, 33, 89, 117, 144–48, 173, 179, 183, 193, 202, 209, 254, 268, 281, 299, 323, 328, 383, 386, 388, 420–21, 424, 433, 435, 438, 440, 442
  common/vulgar, 24–26, 35, 37–39, 45, 76
  of change, 34, 38, 60–62
  of existence, 38
  formulation of, 35–36
  illusory, 39–40
  moral, 26, 42–43
  of obligation, 114
  of order, 114
  philosophical, 24–26, 34, 36–40, 42, 45

  of plurality, 38
  probable, 41, 42
  psychological, 64, 135–36
  scientific, 24–25, 36–40, 45, 129–30
  social, 314, 334, 370
  theory of, 42, 316
  typology of, 24, 26, 36, 45
faculty, 56–57, 59, 69–70, 129, 204, 270–71, 403, 427
faith, 6, 12, 48–50, 164, 169, 176, 255, 351, 419, 433–34, 445
family, 155–56, 258–89, 278, 286–88, 303n2, 308, 317, 319, 335, 348, 353, 360, 381, 385, 390, 411
fascism, 416, 417, 420, 422, 430
Fermi, Enrico, 281
Final Cause. *See* cause
finality, 114, 141, 189, 204, 247–48, 257, 284n9, 302, 438–39, 443
force, 11, 109, 164, 186, 192, 194, 207–8, 215, 235, 245, 251, 258, 268, 296–97, 308, 313, 318, 319, 375, 392, 421, 427–36
  active, 153
  of authority and liberty, 424
  of error, 273
  of exploitation, 380, 436
  external, 158
  ideological, 353
  inhibiting, 218
  legal, 428
  nonrational, 218
  right-wing, 417
  of truth, 442
  unconscious, 219–20n4
  See also violence
formal cause. *See under* cause
form, 23, 28–29, 33, 36, 42, 45, 47, 51, 59, 78, 95, 118, 132, 134–36, 153, 181, 185, 189, 197, 205, 208–9, 212, 217, 246, 269, 283, 297–98, 310–11, 317, 341, 369, 392, 393, 415, 427
  of action, 122, 158–59
  of being, 55, 110–11, 407
  of common good, 349–50
  determined, 72–73, 210

formless and unformed, 178, 215, 253, 255
of happiness, 182–83
of intending, 338–39, 346
of last end, 190–91
of life, 46, 55–57, 104
logical, 20, 82, 258
and matter, 68, 75–77, 123, 199–200n3, 331, 349–51
scientific, 40, 41, 143
of sociability, 218, 312
fortitude. *See* courage
Fourier, Joseph, 241, 245, 255
France, 3, 4, 11, 367, 416–18, 431–32, 436
freedom, 31, 33, 62, 132, 194, 198–99, 263, 265–66, 285, 298, 315, 341, 343, 350, 392, 424, 432
as active and dominating indifference, 196, 202–3, 214–16, 293, 344
authority and order, 176, 269, 271, 301, 347
autonomy, 269–72, 290
causes of, 46, 217
community, 108–9, 352
determination and indetermination, 78, 176, 178, 193, 202, 204, 249, 274
Epicurean indetermination, 7, 176
and equality, 379, 381
from exploitation, 380, 395
human freedom (see *under* humanity)
indifference of judgment, 204–5, 213, 215, 217
of the intellect, 273–84, 397
life of, 219–20n4, 419
spontaneity, 193, 286, 297
as superdetermination, 6, 173–74, 196, 200n4, 202, 209, 214
suppression of, 137, 139, 219–20n4
terminal, 5, 269–71
theory of, 147, 177, 212, 296
use of, 26, 43, 270, 286, 354, 369, 418, 446
voluntariness, 178–83, 219n2
from work, 354, 410, 411, 413

freedom of choice, and free will, 5–8, 21nn14–15, 44–47, 65, 67, 137–38, 147, 167, 174–75, 192–94, 196, 199–200n3, 200n4, 201, 203–5, 208–9, 212–15, 219n2, 219–20n4, 249, 269–71, 290, 308
free will as active and dominating indifference, 7, 196, 202–3, 215–16, 296, 344
French Revolution, 3, 327, 391, 417, 429, 431
friend, xiii, 3, 10, 11, 19n5, 91, 94n3, 120, 124, 150, 165, 179–80, 189, 193, 246–47, 252, 254, 257, 318–19, 381, 408, 434, 443
friendship, 17, 50, 69, 175, 280, 339, 351, 353, 381, 434

Galilei, Galileo, 238, 282, 406, 443
genus, 76–78, 96, 115, 128, 158, 181, 210, 218, 342
Germany, 19n5, 268, 367, 417–18, 430–31
Gilson, Étienne, 5, 27, 48
goals, 20n9, 73, 91, 174, 199, 206–8, 223, 292, 332, 378, 396, 417, 418, 422. See also ends
God, 4, 7, 20n9, 48, 49, 132, 219–20n4, 271, 276–77, 283n5, 294, 309, 373, 431, 445
and analogical discourse, 97, 101, 106
and angels, 73, 98, 110
being (*esse*) of, 57, 71, 96, 440
conservation of, 57, 62, 71
creative action of, 57, 71
"definition" of, 113
designated by, 335, 348
desire to know, 114, 145, 186
divinized by, 153
existence of, 174, 268, 280
for the sake of, 286, 296, 298
freedom and liberty of, 429
goodness of, 74, 101, 440
identity of "to be" and "to know" of, 57–58, 110, 113–14
image of, 131, 216, 297
infinity of, 101–2

God (*cont.*)
  intellect of, 97, 110, 113, 327
  as last end, 189, 191
  law of, 112, 191
  life of, 53, 57, 73, 104
  mother of, 102
  omniscience of, 60
  perfection of, 57, 73, 101–2, 104, 106
  will and love of, 113, 327
Gompers, Samuel, 374n13
Gonseth, Ferdinand, 414n8
good, 7, 69, 71–72, 89, 96, 100, 119–20, 196, 206, 223, 253, 296, 301, 342, 393
  Absolute and supreme, 4, 278, 309, 440
  common good (*see* common good)
  comprehensive, 173–75, 181, 192, 201–3, 207–8, 212, 213–14, 219n2, 310
  created, 189, 191, 200n4
  disposition, 160, 244, 254
  economic, 376, 378, 413
  and evil, 43, 68, 201, 243, 257
  goodness and nongoodness, 193–94, 202, 208
  greatest of the greatest number, 312, 335, 422
  and happiness, 187, 189, 192
  inclination to, 144–45
  infinite, 310
  as man, 226, 232, 256–57, 260, 262
  for man, 132, 144, 192, 200n4, 207–8, 224, 248, 258, 264, 292–93, 321, 357, 359–60, 370, 405
  of moral virtue, 148, 180, 189, 251, 256, 270
  not in mathematical entities, 141, 443
  particular, 193–95, 200n4, 201–3, 207–9, 213–14, 274
  social, 341
  surplus of, 194–95
  use, 26, 43, 133, 147, 221–22, 227–34, 286, 405
  will, 50, 138, 154, 159, 229, 233, 288, 346, 350–51, 387
  of worker, 413

government, 302–3, 311, 318, 327, 332–33, 337, 347, 356, 366–67, 370, 382, 390, 416, 417, 421–23, 428, 436, 445
  civil, 321, 380
  political, 367, 374–75n13, 380
  of self, 300–301, 374n12
Goya, Francisco, 13
Gurian, Waldemar, 19n5

habit, 26, 88, 211, 220n4, 249, 252, 254, 262, 297, 384, 395, 439
  vs. *habitus*, 222–24, 234–39, 241–42, 406–7
  involuntary, 223, 235, 242
  mental, 24, 236, 238, 246, 250
  power of, 190, 296
  subjective, 223, 236–37, 242, 250–51
habitus, 5, 50, 173, 223–24, 234–39, 241–42, 246, 254, 299–300, 407–9, 411, 413
happiness, 6, 181–87, 189, 192, 194, 207, 254, 277, 363, 421, 424
Heraclitus, 34
heroic faith, 419, 433–34
Hilbert, David, 238, 239n4
history, 9, 10, 29, 112, 140, 164, 176, 187, 192–93, 265, 269, 276, 283n4, 285, 295, 316, 318, 326, 333, 364, 370, 379, 407, 410, 420, 432, 435, 436, 440, 433, 445
  of culture, 275
  of economic life, 385
  of idealism, 77
  of ideas, 16, 32, 365, 438
  of labor relations, 441
  of mankind, 165, 362, 416, 418, 444
  of modern times, 380
  of morals, 418, 442
  of philosophy, 25, 26, 39, 49, 79, 234–35, 263
  of sciences, 156, 250, 282, 406
  of socialism, 367
  of voluntarism, 328
Hitler, Adolf, 268, 431–32
Hobbes, Thomas, 131, 407

Holmes, Oliver Wendell, Jr., 282
human action, 51, 106, 137, 154, 156, 162, 168, 187, 206, 223, 234, 255, 328–29, 333–34, 356, 360, 366, 373n7, 444
human life, 119, 144–45, 157, 185, 199, 241, 257, 274, 277–78, 287, 300, 319, 371, 388–89, 402, 408–9
human nature, 4, 26, 112, 130, 133, 135, 144, 146, 186, 224, 249, 257, 260, 263, 266, 267, 337, 444, 445
humanism, 9, 16, 181, 182, 186, 300, 398, 414, 443–46
humanity, 131, 141, 277, 389, 443, 445
   action (*see* human action)
   affairs of, 28, 133, 177, 199, 254, 260, 327–29, 418, 444
   appetite/desire and will, 71, 108, 138, 139, 182, 186, 216, 272, 286, 399
   aspiration, 20n9, 144–45, 182, 184–85, 223
   and being, 4, 132, 155, 173–74, 227, 256–57, 260, 308, 327, 397, 418
   community, 263, 317, 353, 418
   condition of, 50, 133, 245, 308, 436
   dependability, 234, 246, 255
   effort, 182, 162, 364, 367
   excellence, 249–251, 288, 361, 363
   freedom, 5, 50, 133, 146–47, 173–200, 217, 354, 369, 418, 446
   goals and purpose, 28, 133, 155, 223, 300, 363
   and intelligence, 59, 61, 71, 73
   knowledge, 108, 127, 129, 150, 282
   labor, 300, 353, 389, 393–94
   life (*see* human life)
   mind, 13, 49, 69, 152, 187, 197, 205, 214, 238, 275–76, 289
   nature (*see* human nature)
   needs, 232, 260–61, 300–301, 373–74n9, 374–75n13, 377, 387–89, 394, 405, 409–10, 418
   reason and will, 201–20
   society, 145, 148, 330, 336n4, 339, 371, 378, 421
   soul, 11, 15, 137–38, 222, 228–29 (*see* soul)
   superhuman virtue, 394
   use, 50–51, 133, 146, 148, 163, 221–34, 313, 370
Hume, David, 236, 250–51, 407, 414n5
Hutchins, Robert M. 402, 404–5

idea, 78, 111, 124
   clear and distinct (Descartes), 116
   and object, 72, 85, 11
   as representation, 77, 95, 98, 111, 125
   sensorial and *species sensibilis*, 126
   and thing, 77, 83, 125
idealism, 77, 124, 143–44, 257
imagination, 44, 47, 120, 125–26, 135, 138, 146, 176, 192, 197, 199, 204, 210–11, 257, 295, 377, 390, 395
inclination, 145, 210, 257–61, 271, 278, 281, 286, 290, 344
   correct judgment by and knowledge by, 164–68, 170, 259
   dependable and sound, 235, 318, 331, 333
   of nature, 133, 144, 254
   of the heart and love, 153–54, 165–66, 214, 291
   of virtue and virtuous will, 153–54, 160, 167, 262
   See also tendency
indetermination, 7, 176–78, 194, 196, 199, 202–3, 209, 214–16, 271, 387
individualism, 283n6, 292–93, 312, 327, 334–35, 362, 378, 422, 442
industry, 3, 139, 187, 232, 277, 299–302, 303n2, 360, 362–63, 366, 371, 374–75, 377, 394–95, 397, 441, 443
instinct, 118, 153, 159, 164, 188, 189, 202, 211, 213, 258, 267, 311, 330
intellect, 67, 108, 113, 125, 209, 412, 413
   angelic, 85
   culture, 299, 401–3, 406, 446
   divine, 97, 109, 112, 326
   freedom, 263–84, 397
   habitus, 300, 406–8, 411
   as immanent action, 37, 71
   interpretation and reading, 36, 38–39, 41

intellect (*cont.*)
   and judgment, 65, 83, 117
   object, 35, 65, 83
   and sense, 126
   virtues, 46, 236, 397, 402–6
intention, 58, 70, 83, 94n3, 97–98, 297
Italian Fascism, 416, 430, 431, 441

James, William, 231, 236, 239n2
Jeans, James, 176
John of St. Thomas, 7, 21n18, 29, 100, 114n1, 170n2
John of the Cross, 102
joy, 17, 69, 71, 120, 183–86, 207, 213, 217, 235, 280, 311, 435
judgment, 117, 129, 133, 143, 163, 180, 204, 218, 253, 297, 318, 340–42, 425–26, 430
   of animal intelligence, 135, 211–13
   by cognition and rational, 87, 159, 166, 168, 213
   defined, 83
   existential and factual, 35–36, 38, 39
   free, 196, 201, 205, 213
   identity of object and thing in, 83, 86–87
   by inclination, 164–66, 168, 170, 331
   indeliberate, 214, 217
   indifference of, 201–3, 206–9, 213–16, 274
   instinctive, 118, 211
   judicative synthesis, 83, 86–87
   moral, 26, 43, 149, 163, 408
   practical, 153–54, 158–59, 166, 196, 212, 298, 331, 349, 424, 426
   prudential, 13, 154, 160, 242, 258, 260, 426
   sensorial, 83, 129
   ultimate practical, 154, 158–59, 189, 194–95, 331
justice, 43, 49–51, 69, 76, 170, 181, 184, 198–9, 203, 219–20n4, 247, 262, 319, 347, 384, 435
   divine name of, 106, 109, 429
   economic, 6, 376–95
   equal, 436, 432
   essential nature of, 326
   in exchange, 168, 390
   natural, 167
   rule of, 168, 318, 382, 427
   sense of, 246, 260, 318
   truth and, 109, 418–19, 434
   virtue and *habitus* of, 234, 244, 251, 256, 261, 405

Kant, Immanuel, 134, 249, 410
Khrushchev, Nikita, 374n12
Kierkegaard, Søren, 170, 259
Klubertanz, George, 13
knowledge, 5–6, 8, 30, 69, 85, 89, 91, 122, 156–57, 185, 239n4, 242, 250, 264, 267–68, 300, 309, 313, 344–45, 351–52, 367, 403, 440, 445
   affective and connatural, 151, 153–54,164, 167, 170
   angelic, 80
   definition of, 76
   divine, 106, 110
   of fact, 37, 43
   human, 4, 5, 108, 127, 129, 150, 282
   incommunicable, 163, 167, 265, 280
   as immanent action, 55–78, 322
   mathematical, 29, 141
   metaphysical, 75, 98, 110, 136, 289
   moral, 137, 149–70
   objective and extramental, 55, 58–59, 79, 83, 87, 90, 97, 111
   of persons and society, 131–48
   physical and sense, 115–17, 140, 145, 314
   rational and philosophical, 48–49, 150, 152, 343
   salvation through, 142–43
   scientific, 29, 142, 154, 236, 246, 276
   of the soul, 133, 134–35
   theory of, 77, 91, 110, 257
   of truth, 83, 84, 297, 413
Kuic, Vukan, 19nn6–7, 239n1, 352, 373

labor, 299–301, 353, 359, 370, 373nn6–7, 378–80, 395, 422, 441
   human, 389, 393–94
   intellectual, 65, 205
   manual, 299, 356, 398, 412

movement and organized, 302, 352, 394
union, 302, 367, 394
Lafayette, Marquis de. *See* Motier, Gilbert du
law, 59, 81, 118, 127, 132, 138, 147, 153, 155, 162, 185, 190, 205, 240, 249, 270–71, 281–82, 290–91, 301, 317, 365, 378, 379, 384, 400, 446
  of abstraction, 100, 106
  of analogical order, 110, 198
  of causality, 61, 176
  definition of, 325, 328, 335–36
  natural (*see* natural law)
  positive, 278, 427–28
  of progress, 262, 269, 316, 425
League of Nations, 416, 419, 428, 430–31
Legendre, Adrien Marie, 236
Leibniz, Gottfried Wilhelm, 134, 410
leisure, 354, 370, 398, 409–12
Lenin, Vladimir, 367
liberalism, 263–65, 273–79, 319, 342, 361–62, 368, 371, 376–77, 381, 390–91, 421–25, 429, 436–37, 442
liberty, 6, 73, 102, 133, 199, 219–20n4, 268, 270, 287–88, 311, 341, 345, 373n5, 377, 382, 392, 417, 434–37
  and authority, 97, 108, 337, 347, 424
  divine name of, 108, 269, 429
  goddess of, 429
  and necessity, 204
  negative, 285
  progress of, 424
life, 17, 71–73, 102, 121, 129, 135, 186, 204, 229, 303, 311, 312, 321, 382, 393, 400, 435
  animal, 5, 41, 104, 199, 311
  biological vegetative, 74, 104, 108, 270
  Christian, 351
  common, 273, 294, 321, 342, 353, 425
  community, 295–96, 314–15, 319, 353
  contemplative, 264, 292–93, 362, 368, 398
  daily, 212, 269, 390
  divine and perfect, 57, 74, 104, 105
  economic, 251, 319, 391, 395, 442
  eternal, 120, 413, 446

  family, 287, 319, 353
  form of, 55, 57, 104
  of freedom, 219–20n4, 419
  human (*see* human life)
  of leisure, 410–12
  of the mind, 28, 125, 187, 281, 413
  moral, 240, 350, 381
  motionless, 104–5
  political and public, 264, 265, 279, 302, 314
  of self-motion, 104–5
  social, 148, 185, 272, 278, 282, 294–95, 300, 309, 320, 352, 389, 397, 401–2, 409, 436
  spiritual, 4, 61
Locke, John, 23, 373n7
logic, 4, 29, 33, 89, 105, 114, 163, 169, 177, 196, 259–61, 274, 276–77, 294, 318, 331, 402
  being of reason, 81, 88, 92
  definition of, 91, 227
  essence, 46, 411
  formal, 20n9, 258
  material, 21n18, 447
  properties, 81, 88, 92
  symbolic, 82, 330, 410
  term, 46, 90, 99, 102, 106, 121
loneliness. *See* solitude
Longfellow, Henry Wadsworth, 360
love, 72, 102, 120, 141, 152, 182, 212, 311, 314, 318, 320, 321, 322, 355, 409, 429, 436, 433
  "amor transit in conditionem objecti" (John of St. Thomas), 153, 170n2, 331
  of common good, 343, 345–46
  divine, 106, 113, 312, 439
  "free," 297, 386
  of freedom, 176
  and friendship, 339, 351, 353
  of God, 113
  intelligence becoming pupil of, 153
  for law, 290–91
  of truth, 8, 17, 264, 273, 349, 354, 367–69, 396, 413
Lowell, James Russell, 360, 373n6
Lucretius, 134, 177

Maistre, Joseph de, 276
man. *see* humanity
man and woman, 163, 261, 286, 296, 335
Maritain, Jacques, 27, 28, 48, 49, 51, 94n3, 150, 219, 250, 258, 291, 338, 400–401, 409, 417
  correspondence with, xi, 19n4
  friend of, 254, 257
  homage to, 9–12
  as mentor, 3, 5, 7, 12
marriage, 51, 168, 278, 286, 294, 296–97, 439
Marx, Karl, 58, 341, 359, 373n7
Marxism, 58, 76, 365–66, 374n12, 421
material cause. *See under* cause
materialism, 88, 177–78, 413
mathematics, 16, 27–29, 48, 49, 92–93, 95, 113, 132–33, 186, 233, 236–38, 239n4, 242, 275, 277, 281, 283n4, 327, 330, 363, 370, 378, 403–4, 210
  abstraction, 13, 141, 329, 443
  entities/objects, 92, 93, 443
  interpretation, 117, 141, 145, 444
  logic, 410
  physics, 23, 31
matter, 40, 120, 198, 248, 291, 297, 339, 340, 438
  contingent and necessary, 92
  and form, 68, 75–76, 110, 123, 185, 190–91, 200, 311, 326, 331, 349, 350–51
  of justice, 51, 160, 170, 428
  organic, 209
  practical, 343
  prime, 215–16
  transcendent, 265, 278, 282, 283n6, 295, 319
  of truth, 351
meaning, 9, 31, 47, 73, 95–96, 99–102, 106–7, 117, 120, 128, 136, 149, 163, 168, 181–82, 259, 267, 273, 276, 277, 280, 294, 301, 328, 336, 422, 439, 444
  of abstraction, 383
  of autonomy, 291, 302
  of axioms, 329
  of *bonum in communi*, 181
  of capitalization, 390
  of causal power, 61
  of culture, 399–401
  of experimental absolute, 130
  of force, 427
  of human life, 277
  of ideal type, 383
  of image of God in man, 13
  of last end, 189
  of law, 427
  of liberty, 436
  of myth, 419
  of natural science, 444
  of objectivity, 236
  of use, 225
  of value, 244, 254
  of virtue, 244, 254
  of words, 32, 422
means, 261, 421, 435
  as bearer of a form, 191, 199–200n3
  as intermediate end, 189–90
  ordered to a means, 385
  ordered to an end, 189–90, 335, 339, 345
  ordered to the common good, 187, 334, 344–45
  proper, 343, 427
  true and false, 199–200n3, 205, 270–71, 344–45, 356
measure of human action, 328–29, 334
mechanism, 116, 128, 139, 248–49, 257, 444
Megarians, 87
memory, 88, 90, 111, 119, 120, 124–27, 146, 150, 159, 192, 222, 228–29, 231–32, 239n2, 253
metaphysics, 20n9, 28, 97–98, 108, 110, 112, 131–32, 137, 279, 281, 289–90, 401, 440
  of contingency and necessity, 92
  experimental foundation of, 197
  of knowledge, 75
  of religion and theology, 187, 267, 276, 445
  See also ontology

Meyerson, Emile, 283n4
Michelangelo. *See* Buonarroti, Michelangelo
Mill, John Stuart, 134, 425
mind, 38, 39, 43, 47, 63, 65, 73, 83, 87, 112, 121, 150, 152, 154, 197, 206, 208, 238, 250, 252, 274, 281, 302, 397, 403, 407
  affective dimension of the, 171, 174
  angelic, 85
  assent of the, 205, 207, 276, 343
  conforming to reality, 84–85
  divine, 112
  human, 13, 49, 69, 152, 188, 197, 205, 214, 238, 275, 276, 289
  metaphysical, 34, 37, 44
  mind-independent, 79–80
  objects in the, 88–90, 126
  operation of the, 33, 100, 102, 354, 371
  philosophy of the, 132, 136
  and physical nature, 125–36
  reflection on itself, 80, 86, 111
  scientific, 24, 37, 44, 141, 283, 343
  and truth, 96, 273
Montaigne, Michel de, 245
moral philosophy, 27, 50–52, 149, 154–55, 161–64, 240, 243. *See also* ethics
morals, 12, 16, 47, 112, 146, 170, 176, 200, 221, 229–30, 285, 287–88, 290, 300, 339, 348, 351, 353–54, 367, 371, 376, 406, 439, 440
  axioms/principles, 242, 256, 257, 258, 416, 419
  character, 132, 252, 254, 255
  conscience, 313, 441–42
  debasement, 25, 161, 402
  and evil, 102, 148
  facts, 26, 42–43
  judgment, 26, 43, 149, 408
  knowledge, 137, 149, 152–67
  problem, 133, 166, 247
  psychology, 137–38, 199, 267
  truth, 268, 269, 397, 442
  virtue, 8, 69, 160, 234–35, 240–62, 350, 405

Morgan, Angela, 373n6
Motier, Gilbert du, 363
motionless activity, 57, 70, 105, 120
motive, 34, 176, 192–93, 195, 203, 219n4, 220, 242, 255, 378, 427
movement, 56, 71, 84, 88, 116, 120, 127, 153, 210, 211, 247–48, 271, 324n2, 359
  of aversion, 208
  of desire, 152–53
  labor, 352, 360, 367
  liberal, 273–74
  nonfree, 202, 213
  personalistic, 291–92, 302
  social, 363, 371
multitude, 69, 185, 198, 301, 313, 314, 323, 335, 338, 343, 426, 439
Mussolini, Benito, 11, 429, 431
mystery, 26, 28–29, 133, 147, 248, 274, 311, 433, 439
mysticism, 10, 102, 154, 362, 446
myth, 418–19, 432–34

Napoleon. *See* Bonaparte, Napoleon
natural law, 51, 98, 112–14, 133, 144–45, 151, 165–68, 243, 249, 258, 326–28, 331–35, 427–28, 431, 434, 444–45
natural science. 25, 36, 142, 146–47, 264, 444
nature, 24, 57, 59, 61, 63, 68, 72, 74, 89, 118, 135, 138, 140, 156, 172, 182–83, 198, 209, 216, 248, 271, 300, 319–20, 335, 356, 399, 422, 438, 444
  activity of defined, 56, 64
  of the common good, 312–13, 315
  defined, 291
  exploitation of, 363–65, 373–74n9
  God as author of, 106, 112–14
  goodness in, 255, 426
  human (*see* human nature)
  inclinations of, 144–45, 154
  laws of, 249, 269, 327–28, 254
  mathematical science of, 133, 141–42
  physical (*see* physical nature)

nature (*cont.*)
   of reason/rational, 37, 71, 187, 191, 311
   sensorial, 119, 123, 126–27
   teleology of, 187, 193
   and use, 220–22, 225–34, 255
   and use in social science, 145–47, 162–63
   of will/volitional, 47, 71, 181, 191, 311
   of work, 371, 378, 397–98
Nazism, 416–18, 420
necessity, 182, 214, 217, 241, 263, 297, 299, 332, 378, 388, 395, 397, 413, 425–26
   absolute, 49, 92, 130, 205, 320
   and contingency, 92, 430
   essential, 17, 49, 193, 350
   extreme, 166, 260, 318
   and freedom and liberty, 204, 270, 274
   mathematical, 275
   metaphysical, 185, 248
   natural, 147, 177
   objective, 15–16, 236–38, 251, 281, 406–9
   of principles, 49, 205, 275
   rational, 15, 275, 320, 330–31
   subjective, 222–23, 236, 251, 257, 407
   universal, 92, 332
Nef, John U., 19n6
Nietzsche, Friedrich, 181–83, 311
nominalism, 97, 100, 191

obedience, 296–98
   and disobedience, 270
object, 23, 28, 33, 45, 70–73, 91, 101, 124, 125, 153, 191, 195, 207, 210, 321, 427
   of appetite/desire, 120, 152, 159, 182, 186, 192, 310, 323, 385
   of choice/will, 181, 228–29, 216, 271
   of common action, 317, 321–11
   identity of object and thing, 75–76, 80–87
   of inclination, 184, 189, 259–60
   of logic/reason, 88–90, 92, 94n3, 121
   mathematical, 93, 443
   metaphysical, 34, 101, 277
   in the mind, 88–90, 91
   necessary, 200n4, 205, 299
   phenomenal, 83, 85
   physical presence of, 121–22, 126–28
   proper, 117, 127–29
   scientific, 69, 75, 206, 343, 445
   of sensation, 24, 34–36, 75, 83, 121–23, 127–28
   sense union with, vs. matter-form union, 75–76, 110, 122–23
   social, 143, 148
   of thought, 14, 24, 35–36, 63–65, 76, 83, 86, 90, 111, 122, 145, 154, 195, 196, 215, 250, 323, 407
   objectives, 55, 124, 145, 153, 169–70, 206, 250, 259–60, 275, 282, 322, 371, 372n2, 378
   determination, 71, 242
   existence, 76, 90, 91, 98, 111, 297
   goal, 223, 257
   habitus, 223, 252, 253–54
   laws, 282, 427
   necessity, 15–16, 236–38, 251, 406–9
   relation, 251, 312
   "transobjective," 80, 85–87
   type, 75, 123
   union, 59, 75–76, 97, 110, 116, 123, 126–27
objectivity, 77, 86, 124, 146, 236, 254
   and activity, 59–60
   of knowledge, 5, 58–59, 297
   "transobjectivity," 85–87
ontology, 33, 57, 64, 81, 98, 113, 117, 135, 214–15, 223, 376
   analysis, 115, 155
   "disontologized," 29
   nonontological, 186, 192
   See also metaphysics
opinions, 16–17, 33, 89, 117, 139, 205–6, 254, 287, 314, 320, 353, 392, 408, 418
   common, 15, 119, 203, 347, 263, 393
   "in my opinion," 10, 49, 227, 233–34, 245, 250
   See also beliefs

optimism, 28, 282, 420, 422, 438, 440, 442, 444
order, 12, 29, 38, 41, 37, 81, 85, 95, 97, 112, 159, 176, 184–85, 203, 285, 293, 297, 301
  and abstraction, 103–6
  analogical, 97, 110, 197
  of being, 63, 74, 77–78, 98, 100
  and disposition, 68–69
  of final causality, 190, 204, 292
  of formal causality, 104, 190, 204
  of inclination, 144, 182
  of intelligibility, 132, 308, 427
  international, 415–16, 419, 429, 443
  of law, 51, 144, 328
  of material causality, 73, 183
  moral, 200, 256, 258
  of nature, 59, 148, 271, 442
  political 5, 274
  and proportionality, 106–7
  right, 369, 425
  of salvation, 446
  social, 143, 255, 308, 369, 390
  supernatural, 444–45
  of thought, 153, 159
  of truth, 287, 294–95, 309, 319
  in universe, 37, 114
  of a whole, 252, 254
  of wisdom, 326, 355

Parmenides, 34, 365
Pascal, Blaise, 327, 410
passion, 61, 153
  "autonomic," 116–17, 123, 126
  "heteronomic," 116–17, 123
passivity, 73, 118, 120, 122, 215, 395, 439
  pure, 55, 59–60
Pasteur, Louis, 282
peace, 182, 186, 254, 311, 322, 349, 430, 435
Pegis, Anton P., 235, 336
Péguy, Charles, 419, 429
Peirce, Charles Sanders, 227
People's Front, 431
perception, 77, 84, 115, 128, 145, 147, 168, 178, 191, 207, 210, 247, 255, 311, 349

  of discrepancy between particular and universal good, 202–3, 213–14
  exhaustive and nonexhaustive, 85–86
  first principles/axioms, 205, 405, 445
  imperceptible and perceptible to the senses, 41–42, 45
perfection, 37, 38, 69, 102, 110, 118, 132, 140, 167, 180, 184, 185, 209, 229, 261–62, 272, 291, 293, 297, 341, 342, 350, 412, 425
  absolute, 101, 108–9
  of being, 61, 96, 111, 136, 186, 215
  certain, 166, 268
  final, 57, 70
  free, 203, 219–20n4, 270
  full, 96
  of God, 73, 96
  legal, 358, 386
  most perfect form, 56
  of order, 291, 413
  pure, 96–97, 269
  qualitative, 56, 70
  self-perfection, 5, 55, 57
  subject, 57, 71
  supreme, 57
  transcendental, 97, 108
person, 65, 199, 223, 230, 245–46, 252, 254, 287–88, 296, 302, 350–51, 372n2, 376, 424–25
  in authority, 340
  designated, 335, 348, 369
  and freedom, 285, 301
  good, 4, 301, 338
  personalism, 291–92, 301
  private, 345–46, 348–49, 379, 393
  public, 349
pessimism, 420–21, 439–40
phenomena, 36, 84–86, 136, 139, 177, 220, 238, 271, 400, 432
philosophy, 16–17, 29–30, 32, 47, 155, 233, 327, 329, 360, 389, 411–12, 418
  Christian, 12, 26–27, 48–50
  and common sense, 25–26, 39, 44–46, 60
  contemporary, xii, 5–6

philosophy *(cont.)*
  disagreements of, 15–16
  facts, 24, 34, 36–40
  history of, 25–26, 39, 79, 234–35, 263
  mechanistic, 257, 444
  method, 4, 23–52
  modern, 131, 133, 149, 240–41, 243, 368, 407
  nominal definition of, 25
  Plato's definition of, 264
  progress of, 40, 72, 234, 438
  and science, 5, 15, 26, 31, 33, 36–37, 40, 42, 134–35, 187, 191, 197, 236, 282
  of society, 148, 245, 401
philosophy of mind, and philosophical psychology, 9, 126, 134, 136. *See also* psychology
philosophy of nature, 25, 42, 131–32, 134, 136, 187, 197, 249, 444
philosophy of science, 31, 117, 249, 396
physical nature, 15, 73, 88, 97, 112, 125–26, 132, 142, 176, 248, 291, 364–66, 368–69, 371–72, 412, 427, 444
physical premotion, 66, 73
physics, 16, 23, 27, 29, 49, 92, 115, 116, 124, 134, 135, 140, 176–77, 196, 236, 289, 411, 444
Pieper, Josef, 354, 409
Plato, 4, 6, 13, 20n8, 27, 117, 134, 174, 203, 227, 236–37, 245, 255–57, 263, 264, 330, 370
pleasure, 183–85, 189–91, 193–94, 218, 229, 268–69, 301, 330, 389, 431
Poincaré, Henri, 239
political philosophy, 6, 12, 146, 151, 263, 285, 337
Polo, Marco, 400
positive psychology, 134–36, 138. *See also* psychology
positivism, 117, 187, 276, 283n4, 364
postulates, 33, 77, 143, 147, 176, 209, 275, 316, 329, 341, 371, 376, 389, 401, 403–4, 435, 442

potency, 59, 62–63, 65, 69, 96–97, 100, 104–5, 107, 194, 198
potentiality, 56, 59–60, 68, 102, 192, 196–97, 200n4, 214–15, 253, 255, 260, 400
practicality, 44–45, 162, 167, 207, 238, 241, 259, 264, 331, 367, 370
  and ethics and morality, 277–78
  historico-practical truth, 268–69
  and indifference, 201, 206, 208, 213, 274
  and judgment *(see* practical judgment)
  and knowledge, 5, 49, 150, 152, 343
  and knowledge of social science, 143–45
  and philosophy, 5, 6, 27, 49, 352
  practically practical knowledge, 6, 150, 418
  and proposition, 208, 267, 343
  and psychology, 136–37
  and science, 132, 136–37, 155, 163
  and thought, 50, 150–51, 154–56, 158–59, 161, 163
  and truth, 152, 343–44
  and wisdom *(see* practical wisdom)
practical judgment, 153, 159, 163, 166, 196, 202–4, 209, 215, 217–18, 298, 344, 424, 426
  last, 154, 159, 194, 331
practical wisdom, 4, 25, 152, 158, 169, 242, 295, 350, 404, 415, 418–19. *See also* prudence
pragmatism, 15, 227, 232, 280
predetermination, 72–73, 177
premises, 155, 166–67, 256, 258, 312, 331, 333
  absolute/axiomatic, 168, 205, 206, 329
  first/indemonstrable, 275, 329
  revealed, 11–12
presence, 33–34, 36, 37, 65, 85, 119–23, 127, 153, 208, 249, 270, 292
Pre-Socratics, 365, 418
principle, 135, 153, 173, 176, 211, 265, 270, 300, 316, 332, 338, 370, 385, 405

of actuality of the cause, 193–95, 197
of authority, 426
of autonomy, 393
of causality, 77, 284n9
of efficient causality, 45, 196–97
of equal justice, 432, 436
of essential causality and resemblance between cause and effect, 106, 197
of ethical neutrality, 146
of family life, 319
of final causality, 45
of free choice/freedom, 177, 214
of gravity, 248
of identity, 45, 49
of indeterminateness, 438
of materiality, 45
of noncontradiction, 46, 274
of otherness of the cause, 197
of rationality/sufficient reason, 45, 200n4
of subsidiarity, 377
of united action, 344–45
privacy, 260, 278, 307, 309, 312–13, 317, 333, 335, 345–46, 348–49, 351, 362, 377, 379, 393
production, 57, 62, 69, 71, 74, 119, 126, 209, 300, 322, 357, 378, 384, 388, 408
cost of, 386–87, 389–91, 393–94
progress, 14, 254, 271, 423, 429, 438, 440
of applied psychology/social science, 138, 140
in explanation, 51, 164
of freedom and liberty, 424
in moral conscience/natural law, 168, 442
of philosophy, 40, 42, 234
scientific, 142, 186
of society, 347, 427, 430
technical, 316, 441
property, 319, 386, 435, 437
essential, 70, 89
labor source of (Locke), 373n7
logical, 90, 121

private, 278, 286–87, 294, 377
theory of, 318, 373n5
of a thing, 40, 63, 173, 241, 247, 272, 403
proposition, 80, 89, 284n8, 318, 344
axiomatic, 45, 168, 275, 329–30, 403
of common sense, 44–45
contingent and necessary, 92, 332–33
demonstrated, 15, 45, 205, 280–81
philosophic/metaphysical, 16, 44–45, 265, 281, 289
practical, 208, 267, 343
scientific, 142, 283, 343
transcendental, 276, 294
verifiable, 276, 279, 281, 282, 294
Proudhon, Pierre-Joseph, 6, 359–60, 373, 377, 391–92, 425
prudence, 287, 350
and animal sagacity, 330
and authority, 426
incommunicability of, 163
and intellectual virtues, 402–6
judgment, 12, 153, 154, 160, 258, 260
legislative, 327, 333
and moral virtues, 162, 234, 246, 251, 387
political, 51, 133, 313, 318
See also practical wisdom
psyche. See soul
psychoanalysis, 168, 241, 254
psychology, 9, 81, 132, 146, 330
applied, 137–38, 139
facts, 64, 135
modern, 132, 234, 245, 254–55
moral, 137–38, 199
philosophical, 125, 136
positive, 134–38
reality, 88, 90, 124
subjective disposition, 111, 258–59
techniques, 230, 246
and unconscious, 219–20n4
See also philosophy of mind, and philosophical psychology
psycho-technology, 132, 227, 234, 241, 245
public powers, 390, 393, 395

qualitative readiness, 242, 246–47, 249, 252, 256. *See also* existential readiness
quality, 46, 56–57, 67–70, 99, 104, 122, 126, 155, 215, 236, 239n2, 246, 251–56, 268, 289, 350, 405, 407–8, 414n5
  intellectual, 299, 404, 406
  moral, 69, 146, 161, 402
  sense, 127–30
quantity, 56, 68, 99, 127, 194, 215

rationality, 112, 155, 187–88, 203, 251, 308, 327, 445
  analysis, 9, 86, 118, 407
  appetite, 135, 194, 201–2, 209
  apprehension of moral principles, 257–58
  communicability, 284n8, 338, 343–44
  determination, 15, 152, 205–6, 274
  ethics, 50, 51
  evidence, 29, 45, 167
  irrational/nonrational, 138, 159, 179, 188, 202, 203, 210–12, 214, 218, 258, 389
  knowledge, 48–49, 81, 258
  necessity, 15, 275, 330–31
  psychology, 9, 134, 136
  rationalization, 168
reality, 7, 102, 143, 236, 257, 434
  extramental, 55, 83
  of freedom/free will, 47, 219n4
  historical, 48, 273
  judgment and, 152, 159
  logical, 90
  mathematical, 239n4, 330
  mind and, 80, 85, 277
  object and, 85–86
  physical, 98, 110, 117, 130, 145
  psychological, 88, 124, 259
  social, 314, 323, 349
reason, 14, 135–36, 145, 188, 219n4, 271, 424–25, 445
  being of, 80–81, 88–94, 121, 127, 143
  intuitive, 403
  judgment of, 212, 213

  and law, 325, 331, 336
  practical, 331
  public, 246, 346, 397
  rule of, 300, 335
  sufficient, 24, 200
  and will, 5, 47, 71, 201, 326, 346
  work of, 166, 211, 328–29, 331, 333
Reed, Louis S., 374–75n13
Reichenbach, Hans, 239n3
relations, 65–66
  causal, 66, 96, 197, 209
  to common good, 327, 335, 350–51
  between fact and value, 316
  between form and matter, 123, 190
  between idea/object or thought and thing/reality, 77, 83, 84, 125, 277
  interdependent/interpersonal, 99, 262
  of man and woman, 163, 286, 296
  of man/nature to God, 112, 276
  of mathematics to reality, 93, 330
  of means to end, 190, 199–200n3
  between nature and use, 221, 231, 233–34
  predicamental/pure vs. transcendental/mixed, 104–5
  real, 93–94
  of reason, 93–94
  of sense to object, 127
  social, 143, 244
religion, 28, 31, 32, 187, 267, 276, 278–79, 283n6, 310, 395, 432
Rembrandt. *See* van Rijn, Rembrandt
Renouvier, Charles, 134, 274
representation, 14, 35, 43, 58, 76–77, 94n3, 118, 123, 125–26, 211, 420, 433
revolution, 169, 236, 247, 313, 359–60, 382, 389, 392, 433, 437
  democratic, 380, 381
  French Revolution, 6, 327, 391, 421, 429, 432
  Russian Revolution, 367
right, and wrong, 26, 43, 50–51, 145–46, 148, 162, 168, 181, 221, 225, 251, 255, 257–58, 260, 313, 381

rights, 11, 169, 226, 244, 246, 247, 256, 268, 269, 318, 326
   action, 26, 241, 255, 343
   desire, 159–60
   form vs. matter, 350–51
   human, 287, 294, 319, 372n2, 424, 432, 436
   inclination, 164–65, 167–68, 260–61
   method, 15, 17
   natural, 165, 167–68
   to private property, 286, 392
   of society, 277–78
   use, 132–33, 161–62, 222, 225, 230–31, 250, 354, 398, 405
Romanticism, 245, 254, 299, 364
Ross, W. D., 403–5
Rousseau, Jean-Jacques, 241, 245, 327
Rubens, Peter Paul, 13, 17
rules, 28, 133, 138, 154, 265, 277, 278, 279, 281, 291, 301, 302, 303, 310, 326, 330–32, 334–35, 348–49, 353, 358, 384, 386–87, 393, 412, 414, 424, 425
   of action, 146, 155, 157, 167, 234, 294, 311, 318, 328–29, 333–34, 343, 382, 406, 426–27
   of civil community, 333
   of ethics and morality, 180, 227, 278
   of justice, 168, 318, 382, 427
   of law, 278, 280, 290, 328, 332–33, 427–28
   of method, 15, 407

Saint-Simon, Henri de, 21n16, 363, 366
Saint-Simonism, 363–67, 371
Scheler, Max, 292
Scholasticism, 9, 10, 19n4, 24, 410
science, 23, 41, 73, 172, 205, 219–20n4, 246, 250, 343, 404, 407–8
   empiriological, 36, 39, 294
   as a *habitus*, 236, 238
   history of, 156, 250, 406
   interpretation, 31, 117, 145, 236, 249, 396
   mathematical, 31, 133, 283n4, 330, 443
   modern, 26, 116, 131–32, 141, 236
   natural, 25, 36, 127, 132, 133, 141–47, 264, 444
   philosophical, 32, 49, 115, 134, 136
   and philosophy, 32–33, 40, 42, 44–45
   physical, 116–17, 121, 140, 191
   positive, 28, 30, 31, 115, 134–37, 187, 281–82
   practical, 132, 136, 155
   social, 132, 137, 140–47, 194, 314, 353, 444
   of the soul, 134–36
   speculative, 154–55, 333
   theoretically practical, 162
scientism, 31–32, 42, 138
self, 174, 290, 296, 297, 298, 425
   actualization of, 55, 57, 104
   consciousness of, 110, 397
   determination of, 5, 7, 286
   evidence of, 24, 154, 275
   government of, 300–301, 374n12
   mastery of, 5, 217, 286
   motion of, 104–5
   perfection of, 5, 55
sensation, 24, 34–38, 41–42, 75, 80, 83, 88, 115–30, 210, 215, 330
sense, 24, 37–38, 72, 122, 123, 125, 126–28, 129
   as autonomic passion, 119
   common sense (*see* common sense)
   experience, 14, 116, 117, 121, 265
   external object of, 75, 83
   judgment of, 202, 213
   organ, 16, 112
   truthfulness of, 117, 130
sensibility, 23, 36, 37, 38, 55, 61, 76, 78, 126, 132, 155, 311, 333
   common sense, 115, 117, 128
sex, 144, 164, 168, 229
Shakespeare, William, 249, 400, 445
Simon, Anthony "Tony" O., xi–xiii, xivn4, 17n1, 372n3, 449
skepticism, 38, 84–85, 116, 407, 429
slavery, 373n9, 379–81
Smith, Adam, 375n15

sociability, 163, 185, 245, 254, 280–81, 322, 349, 356, 359, 370
  activity, 368
  causality, 143–44
  Darwinism, 286
  fact, 314, 334
  group, 354, 369–71, 424, 433
  leisure, 411–12
  life, 278, 282, 294–95, 300, 309, 314, 320, 392, 401, 409, 436
  order, 143–44, 255, 308, 369, 389
  progress, 424, 430
  relations, 143, 244, 442
  thinker, 143, 146, 199, 370, 424
  unity, 338, 424
  whole, 218, 255, 320
social engineering, 132–33, 144, 241, 244–45, 255
socialism, 360, 364, 367, 391, 395, 420, 433
social sciences, 143–48, 199, 314, 353, 444
society, 131, 145, 148, 157, 165, 219–20n4, 266, 278–79, 289–91, 307–9, 345–46, 401, 421
  civil, 283n6, 286, 294, 319, 321–24, 334, 336, 342
  community vs. partnership, 321–24
  contemplatives in, 292–93, 361–62, 368
  debt to, 360–63, 367–68
  prudence of, 426
  science of, 132–33, 141, 143, 147
  service to, 354, 356–59, 361–62, 369
  technological, 15, 142, 302
  temporal interest in transcendent, 282, 294–95, 317
  "wealth leaks out of" (Proudhon), 358, 360, 367, 377, 386, 391, 394
  wisdom of, 287, 295, 319, 387
Socrates, 4, 174, 242, 246, 263
solitude, 17, 32, 285, 322, 362, 434
Sorel, Georges, 434
soul, 11, 15, 67, 132, 137
  common good contained in, 308–9
  divinized, 153
  "is in a way all things" (Aristotle), 75–76
  just soul, 62, 318
  knowledge of, 133–35
  part of, 126, 136, 203
  powers of, 64, 68, 133, 146, 191–92, 222, 228–29, 234
  science of, 134–36, 138
  in a state of grace, 62
Soviet Union, 366, 417, 418
space utility, 357, 384
Spanish Civil War, 10, 11, 417
species, 45, 63, 68, 76, 89, 99, 103, 105, 115, 116, 126–27, 158, 188, 210, 280, 317, 342, 364, 427, 439
Spinoza, Baruch, 16, 92
spirit, 9, 14, 19n4, 31–32, 34, 56, 69, 71, 177, 181, 229, 269, 270, 275, 278–79, 285, 290, 297, 303, 311, 323, 373n6, 413, 421, 424, 430, 434, 445–46
  created, 74, 98, 110
  of French Revolution, 429, 432
  pure, 61, 73
  scientific, 313, 356
  of society, 313, 36
  See also angels
spontaneity, 10, 38, 62, 63, 64, 84, 91, 166, 193, 194, 196, 205, 219n2, 249, 252, 271, 279, 296, 333, 334, 369, 374, 400, 401, 422, 433
  absolute, 47, 73
  freedom of, 286, 297
  natural, 207, 241, 244–45
state, 127, 225, 285, 302, 314, 336n4, 376
  of affairs, 81, 119, 141, 184, 276, 365, 388
  of character, 221, 234–35, 242, 252, 405
  Christian, 11–12, 49
  civil, 51, 279, 294–96, 308
  democratic, 303, 395, 416, 421
  fallen, 27, 308
  of grace, 62
  intervention, 377, 395, 422

management, 395
of perfection, 272, 292
of philosophy, 11–12, 16, 48–19
of potency, 69, 100, 112
of real achievement, 183–84
socialist, 374n12, 391, 393, 395, 433
totalitarian, 139, 292, 366, 416, 420, 421, 436–37
"withering away of," 367, 374n12, 391, 420
Stoics, 27, 102, 181, 261–62
subject, 34, 46, 57, 60, 68, 72, 75, 79, 272
acting, 61, 66–67, 70–71, 104, 120, 324n2
"in der Subjektivität liegt der Wahrheit" (Kierkegaard), 170, 260
intersubjective, 30, 236
knowing, 59, 70–71, 153, 247
logical, 81–82, 89–91, 121, 168, 403, 410
subjectivity, 30, 55, 59, 100, 116–17, 123, 124, 149, 162–63, 170, 223, 236, 242, 250–54, 257–60, 297–98, 372n2, 407, 409, 427, 428
substance, 24, 40, 44, 99, 144, 201, 204
and accident, 105
extended vs. thinking (Descartes), 116
form and matter, 60
suffrage, 435–36

technology, 10, 133, 137, 139, 142, 287, 301, 352, 366, 387, 388, 413, 414, 415
"psycho-technology," 132, 231, 234, 241, 245
society and, 15, 302
temperance, 43, 50, 69, 138, 160, 246, 251, 260–62, 387, 405
tendency, 72, 159, 176, 182, 216, 219, 222–23
of desire, 152–53
to exist, 144
to good or bad use, 228–34

to know, 168
natural, 154, 184, 209, 224, 267
to the right matter, 350
satisfaction of, 184–85
to the truth, 154, 264, 267
See also inclination
terminal act, 6, 63–69
Thales, 140, 365
theology, 6, 12, 19n4, 28, 29, 187, 198, 276, 357, 384–85, 404
thing, 14, 37, 45, 49, 58, 60, 76, 78, 83–84, 96, 120–22, 127, 130, 155, 181, 190, 225
"all other things being equal," 220–21n4, 301, 316, 332, 345, 403
desirability/goodness of, 190, 199, 204, 208, 312, 368
human use of, 227–28, 233–34
and idea, 77, 111, 125–26
intentional object and extramental thing, 79–94
nature of, 75, 113–14, 221–22, 236, 257, 267, 321, 338, 344, 381, 426
right, 165, 232, 241, 247, 256, 261, 350
Thomas Aquinas, 6, 9, 12, 23, 25, 29, 48, 97, 102, 107, 111, 116, 118, 134, 150, 162, 235, 316, 318, 326, 331, 340, 385, 396, 397, 438, 439
Aquinas Lecture, 337, 378, 447
Aquinas Medal, xi, 7, 13
bonum in communi, 181
knowledge, 297
law, 144, 325, 328
liberty, 108
nature, 291
Summa Theologiae, 75, 132, 174, 202, 328, 262n2, 350
Thomism, xii, 6, 7, 8, 31–32, 48, 116, 150, 181, 235, 240, 243, 266, 325, 397, 417
thought, 62, 73, 81, 113, 118
act of, 66–67
common sense, 64, 67
ethical, 89, 240
habits of, 250, 384, 406, 407

thought (cont.)
  metaphysical, 61, 64
  object of, 63, 83, 86–87, 407
  philosophical, 25, 37, 39, 42, 48, 155, 194, 368–69
  practical, 30, 150, 153–63
  scientific, 16, 28, 37, 69, 276, 283n4, 343
  and thing/reality, 83–88
time utility, 384
Tocqueville, Alexis de, 379
Todoli, José, 375n14
totalitarianism, 139, 292, 308, 366, 391–92, 416, 420–21, 436–37. See also absolutism
transcendence, 97, 108, 114, 183, 287, 264–65, 294–95
  definition of action, 56, 63–65
  vs. predicamental relation, 104–5
  system vs. positive system of truth, 276–80
  and truths, 279, 283n6, 296, 309, 319
truth, 16, 25, 48, 79–81, 96, 132, 151, 205, 263, 403
  communicability and incommunicability of, 265, 293, 280–81
  in judgment, 24, 83, 117
  love of, 7, 17, 264, 267, 269, 273, 349, 354, 396, 413
  moral, 268–69, 397, 442
  mystique of, 419, 434
  objectivity of, 84–85, 297
  order of, 287, 295, 309
  positive, 205, 279, 282
  practical and historico-practical, 152, 168–69, 343–44
  search for, 23, 189, 263, 267, 279, 295, 368, 397
  theoretical/speculative, 154, 206, 280
  transcendent, 265, 279, 282, 283n6, 284n7, 287, 295–96, 319
  unity of, 267–69
tyranny, 139, 203, 218, 391, 424, 436, 442

unanimity, 280, 281, 332, 338, 342–44, 348, 425
understanding, 88, 113, 126, 161, 167, 193, 204, 236, 309, 330, 402–6, 444
United States, 3, 4, 18n2, 283n5, 324, 357, 418
unity, 26, 44, 67, 69, 99–103, 105, 118, 204, 264, 279, 318, 339, 349, 433
  of action, 314, 332, 338, 342, 425, 426
universals, 15, 47, 49, 63, 92, 100–101, 154–55, 185, 194–95, 196, 202, 272, 335, 343
universe, 37, 71, 76, 102, 111–14, 143, 174, 176, 186, 238, 248, 276, 283n4, 291, 309, 317, 343, 404, 443, 444. See also world
University of Chicago, 3, 19n6, 20nn10–12, 240, 337, 352, 372n3, 402, 459
University of Notre Dame, 3, 19n5, 20n9, 459
univocality, 67, 95, 99, 101–2, 105, 107, 147, 181, 196
use, 26, 43, 50, 132–33, 146–48, 161–63, 174, 221–22, 225–34, 246, 252, 314, 405
  definition of, 225
utopia, 138–39, 285, 342, 377, 421, 433–35

values, xiii, 25, 26, 43, 80, 95, 133, 143, 144, 145, 164, 219n4, 257, 285, 287, 302, 316, 357, 360, 362, 376, 377, 378, 393, 421
  equality of, 169, 381–82, 385–86, 390
van Rijn, Rembrandt, 13
Veblen, Thorstein, 370
Vienna Circle, 30
violence, 11, 47, 182, 279, 280, 302, 333, 387, 428. See also force
virtue, 180
  cardinal, 27, 69, 234, 241
  of charity, 193
  and common good, 345–46, 348, 350

of courage (*see* courage)
definitions of, 221, 240–43, 252, 256, 404
and dependability, 244, 246, 254, 256
as disposition, 223, 252, 259
as existential readiness, 8, 242, 246–51, 256
of faith, 12, 48–50, 164, 351, 419, 433–34, 445
as *habitus*, 223, 235, 242, 406
of hope, 146, 213, 351
inclination/instinct of, 153, 262
intellectual, 46, 235, 350, 397, 402–6
interdependence of, 260–61
of justice (*see* justice)
knowledge/science and, 246, 251
law of development, 262, 290
moral, 8, 69, 160, 235, 240, 242–43, 249–51, 256, 260, 262, 350, 405
of prudence (*see* prudence)
substitute for, 132, 222, 240–41, 154
of temperance (*see* temperance)
volition, 65, 66, 181, 207, 223, 298, 339, 345–46, 350. *See also* will
voluntary action, 186, 191–92
    and free choice/will, 178–80, 189, 210, 219n2, 249, 251, 298, 436
    for the good, 181, 187–89
    for happiness, 183, 187, 189
    and involuntary action, 159 159, 178–80, 189, 210, 223, 235, 242, 255, 280, 379
    for a last end, 187–89
    and nonvoluntary action, 207, 219n2
    and spontaneity, 196, 207, 219n2, 271, 286
von Hildebrand, Dietrich, 292
Vuillemin, Joseph, 32

Watteau, Jean-Antoine, 13
wealth, 7, 140, 185, 189, 296, 344, 352, 353, 354, 373n7, 385, 388–90, 392
    "leaks out of society" (Proudhon), 358, 360, 367, 377, 386, 391, 394

Weil, André, 237, 239n4
whole, 78, 118, 177, 247–48, 291, 299, 301, 313
    accidental/substantial, 161, 191
    dynamic, 69, 185, 252–53
    homogenous, 26, 41
    order of, 252, 254
    parts and, 67–69, 252, 300, 307, 308, 403
    qualitative, 68
    quantitative, 56, 68
    social, 218, 256, 320
will, 47, 68–69, 94n3, 132, 136, 146, 180, 191–92, 218, 271, 311
    adherence to/object of *bonum in communi*, 181, 201, 207–8
    angelic, 85
    of common good, 318, 338–39, 346, 348–50
    determinate, 158, 195, 201, 205
    divine, 57, 112–13
    free will (*see* free will)
    good, 43, 50, 138, 152–54, 159–60, 229, 233, 288, 346, 348–51
    as immanent activity, 56, 64, 67
    and last practical judgment, 194–96, 216
    and law, 326, 328–29
    rebellious, 290, 298
    strong, 222, 229, 231, 233
    "superdetermination" of, 6, 173–74, 196, 200n4, 209, 211
    surplus of goodness and, 194–96
    weak, 199, 202, 206, 214, 216, 222, 229, 231
    See also volition
Williams, Raymond, 414n4
wisdom, 31, 156, 157, 189, 235, 287, 331, 355, 394, 402, 404–8
    divine, 98, 326, 439
    practical, 9, 20n9, 25, 152, 158, 242, 295, 350, 404–5, 418–19
        (*see also* prudence)
    of society, 257, 294–95, 319, 387
    speculative/theoretical, 4, 20n9, 25, 415

work, 182–83, 269, 352–55, 356–58, 373n6, 379
  of art, 183, 198
  and culture, 408, 410
  definition of, 359, 368–69
  manual, 365, 371, 394, 413
  mental, 33, 86, 100, 371, 413
  of reason/thought, 135, 166, 276, 328, 331, 333, 445
  technical, 365, 413
  of the will, 328–29
workers, 321, 353–55, 357, 369–71, 372n2, 377, 378, 389, 397, 413–14, 422
  assembly line/industrial, 259, 300
  ethics of, 359–63, 367–68
  farm, 300–301, 435
  manual, 371, 398, 413
  skilled, 299
  unskilled, 435
world, 114, 236, 247
  "best possible," 121
  changeable/mobile, 136, 197, 317, 404
  created, 73, 101–2
  of experience, 37, 46, 98, 108, 110, 281, 383
  physical, 44, 136, 141, 239, 444, 446
  moral, 112, 165
  real, 89–90, 93, 143, 146, 275
  sensible, 55, 117–18
  See also universe
World War I, 3, 380, 429, 438
World War II, 4, 264, 416

YVES R. SIMON (1903–1961)

was professor of philosophy at the University of Notre Dame and the University of Chicago. He was the author of numerous books, including *A General Theory of Authority* (1991) and *Philosophy of Democratic Government* (1993), both published by the University of Notre Dame Press.

MICHAEL D. TORRE

is associate professor of philosophy at the University of San Francisco. He is the author and editor of twelve books, including *Do Not Resist the Spirit's Call: Francisco Marín-Sola on Sufficient Grace*.

www.ingramcontent.com/pod-product-compliance
Lightning Source LLC
Chambersburg PA
CBHW071353300426
44114CB00016B/2053